In My Father's Name

a family, a town, a murder

Mark Arax

Mark Arax (signature)

SIMON & SCHUSTER

New York

London

Toronto

Sydney

Tokyo

Singapore

SIMON & SCHUSTER
Rockefeller Center
1230 Avenue of the Americas
New York, NY 10020

Copyright © 1996 by Mark Arax

SIMON & SCHUSTER
and colophon are registered
trademarks of Simon & Schuster Inc.

Designed by Elina D. Nudelman
Manufactured in the United States of America
1 3 5 7 9 10 8 6 4 2

Library of Congress Cataloging-in-Publication Data

Arax, Mark
In my father's name: a family, a town, a murder/Mark Arax.
p.   cm.
1. Murder—California—Fresno—Case studies.   2. Arax, Ara,
1931–1972.   3. Armenian Americans—California—Fresno—Biography.
I. Title.
HV6534.F74A73   1996
364.1'523'092—dc20

[B]   95–30026
                                                              CIP

ISBN 0-684-80845-5

For Ashley and Caitlan and Alyssa
and Joseph and Adrienne and all the ones
yet born, my parents' grandchildren, so that
they might know them and those who came before.

A FAMILY TREE

Dad's Side

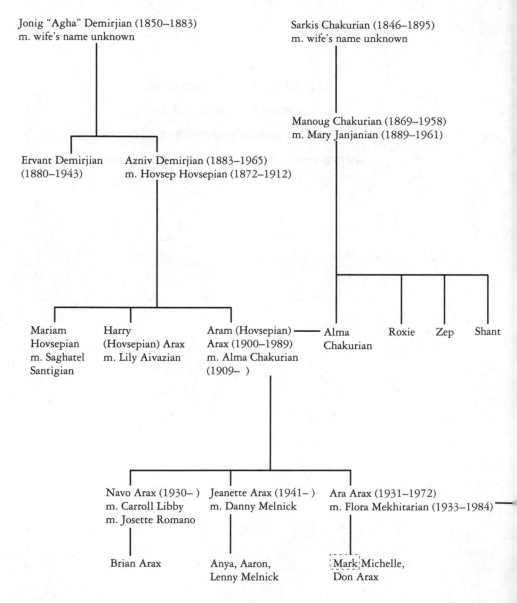

Jonig "Agha" Demirjian (1850–1883)
m. wife's name unknown

Sarkis Chakurian (1846–1895)
m. wife's name unknown

Manoug Chakurian (1869–1958)
m. Mary Janjanian (1889–1961)

Ervant Demirjian
(1880–1943)

Azniv Demirjian (1883–1965)
m. Hovsep Hovsepian (1872–1912)

Mariam
Hovsepian
m. Saghatel
Santigian

Harry
(Hovsepian) Arax
m. Lily Aivazian

Aram (Hovsepian)
Arax (1900–1989)
m. Alma Chakurian
(1909–)

Alma
Chakurian

Roxie   Zep   Shant

Navo Arax (1930–)
m. Carroll Libby
m. Josette Romano

Jeanette Arax (1941–)
m. Danny Melnick

Ara Arax (1931–1972)
m. Flora Mekhitarian (1933–1984)

Brian Arax

Anya, Aaron,
Lenny Melnick

Mark Michelle,
Don Arax

Mom's Side

Bagdasar Mekhitarian (1855–1915)
m.wife's name unknown

Khorshood Mekhitarian (1875–1915)
m. Atlas maiden name unknown (1880–1915)

Perouz Sarkisian "Big Momma"
(1881–1963)
m. husband's name unknown

(The entire family—including 7 children—
massacred by Turks. One child survived.)

Lucine Sarkisian

Hamayak Yegishe Mekhitarian (1900–1985)
m. Lucine Sarkisian (1903–1936)

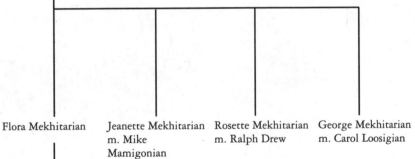

Flora Mekhitarian

Jeanette Mekhitarian
m. Mike
Mamigonian

Rosette Mekhitarian
m. Ralph Drew

George Mekhitarian
m. Carol Loosigian

Be patient toward all that is unsolved in
your heart and try to love the questions themselves.

—Rainer Maria Rilke

Introduction

On a cold January night in Fresno, California, in 1972, when the tangerine tree in our backyard was pure sugar and the air smelled smoky and was full of fog, two white men in their early twenties walked into my father's nightclub wearing gloves. It was Sunday and the bar was empty and he was working on the quarterly taxes in a small office in the back. They ordered two draft beers, played a game of eight-ball that took them past the open door of his office, left, returned ten minutes later and without provocation or a demand for money, shot him to death. The only witness, a female bartender, was unhurt. They left behind two half-full glasses, absent fingerprints, and a dollar bill.

It was one of the most sensational murders in the history of our town, partly because my father had been a local football hero and a prominent grocer before he bought the bar. And it was never solved, leaving behind endless speculation about drugs and corrupt police and the Mafia.

I tried to reconstruct my life but no one, not my mother or father's brother nor the cops, could tell me how to put back the pieces. If there was a lesson to be learned, they didn't know that either. So I did what any decent fifteen-year-old son would do: I ignored the rumors and made holy my father. In bed at night, surrounded by his athletic trophies and coach's whistle, I devised ways to get even. I tried to picture the killers, not the two young men who gunned him down but the ones who presumably hired them. Did we know these men, a plot dark and hatched? Or were they strangers bearing some petty grudge? I practiced the detachment with which I would coldly announce my name and calmly pull the trigger, and then I fell asleep.

Through high school and college and a career in journalism at the *Baltimore Evening Sun* and the *Los Angeles Times,* I never stopped fantasizing about revenge, even as the questions became more tangled. How could my father move so easily between worlds, the Little League diamond by day and the bar and its underworld figures by night? What side was he on and what did I, his oldest child, owe him? Was it enough to find the truth of his murder and perhaps acquit him in my heart? Or must redemption, like the stain itself, be a public display? Did the discovery of his killers demand something more of me?

I have contemplated these questions of revenge and requital for more than twenty years, a journey through my teens and twenties and now thirties. I must apologize to my loved ones, living and dead, for the ceaseless questioning that has provoked anger and even tears. This may have begun as a chase for killers in my bedroom of icons, but where it ended was someplace else entirely. Perhaps I have been ruthless. I have rifled the drawers of my father's life. I have awakened family and family secrets that date back five generations to Turkish Armenia. I have exhumed our town, Fresno, and the story of California's heartland that William Saroyan never bothered to tell. I have found many answers, the truth about my father and his murder only one piece of our mosaic. But at what price, I still wonder.

Part One

Blood on the Vine

c h a p t e r 1

My father, Ara Arax, bought a bar in Fresno in the spring of 1965 when he was thirty-three years old and I, his oldest child, was eight. He was a grape grower and a grocer. He knew nothing about bars.

The Apartments, as the bar was known, sat near the middle of town close by the Southern Pacific railroad tracks. The neighborhood, like so much else in Fresno, was a salute to bad planning—a hodgepodge of commercial and industrial buildings, stucco ranch houses and open land. To the immediate left was a field Dad named Itchycoo Park after a song on the radio. To the right was a plain cinderblock building that housed a beauty salon and a laundromat where the all-night spin and tumble of the machines concealed some of the biggest crap games in town.

Across the street was a bowling alley called Mid-State (this was the center of California) and just beyond that Motel Drive. It was a gaudy hash of motels, motor inns and prime rib houses where Fresnans caroused weekend nights. The most flamboyant of these establishments was the Hacienda, a sprawling motel and convention complex conceived as a tribute to Spanish architecture and Las Vegas gilt. Among its more florid features were a bar made of leather and handcarved teakwood and an entertainment stage that the local newspaper boasted was "the largest west of the Mississippi." But nothing quite topped the Hacienda's Mermaid Room, a cavernous cocktail lounge ten feet below ground. It had a big picture window that looked out to the bottom of the motel's swimming pool. Drunks ogled showgirls dancing underwater.

Highway 99 ran straight between Dad's bar and Motel Drive, two lanes one way and two lanes the other, splattered with dead chickens and divided by a hedge of weary oleander. From Weed Patch in the south to Red Bluff in the north, Highway 99 stretched some 400 miles through the flatlands of California's Great Central Valley, lacing together farm towns with names like Delano, Earlimart, Visalia, Kingsburg, Fowler, Madera, Chowchilla, Manteca.

My father's father, an Armenian, fled Turkey at age nineteen and arrived in this valley in the wake of World War I. He pruned vines and picked fruit and dreamed of college and a life devoted to writing, dreams left behind in the fields. My father was born in Fresno in 1931 and saw only the promise of this lush land. He was a high school football hero who, after a semester at USC, gave up his athletic scholarship and returned home to the family business. He worked all his adult life beside his father, Aram, and older brother, Navo, first in the vineyards and then in a chain of grocery stores. If he tended to be more careless than Uncle Navo (he was always misplacing keys and money), he was less guarded, too. The customers loved him. Not even the grocery stores going bankrupt dampened his optimism.

Although he knew nothing about bars—he wasn't even a drinker—he told my mother not to worry. The bar business wasn't so much a departure from the markets, and The Apartments wasn't so much a bar. It had been built as a cocktail lounge and dinner house and he would continue serving lunch and dinner. He would manage without Uncle Navo, who wanted no part of the bar business. Grandpa Arax would count the money and pay the bills. Highway 99 would deposit a steady flow of customers.

The Apartments. The name confounded me. Instead of clearing up the confusion, Dad personalized it: Ara's Apartments. I never understood why he kept the name and changed everything else. The food was the first to go.

The rhythm of the bar, its throbs and upside-down time, became the rhythm of our home. New music, the blue-eyed soul of the Righteous

Brothers, blasted from the big Philco in our den. In the grocery business, Dad left for work in the early morning, hours before I awakened, and returned at dinner. We had him for the night. The bar demanded his presence each night right after dinner.

I didn't sleep soundly until I heard his key click in the side door, usually at 2:20 in the morning. If he hadn't come home by 3 A.M., Mom chained the inside lock in protest. On those nights, he rapped on my window and I tiptoed down the long hall to let him in. Sometimes Dad couldn't help the late hour. One night, a quarter past three, I heard heavy footsteps outside my window, and then pounding. "Mark, Mark! Open the door, son." He was crazy with fear, clothes ripped, drenched in sweat. At a stoplight a few miles from our house a customer had waved him down for assistance. Dad stepped out of the car unsuspecting and the man lunged at him with a long blade. Dad won the footrace. We learned later that the man, fresh from a mental ward, had been stalking him for a week.

We lived in a housing tract in east Fresno: me and my father; my mother, Flora; a sister, Michelle; and a brother, Donny. The homes were modest but enough of the lots remained empty that it felt more like country than suburb. Our backyard resembled a small orchard with almond and walnut trees that blossomed pink and white and volunteer figs that popped up everywhere in the mistaken belief that this was still farmland. I practiced my baseball swing against one stubborn fig, hacking away at its limbs all summer long, the soft wood bleeding sticky milk but never yielding.

Everywhere I looked the land was flat and wide and open. Fresno seemed to have been exiled from the rest of the state, 180 miles south of San Francisco and 210 miles north of Los Angeles, a banishment made even more pronounced by the mountains that walled off the valley. The horizon showed nothing but clear sky in three directions; the Sierra Nevada loomed to the east. Before the great dams were built and the rivers shunted to valley farms, this land had been desert and marsh. The weather was not so easily tamed. The valley sizzled in summer and brooded under a veil of wet gray fog in winter.

Here in the middle of California's agricultural heartland, a child could grow up feeling disconnected from the outside world, especially when his father, like my father, detested travel. And yet it was hard to feel deprived in a place that was still so much open space. After school, I'd climb into a miniature, three-horsepower Model T Ford once used to promote our grocery stores and take a spin down Olive Avenue, past Longs Drugs and Country Boy Market, past the crisscrossing irrigation canals that seemed to scorn gravity, miles and miles under a great wide sky.

Our isolation made every breach from the outside seem even more ominous. The sky, immense as it was, exploded almost daily with jet fighters breaking the buffer of sound, breaking glass. We had become the test range for the Phantoms and Starfighters and B-52 Hustlers that flew out of Edwards Air Force base in the Mojave, the Sierra swallowing more military hardware and young lives than any mountain in America. Decades later they were still pulling them out. Alongside the ditch next to my grandparents' house lurked a tall yellow air-raid siren behind bushes. We were wired for Cold War sound like few cities.

There was no daunting my father. In a matter of three years, he turned The Apartments into the hottest rock 'n' roll club between Los Angeles and San Francisco. At a time when other bar owners in the valley settled for jukebox music, he brought in bands from the big city with names like El Chicano, Zebra and Ballin' Jack. In the summer of 1971, Chuck Berry, paroled from prison, zonked on narcotics, duckwalked across the tiny stage in two frenzied shows.

The businessmen and attorneys who had frequented The Apartments in the mid-sixties drifted away as the cocktail lounge became a nightclub. The customers now were an odd fusion of young whites, blacks and Chicanos who came to dance, bikers and weight lifters who came to brawl, and hippies who came to extol the free love and drugs of the antiwar movement, minus its politics. It was an uneasy mix and Dad tried, desperately at times, to keep things calm. He tried bouncers and $2 cover charges. He tried his own fists.

To soothe Mom, he bought a vacant lot in north Fresno just off Van Ness Extension, the town's most prestigious boulevard, and hired an architect to design a custom home. The builder he chose was a well-known drunk who agreed to construct the home at cost. Except for kitchen cabinets slightly askew, the place was wonderful: 3,200 square feet in all, four bedrooms and three bathrooms, Spanish adobe exterior, wrought-iron gates, a private courtyard and swimming pool.

Our new neighbors must have thought it curious that a bar owner could live among them, though they never quite said that to us. Everyone kept pretty much to himself. We got along best with the Stephan family down the block. Chuck Stephan owned a tractor business and he and Dad talked farming. Brian Stephan was my age and we became fast buddies. On Christmas, Dad gave me a minibike and Brian found a way to raise its top speed beyond 40 mph by replacing the slack spring that governed the flow of gas with a straight paper clip that threw open the floodgates. Fig orchards took up half the neighborhood and we raced the wide smooth rows of hardpan between the trees, chasing jackrabbits. At night, we gigged frogs in a canal that irrigated the figs.

Most of my schoolmates came from white-collar families. My father was the only bar owner. For a long time, I felt ashamed and pretended that Ara's Apartments was a steak house. Once I reached junior high, with all my friends buzzed on Boone's Farm Strawberry Ripple, the bar became something to actually feel proud about. I began spending Saturdays there with Dad. We would arrive by mid-morning, the first to survey the damage from the night before. Five and ten dollar bills, the largesse of drunks, lay crumpled amid the litter of cocktail napkins and broken glass and cigarette butts. A cousin or friend sometimes came along and we raced from opposite ends of the bar in a hunt for the most money. Dad let us keep whatever we found.

No night at The Apartments was wilder than New Year's Eve, and no morning beckoned with more possibilities than New Year's Day. Saturday, January 1, 1972, began with the promise of riches sprinkled on the red carpet, awaiting my arrival. I had turned fifteen the week before and was too small to play Pop Warner football. As consolation, Dad offered the bar as a morning playground followed by a round of afternoon golf. Our day together.

The drive from home to the bar took only five minutes and Dad swore he got there faster by holding the throttle of his Firebird, an apple green Formula 400, at 35 mph and timing all the lights. This practicality struck even me, the vigilant child forever admonishing him to "drive safe," as a sinful waste of horsepower.

The route happened to take us by one of our old grocery stores, lost to bankruptcy and now a carpet warehouse. I don't recall my father ever pointing it out to me or slowing down to gaze wistfully. It was long in the past now.

"Ready on the left," he said, measuring the intersection for safe passage.

"Ready on the right," I said.

"Ready on the firing line," we both shouted in unison.

Just ahead, backlighted in neon, beckoned the future. It was topped with a martini glass and a toothpick-skewered olive, and in large bold letters, high enough for the world to see, shouted: ARA'S APARTMENTS.

The building itself, if not windowless and painted gold, might have passed for just another stucco tract house. My father tried his best to spruce things up on the outside. He planted palm trees, shrubs and flowers and hired another notorious drunk, this time a stone mason, to erect a new façade.

Stepping inside from daylight was like burrowing into a dark, dank cavern heavy with stale smoke and the sweetness of rum. Gradually, I could discern booths, tables and a fireplace along the periphery, a terrazzo dance floor in the middle and a corner jukebox that poured out Top 40 when the band wasn't playing. The carpet was royal red flecked with black. On the walls hung pewter coats of arms, large mirrors veined in black and two oil paintings of a beautiful redhead with bare breasts. The bar extended some sixty feet and was topped in light blue Formica.

Standing there, not a thing disturbed from the night before, I tried to reconstruct New Year's Eve from the evidence at hand: lipstick-stained glasses, phone numbers on bar napkins, panties in the parking lot. Here were things that could only be guessed at. What had the bar looked like hours before, 200 bodies packed tight, throbbing music and pounding strobe light? Whose phone number got left behind? Whose panties and how? What about the naked redhead on the wall?

On the carpet beneath a long row of bar stools, I scooped up dimes, quarters, a fifty-cent piece. Not exactly the riches I anticipated. The red and white pills I found—and which Dad flushed down the toilet—were worth lots more.

He threw me a towel soaked in soda water and I cleaned the booths and tables top to bottom. He inspected every inch of my work and I grumbled and marveled at his fastidiousness. He didn't consider the job done until I had scraped off every piece of chewing gum from under the tables.

"This is a bar," I reminded him. "Who cares about a little gum?"

"This is *my* bar," he reminded me. "I care."

Once a week he scoured the walls and air ducts with a steam cleaner. It wasn't enough to sweep the parking lot; he had to wash it down with a hose, too. All over the men's restroom, urine stuck to my tennis shoes like spilled lemonade. With bare hands I plucked cigarette butts stuck in the deodorant nets that lined each urinal. The women's restroom was fancier and far worse. Vomit stained the sink and shag carpet, and tampons clogged the toilets.

On that Saturday I bent over to unplug the mess and a shout from behind jerked me skyward. Mike Garvey, the bar manager, tall and slick, stood there chuckling.

"You sure are spending a lot of time in here, Markie. What are you doing? Sniffing the toilet seats again?"

More than once Garvey picked the women's stalls to rattle me this way. Each time I promised myself the next time would be different, and I'd be prepared. I never was.

Serious men shaking Tabasco into drinks already red occupied a few barstools, cheering the New Year's Day bowl games. Dad didn't want me around the drinking and man talk so he handed me a submarine sandwich, potato chips and a Shirley Temple topped with a maraschino cherry and told me to eat in his office.

Try as he might to protect me from the seamier side, it was hard not to pick up things. I knew that Garvey had the Ping-Pong clap. I knew he booked bets and my father told him more than once to knock it off. I knew he had been arrested for setting up abortions on behalf of bar patrons. The investigation into Garvey's actions made clear that Dad wasn't involved—the $500 Garvey demanded for each referral went straight into his pocket. Garvey pleaded guilty and got probation.

I tiptoed back into the main room and watched from a booth in the far dark corner. My father, who had turned forty a few months earlier, was the star of the show. He appeared at ease and the banter of the bar—sports and city hall politics—suited him fine. He knew just about everyone in town or so it seemed, his popularity made clear to me each fall at Ratcliffe Stadium, the home of the Battlin' Bulldogs from Fresno State. All of halftime and the first five minutes of the third quarter were spent in a walk to and from the concession stand. It took that long for Dad (and me) to shake hands with every person he knew.

That afternoon, we left to play golf at Fig Garden, a public course carved out of the San Joaquin River bottom where the regulars liked to tell stories about my father's prowess with a One Wood. His power sacrificed almost no accuracy and on some of the shorter par fours, 300 to 320 yards, he would land on the green with his tee shot. Dad was determined to correct my slice and we proceeded first to the practice range. "Damn it, Mark," he abruptly interrupted my backswing. "Drag the clubhead straight back." It was hopeless. I was raining golf balls off the practice range and onto the ninth hole green, interrupting the players. We never made it onto the course that afternoon.

That night Mom joined Dad at the bar, something she hadn't done in months. They got home late, arguing about the hours he spent working and playing golf. It had been like this since summer. That's when Dad, without telling Mom, invested $18,000 in a bigger nightclub in a better part of town. "Ara-boy, you've got one piece of junk already," my grandfather told him. "Why buy another?" Dad explained to Mom, well after the fact, that this second nightclub had the size and acoustics to better accommodate the big rock groups he wanted to bring to Fresno. Mom wasn't placated.

I stood at the edge of my room and peeked down the hall to the den where she confronted him, out of view. I could see my little sister, knock-kneed, standing at her doorway, too. I begged my mother in whispers not to taunt him.

What kind of life is this? She shouted, flaunting a streak of stubbornness that trailed back to her father and the whole headstrong Armenian race. Dark hair and olive skin, she otherwise bore little resemblance to an Armenian. Her nose was small and narrow, flawed only by a childhood scar faint across one nostril. It looked nothing like the Armenian hook nose, and the jealous church ladies speculated over its origin. *You call yourself a provider? What a joke. I've got news for you—you don't provide shit except a paycheck!* Flora Mekhitarian had been prized as one of the prettiest Armenian girls of her generation and she had kept her figure, five-foot-one, 105 pounds, full breasted, through sixteen years of marriage and three children. The daughter of a priest, she blamed the bar business for her less-than-chaste mouth. *Big Ara. Ara's Apartments. Name in lights. Mentor to all the creeps and whores. These kids have no father. I have no husband!* She stood toe-to-toe with Dad, snarling questions without the question mark.

He was nearly ten inches taller and 100 solid pounds heavier. He was an exercise fiend. He ran and lifted weights and made himself walk the eighteen holes, the bag of clubs slung across his back. His legs were compact and powerful, buttocks humped. If his stomach had spread a little since USC it just meant that his shoulders, chest and forearms were thicker, too.

In some adult faces you could glimpse the child. Not so with my father. His golden hair, rare for an Armenian, had darkened to a dull brown and receded prematurely, the broad brow broader. His ears and nose, already prominent, seemed bigger, too. His forehead bore a small scar from the shrapnel of a tractor disc; there was a patch of discoloration on one arm and leg from burns suffered when he defied his father and poured gasoline on uprooted fig trees against a strong wind. He had a soft face and velvety brown eyes that could surrender their gentleness in an instant. His two front teeth were gapped and he talked in a sputter and slight lisp. When he got angry or excited—the latter pretty much a constant state—everything came out in fits. I couldn't always understand him.

As long as he refused to be provoked by Mom, I assured my sister, everything was all right. At the first sudden sound of his fury, I sprang to stop him. *Look at me! Look at me!* I was an actor and the more dramatic my portrayal the better chance of diverting his attention. I knew from past fights that Dad flung objects, not punches. This was slight solace, however, for he possessed pinpoint accuracy and the choice of objects to launch was indiscriminate. He threw the first thing he could lay his hands on.

He grabbed a thin junior volume from the Encyclopedia Britannica set and flung it sideways at Mom. I blocked it with my arm. Then he heaved a stout senior volume, barely missing our heads. Mom never stopped swearing. When the tirade finally ended and he stormed out the side door, the entire forty-volume set of Britannicas lay scattered across the family room.

○ ○ ○

I didn't hear him return that night. By the time I awakened the next morning, peace had been restored. My mother was upset with *me*.

"If you think you're staying home, you've got another thing coming, mister," she said. "You're going to Sunday school. All your cousins will be there."

"Sunday school? . . . I'm in the ninth grade. It's the same old crap over and over. I know it already."

"*Ooooffff,* what do you know?" she said, a dismissive wave of the hand.

To be an Armenian kid was to be spoon-fed a legacy of firsts. We were the first people to mine tin and copper and produce bronze; the first grape culture; the first Christian nation, the first builders of eight-sided church domes that rested not on pillars but on square foundations; the first choice of anthropologist Margaret Mead who was looking for a perfect, unambiguous language; the first victims of twentieth-century genocide, the "forgotten genocide" we called it. Some of these firsts, I learned later, were more unassailable than others.

Then there was the inevitable list that accompanied every primer on Armenians, the list of who's who: writer William Saroyan; painter Arshile Gorky; football coach Ara Parseghian; TV's "Mannix" Mike Connors; Portugal's oil magnate Calouste Gulbenkian; French singer Charles Aznavour; Soviet composer Aram Khachaturian; Soviet President Anastas Mikoyan; Soviet MiG designer Arten Mikoyan: You got the idea real fast. We were small but hardly insignificant.

Church was a place to celebrate Armenian culture and these temporal firsts, but on Sundays, in football season, all I cared about celebrating was the team Dad and I rooted for, the San Francisco 49ers.

Sunday mornings began with a tug whenever the 49ers played on TV during the church hour. Mom's father was a priest at the red brick Armenian church downtown. Our attendance, Mom and the three children, was expected every Sunday. Meanwhile Dad, the agnostic son of an atheist, got to stay home and watch the 49ers on television.

"Ara! Tell this kid," she persisted. "All the cousins will be at church."

"Oh, let him stay . . . it's a big, big game . . . the Dallas Cowboys."

He reminded her of the stakes—the winner would advance to the Super

Bowl—and she backed down gently. I think she even stayed home this time to watch the game with us.

My father's addiction to the 49ers began in grammar school when his father moved the family to San Francisco to find work. Over the years, the team secured its place in gridiron lore as one of the great also-rans, but my father stuck by them, his faithfulness finally rewarded with back-to-back divisional titles in 1970 and 1971.

The 49ers had lost to the Dallas Cowboys 17–10 in this same championship game a year ago. Dad approached the rematch with all the solemnity due an arcane religious rite. He wore boxer shorts, a red and gold team hat and wrapped himself in a wool blanket. He sat on a section of sofa deemed lucky and moved only when things started to look bleak. On key plays he thrust a "horn's hex" sign—the index and pinkie fingers extended—toward the half of the tube where the Cowboys played.

On that Sunday, my father's infinite contortions notwithstanding, 49ers quarterback John Brodie was stifled by a Dallas defense nicknamed Doomsday. In the fourth quarter, Cowboy Roger "The Dodger" Staubach displayed an elusiveness I had not seen before, directing an eighty-yard touchdown march that vanquished all hope. Cowboys 14, 49ers 3.

My father was still upset hours later when he left for the bar. He almost never worked Sunday nights but a phone call had summoned him, and he asked if I wanted to go along. I don't recall if I said no or if he couldn't wait while I finished taking a shower. "Markie, I'm leaving," he said. "I'll be back in an hour."

All these years later, when I return to that day, my father now dressed in glorious colors, moments between us purfled in myth, I want to say he kissed me and my last words to him were, "Drive safe."

Mom cleaned the kitchen. I watched TV in the family room. President Nixon, renewing a promise to end the war in Vietnam, pledged to continue the troop pullout. Then the phone rang.

I think now that before it rang a second time I already knew. Maybe it was the in-between hour, one parent unaccounted for. Or that this ring followed Dad's departure so precisely, with just enough built-in minutes for accident, discovery of wrecked body, calls to police and ambulance and now a call to us. Maybe it was me, the nail biter who halfway expected this all along. Whatever, this ring at 7:15 P.M. was different.

My seven-year-old brother raced to answer the phone. Linda Lewis, the bartender on duty, asked to talk to Mom. *Ara was shot a few minutes ago in the office. The ambulance is taking him to St. Agnes. . . .*

"Your father's been shot! He's been shot! . . . Oh, Ara. Ara. Ara. Ara."

Every step from that step on was not mine. I darted to my bedroom, fought to put on pants and ran back into the kitchen. Mom was dialing Uncle Navo.

"Navo! Navo! Ara's been shot at the bar. They've taken him to St. Agnes."

I bolted out the side door. Heavy fog, week-old tule fog, hushed the street as I sprinted toward the Stephans' house, alone, delirious, howling, "My dad's been shot! My dad's been shot!"

I pounded both fists against their front door and screamed for someone to please open.

"It's Mark Arax. Please. My dad's been shot!"

Mr. Stephan braced my shoulders.

"Where, son?"

"At the bar. He was shot at the bar. They're taking him to St. Agnes."

I ran back home and grabbed my Bible. Mr. and Mrs. Stephan were already outside, waiting to drive us to the hospital. My mother thought it best that my little sister and brother stay behind with other neighbors. In the backseat the two of us held each other the whole way there.

"He's going to be all right, son," Mr. Stephan promised. "We're going to get him out of that damn bar business and put him back in the vineyards where he belongs."

Uncle Navo was waiting outside the emergency room door. The expression on his face hovered between glum and composed and I tried to read in it some clue about Dad's condition. It was no use. He smiled stiffly and sat us down.

"They say Ara's blood pressure has dropped to fifty over zero. But he's fighting. They're not sure how many times he's been hit."

"Is he conscious?" Mom asked.

"Yeah . . . he's cussing like a sailor."

We waited forty-five minutes without another word. I opened my Bible and began praying over a picture of Jesus preaching at a rock surrounded by believers. Weeks later I would go back to that picture and the face of one believer had become the face of my father. A policeman approached Uncle Navo and whispered into his ear; my uncle shook his head no, and the cop wrote something into his notebook.

"They still haven't taken him to surgery," he said. "His blood pressure has dropped a little more but he's still alert and he keeps asking for Doctor Marius."

Dr. Fitzalbert Marius (my father called him Bertie) was a surgeon and longtime friend. He moved next door to us in 1958 and the entire block of white residents (Marius was black) lined the street with For Sale signs. My father, who had felt the sting of real estate codes preventing Armenians from living in certain neighborhoods, stood beside Dr. Marius. Mom and Dottie Marius became friends and April Marius and I playmates. It was Dr. Marius who had alerted Dad that The Apartments was up for sale. They talked about buying the bar together. When I suffered a hernia in grade school, Dad trusted only Dr. Marius with the surgery. He ushered me gently to a state of unconsciousness by counting back from the number 100 and his kind face and elegant hands floated over me as I awakened. "Yur all right, Mawkey," he said in a soothing West Indian–Harlem drawl. "You came through just fine, just fine."

It wasn't ten minutes later that Dr. Marius, his tall slender body swaddled in surgical gown, emerged from Dad's room. My hopes swelled. He walked straight to Mom and rested a hand on her shoulder.

"Flo and Mawkey," he said, shaking his head. "I'm sorry, but Ara is dead."

My mother cried no and I rose from the seat and flung my Bible across the waiting room floor. No force on this human earth could bring my father down. I damned God again and again and again. A nun bent over and picked up the Bible. A second nun escorted us away from the strangers in the emergency waiting room, to an anteroom with couches and crucifixes. A nurse walked in with a tray of sedatives and a needle. "Get that away from us," I shouted. "We don't need any of that crap." I moved quickly from relative to friend, surveyed each one of their faces. I had never seen grown-ups cry. Thin arms rigid and pounding, I made each one of them a witness to my promise: I would someday become a star athlete (I believe I said a pro football player) and find the man who killed my father. I swore this over and over until I saw my mother's face. Her tiny body, now frail and distorted, slumped in a chair. She looked up at me, her fifteen-year-old son, weeping.

"What am I going to do, Mark?"

I stood over her, cradled and stroked her head and promised that I would take care of things now. She wept more, and for an instant my tears froze and I understood one thing deeper than I had ever understood anything before. Nothing would be the same again. Not me. Not Mom. Not love. Not hate. What ended in the hospital that night was more than my father's life.

c h a p t e r | 2 |

$\mathbf{I}$ imagined on the way home he was riddled with bullet holes and that's why we couldn't see him. I wondered what they did with his body, the fat callouses on his feet that he picked with a pocket knife while reading the newspaper, the penis that was different from mine—uncut the old country way. Would they keep him overnight in the emergency room? Or would they shove him down some stainless steel chute into a basement to await disposal the next morning? When would his body, like the frogs I gigged, stiffen? I asked none of these questions. I tried to picture him again flush in life: The way he looked three hours earlier when he left me behind in the shower; Christmas Eve just a week earlier when cousin Brian and I accompanied him on a last-minute shopping frenzy and he bought Mom a four-slice toaster, an Osterizer, a carving knife, a can opener and a mashed potato mixer, all in the same avocado-green color, and Michelle a ten-speed bike and me clothes and the new Santana album, none of the presents ever wrapped; the day he disobeyed Mom and took us to Buster Brown shoes and told us to pick out whatever style we wanted, liberating our pigeon-toed feet from the straitjacket of corrective shoes forever; the first baseball mitt he bought me, a James Davenport "pro-styled, nylon-stitched" special he hid beneath my covers one night, the leather pocket already supple with oil and wrapped around a brand-new hardball; his motto that you could measure a man by the firmness of his handshake and the sheen of his shoes. I tried to crack knuckles when I shook hands, and each week I was given the chore of polishing the dress boots that lined his closet; his little phobia when his clothes came back from the cleaners, not simply content to throw away the plastic bags but making sure they were riddled with holes—*pop, pop, pop, pop.* He did this to protect my little sister and brother from accidental suffocation. Now, they were not even aware of the terrible truth we were taking home. How lucky they were to have all the rest of their lives those extra minutes of deception, of our father still alive.

Donny had been tucked into bed, a portable TV trundled into the room to lull him to sleep. He was still wide awake, his mind racing with possibilities. *Dad's going to walk in. He's going to be on crutches or maybe in a wheelchair. He's going to be hurt but he'll be coming in.* He turned off the volume and waited for the sound of crutches or wheels down the long hallway. He never heard those sounds. The only light in the room was the flickering light of the TV and the only voice was Mom's soft voice. He could see tears in her eyes but she wasn't sobbing. She hugged him and said, "Your dad's gone," and he tried not to cry. She kissed him goodnight and told him to fall asleep. He lay in bed trying to conceive the murder. Years later, each time he watched the Zapruder film of President Kennedy's head being blown off, he would visualize the shooting of Dad and the two murders would always be seared as one. He tried to sleep but the house was already filling with family and friends.

Uncle Navo left to break the news to Grandpa and Grandma at their house. They had just returned from an art exhibit when he confronted them in the small hallway as they were hanging up their coats.

"Ara died," he blurted in Armenian.

"What are you talking about?" Grandma said. "Ara's not sick."

"They killed him . . . he was shot tonight at the bar."

"My Ara-boy! My Ara-boy," Grandpa screamed, calling out my father's childhood nickname.

"No! You're lying," Grandma protested. "How could he die?"

"What do you mean, 'How could he die?' When you shoot someone, Ma, they die."

Uncle Navo stood there with the small dull expression he wore at the hospital, and Grandma pounded him with her fists.

"Shut up . . . get out . . . go away!"

Cousin Brian, who was staying with my grandparents, fled behind a bedroom door trying to drown out their cries. He had never heard such sounds. Suddenly there was silence; Grandma could not be found. Uncle Navo moved room to room calling her name. Inside a bedroom closet he heard movement and sliding open the door he found her in the corner, tucked like a fetus, gabbling nonsense. He lifted her onto a chair and she gradually worked back to lucidity, rambling on and on how she foretold this day.

"Isn't anyone going to Flora's house?" she asked. "Don't you think we should be there? . . . The children. . . . Oh my God, the children."

I was huddled in a corner of the dining room, hiding behind a white curtain in darkness, when I heard my grandmother calling my name.

"Mark, Mark . . . is that you? What are you doing behind there, honey?"

She started to sob and kissed both my cheeks, fretting over the wetness she left behind. Years later, she reminded me what I said: "What's going to happen, Grandma? How am I going to take care of us?"

She didn't have an answer. She hugged me. "I told your father, 'Ara, this is not your business. Bar business is not your business.' He said, 'What shall I do? I've got $25,000 to invest.' I said, 'I'll tell you what. You are a grocer. A good grocer. Any big market will hire you. They pay big money. And then maybe you can go back to school and be a coach or teacher. I don't want that bar. It's a dirty business. You can't keep the people out.' . . . I knew it . . . I warned him.

"I told him so. Then I told your mother, 'Don't sign those papers, Flora! Don't sign them!'"

Grandpa staggered into the dining room, wailing. "My Ara-boy." He grabbed me hard to his chest and pulled my hair. He wouldn't let go. "What has happened, *tsahkis* (my little one)?"

He led me by the hand into the family room where by now fifteen to twenty people had gathered. Each time someone offered condolences I restated my pledge to Dad. One of his friends suggested that perhaps professional football was too lofty a goal and high school sports might be a more realistic way to honor him. Another tried to quell my anger. "You're a man now, Mark. Your mother's counting on you. Be tough for your old man."

I looked around the room for Uncle Navo. He was a small man, not much taller than myself, yet there was something imposing, almost regal about him. He was always tough, always a man. I wanted him to comfort me, to shore me up, to tell me that Dad hadn't suffered, that there was a heaven and he was going to it, that everything was going to be all right. He was busy on the phone telling the news to relatives and working out the funeral details. Someone had to tend to business and Uncle Navo wore the no-nonsense face of the business at hand.

"The funeral looks like it will be Wednesday, Flora," he said. "Jack Sarafian will come by tomorrow to discuss the plans. He said he'll call first. If you want, I'll be here to meet him."

Mom nodded yes.

I never saw my uncle leave, my eyes fixed on a hulk of a man who had squeezed through the side door and into the kitchen. He wore cowboy boots and a leather belt with a Harley-Davidson buckle and the name "Armond" embossed on back. Armond Bletcher stood six-foot-three, 330 pounds, almost all of it muscle. He looked like Bluto, Popeye's nemesis, only bigger. He offered condolences to Mom, shook hands with Uncle Mike and took me into the foyer, away from the others.

"I just got into town from San Jose when I heard what happened," he said. "Your mother needs you strong. You gotta show some soul. You're the man now."

I lifted my head.

"If I find out, pardner, I'll tear out their fuckin' hearts. Your old man was one tough hombre. Even I wouldn't go messin' with Ara when he got angry. You should be proud. Your Dad died a hee-row."

Armond was twenty-nine years old and made his living collecting bad debts. He rode a big orange Harley and hung around the Hell's Angels.

The first time Dad brought him home the previous summer, we played billiards in the family room. At his behest, I racked the balls extra tight and he warned me to stand way back. He broke the cluster with such concentrated force—not unlike the methodical explosion of a shot putter—that several of the balls came whizzing off the table and the cue stick splintered in his hands. At dinner he leaned back in the wrought-iron chair and snapped it in half, apologizing sheepishly to Mom. He was anything but clumsy when fighting. His black leather shoes were specially made for street brawling, toes pointed and soles that grabbed the pavement. He could kick as high as he was tall, Dad had said. As a precaution against attacks from the rear, Armond moved through the world back to the wall, all motion in front of him.

After that first visit, he brought his wife Janice over once or twice for dinner. This was something of an honor since Armond's usual practice was to keep Janice at home, tucked away like some china doll. She tended to him in the manner of a geisha, tiny and delicate with a voice that could not have been softer or sweeter. I wondered how they did it, certainly not his 330 pounds on top. At meal's end, toothpicks in hand, they took turns picking clean each other's teeth.

"I wanted to leave San Jose earlier and I would've probably been at the bar when this happened. But I got hung up. I'm sorry."

He unfolded a thick wad of hundred dollar bills from his pocket. "People are going to say I was your father's friend because of money. Don't believe 'em. . . . I don't need money." He fanned the bills in my face. "See, I've got plenty of it."

He left and came back a few hours later, packing a gun. We were afraid to be alone and he offered to spend the night, along with a few relatives. I watched him fall asleep on my sister's bed, the sheer weight of his mass folding the mattress around him, the .357 a plaything at his side.

The three of us went to bed that night with our mother. For years afterward, we took turns sleeping beside her. I am ashamed to say that I found sleep that night, beguiled by a voice assuring me that none of this was happening, the same voice that comes in bad dreams and whispers *you are hurtling through the pitch black air and death below is certain but trust me, trust me, I will awaken you just when you think it's too late.* I awakened that first morning sick to my stomach to the truth of us side-by-side, Mom curled up in the cavity where Dad slept. She got up first not knowing we were awake and tried to sneak into the kitchen. My sister and I slunk close behind. As she reached into the drawer, the one with the butcher knife, we pounced from different directions.

"I'm making a pot of coffee," she said, a sullen smile. "I'm not going anywhere."

My father made the front page of the *Fresno Bee* that afternoon, above the fold: FRESNO TAVERN OWNER IS SHOT, KILLED; PAIR SOUGHT. Nothing seemed completely real about that night until then: face-to-face with his picture, the white wedding tux, the black bow tie, the gap-toothed smile.

I learned that not one but two gunmen were involved, both of them white and in their early twenties. Dad was working on the quarterly taxes when they walked in and without a word began firing. Linda Lewis, the only witness, ducked behind the bar and was unhurt. Dad had been wounded five times, in the chest, stomach, legs, wrist and head. No money had been taken from the till and $135 was found in his pocket.

Police called the murder a hit but the two gunmen and the person or persons who hired them were never found. Because of the bar's rough clientele, most of the speculation centered on drugs and drug smuggling, with Dad somehow involved. Absent a clear motive, the reason for the murder somehow went down in our town as a transgression by the victim. However lopsided the response, people reasoned, Ara Arax must have committed his own flagrant wrong.

I *often think back to my promise to you, that half-pitiful child* (I'm going to be a professional football player!) *and half-wishful adult* (I'm going to find the killers!) *and I wonder. Did that fifteen-year-old boy, hands clenched into fists, know something? Why had he assumed the cops would not find them? That it would be left to him?*

I never made it to the pros, much less to the college gridiron. There wasn't much market for a five-foot-eleven prep quarterback, heavy of foot, who operated best from the shotgun position. I told myself you'd understand. It is that second half of my promise that I could never let go of, and that would never let go of me.

On a foggy night in January, 1989, seventeen years after that night, I came home to Fresno to find the truth of your murder. It is a hunt for more than killers. It has to be more, or else I would hire a good private detective and be done with it. I am trying to understand a life, a family, a town. I want to know you, shorn of rumor and myth. I want to reclaim that part of you, and me, that has nothing to do with murder.

My return here is not as prodigal son but as wary man, a husband and father now, thirty-two years old, with an assumed name and the first gun I've ever owned. We moved into one of the new gated apartment complexes built on fig orchard land where I rode the miniature motorcycle you gave me as a kid and where I drank beer

*in high school on autumn nights warmed by bonfires. I checked the list of tenants be-
fore moving in. I burned my notes rather than trust the communal garbage bin.*

*I try hard to shield my wife and your two-year-old granddaughter from aware-
ness of the men who tease my days and torment my nights. This is not an easy thing
to do, surrounded as I am by mounds of criminal files and court cases, records of investigations of old drug smuggling rings, mug shots, fingerprints, lie detector tests
and newspaper clippings going back a hundred years.*

*In case I have forgotten the old rumors, there are still a few brash voices around
to tell the son what they really thought of the father. "Ara's Apartments. Ara
Arax. The crook," said Todd Lofgren, one of my first contacts. The state narcotics
agent had been transferred from Fresno to Sacramento long ago but he didn't need
any cue on the subject of you and your bar.*

*"We used to drive by that place and talk about him. He was one of the reputed
crooks in town. I have to tell you, I've been in law enforcement a number of years
and people don't get reputations like that without being involved to some extent. I've
never seen a man with that kind of reputation unjustly accused."*

*This was not something I wanted to hear, and my protest, so damn sonlike, was
not about to change his mind. I'm not sure I believe it myself. You taught me baseball and football and table manners. You professed clean living, didn't smoke or get
drunk and hated drugs. But I was just a kid, what did I know?*

*The truth, the truth as I know it, is no abstraction. I am not alone in this
world. There is a clan and its proud name to consider. Michelle, Donny, cousins,
aunts and uncles, all those living whose actions I am judging and whose secrets I
contemplate betraying. The reason none of them has risen to shout, "Who gives you
the right?" is that I continue to deceive them. Even as they recall my childhood vows
of vengeance, I insist that I have come home to write about Southeast Asians. The
few I trust with the truth are only too willing to grant me their approval, not
knowing how far I have already taken things.*

*How to prepare Michelle and Donny for the deceit in your life? How to explain
to Uncle Navo, a prudent man who safeguards the family secrets and defends the
family honor, that it is necessary to hide a tiny machine beneath my shirt to record
our conversations.*

*Night after night, I sit and linger in the past. There were four murders in our
family, one in each generation. Murder is what brought us to America. Questions of
murder have become questions of family and questions of family have become questions of history, until I find myself buried in some book about ancient Armenia,*

circa 3000 B.C. *Who were my forebears? What were the forces that shaped you and reached down to shape me? What did it mean for you to be the first generation after the Armenian genocide, the son of a survivor? How did your father's impassioned communism at the height of the McCarthy era affect you and Uncle Navo? What kind of parents were Grandpa and Grandma? How was it that Grandpa and his brother, one a poet and the other a killer, came from the same womb? What possibilities, then, am I to consider about you and your brother, and me?*

Time has played its trick, Dad. The space between us has so narrowed that we are more like contemporaries now, more like brothers. To answer these questions, I am drawn back to where my knowledge of you first took shape, back to our origins, the birth of our people and family and me, back to where your fate became my fate and the murder was like a giant river that swelled through my life, you on one distant bluff and me on the other, carving a way across.

My mother liked to tell people I was bullheaded from the start. It took a whole night of raucous Armenian circle dancing to nudge me down and fourteen hours of push to coax me out. I was born the day after Christmas, 1956, the first grandchild of the Arax clan in America.

It was Armenian custom to name the first boy after a male forebear, usually the paternal grandfather. Had custom been honored, Mom would have christened me Aram, if not the first name at least the middle. She chose Mark Randy instead.

Our last name didn't end in the usual "ian," which in Armenian means "the son of." There was Vosgerichian, son of goldsmith. And Goshgarian, son of cobbler. And Medzorian, son of fat ass. In our case, the oddly truncated "Arax" had nothing to do with a tongue-tied clerk at Ellis Island or the great melting pot. Arax was the mother river that flowed from the mother mountain, Ararat. It was my grandfather's pen name. Our actual, centuries-old last name was Hovsepian, son of Joseph.

My birth punctuated a turning in their lives, the final move from farm to city, from vineyards to the grocery stores. For years, the only piece of art that graced our walls was an oil painting of one such vineyard in early spring bloom, trunks sloughing skin and twisted like an old man, three fruit-bearing spurs pointed east and three fruit-bearing spurs pointed west, leaves tender and translucent, and not a weed in the wide, long rows. It hung there like myth, a dream from the past. I assumed it was one of the vineyards my family farmed before I was born. I assumed my father placed it there, above the hearth, as an intention. When the madness of the grocery stores and later the bar business was behind him and he had saved a little cash, he would return to the vineyard with the girdling knife he kept with the other tools.

My father, grandfather and uncle used the proceeds from the sale of the last vineyard to buy four small markets in poor white neighborhoods. They named the chain Peacock. A big neon bird preened iridescent overhead. It was supposed to be a three-man partnership but Grandpa mostly walked the aisles smoking a pipe and trailing socialist dogma. It was just as well, Dad said. The boys worked fifteen-hour days and didn't need any ideological distractions. They were trying to lock out the union, and the old man was fodder for the other side.

It was the fifties, a sanguine time when the banks were waving big loans in every direction. Uncle Navo, flush with borrowed dollars, decided that he and Dad should take on the big chains, and in the spring of 1959 they broke ground for a fifth grocery. It wasn't just a new market but a supermarket, the chain's flagship, located in a middle-class corner of northwest Fresno.

My father and uncle, neither one yet thirty, poured their energy into the new store. They left the four other markets, the chain's bread and butter, in the hands of a collection of buddies and brothers-in-law and genocide survivors and whoever else was willing to work twelve hours and get paid for eight and not tell the unions and buy into the promise of good times and promotions ahead.

I roamed the wide aisles on Saturday, the whole place mine, dressed in a yellow-orange grocer smock Dad cut to my size. I liked the meat department best, the smell of the sawdust floor and the screech of the butcher's rubber soles like a game of one-on-one. They stuffed me with hot dogs and Cokes and the one time I stole candy and got caught, Dad said I never had to steal again. All I had to do was ask.

Dad was chosen president of the local food dealers association at a time when the big chains were waging a price war with the independents. To compete, Peacock advertised a different staple each week far below whole-sale price. This "loss leader" operated on the premise that once people were enticed inside they would buy other items and the friendly service would woo them back.

But Peacock customers, many of them Dust Bowl survivors, were far too penny-wise for that. They shopped sugar at one market, bread at an-other, milk at a third. Cherry pickers, Uncle Navo called them. The Pea-cocks were buying coffee at $1.09 a pound and selling it for 69 cents and losing $3,000 a week in the process. Uncle Navo, hoping to slow the bleeding, ended the loss-leader practice. People just went elsewhere. No loss leader, no traffic. It was either dying alone or dying with a crowd around.

Dad complained that Uncle Navo called all the shots, lunched with all the salesmen and took off afternoons to play golf while he stayed behind and worked the produce. He blamed his brother for stretching resources too thin by building the fifth store. One by one, in 1961, the stores began to falter and the relationship between my father and uncle degenerated into violence. One Saturday, in front of the vegetable stand, Dad blew up and took Grandpa's head in one palm and Uncle Navo's head in the other and like two melons thumped them together.

Uncle Navo, reading the futility of it all, pushed to file bankruptcy. Dad fought to save at least one store. I awoke one night and found my fa-ther standing naked over my mother in bed, pleading that she wake up. "Flora! Flora!," he cried, not seeing his son until it was too late. "My heart is skipping beats."

The doctor assured Dad his heart was fine. After that, he had a hard time driving the car. He'd stop for no reason in the middle of traffic and telephone Mom to pick him up. The butcher began chauffering him to and from work. Mom told us he had fallen asleep at the wheel and just needed a rest. Every Wednesday we dropped him off in front of this dark, cabinlike house, and picked him up an hour later. Mom said he was visit-ing a friend. Years later I found out that this friend was a psychologist named Donn Beedle; my father had suffered a mental breakdown.

○○○

The Peacocks went into receivership in 1962. My father found two brothers, John and Jack Terzian, willing to buy the best Peacock and hire him as manager with a future stake.

On the comeback, Dad borrowed an air force fitness program from a neighbor and made it even more demanding. Four days a week, forty-five minutes a session, there was a furious unleashing across the den. Jumping jacks, straddle hops, push-ups, sit-ups, leg raises, high knees in place. He bought this torture contraption for the stomach, a little bar on two rubber tires, that he gripped and rolled all the way out to the prone position.

He charted his emotional recovery in a little green book:

> Feb. 16th, felt good, A.M. exercises, 450 running in place, B+.
>
> 17th, felt good, 444 running in place, B.
>
> 18th, felt the greatest, did not get mad, A+.
>
> 19th, felt a little gas, OK, 455 running in place, C+.
>
> 20th, felt bad, gas, tired from work, no exercise, D.
>
> 21st, anxiety P.M., felt good and bad, no exercise, C-.
>
> 22nd, felt excellent, on the way back, did not get mad, P.M. exercise,
>
> 515 running in place, A++.

The surviving Peacock broke even the first year and made money the second and third. Even so, John and Jack Terzian complained that Dad kept erring on the generous side, overstocking the shelves. Dad thought he and John were going to buy out Jack but the brothers pulled a fast one. They wanted Dad out and were willing to pay him $25,000 for having taught them the business. Dad smirked, took the money and bought The Apartments. My mother refused to talk to the Terzians for years, a silence that became a pointed finger after the murder, as if to say, Ara would still be alive if you hadn't connived.

ooo

Armenian? I remember looking up the word in the encyclopedia when I was a kid and finding "an Oriental people." I kept checking my eyes for slants. No historian could say for sure who we were exactly—we were Oriental in the Middle Eastern sense—or how far our country dated back. The best guess traced us 2,600 years to the kingdom of Urartu or Ararat in what is now eastern Turkey. Perched high above the empires of the low-lands, this plateau would become the bridge between East and West. There would be no peace at this crossroads of history.

The first invaders were the Armeni and Hayasa, Balkan peoples who felt duty-bound to impose their Indo-European language and ways on the Urartians. From a marriage of the Urartians and Armeni and Hayasa emerged the Armenians. Like the Jews, the encyclopedia said, we possessed a "remarkable tenacity of race and faculty of adaptation to circumstances." I understood later that this was a polite way of noting that our refusal to give up our ways meant that we had been kicked, like our fellow "wanderers" the Jews, far and wide.

For two centuries before Christ, eleven Armenian kings ruled over a country that at its full flower extended from the Caspian to Mediterranean seas. One of the last of these kings was Tigran the Great, a man of profuse talent and ego, lover of Greek refinements, patron of the arts and land grabber. His reign might be called Armenia's gilded age, for Tigran's dominion hinged on the continued languor of the world's other great powers. At some point, no longer preoccupied with each other, they looked up and discovered that Tigran, the great dilettante, had annexed the whole of Anatolia. A series of military defeats pushed him back to more humble boundaries. For the imperial nation of Armenia, it was pretty much downhill from there.

Several of the kings of Rome, occupiers of Armenia, were Armenian themselves. History recorded Leo V who sat on the Byzantine throne in the early 800s this way: "As to his immediate origin, it is well known that he came from the country of Armenians, whence, according to some, his obstinacy and his bad disposition."

Fresno boasted some 20,000 Armenians but we were scattered from city to farm. My grandparents' generation had come to the San Joaquin Valley in the 1920s in the wake of the Turkish massacres that claimed two-thirds of the Armenian race and scattered the other third across the globe. These elders may have sprung from a culture that survived successive waves of Macedonians, Persians, Romans, Mongols and Tartars, but they were made to look on feebly as their children and children's children surrendered to the blandishments of America.

As a clan, we Araxes had an easier time of it. Not only did our last name lack the telltale "ian" ending, but our looks didn't exactly give us away either. My father's curly blond hair was so unusual for an Armenian that Grandma saw no harm in letting it grow past the shoulders. Strangers glimpsed the two brothers—Navo dark, Ara tumbling white—and remarked how nice it was, a boy and a girl. "No, I boy," Dad would tell them. For the rest of his life, family and friends called him Ara-boy.

I inherited the deep brown eyes and thick long eyelashes (the Armenian blessing) and the stubby legs (our curse). Otherwise, I stood out from the kids at Sunday school. I had a mix of my father's light coloring and my mother's small features. Every August, gathered at the fairgrounds for the harvest picnic, the matrons with bloated ankles and bloated feet, nylons rolled mid-calf, fussed over me.

"You're Armenian? Full-blooded?"

"Yes," I would nod.

"Oh, *ah-bris* (may you live a long life)."

I had once been fluent in Armenian, as fluent as a five-year-old could be, but one day of kindergarten took care of that. I insisted on English only, and Mom and Dad didn't press me. Grandpa Arax spoke Armenian, Turkish, English and a little French, and suffered more or less kindly my loss of the mother tongue. He called it the "white genocide." He wrote of his seven grandchildren, none of whom could speak Armenian: "The mellifluous music mute on their lips."

At times I felt the compulsory chauvinism of a people only six million strong. Mostly, though, I felt confusion over the elaborate politics that split us Armenians into two warring camps. There were two of everything. Two churches, two commemorations to mark the Genocide, two picnics to bless the grapes, two youth groups, two Armenian Olympics. There were two of everything except one cemetery, Ararat.

To the child the feud seemed about two flags. Holy Trinity Armenian Church proudly displayed the red, orange and blue flag of independent Armenia (1918–1920). St. Paul's Church down the road preached solidarity with Armenians abroad, and whenever a bigwig from Yerevan came to town the church flew the red Soviet Armenian flag next to the Stars and Stripes.

Sadly, the Armenian church had been one entity for more than a thousand years until a dispute over the two flags ended in the sensational 1933 murder of the Archbishop in New York City. Detectives traced the motive to an insult at the Chicago World's Fair that summer but the murder was actually decades in the making, a blood feud appeased but never extinguished.

At the 1933 World's Fair, Archbishop Leon Tourian had refused to speak with the old flag of independent Armenia unfurled behind him. Tourian insisted that the flag of Soviet Armenia, where the pope and mother church were based, be flown instead. This was an affront to some audience members who belonged to the Dashnak Party, a revolutionary group holding fast to the dream of a free Armenia.

The Dashnaks traced Soviet Armenia's wretched condition in the 1930s to the Bolshevik Armenians who were so willing to throw their lot behind Lenin as savior. The Bolshevik Armenians blamed the Dashnaks for not recognizing the duplicity of Turkish leaders on the eve of World War I and leading Armenians into slaughter.

On Christmas Eve, 1933, 200 parishioners packed Holy Cross Armenian Church on 187th Street in Manhattan to see Tourian celebrate a special holiday liturgy. In a procession to the altar, he clutched a gold pastoral staff in one hand and a crucifix in the other. As he moved past the fifth row of pews, a swarm of Dashnaks, their presence previously unnoticed in the crowd, thronged about him. Tourian stood six feet tall, towering above the little men lunging butcher knives. Witnesses said he groaned, slumped forward and fell in the aisle, his staff bent by his weight, his face turned in the direction of a painted Crucifixion. The fifty-four-year-old Archbishop died before help arrived. Two of the Dashnak assassins were beaten by parishioners and detained. Three more were arrested the next day.

The murder kindled the passions of both Dashnaks and Soviet supporters who had coexisted more or less in peace under a banner of Armenian solidarity. At Holy Trinity in Fresno, a pro-Soviet Armenia group broke away from the Dashnaks and formed St. Paul's Church.

My two grandfathers, the poet and the priest, split along this obdurate line. I have been pulled back and forth most of my life.

Grandpa and Grandma Arax were Bolshevik Armenians affiliated with St. Paul's. On Labor Day weekend, I'd accompany them to socialist functions that always extended late into the night and always featured Grandpa as closing speaker. He was roly-poly and barely taller than the lectern itself, and even though I understood only a few words of Armenian, it was easy to sense the power of his speech.

My mother's father, Reverend Yegishe Mekhitarian, was no less formidable. A Dashnak Party leader and red baiter, he had fought all his life to free Armenia from Soviet rule. And he fought straight from the pulpit as the priest of Holy Trinity Church. The title "Grandpa" didn't quite fit the man, proper and fastidious and never caught without his priestly collar. So we grandchildren took a cue from our parents and called him *Hyreek*, which means father in Armenian.

I don't recall my mother's father ever quoting the Bible outside of church or thumping a dog-eared edition at home. Hyreek poked fun at born-again rapture and his liturgy demanded little vocal participation from the assembled. There were no trips around a rosary bead, no Hail Marys. As the first Christian nation, we Armenians observe Christianity a lot like the Reform Jews observe Judaism, with an emphasis on history and suffering, tradition and ceremony. Hyreek didn't saddle his parishioners with guilt but neither did he steel them with unquestioning faith.

When it came to the children, my grandparents and parents chose not to burden us with history—not of Armenia, not of Fresno. We were never told that our city resisted absorbing Armenians to the last. Whether Christian or Bolshevik, Fresno didn't want them.

The discriminatory real estate codes that prevented two generations of my clan from living on the north end were a thing of the past when I was growing up. We Armenians no longer ate our watermelon on the front porch, sparing longtime Fresnans with midwestern roots who believed life was to be conducted decorously behind the front door. Likewise, I rarely heard our language spoken in public, at least in places that were not comfortably Armenian.

A few symbols of intolerance persisted. If you wanted to be a Shriner, you had to go to the San Francisco chapter to join. City hall blackballed Armenians, patronage controlled by the Volga Germans from Russia. So did the local newspaper, the *Fresno Bee,* on its editorial side. Sunnyside Country Club wouldn't allow an Armenian member, no matter how well-to-do. I knew this because the golf pro at Sunnyside made the mistake of walking into The Apartments one day. Dad let him order a drink and he let the bartender serve it. Then he leaned over and informed the man, "I can't belong to your country club and you can't drink in my bar."

I'd like to think my father's temper had something to do with this hide-bound past. He was quite capable of laughing at himself but responded to even the hint of put-down, ethnic or otherwise, with explosive anger. This made for some unforgettable scenes. Our good-bye to the old neighborhood when I was not yet eleven ended in one such spectacle, although my father tried his best to avoid it.

He had been generous to the man who bought our house. When Terry couldn't swing the financing on his own, Dad offered to carry a second mortgage. A week before the deal closed, Dad gave Terry a tour of the house, explaining in great detail what worked and what didn't work. Mom complained he was being too honest. A family member died a few days later and we needed an extra weekend to move. A perplexed Terry showed up at our front door in coat and tie.

"What's the delay, Ara?"

Dad invited him inside. "It's been a tough week, Terry. The funeral set us behind. I know you said you had an extra week on your lease. Would it be all right if we stayed until Sunday?"

Dad offered to pay rent for the extra two days. Terry thought for a second.

"You guys can sleep in the garage."

At first I thought this was Terry's idea of a bad joke, for he said it with such aplomb. But he offered nothing in the way of a punchline. Only silence.

Dad's face froze. "Sleep in the garage. Sleep in the garage. Sleep in the garage," he muttered, first in apparent disbelief and then with an anger that billowed. Each time he repeated the phrase the affront became clearer and clearer.

His lower lip curled tight under the glint of teeth. I knew very well what came next. Terry never saw it. Dad wound up and backhanded him, one bearlike swat to the cheek. He flew across the kitchen and landed at my feet. As he tried to shake off the blow, I got carried away and gave him a swift kick in the ribs. Mom restrained Dad long enough for Terry to stumble outside. When he reached his car, he turned around and wagged a defiant finger at Dad.

"I've been waiting for this," he cried. "I'm going to sue you! Did you hear that? Sue you!"

If Terry had been smart, he'd have gotten into his car right then and drove off. Maybe he thought the light of outdoors afforded him protection the inside of our house did not. If he had been dealing with any other man, he might have been right. But Dad wasn't thinking right then about lawsuits or eyewitness accounts. All he could see was this pip-squeak who had needed his help to buy his home, who had stood in his kitchen and pointed to his garage as a solution to a two-day delay caused by a death in his family, standing before him still wagging his finger.

"When my lawyers get through with you, this house will be mine," Terry said. "I'm going to sue! Did you hear that? Sue!"

"Lawyers?" Dad seethed. "Sue?" Dad marched across the front lawn to where Terry stood and jerked his tie. I winced. He spun him through the air once, twice, before the knot in the tie gave way. Dad was still holding the tie when Terry burned rubber down the block. Whether we stayed the weekend, whether Dad answered charges of assault and battery, I am not sure.

It occurs to me now that an offer to "sleep in the garage," simply asinine to me, might have come across as a racist code to someone weaned on "No occupancy by Negro, Chinese, Japanese, Hindu, Armenian, Asiatic or natives of the Turkish Empire or any descendants of the above." The Golden State, after all, was where housing officials had declared Armenian immigrants to be undesirably flawed by antisocial traits. It was where insurance companies once refused coverage to Armenians because, in the words of one insurer's letter, "there is a certain feeling against this class of people which renders their risks undesirable by reason of the moral hazard which is engendered because they have enemies."

Only once or twice growing up did I find myself face-to-face with an ethnic slur, wondering how best to react. A few months after Dad bought The Apartments, I took some menus to school hoping to prove that what we owned was a restaurant, not a bar. A sixth grader named Kovacevich grabbed one menu—steak, lobster and a daily Armenian special—and laughed. I thought he was mocking my assertion that this fare, so sparse, constituted a restaurant. In fact, it was the word Armenian that provoked him.

"So you're a Fresno Indian." He began dancing in circles. *"Wu, wu, wu, wu. Wu, wu, wu, wu. Wu! Wuuuuu!"* He held the menu teasingly past my reach and I tried to punch him in the nose but he kicked me in the nuts first.

The next year, I got into a shoving match with the Mormon kid who sat behind me. He shouted "dirty Armenian" and before I could respond, our teacher Mr. Unruh stood between us and led me outside. He calmed me down and even got me to agree to a handshake. I walked to the back of the room fully intending to carry out my part of the agreement. Something snapped halfway there. Feigning the look of apology, I buried my head into the blond boy's chest and flailed both fists. I was sent home for the day.

That night, he visited our house bandaged and accompanied by contrite parents. I had cracked two of his ribs. Under the expectant gaze of our fathers, we shook hands and apologized. For several years after that, at Christmas, he showed up at our front door with a plate of cookies his mother had baked.

Proud as I was to be Armenian, I did feel ambivalent about the men and women I encountered at church and Sunday picnics at the fairgrounds.

They cherished old folks and children, savored pomegranates and persimmons, swapped gossip and told fortunes from the coffee grounds of an upside-down demitasse. They branded you for life. One poor guy stole a crate of raisins during the Depression and forever lost his name. He was known all the rest of his days as the *chahmich gogh,* the raisin stealer. Forty years later, an old lady seated on an aluminum lawn chair at the fairgrounds pointed to the teenager standing in the shish kebab line. "That's the *chahmich gogh*'s grandson," she said. All the old ladies in aluminum lawn chairs nodded their heads vigorously.

They never forgot their provincial differences. That group over there hails from ancient Van. They're from Bitlis. They're from Moosh. You can't come between a native of Van and a dollar. The people of Bitlis have Jewish blood, shrewd businessmen. The Moosh natives are plain stubborn, warriors. That group over there is made up of big-city dwellers, educated, polished. That group over there comes from the mountain, crude.

Maybe I was mixing up the foibles of the human race with the foibles of the Armenian race, but they seemed to me to be especially small and petty. They thought nothing of dropping tens of thousands of dollars on weddings and bickering over a few cents in the price per ton of raisins. They could keep a grudge like no one. It didn't matter who had hurt them—a brother, sister or cousin—for they were quite capable of carrying the pique to the grave. Too often the reason was money. They were great orators and benefactors. Their weeklies and monthlies were filled with the news of speechmaking and philanthropy. Everywhere I turned in church was another gold plate telling me this room or that font or this drinking fountain had been donated in the name or memory of so and so.

And just when you had them solved, infinite sufferers and begrudgers, they would confound you with a nobility of spirit, a dignity, laughter in the face of great tragedy. When they had nothing, they gave you everything. They had somehow managed to hang on, their language and religion and mirth still glowing, long after the candle of their Indo-European cousins—the Assyrians, Macedonians and Hittites—had been quenched.

It was no coincidence that our father's mother, Alma, the one grandparent born in America who spoke English without fracture, a thoroughly modern woman, was our favorite. My sister and I used to beg Mom to let us spend the weekend with Grandma and Pop even though it surely meant being dragged to one of their insufferable card nights. The houses where these games were held all looked and smelled the same. Doilies and mothballs. The sound was the fullness of dissonance—Communists, capitalists, artists, backsliders and libertines, blowhards, the former seamstress to the Castro family of Cuba and the fat, cigar-chomping proprietor of a downtown hotel for whores.

As soon as we walked through the door, Charlie Margosian grabbed my ear and pulled and pulled until I screamed. This was a common, if annoying, Armenian greeting for children, much like the question "Who do you love more—your mother or your father?" Then Mr. Margosian reached into his pocket and handed me a quarter and said, as if I had to be grateful, "I used to give your father, who had bigger ears, a nickel."

They played past midnight, one game folding into the next. "We're going to play baseball now," Grandma said. "I need your help, Markie."

Why they called it baseball and why she thought she needed my help I'll never know. The card game shared not a single trait with my game. I

kept quiet knowing sooner or later they were going to break out the plat-
ters of watermelon, peppers pickled in garlic vinegar, string cheese and
slices of cured beef called basturma, whose seasonings affected the smell of
your urine like asparagus, only stronger, and for a full forty-eight hours.

Whenever we spent the night, my sister and I shared the fold-out couch
in their living room, and Grandma did a final body check before tucking
us in. "I was reading an article the other day that it's nice to let your body
breathe," she said. "Why not take off your socks?"

The next morning after showers she bundled us in two layers and ran
her fingers through our hair to make sure it was completely dry before we
played outside. Breathe by night, suffocate by day, it was Grandma's pleasure.

"Kitty, I'm taking Markie to Sambo's," Grandpa said. "We'll be back in
an hour."

They called each other Kitty, short for kitten. When he wanted to toy
with her just a little, he had a second nickname, Mademoiselle Fifi, which
I learned later came from a Maupassant short story. Sambo's was a breakfast house on Blackstone near the railroad tracks. I gathered from the mosaic on the wall that Sambo was a little black boy who got chased by a
tiger and turned into butter.

"Order anything you want, *dugh-ahs* (my boy)."

"Can I have steak and eggs?"

"Why not?" he smiled. "You're paying."

He wasn't in any hurry like Dad. He drank four or five cups of coffee.
"These are the best mugs in town, Markie. I can't stand drinking coffee
from stir-a-foam cup. It doesn't taste the same."

He reached for the bill and cussed in Turkish.

"What's wrong, Pop?"

"Kitty took my money," he said, holding up an empty wallet as proof.
"Did you bring any cash?"

I was ten.

"How come you never carry cash? Have you washed dishes before?"

He had me going and my face showed it. He waited a moment or two
for full effect, then pulled out a crisp twenty from his shirt pocket and
broke into laughter that was something less than kind, a sly laugh that
stayed stuck in his throat. I was way too serious for my own good and he

was going to have a little fun at my expense. I remember climbing into the car still stewing. For years after, whenever we ate at Sambo's, he would try the same stunt knowing it was doomed, until one day I called his bluff and pulled out my own crisp twenty. He let me pay.

The history that made Armenians tough seemed to have taken an extra toll on my mother's clan.

My great-grandmother, Perouz, survived the Genocide only to see her two daughters die of pneumonia in their twenties. One of these daughters, Lucine, was the grandmother I never knew. She left my six-year-old mother and three other children, one of them a baby boy, behind in France. Perouz, whose name meant the blue rock of the Persian Gulf, stepped in as caretaker.

They said her enormous blue eyes spilled tears every day for two years after her daughter's death. She stopped mourning only to do battle with the woman who my grandfather, Hyreek, brought home to care for my mother and her siblings. It was less a marriage than an arrangement, and Perouz naturally took offense that a simple widow who could neither read nor write could replace her cultured daughter.

She worked hard to sabatoge the marriage, packing her bags more than once knowing that the four small children, her blood, would only call her back with their tears. She heckled and jeered the stepmother and ascribed selfish motives to the most generous of gestures. Stepmother would serve pilaf to Perouz and the children first, taking for herself morsels left on the bottom. "Look," Perouz would say, gesturing with her chin, "your step-mother gives us the bland on top and takes for herself the buttery on the bottom."

In America, years later, Mom and her two sisters weren't ready to put Perouz in an old age home, so it was decided that they would take turns caring for my great-grandmother, a few months at a time.

I remember the first time she came to live with us, *Medz Momma,* we called her, Big Momma, her hair wild and white, stalking the halls at night cursing the Turks and chanting scripture from a torn Armenian Bible. She sat most of the day staring out the window, her long nails tap dancing on the wooden sills. I was no more than seven or eight and the noise, unremitting, drove me mad. At dinner one night, I flung an aluminum pie plate across the table and struck the top of Big Momma's head. To my horror, it cut open her scalp, as thin as parchment, and she fell over bleeding. If I felt a fleeting moment of triumph in the delivery of a perfect strike, it gave way quickly to fear and remorse, the old lady crumpled on her side, holding her head in her hands and murmuring something ancient in Armenian, and my mother shrieking, "What have you done?"

Big Momma eventually agreed to a nursing home. Years after her death, thousands of tiny depressions dug by her nails still pocked our house. Whenever I see distressed wood, I think of my great-grandmother.

Grandma Mekhitarian's status as step-grandmother was supposed to be this big family secret. Cousin Michael broke the news to me. "You know she's not our real grandmother? Our real grandmother died in France." This may well have been the first of a hundred blood secrets exposed and myths decoded, but I can't remember my reaction. I better recollect another time when Michael—two years older, my window on the adult world, my defiler—lifted another veil.

"I know the dirtiest word in all of America," he boasted on the playground.

"Well, what is it?"

He wouldn't tell me no matter what I promised. "You're too young."

I was eight or nine. I begged and begged and then I extorted. "If you don't tell me, I'll never be your cousin again."

I made him repeat it. I made him spell it. But for some reason I never asked him what it meant. I'm not sure he knew.

That night, driving to the Italian Kitchen, our weekly out-to-dinner treat, I sat in the backseat and sang "I Wanna Hold Your Hand" with the Beatles: "It's such a feeling that my love, I get fucked, I get fucked, I get fuuuuckkkkked." I can still see Dad and Mom trying to suppress their laughter in the front seat of the 64 Grand Prix.

Their reaction seems oddly charitable, looking back. This was part of the enigma of my parents, guessing how they might respond. Some things set them off and some things, like the f-word, didn't. It was hard to predict. They were hard to predict. They seemed genuinely confused about what to hold onto, what to discard.

My mother knew the words to singer Varoujan's "Armenian Classics" and the Jefferson Airplane's "Surrealistic Pillow." She could name the Giants opening day lineup and the jersey numbers of Mays, McCovey and Marichal. If she thought us shortchanged at school, she'd march right over and tell off the teacher and, if need be, the principal, too. She dressed for the times. In the sixties, she wore beehive wigs, short skirts and fishnet stockings. She spoke beautiful Armenian and sang in the church choir. Around her neck hung the alabaster and turquoise eye to ward off evil. Whenever Hyreek came to visit, she scurried to hide all traces of her smoking habit. We'd catch him opening the drawers in the kitchen and bathrooms, rubbing and sniffing each ashtray. It wasn't until cousin Michael and I snitched on our mothers that Hyreek knew for sure his daughters smoked. Mom preferred some forms of old-country punishment (black pepper in a sassy mouth) and some forms of new (wood hanger across the backside). She once tried her grandmother's custom of "cupping," applying a heated glass to my lungs to suck out the congestion. I walked around for days with ovals tattooed all over my back and chest.

My father surrendered a lot more. Even his Armenian was broken. He edged his entrepreneurial spirit with touches of Grandpa's politics. He'd tell customers, "I am a capitalist. I am a Communist. I am both." It seemed deeply felt and possible in the sixties. What I recall of his library, paltry as it was, was a curious melange that seems to have reflected this contradiction. There was an inspirational tale about golfer Billy Casper fighting cancer through the Mormon faith; the story of the brave Red Army during World War II called *Russians Don't Surrender;* a few paperbacks on the Mafia, including *Grim Reapers* and *The Valachi Papers;* and *Soul on Ice,* Eldridge Cleaver's polemic on the black man.

"What is this junk?" my mother demanded, holding up the Cleaver book. "He blames white women for all the problems of black men. 'The ogre. White witch. Your white skin is nightmare food.' So he rapes them?"

Dad sloughed her off with one of his quips: "Don't get down on something you're not up on."

I don't recall ever catching my parents in full embrace, but they must have displayed their affection, I just don't remember. Maybe I did catch them once or twice and was too embarrassed to look more than a glance and have since forgotten. I did catch them kicking it up on the dance floor

once, Dad blessed with fluid feet. Mom told me they had won a dance contest at the Rainbow Ballroom the year before they were married.

While there were happy times between them, happy times that filtered
down to us, the impression that lingers today is one of incompatibility.
The nagging history of Turkish Armenia and the destiny of Soviet Armenia, issues that defined the whole of my grandparents' condition, took a
backseat in our lives to dreams pinned instead on the suburbs. This was
hardly unique. Immigrant families, the first generation especially, strad-
dled two worlds and struggled with paradox. What made it different,
what made our lives so crazy, was the engine Dad chose to chase down the
American Dream. One day out of the incredible blue, he left the house a
farmer and grocery man and came back the owner of a bar.

c h a p t e r 6

The day my father bought The Apartments he brought home a puppy, a peace offering to Mom who had argued against the bar business. It was an ugly mongrel and crazy to boot, confusing my basketball for a lover. Dad got nowhere with the dog but he finally did find a way to mute Mom's criticism about the bar. He made her younger brother, George, his partner. I never understood how he could do business with family again after what happened in the Peacocks.

It's true his relationship with Uncle George was different. Uncle George looked up to Dad—the athlete he never was, the father figure he never had. Grandpa Hyreek was a relic, spoke a different language, fought a distant battle, wore a collar that cramped the style of his only son.

From the outset, the partnership strained family relations. Dad apparently broke a promise to cut Uncle George's brother-in-law a piece of the action. He didn't trust the guy, chin high in bookie debts. Six months into the partnership, Dad learned that Uncle George himself was taking football bets from bar customers and calling them in to Fresno's biggest bookie. Uncle George was getting a kickback from the juice. Dad told him to knock it off, the feds were in town and phones were being tapped.

One Saturday, I was wiping down the tables when Dad suddenly grabbed Uncle George by the hair and hoisted him onto the bar.

"That's it, Ara. Do your crazy bit," Uncle George shouted. "Go nuts. Hop up and down like a wild man."

Dad kept his cool. "I'm not going to have my partner running book," he said. "I want you out. Right now."

Uncle George accused Dad of his own indiscretions, something about a "redhead." Then he made a beeline to our house, showed Mom the clump of missing hair: "See what your maniac husband did to me?"

When we got home, Mom laid into Dad. "Can you believe it," he turned to me. "She's chosen her brother over me?"

Uncle George demanded his $10,000 back plus a hefty interest payment. Dad gave the money willingly.

My father learned very early the fickleness of the booze crowd. He hustled constantly to keep old customers and lure new ones. He knocked out the kitchen (the profit margin on food was as thin as the profit margin on produce) and put in a game room. He dressed the bartenders in black knit shirts, their names stitched in white on one breast and ARA'S APTS on the other. Matches and ash trays carried the same motif.

From four to six, usually a dead time, he offered a 35-cent-a-cocktail "Happy Hour" that drew salesmen from throughout the valley. Other bar owners let the jukebox vendors pick the music—a stale mix of oldies, country and western and pop. Dad scoured the music stores in search of the latest singles and made friends with deejays who slipped him hot 45s.

Except for a few beer joints near the college, Ara's Apartments was the only nightspot in town where you could hear The Beatles, The Rolling Stones, The Who, Jefferson Airplane, The Mamas and the Papas, The Byrds, The Righteous Brothers, Marvin Gaye, Smokey Robinson, James Brown, The Supremes and The Temptations.

He liked bringing people together who inhabited different worlds by day. If the mix wasn't right, he'd tinker with the music. On any given night in the early years, you'd find Mayor Floyd Hyde in his white patent leathers, prosecutors, doctors, lawyers, high-class hookers, bookies, police detectives, black newspaper publisher Les Kimber and luminaries from the jock world like Fresno State football coach Daryl Rogers and Oakland Raiders quarterback Daryl Lamonica, the Mad Bomber.

Dad had a real gift. He connected with people. They felt comfortable around him and invested their trust. The bar became his forum. He took ideas from TV and the newspapers and added to them in a way that made them his. Then, behind the bar, mixing drinks, he'd try his routines on patrons.

All our taxes are going to bankroll the war machine. We're being screwed. What if each of us withheld that percentage of taxes that went to the Pentagon? It won't get us in trouble because it's a good gesture, an honest gesture. It's what we should do.

He'd talk about unionizing the farmworkers and the good work Cesar Chávez was doing. *It's for the love of this country that we have to do justice by these Chicanos.*

Or socialized medicine. *Think about so-and-so who's sick. Think about how he's being bankrupted by doctor bills.*

He blended the blood-and-guts American patriotism of the forties and fifties with Grandpa's leftist rhetoric. "Ara's Populism," my uncle Danny called it. He invented his own brand of idealism right there on the spot. It didn't matter that it was pure fantasy or at times seemed a put-on. It had its own beauty and power. The utterance is what counted, the performance—and he succeeded. The Apartments was a huge hit. It was all Dad. It wasn't anything or anyone else. He commanded that place. Not his father or his mother or his brother, Navo. It was his creation.

We lived well. Dad gave Mom a $125-a-week allowance and what she didn't spend on groceries she spent on clothes and shoes from the best shops in town. Our Sunday ritual was dinner out followed by two scoops of Jamoca Almond Fudge at Baskin Robbins. There were no limits with Dad. We grabbed all the change we wanted from his pocket. A trip to the store with him for milk might last an hour. It was like roaming the aisles of Peacock again, everything mine for the taking.

Waiting up at night for Dad meant some weary days at school. It also meant that he was home when I got there, the hardball and mitts on the front lawn. For the longest time we'd stand under the shade of two big walnut trees and not say a word. There was a measured flow playing catch as surely as the rhythm of a song or poem. We were trying to find it, chewing sweet crabgrass, listening to Russ Hodges and Lon Simmons do the play-by-play from Candlestick. And when we found it—that *pop* . . . *pop* . . . *pop* . . . *pop*—Dad would begin his lesson for the day.

Don't aim the ball, son. Trust yourself. Let it fly. I'd rather have you just wing it way over my head than guide it to me half armed. That's it. Reach way back. Keep your head right here. Don't overstride. Remember your base of power. The belly button. It all comes from the belly button. Picture an explosion. Lead with your elbow. Drive off the right foot. Remember to keep that neck tucked into the shoulder now. That's it. That's it. Now explode. Whooooooossshhh! Beautiful, Mark. Just beautiful. Cepeda steps out. Checks the sign at third. Grabs a handful of dirt. Now he's ready. Drysdale winds up and the two-two pitch. There's a drive to left field. Deep. Way back. Way back. Way back. You can tell it . . . BYE . . . BYE . . . BABY.

It wasn't enough that I could hit with power from the right side, he wanted a switch hitter in the family. Switch hitters were prodigies. Mantle was a switch hitter. The advantages were multiple, he explained. Most pitchers are right-handed and their curve balls break away from the right-handed hitter. Not only could I see the curve ball better from the left side, but left-handed hitters stood two steps closer to first base. I was slow down the line and could use that two-step advantage. It made sense except that nearly all the pitchers in Little League threw right-handed, which meant I was hitting almost exclusively from the awkward left side. And none of these righties threw a curve ball worth worrying about anyway.

He coached my baseball team in a mixed black and Chicano section of southeast Fresno, a poor league in dire need of boosters. Dad agreed to sponsor our team using the name Ara's Apartments, only to learn that city rules prohibited uniforms emblazoned with the name of a drinking establishment. So he sponsored the team as an individual, "Ara's," the only coach/sponsor in the league. And when the league president quit, he agreed to perform those duties, too.

It placed him in an awkward position: the coach and patron of one team who had to fairly represent the interests of all five. The league floundered and Dad chipped in to buy bats, balls and uniforms for several teams. If a kid came ill equipped, no matter if he was on our team or not, Dad would catch up with him after practice and offer a ride home. He'd size up the kid's hands and feet and off we'd go, to Blosser's Sports downtown. We stayed in the car while Dad shopped. He insisted. It took more than one trip in and out before he found the perfect fit. Even so, he must have figured he was saving time. What could be worse than trying to shop with us kids in a sporting goods store, the perfume of leather stupefying? And yet there is a part of me that believes he wasn't trying to save time at all. He had all the time in the world. What he wanted, I fancy, was to save the kid the embarrassment of deciding between the most and least expensive.

I wanted to play third base, where I could be moored at the bag. He stuck me at shortstop, adrift in a sea of dirt and rock. The grounders he hit me during infield practice were rockets, short hops, bad hops and 'tweeners. Not a routine two bouncer in the lot. Pull up on a short hop and take it in the eggs. Turn your head on a bad hop and take it in the ear. Hesitate to charge a 'tweener and disgrace yourself and family. *Stay down, Mark. Stay down.* We finished with pop flies. Mine were cloud busters. Batting practice was no different. He threw hardest to me. So hard that he sometimes couldn't find the plate. He'd have to recruit one of the other fathers to pitch to me.

I enjoyed football season a lot more, mostly because Dad had the good sense to sit it out, content to watch from the stands like the other fathers. He was the star fullback who gave up a full ride to USC. I was the little guy who couldn't quite make the eighty-pound minimum for the Pee-Wee division.

Dad had spent a lifetime fighting off his mother's urges to feed him so he figured who better to fatten me up. My grandmother served up food like a piledriver, but not even she could take me over the hump. I was the team quarterback, and that first game my coach talked the official weigher into letting me hop on the scale with my helmet. What they didn't know is that beneath the webbing of the helmet Dad had stuck a bank bag full of pennies weighed out to precisely 1.5 pounds.

There was no guarantee that the next official weigher would be as kind or blind, so Dad had a friend fashion a lead cup to stuff into my jockstrap. I hid behind the locker and snapped it into place—a crudely sculpted hunk with bumps and folds that chafed the inner thighs and hampered my walk to the scale. Week after week I escaped detection and removed it minutes before kickoff. By season's end, the jockstrap had lost its elasticity. The mass of metal hung halfway to my knees.

I never thought my father was living through me, but he could be an unsparing teacher, on and off the sports field. He caught me shooting a bird with a friend's pellet gun and preached that I and the world would be better served with "hands gripped firmly on a shovel." Racial epithets were strictly forbidden. I called Robert Ambers a monkey for spiking me at second base. Robert, who was black, nearly took off my head. Dad had to explain that monkey, my term for hot dog, meant something else entirely to Robert. That next year Dad contrived an elaborate trade for Robert (a trade in Little League?) and nudged the two of us closer.

He showed no mercy at the dinner table. *I don't want to see elbows. Bridge the knife across the upper plate when not in use. Cut your meat with knife in right hand and fork in left and then switch the fork to the right hand before placing in mouth. Back straight, chin proud.* He thought exiling me to the back porch to finish the meal was punishment; I had news for him. When I reached the seventh grade, he wanted me to read a book a week and discuss its themes at this same dinner table.

Even when he wasn't playing teacher, he had an intensity that bowled me over. I never knew what was coming next. He'd burst into the room and we'd wrestle and then he'd get distracted by something and burst toward that. Then he'd want to show Mom something or watch the news or read the paper. And then he'd come back and wrestle some more and swing his 9-iron hard on the carpet and do his Air Force exercise routine. Still in boxer shorts, he'd give the dry cleaning man a golf lesson in the driveway. He'd lose his keys and it was my job to find them. I'd run from kitchen to living room to den to bedroom, turning over pillows and sections of sofa and groping under beds. I got very good at finding things lost.

I envied my little brother and sister. They had such an easy time with him. Donny, the little guy, was built just like him, the same spark. Michelle was Sissy Missy. She could do no wrong. As soon as Dad got home she started working on me, small provocations that any other time I'd stifle by pinching the life out of her cheeks or punching her in the stomach. She'd stand behind him and stick her tongue out and if I took one single step forward, I'd get yelled at, or worse. Maybe he felt bad because so much of his free time was consumed by me and sports. Maybe he felt this was counterbalance to Mom's inclination toward boys. Either way, he handled Michelle like something fine and rare.

We all had these big boney knees that grew before everything else and somehow compounded our pigeon toes. I hid mine in pants. I had to fall asleep wearing these special shoes that screwed into a thick metal bar, my feet locked all night in a wide V position, my body unable to move from side to side. Michelle wanted surgery. Dad swept her up in his arms and hugged her tight. "One day Sissy Missy you're going to grow into those knees and be a movie actress. I promise. Your legs are going to fill out." And they did.

c h a p t e r $\boxed{7}$

The Peacocks had been Marx Brothers
places, arenas of anarchy. Dad reproduced this topsy-turvy atmosphere in
The Apartments. He paid Grandpa, officially retired and collecting Social
Security, $75 a week cash to manage the books. Most of the bartenders
were former customers, single guys who spent their days gambling on the
golf course. Behind the bar on a busy weekend night, they had a license to
steal.

The whole operation was seat-of-the-pants. Dad tolerated chaos. He
seemed to thrive on it. He let customers accumulate huge bar tabs that
wouldn't always be paid. Those who were skilled at a trade, say plumber
or mechanic, were sent to our house to work off the debt. Our patchwork
sprinkler system—one station spraying half the yard and another flooding
a single plant—was installed by a bad check artist. Dad cosigned car and
stereo loans for Fresno State football players as a favor to Coach Rogers and
ended up having to pay them off. He gave one customer fresh out of jail
$1,500 to buy a water truck for a highway project near San Jose. The guy
used the money for a drug deal.

"You'll never learn your lesson," Mom protested, rightly so. Invariably,
on Thanksgiving and Christmas, as she was about to serve an elaborate

meal blessed by her father, Dad would show up with some poor soul from the bar who had nowhere else to go.

Occasionally, he got back what he gave. I remember Larry Joe Cameron, a stonemason who wore bib overalls and lived in the Sierra in a green flatbed truck with two half-breed dogs that accompanied him everywhere. He'd come down from the mountain every few weeks with granite he had quarried and cut, stop in the bar and get sloshed. Dad took care of Larry Joe and Larry Joe took care of Dad. In one of Dad's offbeat deals, Larry Joe agreed to erect a planter box out front in return for a few dollars and all the bourbon he could drink.

What was supposed to be a small touch of ornamentation evolved into a new façade for Ara's Apartments. It was a wonderful piece of work. Larry Joe in his besottedness had transformed the bar into a fortress of white rough-hewn rock that twinkled in the light.

I was there the Saturday Larry Joe put the final rock in place and was fixing to return to the mountain. Partway through a quart of Jack Daniels, he walked outside to check on his beloved mutts. They knew enough about the old man's habits to understand that when he parked it would be awhile and not to yap. He heard a piercing, plaintive howl and then was confronted by a ghastly sight. One of the dogs was in high mourning, the other dangling outside the door of the truck at the end of a rope Larry Joe had tied to the steering wheel. The dog had squirmed through the open window only to be pulled up short by the rope. In his care not to manacle and suffocate the dogs, Larry Joe had given just enough slack and half window for the perfect gallows. He tried mouth-to-mouth but it was too late. Dad tried comforting Larry Joe but the hillbilly, bawling like a baby, wouldn't let go.

My father struck a similar barroom deal with the drinker who built our house. As much as Dad poked fun at Fresno's nouveau riche, he measured success the same way everybody else did in town: a big house on the north end near the San Joaquin River. There was an element of mollifying Mom in his plans but what I noticed more was the pride that beamed plain on his face every time we drove out to mark its progress. I'll never forget our first year there, 1969. Mom and Dad got along better. I won the elementary school's outstanding athlete award. Our baseball team, Ara's, coached and sponsored by Dad and nourished by Mom, breezed through the league undefeated before being upset in the finals of the City Championships. I quarterbacked my Pee-Wee football squad to the National Pop Warner Junior Raisin Bowl, the biggest youth football bowl in the nation. We played a team from Southern California in the morning and the afternoon game pitted the Kalani Colts from Hawaii against a local team sponsored by Dad. He had been shocked by the quality of the equipment and led a candy drive to raise money to outfit the players in safer helmets.

It was the year the family took on a whole new tincture for me, the year Dad succeeded in getting his uncle, Harry Arax, paroled to Fresno. Grandpa's brother had spent the years 1934 to 1950 in San Quentin, a killer at the top of the inmate pecking order. He had been back to prison twice after short breaths of freedom. The official family version of his original crime was that Uncle Harry ran rum from Mexico to California during Prohibition. His partner in crime happened to be a dirty Long Beach policeman. They were about to be arrested when the officer told Harry to run and he would shoot at him and miss. Harry ran and the officer shot and hit him in the back. Double-crossed, Harry reeled around and fired once and killed the cop.

None of this was true, of course.

He showed up at our doorstep that July smelling of leather and unfiltered Camels and looking just like Mister Magoo. It was decided that he would live half the summer with us and half with Grandpa and Grandma, by which time he would presumably have a job. The first time I saw my grandfather and his brother side-by-side I thought how completely bland and colorless Grandpa's presence was. Uncle Harry had what the Turks call *cha-lum,* a dash, a sparkle, a bullshitter's dexterity. He could charm snakes out of holes.

He had been the head nurse at the prison infirmary and was something of an expert on planter warts. For the plump, seedy one on my index finger he recommended an application of apple cider vinegar three times a day for two weeks. When the two weeks were up, he took out a spool of thread and cinctured the wart, cutting it ever so slightly. Then he told me to follow him outside where he buried the thread beneath an inch of topsoil. "Your wart will be gone in seven days," he vowed.

It was Uncle Harry who taught me the birds and the bees, the firm but gentle touches promised to drive a woman wild. "It works like magic," he smirked, rubbing his thumb and index finger together. It never occurred to me to ask, "What the heck do you know?" I mean, Uncle Harry had spent practically his entire seminal life behind bars.

He had also mastered the art of making leather goods and was determined to pass the skill on to me. We made leather purses for the women in the family and leather wallets for the men. He tooled mine with a dog on one flap and an American Indian on the other. Then one day, the wart still fat on my finger, I awoke and the man who talked out of the side of his mouth was gone. No one knew where.

My father met the sixties head on. Where others saw only tumult, he glimpsed opportunity. "You know, Mark, the problem is the young generation just doesn't have a decent place to go at night." To rectify this, he doubled the size of the bar's dance floor and added blinking lights along the perimeter and go-go dancers on a platform. When the competition followed suit, he responded with amplified sound and psychedelic strobe lights. Every six to twelve months he'd add a new wrinkle. The hotspot cycle, he called it. The first sign of stagnation or the unveiling of a new club in town meant he had to strike quick with something novel.

In 1969, jukebox and dance floor innovations exhausted, Dad said it was time for live rock 'n' roll. He tore out the side wall, added a bandstand and doubled the seating. To pay for bands from the big city, he imposed a cover charge—the first bar owner in the valley to do so. The $2 door fee not only helped defray the costs of groups like Country Joe and the Fish (minus Country Joe) but kept out some of the less desirable customers.

The more the bar prospered, the more it took from our lives. Trying to hold onto different worlds, we improvised. Affluent north Fresno by day. The bar and its underworld by night. Dirty Armenians. Dirty Americans. Mom and Dad abused each other. I beat my little sister. Some of the members of the Ladies' Aid for Retarded Children Society whispered that Mom was chewing gum and wearing fishnets. I tasted hash laced with dog tranquilizer and got stoned for the first and last time.

Everything changed with the move to live music. El Dorados, Lincoln Continentals, Cadillac Coupe de Villes—black and white and low to the ground—crammed the parking lot. The mix of patrons now included a leather vest and goatee gang that came straight from the hardtop races at

Kearney Bowl. These men had sculpted their bodies through a garage regimen of bench press and curls, assiduously avoiding all lower body work.
Dad called them "light bulbs"—oversized chest and arms on a trunk of
chicken legs they hid in jeans.

Once a month the "LA man" pulled up in a black lowered El Dorado
and popped open a trunk brimming with leather jackets, purses, sunglasses, military rifles, handguns, bayonets, uppers, downers, weed—all at
bargain prices.

Fresno was the downer capital of California, Dad said. Something about
the tule fog. He even had a name for the red queens: Bummer Bettys.
Mike Garvey, the bar manager, came to work loaded on reds. Cocktail
waitresses turned tricks to support heroin habits. It trickled all the way
down to my junior high school parties where bowls of Eli Lillies were
passed around like potato chips.

The uppers and downers and in-betweeners mixed badly with booze.
Dad hired off-duty cops to guard the door, but the cops were too busy getting drunk or laid to help. One Saturday night, the head of the Hell's Angels in Fresno knocked the son of a prominent black businessman off his
chair. When the black man tried to defend himself, two friends of the
Hell's Angel tore off the metal base of a table and began clubbing him in
the head. Dad and Garvey stopped them but not before the black man had
to be transported to the hospital with a busted skull. He nearly died.

Mom tried to shelter us. It was no use. Someone called and threatened
to blow up the house and she roused us from sleep and drove us to Aunt
Jeanette's. One Saturday afternoon, Dad refused to pay the handyman for a
job poorly done. The big Okie stormed out of the bar cussing and grabbed
a shotgun from his truck rack.

"What are you doing?" I shouted. "Please. My dad! My dad!"

"I'm going to shoot the cocksucker."

Even at gunpoint, Dad continued to gripe. Grandpa stepped in and
waved a fistful of cash in the Okie's face. "We don't want no trouble," he
said in an Armenian accent that seemed to calm the redneck. "Now please
go."

Dad tried surrounding himself with clean-cut guys ten to fifteen years
his junior, former jocks who worked as salesmen and loved his style and
dress and the way he commanded the bar and the generosity he exuded.

Ara's youth brigade, my mother called them. But as much as Dad fed off their admiration—and they off his largesse—they could not give him what he needed most: a front and rear guard.

For the first time he appeared to dread work, the little bounce in his step as nighttime approached gone. And it no longer seemed important to include us, his family, in his daytime pursuits. He was golfing six days a week and spending his idle time in front of the TV mesmerized by zany cartoons and Artie Johnson's silly kraut on *Laugh-In*.

My mother, who had looked the other way the first few years, the bar business sustaining her growing material wants, now had bitter words for Dad. Except for coaching me, which he did for his own ego gratification, he had forsaken us, she said. We did nothing as a family. We had been to Disneyland once and never to Yosemite, a treasure only ninety miles away. She felt trapped. He replied that this was the reason he built her a big, beautiful house. "It's still four walls," she screamed. "They're just bigger and whiter now!"

She was right, but I thought she was going about it all wrong. I mean this was a man who bought her roses every birthday and anniversary, number corresponding to years. She did not offer him a way out. Maybe there wasn't a way out.

It was either prosper in the short run with the drug crowd or go back to being a neighborhood tavern, if not a restaurant. My father put off a final decision and purchased a 40 percent interest in a more respectable nightclub, The Firehouse. He renamed it The Forum. The convoy of low riders simply followed him over. A few days after the grand opening, a man denied entrance at the front door plunged a knife into the windpipe of an off-duty cop, nearly killing him.

How did he not see it coming? How did we not see it coming?

On the night of the murder, driving back from St. Agnes Hospital and later at home in my parents' bed, I pored over these incidents that seemed so disconnected and meaningless at the time and so portentous now. I thought about what he meant to me and the questions I would ask my mother and uncles when the time was better, questions it turned out that neither Mom nor Uncle Navo nor Uncle Mike nor the homicide detectives could ever answer. Did my father have an inkling? Was my father being stalked? Did my father leave behind any clues? He must have known he was being preyed upon, I thought. He must have felt great fear. And what do you do when you're preyed upon? You give yourself some time to make a decision. Because you realize your life is at stake and what you decide is the difference between living and dying. If he did fear for his life, if he was laboring over such a decision, he hid it well from us.

When I go back to those final months and try to assemble our lives, I find myself dwelling on two incidents, seemingly unrelated.

In March, Muhammad Ali fell short of a comeback in a 15-round championship fight against Joe Frazier. A few years earlier, before the courts snatched Ali's title, Dad had taken me to see a closed-circuit telecast of the Ali–Ernie Terrell fight. At the time, my father admired Ali as a master boxer and braggart. His admiration grew into something more when Ali refused military induction ("I got no quarrel with them Vietcong") and refused to cower during a three-year forced exile from boxing. The Ali–Frazier bout was billed The Fight of the Century, and we believed it. As the big day approached, I hung a poster of the fight card, hero and villain crouched in pugilist stances, above my bed and wore the slippers that Grandma Arax knitted in the style of Ali's boxing shoes. That night, the fight blacked out on TV and radio, I listened to a round-by-round synopsis on the Philco in our den. Ali taunted and japed but never took charge. In the twelfth round, Ali needing a miracle, I took down the poster from my bedroom and erected a shrine in the den next to the Philco. Through the science of reverse radio waves, with the poster as medium, my entreaties would reach back to Madison Square Garden and brace Ali. It had worked once with Mays. Hadn't he hit a home run in the bottom of the fifteenth off Spahn? When round 15 came and went, with Frazier packing that savage left hook, I ran devastated to the bedroom and fetched the BB gun. As the scorecard was read and Frazier declared champion, I dissolved into tears and shot the Ali side of the poster full of holes.

Dad was in the next room listening to the wall radio. He walked in, saw the tattered poster, saw the hot metal gun, saw the BBs, saw the little dimples in the wall. Here it comes, I thought, that lecture about guns and shovels. "He lost," I cried. "Can you believe it? He lost." He wiped my tears with his big thumb. "I felt the same way when DiMaggio retired," he smiled. "But heroes never die. Mark my words, son. Ali will be back."

Just before Christmas, a week or so before he died, we got into a nasty row, the subject of which only Dad and I understood. It was about the jeans I wore split up the sides and the Dingo boots with the two-inch hidden lifts I got through mail order and the tall girlfriend who made me forget about sports. It was about the Frank Zappa Taking A Crap poster and my out-of-line golf swing and inappropriate giggles and the pints of ice cream and bags of chips I gorged after late nights at Tenaya Park with friends.

Dad suspected, quite correctly, that I had begun an experiment with drugs. And yet he chose not to confront me directly, never learning that the one time I actually got a buzz from hash I became so dry-mouthed and panicky that I begged a friend to spit in my mouth. Even when Dad probed cousin Michael, he shied away from the real question. "Is Mark smoking cigarettes?" he asked. Years later, I would add to my list of burdens the knowledge that one of the impulses that may have moved my father toward his final act was the fear that I, his beloved son, was now toying with the drug world he had so grandly harbored, exploited and possibly betrayed.

That night a few days before his death in the hall outside my bedroom, he grabbed me by the shirt and tried to shake sense into me. I let my legs go rubber and collapsed on the floor and told him in a flat voice I wanted to die.

"I don't want to live anymore."

I didn't really mean it. I was hoping he would take pity on me and spare me another of his tirades. Instead, he stopped cold for a moment and for the first time in our relationship, rather than toss a grapefruit at my head or throw an empty Coke bottle at my feet or heave his Florsheims through my bedroom wall or dump a glass of cold milk over my head, he raised his open hand and nailed me flush across the cheek. I fell face down on the carpet and he crouched over me, shaking me silly for what seemed a full minute, incredulous.

"You want to die? You want to die? You want to die?"

The fog that muffled the valley for al-
most a week gave way to a glassy freeze that threatened the citrus fields.
The morning of the funeral broke clear and cold and sunny. Two shiny
black limousines stretched the length of our yard. Both were needed to
carry the immediate family: the four of us, four grandparents, Uncle Navo
and my father's sister Aunt Jeanette. My father had preceded everyone in
death.

Armenian funerals consumed whole days and played out in four elaborate acts: a prayer and viewing at the funeral home; the church service; the
burial; and the *hok ah josh,* literally soul meal, at the church hall. You
could count on the lunch being buttered chicken, buttered pilaf, buttered
string beans. And you could count on a certain number of "professional"
mourners whose passing acquaintance with the deceased or someone in the
distant family entitled them to tears and a free lunch. The soul meal was a
tradition debased, an occasion for the freeloaders to grumble about the
taste of the food and to watch the old ladies squirrel away *peda* bread and
half-eaten chicken for home. Mom wanted no part of it and decided instead on a buffet at our house.

I took a seat in the limousine between Mom and Grandpa Arax. He sat there straight and still, a silence I knew well. He was seventy-two years old, a pudgy little man with a shock of gray hair, a pipe protruding perpetually from his mouth and a wet kiss that smelled of strong tobacco. He had a terrible case of psoriasis and I used to inspect the red and white scales that patched his stubby arms and legs and slather them with Vaseline.

He had a quiet resignation, a *tsk, tsk, tsk.* We weren't especially close, those Saturdays at Sambo's notwithstanding. He never came to my ballgames. Dad said he never came to any of his. Not until the previous spring had we found some common ground. Dad had trucked loads of blackened soil from the San Joaquin River into our backyard. If he couldn't return to the farm, then Dad was determined to bring a little farm to North Lafayette Street. Grandpa had long mastered suburban farming, each year producing a bigger crop of vegetables and melons on a tiny plot in his backyard. I awoke early that spring day to the sound of Dad and Grandpa breaking the hardpan outside my bedroom window. I had never seen my father so content. He was completely lost in his shoveling.

Grandpa's lessons were simple ones: You must break up the soil so the plant can breathe. One day of tilling is worth one week of irrigation. When the plant is strong enough, starve it for one to two weeks to force the roots deeper. When the flowers blossom, make sure you don't overwater because flowers, like roots, must take hold. And, finally, the last fruit must be saved and not eaten. Its seeds will be used to plant next year's garden. It was a farmer's duty to think about next year, Grandpa said. The fruits of this year meant nothing without the assurance that they were part of something continuous.

"Ara-boy, dig a little deeper," he commanded. "The tomatoes will need room to spread their roots out."

"I know, Pa. I know."

I removed the plants, their roots plugged tight in a plastic container, and handed them to Grandpa. Each one had to be spaced just so and he broke the soil with one hand and planted with the other. Then he took both thumbs and pressed gently on the roots, pressing until the plant was securely packed, safe. Dad came by with the hose and gave each plant just enough water to prevent wilting under the hot spring sun, yet not enough to discourage the roots from setting deep.

Their relationship had always been somehow private, removed from my world. In our backyard that day, I discovered that we were two fathers, two sons, one grandfather, one grandson.

We had two seasons that summer or at least that's how Grandpa explained it. Mom and her sisters vacationed in Lake Tahoe and the day they were to return I picked bushel baskets of melons, cucumbers, strawberries, eggplants, tomatoes and peppers. I washed each one and placed them on the kitchen counter. That night, Grandpa and Grandma came over and together we marveled at the sight. Mom was impressed. Grandpa said in all his years of backyard farming he had never seen such a crop. I promised him an even bigger one next year.

In the days after Dad's murder, as the first frost descended and blackened what was left of our garden, my Grandpa weathered his single pang of visible anguish. By the morning of the funeral he had retreated back into his safe shell, out of reach, impassive. He looked out beyond the tinted window of the limousine into the crisp sunlight, and what we had shared—the summer garden, the hard hug of winter's death—shrank in the distance.

My grandmother, who was sixty-two, a decade younger than Grandpa, sat behind me next to Michelle and Donny. She offered a soliloquy about the fog's sudden surrender to sun and whether this signaled nature's commiseration. We had grown accustomed to her chatter, the way it flew off at odd angles. She plowed ahead without respect for the moment or a pause to delineate the end of one story and the beginning of another.

She was short and plump all over, with a gnarled nose and slightly hooded eyes. These imperfections she could easily explain. The crooked nose came from a childhood tumble down the stairs; the bend in her legs was nothing more than a deficiency of cod liver oil as a baby.

She took excessive pride in my looks. With both hands, she would press in the hair at my temples and tell me how handsome I was. I thought my left ear jutted out too far and I used to train it like a stubborn cowlick. Grandma did the same thing. She spent hours twisting her nose. Seated on the chair, she'd stretch out her legs and examine the bent shanks. Then she'd move her feet in and out, in and out, while keeping the knees stationary.

Her weary voice fluttered on the edge of a cough and she complained of allergies, overwork and fatigue. But she never stopped moving. She wasn't fond of baking cookies or cakes for these were the foods of leisure and Grandma had no time to sit down with a cup of coffee and enjoy. Rather, she cooked in the finest tradition of short order: cold white bean salad, dolmas, Chinese stir-fry and panfried lamb that she somehow coaxed into tasting like barbeque.

Her mouth, like her kitchen, was constant motion and the nonstop buzz put me asleep sometimes. Behind her back, Grandpa would mimic with his hand like a mouth flapping. But Grandma's chatter was never idle. Always, it seemed to have a purpose: To discredit those inside and outside the family by whom she felt threatened and to keep those she loved out of harm's way. When it came to her brood, Grandma was fiercely protective. Once, after a game of stickball, I reached inside her refrigerator for cold water only to be beaten back by a dire admonition: "Marcus Aurelius, I read an article today that cold water after exercise can cause a heart attack." I poured a glass from the tap instead.

Grandma defined each of us by the forebear she thought we most resembled in character, and in her eyes I was the second coming of Navo, the first son. His real name was Navarsart, New Era, New Hope, in Armenian. I didn't exactly resent the comparison because I loved my uncle deeply. But I wanted to be my father's son. If Uncle Navo and I shared traits, it made him no less difficult to fathom. This enigma was never more real to me than on the morning of the funeral. He took a seat in the rear limousine, his gaze concealed behind dark sunglasses, his visage hollow. He had worn this same face for three days, the only grown-up face I had not yet seen cry.

He was a short guy just past slender, not at all like my father. He sold vacuum cleaners door-to-door, not he personally but a band of salesmen who worked under him. He seemed to be always sucking on a cigar and fondling a gold money clip that pinched a thick wad of hundreds. For all I knew, he owned the entire line of Filter Queen vacuums. He hated excuses from his salesmen or golf partners. "If my aunt had balls," he told one alibi maker, "she'd be my uncle."

He taught me how to swear when I turned two. Old ladies would bend down to kiss me and I'd blurt out "you bitch." I loved going to restaurants with him because he put on such a show. The meals were never good enough or served in the time or manner he thought worthy of himself, and he berated more than one waitress to the point of tears. He had an irresistible wit and a mouth that hurled insults and spewed sarcasm. No group, Armenians included, escaped his skewer. He had a single-word dismissal for anyone else not to his liking, which he delivered in halves: ASS-HOLE.

Unlike my father, my uncle didn't lose his temper, didn't strike his son, didn't let you see what was going on behind that curtain of bluster. He and Dad had spent so much of their time at odds in the grocery business and only in the last few years had they grown closer. Uncle Navo helped coach our Little League team and his son, Brian, played second base. Dad allowed himself once again to envision a partnership with his older brother, this time a restaurant. "Navo and Ara's: Fresno's Finest," he scribbled into his diary.

Trailing in the rear limousine was my father's younger sister, Jeanette, and her husband, Danny Melnick. Only fifteen years separated me and Jeanette and I thought of her not as an aunt but as a distant older sister. In fact, she wouldn't let me call her aunt. To hear Grandma tell it, Jeanette had been a fat, sour child who threw terrible tantrums, held her breath until she turned blue and gave the Bronx Cheer to any adult who happened to admire her in the least. It was easy getting under her skin. I'd call her Fatty, Fatty Two-by-Four and she'd chase me all over the house in her hippie muumuu. She struck back by telling me I'd never reach the height of five feet six but not to worry. Paul Newman wasn't much taller.

She carried the scars of high school, snubs over her excessive weight and bohemian temperament, and she resented her jock brothers for understanding so little of what she endured. She channeled disaffection into painting and folk art and left Fresno in the early 1960s to attend the University of California at Berkeley, where the family's leftist politics finally became a proud badge. Grandpa and Grandma drove me there to visit her once, my first real peek at hippies, and I remember walking up Telegraph Avenue and being struck by the thought that my aunt, so extreme and rebellious back home, was completely tame by Berkeley standards.

She graduated with a degree in history, the first in our family to finish college, and married Danny, a doctor's son who was teaching part-time at Berkeley while completing a Ph.D. in English. He was a slight man with frizzy red hair and black horn-rimmed glasses and a sensitive, hedging manner. The fact that Danny was Jewish and wanted to write novels only enhanced his appeal in Grandpa's eyes. The rest of us felt a little intimidated. Dad called him a genius, but I noticed right off he didn't always say what was on his mind. In fact, it was downright hard to get him to express an unqualified opinion on anything so that it might survive the noise of our sports-obsessed conversation. That Christmas, Danny gave me a rock album and I was pleasantly surprised by the hipness of the gift, until I played it and discovered that The Beatles, The Stones and The Who, my favorite groups, had been set to violins, cellos and flutes.

This was my father's clan on the way to the funeral, January 5, 1972.

The funeral home was really a home, white board and river rock, the greenest lawn on the block. A family must have lived there once. Children. It was dark now, filled with wooden pews, and beyond the pews in an open corner under a pale light rested a sleek copper-colored coffin dressed with red roses and opened at midpoint. I had never laid eyes on a dead person. I didn't know what to expect. The last thing I expected was the man inside to be breathing. Faint breaths from a hollow chest, but he was breathing. Only he wasn't my father. My father never wore a suit, much less a ridiculous gray and white pinstripe. My father was a big man with a proud chest that heaved. His mass never rested. Big white ass clad in boxer shorts, knees and arms pumping furiously, he cut a swath through the living room each day with his Air Force fitness program. The force he unleashed in his golf swing wore divots in the lush carpet. No one person, not even a bar full, could match his energy. My own cries could not still him. This other man was weight, only weight. My sister later told me that she could see the blue skin beneath the caked rouge and the black thread that sealed the lips. It seemed to me that no coercion was necessary. He was a perfect state of neutrality. No hint of happy or sad. Death, I thought, suited this other man fine. Except for a pinkish crease that cleaved the midline of the brow and a small bruise and depression at the wrist, there was no trace of violence or a great struggle waged. My father had swallowed five bullets and would not go down; this other man submitted to death any number of ways. I was about to tell them all to go to hell, that their ornate fraud hadn't fooled me, when my eyes set upon the hands. Even in the gauzy light there was no mistaking the hands. They had been folded and placed at the midsection in a manner that flaunted their splendor. The thumbs and fingers were twice as thick as a normal man's, the veins huge and still protrusive. Nothing about them had been lost to death. They were alive like no other part of the body. These were the hands with which my father had erected and torn down and built again our relationship. The hands that in their brightest, most liberating moments taught me how to make a baseball dance: index and middle finger spread along the center seam for a darting fastball; the same two fingers now together along the outside loop of the seam for a dipping curveball. The hands that in their most inglorious, hysterical moments had hurled a bottle at my feet and a bowl of grapefruits at my head. These hands that lavished love and inflicted pain, these hands that would not be restrained, were now bound one on top of the other by death's pale. I kept a good distance between me and him. As I stood there, in silent awe, my mother's mother hobbled toward me on her cane.

"I am an old lady," she said mixing Armenian, French and English. "*Il fe* Markie, why God didn't take me? *Il fe* God, let it be me."

The funeral attendants closed the coffin and wheeled it outside under a portico where six pallbearers and a limousine waited.

It was a three-minute drive to Holy Trinity Armenian Apostolic Church in old Armenian Town past the Santa Fe railroad tracks and the Basque restaurant and the childhood home of William Saroyan. Much of the neighborhood around the church had been razed to accommodate a convention center and sports arena. Only a handful of Armenians still lived in these houses built early in the century, with wood porches where they ate their watermelons and spit the seeds and talked loud with no mind to the niceties of native Fresnans.

With prosperity came a move north and new immigrants, mostly Mexicans, now spilled out of these houses. Only traces of the past remained— the whiff of *peda* bread drifting from the brick ovens at Saghatelian's Valley Bakery, the creaking plank floors of Arax Market. I used to ditch Sunday school to buy a gumball at the market that shared our last name but no relation, and on the way I'd get stopped by some old-timer who never made it out. I had already mastered the trick of an earnest listener, the willingness to please my elders with my ears, and they thrust upon me the stories of a neighborhood no more. *Sonny boy, see that empty lot behind the church? Did you know it used to be an enchanted forest with rocks and urns and running water? An Armenian lived there and designed and built it himself. One day, he caught his wife with another man and killed her with his bare hands. He spent ten years in prison, got out and returned to his enchanted forest. That's where they found him, hanging from one of the trees.*

Holy Trinity, founded in 1900, the second oldest Armenian church in America, ascended from the corner of Ventura and M streets like a battle-ship. Its design had been taken from the Armenian cross, which differed from the simple cross in that its four arms flared wider as they extended from the center base.

Holy Trinity was red brick and white plaster, arched stained-glass win-dows and two eight-sided copper domes that pierced the sky and beamed ochre in the summer sun. It had none of the marble or stone or gilding that made other churches opulent. It possessed instead an elemental qual-ity that came from the humble meld of wood, glass, masonry. Holy Trin-ity was beautiful.

We filed in last behind the six pallbearers, the four funeral men and the coffin, up steep concrete steps and through the huge double-door entry beneath a stained-glass eye warding away evil. Already the sanctuary spilled with people; the overflow had to be directed up the steps to the balcony, which I hadn't seen filled except for Christmas or Easter.

Down the wide center aisle they rolled the coffin and the wheels of the catafalque pressed heavy into Persian rugs, and a deacon in flowing silk vestment yanked a rope and the church bell pealed maybe a dozen times. We were seated in the first row. To glimpse the raised altar I had to look between the floral wreaths and sprays nailed atop stands that lined the en-tire width of the church. Through the dome's translucent yellow glass, thick shafts of sunlight burst down on the center aisle, painting the coffin a burnished silvery-bronze. The pews too were steeped in a radiance that filtered through the stained-glass renderings of Mary and Jesus, alive with fire. The altar bore the luster of gold and silver-gilt chalices, crosses, radi-ances, candelabras, a red velvet Bible and wood carved Last Supper. Every-thing felt heavy.

The casket rested at the front of the choir rail where my grandfather Mekhitarian had given my mother's hand to my father sixteen years earlier. Incense burned inside a silver censer, and the sweet suffocating smoke puffed skyward to the dome, to the nostrils of God himself.

Reverend Kourken Yaralian wore a simple purple satin chasuble over black robes. In his right hand, he clutched a golden cross veiled in white linen with a belly button of green stone. Over and over the same words in Armenian he repeated: "Merciful Lord, have mercy on the souls who have fallen asleep." The only English words were the names of my father and family members and Little League.

Side by side the pallbearers stood facing the altar. Three of them were members of Dad's youth brigade, two brothers who owned a lighting company and a coffee salesman, decent guys who played sports in high school and saw in my father what they wanted for themselves. It was the other three—Mike Garvey, Armond Bletcher and Dan Hornig—who confounded so many in the church that day. What was Flora thinking? All these lifelong friends and she ends up picking a trio whose relationship to Ara was confined to the bars? Years later I would hear the whispers in the church that day: Perhaps one, or maybe all three, had a hand in the plot to kill my father.

Garvey had been beside my father six of the seven years we owned The Apartments. Bartenders came and went but Dad let Garvey stay. He put up with his boozing and pill popping and gambling. It was simple math. The Garv could juggle fifteen-drink orders, a half-dozen conversations and four girls seated at different spots along the bar, each one believing she was the one going home with him. Sometimes he didn't even bother to take them home. One Saturday morning Dad and I arrived earlier than usual and as I opened the big storage closet to grab the vacuum and broom, a burst of moans and groans stopped me cold.

It was the sound of feminine rapture, the same sound I had heard on my cousin Michael's X-rated eight-track cassette. Through a narrow crack I saw the tall, willowy Garvey, pants around the ankles, bare-assed and prostrate, with one of the cocktail waitresses. He wasn't uttering a sound. I tiptoed out before they saw me and never said a word to Dad.

Armond Bletcher, the fifth pallbearer, was the bodyguard and bouncer who slept on my sister's bed the night of the murder. He showed up at the funeral home in western shirt, cowboy boots and Raybans. We figured he couldn't find a suit on such short notice that would fit his twenty-three-inch biceps and a chest that bench-pressed 610 pounds. The effect of all this mass, topped by an undersized skull, was more than arresting. His glassy blue eyes, feral and transfixed, were set off by thin girlish eyebrows and the longest, most feminine pair of lashes. To dispel nature's equivocation, Armond etched his menace with a surly goatee.

All that week, he had passed word on the streets that sunglasses were required wear for the funeral. Inside the limousine on the way to the church he bragged to the others: "Ara's pretty big, but it's going to take at least twelve of you guys to carry me out." Armond was a notorious figure throughout the state and his selection as pallbearer helped imbue the ceremony with scandal. None of this mattered to me. This was Dad's friend, and watching him stand over the casket, his face registering grief, I was filled with unutterable pride. No less than if John Brodie or Willie Mays or Muhammed Ali himself had seen fit to come to Fresno to honor Dad.

On the other side of Bletcher was Dan Hornig, a partner in the second bar. Hornig was forty-three years old and the only pallbearer older than Dad. I didn't know much about him except that he was Uncle Navo's good friend. I had been told that his father, a craftsman of modest homes, left Germany before World War II and revered Hitler long past the Holocaust. A baseball and track star in high school, Hornig pitched briefly in the minor leagues. He traveled to Germany in the mid-fifties at his father's insistence and took a bride, Ingrid. They married right there in Frankfurt. He returned to Fresno and tried his hand at the construction trade but lacked his father's skill and work ethic. Hornig drank and chased women and played a good enough game of golf to hustle back money lost to bookies.

He was a husky man built along the lines of my father with a big balloon face. I couldn't understand why Dad would want him as a partner. First, Dad did all the work. Second, Dad had a rule that "you don't shit where you eat." This meant not drinking on duty and not bedding the cocktail waitresses. Hornig flouted both. Third, the guy never said a word.

He just sat back with stony eyes and stolid face and listened and occasionally snickered.

Hornig was the original owner of The Apartments. That's how my father met him. He had built the business in 1962 and ran it for three years as a cocktail lounge and restaurant before selling it to Dad. Dad and Hornig barely spoke over the next six years. Then, seven months before the murder, Dad plunked down $18,000 for a share of Hornig's new bar.

As the service ended, a funeral attendant dressed in polyester uniform, not a movement wasted in his bloodless walk, lifted open the top half of the coffin and directed the people in the balcony and those huddled outside to begin a procession past the body. Beholding Armond Bletcher standing sentry over a body cloaked in pinstripes, Cliff Clinger, one of the homicide detectives, muttered just loud enough, "Is this a Mafia funeral or what?"

The parade of people snaked down the side aisle, past the first row where we sat and back up the center aisle where the body rested. White, black, Chicano and Asian; Armenian grandmothers; the kids Dad coached years earlier in Little League; local elected officials and bookmakers; friends from way back and friends from the bar; the police detectives and drug dealers; cocktail waitresses in miniskirts and bikers in T-shirts and leather vests. On and on to the swell of organ music. Each time we saw someone we knew and had not seen since the murder—a memory attached to each one—we cried.

For years afterward, we would talk about the sweep and the number of people as confirmation of Dad's goodness. I will never forget this one old lady who doddered toward the casket repeating an Armenian chant, a village imprecation, against the killers. "Why weren't their fingers broken?" she intoned. "May they wake up with their fingers broken."

As the church emptied and it became our turn to file past the coffin a last time, my mother threw herself onto my father's body and refused to be wrested away. Nothing up to that point had prepared me for the sound of her keening, the spectacle of half her body writhing inside the coffin. Uncle Navo, who never betrayed any emotion, never betrayed any weakness, stood perfectly erect, a single tear in his eye, and he was trying not to show it, fighting, fighting.

We buried my father that afternoon in Ararat Cemetery just beyond the Armenian Martyrs monument next to a field of Thompson grapes. Over the years the vineyard has been razed and the ground beside my father planted with new bodies: my mother, my grandfather, my best friend. I seldom go back there but a red rose I plucked that day from the coffin remains with me, pressed and crinkled inside a plastic sandwich bag, still red, still redolent, bristling with the yellow and green mold of time.

One morning after the funeral, two homicide investigators knocked at our door. Cliff Clinger peppered Mom with questions.

She recalled my father receiving two phone calls before he left for work that Sunday evening, but she didn't know who called or why. She said she couldn't think of any reason why someone would want to kill him. Sure, he had gotten into a few fights lately, but they didn't amount to much.

"How about any business deals that went bad."

"Not that I know of. Ara didn't tell me a lot about the business."

"How about your marriage?"

"Well . . . we've had our ups and down. Like any couple. He had his golf and I had the church and the kids. But it wasn't like we had asked each other for a divorce."

"So what did Ara get ya for Christmas?"

"He bought several appliances for the kitchen. A toaster, electric can opener, electric knife, stuff like that."

"You mean he got ya a toaster and can opener for Christmas? You must have been pretty sore?"

"No."

"Flora, I know this is hard but it'll get a lot better soon," Clinger said, closing his notebook. "You're a good-looking lady. You'll have no trouble finding another man."

"What kind of crap is that, Cliff?" Uncle Mike snapped. "For Christ's sakes, she just buried her husband."

"Well, we're done," Clinger said.

Clinger was a puny redhead with a purple knobbed nose and thin lips befitting a contemptuous little man's spirit. There was no love lost between Clinger and Dad. He had been one of the officers hired to check IDs at The Apartments front door and keep a lid on the violence. It was a common practice for Fresno police to moonlight at bars. They made $75 to $100 a night and all they could drink, for as little as four hours of work. The arrangements bordered on a protection racket.

Clinger wasted no time proving himself wrong for The Apartments job. He would drink himself into a dark mood and pick fights with guys twice his size and half his age. Dad finally had to let him go.

I was willing to forgive Clinger for his indiscreet remark about a "Mafia funeral." The same image had crossed my mind. But how could he sit across from my mother and talk about things like Dad's $75,000 life insurance policy and Mom dating other men. Fortunately, we didn't have to suffer him long. My uncle complained about his behavior to one of his commanding officers and he was taken off the case.

In those first days I locked myself in my room and emptied my anger into pillows and mattress. I was no longer mad at God. How could I have expected God to intervene when I had forsaken him all those years? What had I given God, what faith had I demonstrated, to deserve that Dad's life be spared? I thought back to my Pop Warner football coach who preached a simple gospel: Practice hard because practice is like a bank account—only what you deposit can you withdraw on game day. I had neglected my bank account with God and on game day, I came up empty.

My father's closest friends knocked at my door and sought to quiet my fury. Terry Ashjian told me he was fifteen, the oldest of four children, when his father died suddenly. "I had to grow up overnight," he said. "I know you can do it, too."

Voices dripping stale grief. Face-to-face testimonials, telephone calls, letters, cards. Half of mankind had lost a father young, Mark. Why, this was no exclusive club.

Uncle Mike tried to return me to childhood. He was married to my mother's oldest sister, Jeanette, and he and Dad were about as close as two brothers-in-law could be. He sat across from me, the stench of whiskey on his breath as it had been since the night of the murder, and ran rough carpenter hands gently down the sides of my cheeks. "Mark, you're just a fifteen-year-old boy," he said. "These people mean well but don't listen to them. You're not a man. We're not expecting you to be a man."

I wanted to believe Uncle Mike, to romp untroubled with my cousins and friends, to escape outside into lightness and sprint across the green rye grass Dad planted that winter. I wanted to come inside when it was dark and time for dinner, all these mourners bearing hams and turkeys and enchiladas and cakes vanished, and just the five of us left seated around the wrought iron table, Mom divvying up the round roast and the three of us fighting over the burnt caramel piece at the end and Dad shushing because the Vietnam body count on TV and our meal were being served up at the same time.

No longer did I have the patience for child's play. Cousin Brian broke the quiet of our house with a loud pop. He was a goofy kid, buck teeth and floppy ears, pestering with incessant finger-hand-mouth sounds. This time I couldn't be sure if he was mimicking gunshots or a car backfiring. Either way the sound of disrespect filled my ears. I tore after him, chased him into the kitchen and grabbed his shirt with my left hand, my right fist poised to strike. He didn't know what wrong he had done. I hesitated for a moment, long enough for one of the grown-ups to grab me from behind and pin back my arms.

Even my little brother became a target of my rage. Donny had showed almost no emotion and I began to resent his ability to slough off Dad's death. What did I know that he was just seven years old? He hadn't cried once since the killing and now he crawled into bed and was sobbing over some stupid slight. I held him by the shoulders and shook him like a rag doll.

"You don't even cry about Dad and you're crying about this? You don't get it, do you? Our father is dead. He's gone. He's gone. He's gone. Get that through your damn skull. He's never coming back."

He looked at me as if face-to-face with a madman. Then he began to bawl, this time real tears. Whether he was feeling guilt or genuine sorrow or the shame of my reprimand, it didn't matter. "You've got to let it out," I said, hugging him tight. "It's not good to keep it in."

The elders congregated those first nights in the big family room to discuss Mom's finances. There were so many questions. Should she sell one of the cars? How long before reopening The Apartments? Could Mike Garvey be trusted to manage? What would Dan Hornig do with the second bar, The Forum? I grew weary of this talk and gathered my cousins in the den. I shut the hallway door that led to the family room and put on the Santana album Dad had given me for Christmas. All at once the hallway door was thrown open and there stood Mom, glowering at me.

"What are you doing? This isn't any time for music. Your father was buried four days ago. Have you forgotten?"

Four days. Had it been that long? No, I hadn't forgotten.

She marched over and yanked the plug. "They'll be no music in this home for forty days."

It was Armenian custom. Forty days of mourning. Forty days of black garb. Forty days followed by a church service, a prayer for the dead, a visit to the cemetery. The whole thing all over again. We abided by it. Everyone except Uncle Navo. He married his girlfriend, Josette, thirteen days after the murder. He asked Mom if she objected. What was she going to tell him? Then he invited her to join them on the honeymoon. She politely declined.

The murder made us crazy. In the absence of motive and killers, we found culprits in ourselves and each other. I was certain our whole world would crumble if pushed just so. My mother greeted Uncle Navo's return from the honeymoon with cool indifference. He stopped coming around the house and the burden of guiding us through a thicket of lawsuits and financial problems fell on Uncle Mike, who wasn't even blood. Mom tried not to badmouth Uncle Navo in front of us but others in her family weren't so discreet. He bought a new house, found a new job and surrounded himself with a new set of friends. I got the sense we were damaged goods in his eyes, thieves trying to grab from his new life. I tried not to hate him but the family had split in two, and he had too much pride or too little regard to fix things. One afternoon, Mom and Grandma got into a big fight that had been smoldering for months. The agent provocateur was Mom's sister Rosette.

Aunt Rosette and Grandma Arax at the same table was like two Sumo wrestlers belly-to-belly in the ring, each trying to budge the other with the immensity of her will. Both were full of opinions and certain of those opinions. Both were skilled users of guile as a complement to will. Both liked to stir the pot. Both cared deeply about their respective families and out of that concern flowed the gestures that brought us together and the gestures that set us apart.

The difference was that Rosette had married into wealth. Her husband, Ralph Drew, was a Fresno blueblood if there were such a thing. They lived on Van Ness Boulevard, the town's finest street, in a house given to them free and clear by Ralph's parents. They vacationed in Europe and at their summer home in Lake Tahoe. While Uncle Ralph manned the appliance warehouse handed down from his father, Aunt Rosette busied herself with the white-gloved teas at the Fig Garden Woman's Club.

This irked my grandmother, the socialist, but not for the reasons you'd expect. She seemed to begrudge anyone who had an easier time of it and sitting around the kitchen table that afternoon were three women who had an easier time of it—Mom and Aunt Rosette and Rosette's society friend, Dorothy, a beehive blonde with oversized sunglasses and a scarf concealing a dewlap. It didn't help matters that Dorothy was drunk and cackling.

"Lady, do you realize my son was just killed?" Grandma said. "This is not a happy house. You think you'd show some respect."

Dorothy continued to laugh and snort. Mom had welcomed her to lighten the mood and now she too grew annoyed.

"I don't know who you are but I think you'd better leave," Grandma said.

"What? This isn't your house, old lady," Dorothy huffed. "This is Flora's house. And you've got no business telling me to get out."

"This is my house and I want you out!" Grandma snapped.

"Alma," Mom said, finally speaking up. "I'm not going to have you come here and dictate to us like you've done for the last sixteen years. It's not business as usual anymore."

"My son's dead and you're the one who killed him!" Grandma shrieked. "It's all your fault!"

"You know you're crazy," Mom said. "I didn't kill Ara. Look at the way you treated him all these years. 'My son? My son?' He could never get in your eyes. He could do somersaults and you wouldn't accept it. 'Navo, Navo, Navo, Navo.' You're to blame for what happened to Ara. I think you'd better leave, Alma."

Grandpa had to drag her out. Mom and Grandma didn't speak for two years. Mom would drop us off in their driveway once a week and honk the horn a few hours later to pick us up.

Those first weeks we were never alone. The mystery of murder awakened deep fears. We didn't know who or why, and we could never be certain that the killers weren't coming after us, too. One, two and three relatives spent the night. The more the better. We hadn't gone back to school yet and no one cared what time we went to bed. We stayed up long into each night, a bizarre slumber party. It was as if Christmas vacation had been extended indefinitely with friends and family dropping by and always guests for dinner. Then, almost overnight, everyone left and it was just the four of us. We changed our phone number. The drapes stayed drawn day and night.

One morning I awoke to the rasp of saws and the whiz of drill bits. Uncle Mike, tool box in hand, was boring a peep hole and fastening the front and back doors with dead bolts and chains. I stood in the hallway and watched him cut pieces of wood to precise lengths and then jam the pieces into every window and sliding glass door frame.

"That should do it, Flora," he said. "The place is as tight as a drum."

Uncle Mike, who wanted so badly for me to believe in childhood, had locked us inside. Thereafter, family and friends visited through the side door. Any knock or ring at the front door sent us scurrying. Mom's eyes twitched endlessly. She lost tufts of hair. I began to fear life itself, not only calculable dangers arising from the murder but unrelated ones as well. Whenever Mom was a few minutes late, I paced the concrete divide of the front yard and conjured up an accident. If she didn't make it back home by the count of 100, she was hurt. At 200, she was dead.

I dreamed about killers suddenly appearing outside, big men in dark clothes surrounding the house with machine guns. We moved from room to room trying to elude them. One door or window was always open and it was a race between me and them to see who would get there first. I always lost and just as they entered the house and were about to harm my mother, I awakened in sweat. I dreamed that Dad came home a wounded Army soldier in a wheelchair. I dreamed that we were never told his condition and discovered him, years later, in another town with another wife and child. I could accept every possibility right up to the moment of his dying: that he was crippled forever, that he survived even if it meant abandoning us for another life. But how could my father succumb to death? How hard could it have been for him to live?

That first day at school I felt braced by a strange, newfound pride. I was the son of a sensational murder and it shadowed me everywhere, breathing into my life an exhilarating edge even as it haunted. One teacher presented me with a sympathy card the whole class signed. Dean Kourafas, a Greek kid Dad coached, shepherded me through the first day. He told me not to dwell on the bad things and that my father wouldn't want me to think about him in the course of certain activities, such as screwing. It was premature counsel to say the least. I had turned fifteen without a pubic, facial or underarm hair on my body.

My sister and brother, perhaps because their classmates were younger and more ingenuous, came home that first day bruised and scraped on the inside. They were not like the other kids now. Michelle said she could feel the stares. A girl walked up at lunch and said, "So-and-so says your father was involved in drugs." Michelle didn't know how to respond so she said nothing. Donny said a kid named Rod greeted him first. He sputtered "Your dad died," and a girl marched up and scolded him. "Shush—you're not supposed to say that. You know the teacher told us not to say that." After school, the girl in the big house in the cul-de-sac taunted Donny. "My dad says your dad was a big drug dealer." Michelle asked Mom if that was true. Mom told her that you have to believe what's in your heart. She told us the same thing when the old ladies at Holy Trinity Church started wagging their tongues. "They're just bored," she said. "You can't stop people from talking."

The Apartments reopened two weeks after the murder as a country-

western joint with Mike Garvey at the helm and Uncle Mike close behind.
They packed the place that first Saturday night, the curious ogling the
spot where Dad went down, where the bullets reamed the wall. By the end
of January, business had slumped to such lows that it took a full week to
gross what Dad had grossed in a single night.

To keep The Apartment afloat, Mom used a chunk of the $75,000 life
insurance policy and $25,000 borrowed from Uncle Mike and Uncle
Ralph. Garvey had worked beside Dad for six years but didn't know the
first thing about running the business. Mom had to fire him.

It was hard enough luring patrons to a bar stained with murder. How
would we ever find a buyer? We needed a different image, a clean break,
Uncle Mike said. He hired a new manager, a black man with a huge Afro,
who changed the bar's name to Bump City, the title of a Tower of Power
song. For a time Bump City exceeded even the best nights of Ara's Apartments. But the police department said the new manager was running
drugs and whores through the bar and would have to go. Over the next
two years the bar went through a series of transformations. First, it was a
hard rock club managed by one of Dad's old bartenders, then Jimbo's
Country and Western run by a former truck driver, then a topless bar
without a name managed by a tough-talking waitress. Mom wrote checks
to dancers Candy, Pilar and Lulu.

Each of us children reacted differently to shock, to grief, to fear, to gossip,
to money woes, to the indignity our lives had become. And in response to
the accumulation of these forces, to the whole compass of change, we re-
constructed ourselves in profoundly different ways. Everything intensi-
fied; our best traits became better, our worst traits worse. Donny didn't
dwell on the murder. All that mattered to him was having a good time.
He blamed teachers for his poor grades and citizenship. Michelle, who
brought out a tenderness in my father, grew sullen and possessive and
spent long hours inside her bedroom, everything in its place, ordered, perfect. I used the murder and all that came with it as a driving force, relentless and consuming. I was going to achieve to spite people; there was no
room for mistakes.

I crammed each day of the monthly calendar with tasks and deadlines.
Every aspect of my life found its way onto a list: long-range goals to im-

prove the house, health, school and intellect. Every time I crossed out a completed task I added a new one to do. My older cousin Michael joked that not even my bowel movements escaped regimentation. Weekends were spent perfecting the front, back and courtyards. No one was allowed to step on my lawn, and I knew from the placement of the redwood chips if someone had trudged across the flower bed. I banished my brother to a small plot of forgotten dirt in the backyard, fenced off from the world.

Each artifact of my father's life I clutched dear. I carried his silver brush in my back pocket, my coarse auburn hairs mingled with his wispy brown ones. I lined my bedroom with his athletic trophies and dangled from the bedpost his coach's whistle. To the leftover pages of his tattered scrapbook I added my own sports feats. My mother never fixed the new sofa he ripped in a last outburst of anger. The same with the adobe fireplace he splattered with a cube of butter. I tried to remove the stain once with sandpaper but stopped partway into the job. It was a piece of him, however ignoble. Mementos were all we had.

Even the saddest of the bar's clientele we regarded as cherished relics of Dad. Mom said they branded our house as the hobo brands the house of a benefactor. But as much as she groaned about Dad's indiscriminate giving, she continued the open-hand, open-door policy. Broken hearts, lonely hearts, the depressed and beef-witted—all manner of infirm and afflicted—found their way to our house. She'd sit for hours and listen to their woes, feed them, nurse them.

Several months after the murder, a frail man in his late twenties, bald at the crown, leftover hair long and greasy, clothes threadbare, knocked at the side door. The top third was window and through the loosely woven curtain I caught sight of him. Any other time I would not have answered the door but there was something faintly familiar about him.

I opened the door and asked what he wanted. He studied my mouth and in an attempt to answer pushed out a mush of words, the hard sound of consonants missing.

"O-man," he said. I waited a good five seconds for the rest of the sentence. "O-man . . . die . . . O-man . . . frwhen."

He nodded up and down telling me it was all right to let him in. He followed me into the kitchen where Mom was cooking dinner.

"Mom . . . this is a friend of Dad's. . . . What's your name?"

She glanced up a little startled.

"Ja-we," he said, holding out a blackened hand. "O-man . . . die. . . . I saw-we."

Mom served Jerry coffee and he kept staring at the pool table. I asked if he wanted to play and he had a smooth, perfect stroke from the left side. Then I remembered. A few years back, a deaf man had walked in off the streets and asked Dad for a job and Dad felt bad and gave him a sandwich and beer and some quarters to shoot pool. I never saw him again but Dad said he showed up every few weeks, broke and hungry and itching to play. Dad gave him odd jobs to do and he became a kind of mascot. Teachers in grade school had wrongly evaluated him as retarded when he actually suffered a severe hearing loss. He had taught himself to read lips.

Mom asked Jerry to stay for dinner and we watched in awe as he ravaged several pieces of baked chicken, picking clean every bit of flesh, fat and sinew until there was nothing left but gray polished bone.

"Now that's the way you kids ought to eat chicken," Mom said, breaking the silence of our stares.

We shot a few more games of eight-ball and he followed me into the bedroom. "You have any gwass?"

"What?"

"Gwass? . . . Ma-wanna?"

"Oh, marijuana . . . no, I don't have any."

"Do you know where I get some?"

"No, I don't . . . sorry."

I was bothered by his assumption. He had seen the small collectible bottles of vodka, gin and rum in my bedroom and maybe he figured marijuana was even chance. But his question struck me as something else, that I, the son of Ara Arax, would surely know a thing or two about dope. For a time, Jerry continued to show up at our back door, filthy as ever. He'd reaffirm his sympathies that Old Man had died, Mom would invite him to stay for dinner, we'd play a few games of pool and between the last thank you and the handshake good-bye, he'd ask if I knew where he could score a lid.

Aunt Rosette wanted us to break all ties with the past. She talked a great deal in a loud voice that chided Mom: "Who are these people? You're doing the same thing Ara did, accepting all these creepy people into your house. I mean, Jesus Christ! That's not the kind of people you do that with. You do that with people of your own level."

She badgered Mom to get rid of Dad's clothes. It wasn't healthy to hold onto them, she said. Mom emptied Dad's side of the huge walk-in master closet and gave everything to Uncle Mike—payment, I thought, for shouldering the thankless task of managing The Apartments for us. Uncle Mike said Dad would have done the same for him had the tables been turned. He stopped taking lucrative out-of-town carpenter jobs so he could stay close by the bar. He started pouring the hard stuff and didn't stop for two years.

Every time I attempted to glean something more about Dad's life and death, something beyond the icons, Mom rebuffed me. *Don't spend your time in the past, Mark. What's done is done. Leave well enough alone. Let sleeping dogs lie.* The *Fresno Bee* ran a monthly column of unsolved murders and asked readers with information to call a secret witness telephone line. A $2,500 reward was being offered for any tip that led to prosecution. Dad's case was featured prominently accompanied by a composite of one of the gunmen drawn from the memory of Linda Lewis, the sole witness.

I began seeing the composite in every male I encountered who was between twenty-five and thirty and had chisled hard features and mustache. It didn't matter where I was, the pizza shop or the grocery store or en route to a friend's. I'd jot down or memorize the license plate number and dash home to call the police. At one point I suspected the man who lived next door to Uncle Mike.

"No way, Mark," cousin Steven said. "The guy works for the post office. He's a mailman."

"I don't give a shit what he does, Stevey. He looks like the man who shot my father."

Mom and Uncle Mike believed that the murder was tied to one of the bars, and possibly to drugs. They assumed the best, that Dad had tried to stem the flow of the illicit traffic and was killed in a crossfire between the cops and drug dealers. How they arrived at this belief, I did not know and they did not tell me. We kept on hearing all sorts of rumors to the contrary, though. That Dad owed vast sums of money to Fresno's version of the Mafia. That he reneged on a drug deal at the last minute. Behind Mom's back, I began posing questions to people outside the family and scribbling their answers into a small notebook I hid in my desk. I searched for clues inside Dad's datebooks and business records.

Then came a surprising discovery. In the month before my father was killed, he had made repeated visits to the Fresno Police Department. A family friend who saw him there said he was upbeat and "looked like he was on top of things." The friend assumed Dad was cooperating with a police investigation.

It was what I wanted so badly to hear, and I decided to call the detectives to find out more. Uncle Mike had equipped the telephone with an extra-long cord that stretched into the bathroom. I shut the door and dialed police headquarters and stuck a tape recorder to the receiver. I asked the sergeant how the investigation was going and passed along a rumor from a schoolmate whose brother hung out at the bar. I was doing a fine job leading up to the point of my call when Mom, apparently alarmed by the twenty-foot cord pulled taut behind a closed door, barged in.

"What are you doing in here?"

I had managed to hang up the phone but the tape was still running. "I was talking to one of the detectives."

She had scolded me once before about keeping the names of sources and suspects in my desk drawer. Now she was pleading.

"I don't want you pursuing this. Please, Mark."

I smiled.

"I mean it. Promise me you won't pursue this. You can't fool around with these people. It's not worth it."

"But it's only one of the detectives."

"Promise me."

"Okay, I promise."

My sister, Michelle, was the first to break the every-third-night pattern of sleeping with Mom. Instead of applauding it as a healthy gesture, a cue for me and my little brother, I dismissed it as a function of her growing sulkiness. The way I saw it she was breaking our united front. Donny and I continued switching off bed duties, mostly because Mom never told us it was no longer necessary. I cannot say that it ever felt deep, dark and

Freudian, the divide between us always two feet. It was the most comfortable mattress in the house and half of it lay open and it was the one room besides the family room that had a TV and it felt like camping out. Perhaps I might have questioned our mutual dependence, brooded over its pathology and resented Mom for it had I not been born with such a need to please. And steadily, she allowed me to take over the house.

Somehow, in the paroxysm of grief, manhood found me. Everything stretching and growing. From the ninth to twelfth grade I grew almost ten inches—three inches in a single summer. I had watched my father shave so many times and yet there were questions I wanted to ask. Straight edge or electric? Cold water or hot? How far up the cheeks do I go? What direction? In the cabinet beneath the bathroom sink Mom had saved his razor, badger-hair lathering brush and cut medication. I taught myself how to shave.

Mindful of my deathbed promise to him, I spent summer mornings at the neighborhood grammar school performing a harsh regimen of long distance running, wind sprints and football drills designed to make heavy feet lighter. One afternoon, at the end of a particularly grueling workout, the school janitor walked over to the track and began to chat. He confided that my brother had spent a good deal of the previous academic year in the principal's office.

"All these rich kids hear it from their parents," he said. "Your father was dealing drugs. He owed a big debt to the mob. You should be proud of your brother. I've never seen him lose a fight yet."

At Bullard High School, I played third base in baseball and linebacker and quarterback in football. I wore Dad's number, 44, and carried his picture in the webbing of my helmet. One game I came off the bench late in the fourth quarter and completed six straight passes to pull out a victory. The next day's sports page headlined the story: ARAX IS HERO. I started the rest of the season at quarterback. It was the closest I got to fulfilling that promise.

Mom couldn't afford to buy me a class ring and the $9 check she wrote for the yearbook ended up bouncing—twice. She cried in bed at night and cursed Dad. I found a bottle of Lithium in her bathroom and, not knowing what it was, I called a pharmacist. Mom explained that a friend had given her a few pills to calm the nerves but she hadn't taken any yet. "This isn't for calming the nerves," I yelled. "This is for crazies." I buried the bottle in a fig orchard behind our house.

A sizeable chunk of the life insurance money, our nest egg, was being squandered on legal problems. Mike Garvey sued Mom to recover a portion of his investment in The Apartments and won. The house band sued over stolen instruments and won. The landlord sued, claiming that Dad's expansion had encroached on property not covered in the lease, and won. When we sued Dan Hornig to recover the $18,000 Dad invested in The Forum, he returned less than half of the money and filed bankruptcy.

Uncle Mike was certain that as soon as enough time had passed and the murder faded in the public mind, the bar would sell and we could get on with our lives. I told myself that he was just trying to shore up Mom as he had once tried to shore up me. I doubted the bar would ever sell and imagined the crushing weight of this millstone someday bequeathed to me.

He and Mom sat at the kitchen table night after night drinking coffee and plotting strategies to stretch the dollar. Long after the others, he continued to mourn. "Your father and I were closer to each other than to our own brothers," he'd tell me, eyes twinkling. When the battery in the car gave out, Uncle Mike bought us a new one. When the tires needed replacing, he drove the car to a friend's station and had the job done half price. Sometimes he'd surprise us with a piece of London broil and stay for dinner. Sometimes he'd come over with son Steven and just putter around. If Uncle Mike tended to overdo things, I'm not sure we noticed. As for the wife he left behind, we gave little thought to that, too.

I stopped taking Uncle Mike for granted the night he brought his wife Aunt Jeanette over for a rare visit and Mom banished us to the bedroom. This was serious business. Through the closed hallway doors I could make out only fragments of their conversation. Evidently Aunt Jeanette had been warned by friends to be more vigilant: People are wondering why your husband is spending so much time with your sister. What obviously upset Mom and Uncle Mike was that Aunt Jeanette had not taken the opportunity right then to quell the gossip. She just sat there empty-faced, mute.

Mom wanted to know why she had kept silent? Was it because down deep she had doubts, too? Let's sit crooked and talk straight, Mom said in Armenian.

Aunt Jeanette wasn't talking.

"Answer her, goddamm it!" Uncle Mike yelled.

Years later, Grandma Arax would insinuate that Mom and Uncle Mike had sat much too close on the couch. I, myself, never had any reason to believe that the love he lavished on us was anything but altruistic. The only time I saw anything physical between them was that day four years after the murder when he burst through the door brimming wonderful news. A bartender had put together the cash, $48,000, to buy the stinking joint outright. Mom was so giddy she kissed Uncle Mike on the cheek. With all the lawsuits and legal fees and loans, it was enough to break even.

Displaying the zeal of a born again, Mom was now free to work and plunged headfirst into real estate. In a matter of months she studied and passed her exams, signed on with a growing company and sold enough property to be honored with a plaque naming her salesperson of the month.

My grades were good enough for one of the University of California campuses out of town but I chose to stay home and enroll at Cal State Fresno. The tuition was low, $99 a semester, and Mom took care of the cooking, cleaning and wash. No matter how tight the finances, she juggled things so that I didn't have to work, and on the weekends she always managed to slip me a few bucks on my way out the door. She became a second mother to my buddies, and they confided in her what they couldn't tell their parents. She liked to grumble that her house was no longer her own but she kept on cooking them dinner and bleaching their soiled underwear and nursing their hangovers.

The role of bulwark may have suited
me spiritually but I didn't exactly look the part. Prodded by an old high
school teammate, Sam Titus, I ordered through the mail a 300-pound
Olympic set and bench press from the famed York Barbell Company in
Pennsylvania. We assembled a decent gym in the patio of my backyard
and for the next five years, through the 110 degree heat of summer and the
fog-shrouded days of winter, we pushed ourselves to a realm of physical
agony not previously known.

Sam and I worked out two hours in the afternoon and studied four to
six hours at night. We preened our new swollen bodies in a-size-too-small
shirts and mailed our straight-A report cards to high school teachers who
had forecast our failure. Our heads swelled more than a little, and hubris
knew no bounds. "If you want to talk intellectually, we can do that. If you
want to talk violence, we can do that, too."

Alone in our gym, Sam started to ask questions about my father. He
was captivated by The Apartments era and men such as Armond Bletcher,
and on his own he looked up the newspaper articles at the library and
started to fantasize about solving the murder. "We're going to get bigger,
go away to law school and come back and find out what happened," he'd

say. "We're going to solve it." In one library search he found an article in *Easyriders* motorcycle magazine featuring an exceedingly large Armond astride his swastika-emblazoned Harley, which he dubbed the Big Incher and which looked like a toy scooter between his legs. Sam taped the article to the wall above the bench press as inspiration.

"Do you think he had anything to do with it?" he asked.

"I don't know, Swinger. It's something I've always wondered about. I can believe a lot of things about Armond but I just can't believe he was involved in my father's murder. But to be honest, I'm not sure."

The shadow of Dad's death lingered over Armond. Whenever people ventured a theory, they singled him out as culprit. He was rumored to be Dad's bodyguard or strongarm, and people figured who better than Ara's own hired thug to betray him. Armond's wife Janice assured us that Dad was one of the few men Armond really respected. And yet after the murder he seemed burdened by a strange, morbid remorse. Twice, friends had gone to Ararat Cemetery to put flowers on Dad's grave only to turn back at the sight of a goateed man, bigger than nature intended any man to be, on his hands and knees talking into my father's headstone.

At age twenty-one, after four years of weight lifting, I stood five-feet-eleven inches and weighed nearly 200 pounds. My biceps measured just under eighteen inches and I could bench press 335 pounds—all accomplished drug-free. I had undergone no less than a transfiguration. It was evident from my walk alone (back spread like a cobra's head) that I and this body had just been introduced, intimacy still a way off. Even though the change could hardly have been more dramatic, people still saw me as Little Markie, the boy whose father had been shot dead years back.

I was old enough now to experience the Fresno bar scene first hand and things had changed since Dad's time. The clubs had moved north, disco replacing live rock 'n' roll, downers passé. This was cocaine music. As part of my compact with Dad I swore off drugs and limited my drinking on most weekend nights to a few beers. One Saturday, a stranger in his late thirties took the barstool next to me grumbling about the dearth of female action. Yeah, yeah, I played along. In his day, he recalled wistfully, there was a fleshpot called Ara's Apartments where you could get laid seven nights a week.

Sam Titus and I already had been crowned the "Woodward and Bernstein" of Cal State Fresno's journalism department for an investigative report in which I had gone undercover as a bodybuilder to buy steriods and quaaludes from an old Fresno doctor named O. B. Doyle. I may have been new to this business of journalism but certainly schooled enough to know that you made your own serendipity.

"The Apartments. Sure," I said. "Wasn't the owner murdered or something?"

"Ara . . . Yeah. I didn't know him that well but my girlfriend, Mary Santana, was dating him at the time."

"Oh yeah?"

"She told me that he had a black book with details of a bunch of drug rings in Fresno. He must have known he was going to be killed because he gave the book to Mary. She said after the murder, Armond Bletcher forced her to hand it over."

"What happened to Mary?"

"Nothing. She's still around. We broke up a few years ago. I think she got married."

I got home early that night, everyone asleep, and took out the notebook I'd been keeping since the murder and jotted down the name *Mary Santana* followed by the words *black book.* I knew enough about the bar business to suspect that my father had a fling or two, suspicions only confirmed by my mother's indiscreet remarks during their arguments. So I wasn't surprised to learn that a Mary Santana or someone like her existed. Rather, I felt comforted knowing that there was a woman (or women) out there in addition to Mom who had a part of him I might find one day.

I say women because one night my best friend, Warren, and I met two divorcees at a bar for the older set. We chatted several minutes and bought them drinks and as soon as I muttered "Arax," the younger one, a short blonde, shouted no in disbelief. She took my hand and led me outside, confiding that my father and she had been lovers. She seemed to know a lot about the family and kept apologizing for their affair. We hugged and I had a hundred questions but I didn't ask one. I went to bed that night with her friend. Confused, enfeebled, I apologized more than once and left.

○○○

I knew I couldn't fill the hollow left by Dad or replace the husband my mother lost, and a part of me became convinced that a mate no longer mattered to her. She was in her mid-forties, old by my reckoning, and we children and the promise of our children were plenty enough. Mom would honor Dad, herself and us by doing what Armenian widows had done for generations: perservering without husbands, waiting for desperation to pass, love to atrophy, life to wither.

My mother encouraged this belief. She was a little like Aurora in *Terms of Endearment,* all these Armenian men coming over to the house for long chats and strong coffee. I began to suspect one of them had deeper affections when he gave her a gold ring won at the racetrack.

She busied herself with real estate and the church, and her friends couldn't understand her turning down dates. She was a handsome woman. Though the years and financial woes had bestowed a cleft between her eyes and furrows at the sides of her mouth, she had retained her petite figure and youthful spirit. The hair that had fallen out in the days after the murder had grown back. Her eyes stopped twitching and surgery repaired the weary bags under them.

We thought nothing at first when she began arriving home late from the church committee meetings. The group met afterwards for coffee, she explained. A friend said he had seen a man, balding and bespectacled, driving my mother's car. It must have been a car just like hers, I insisted. Then one day, while searching for Dad's shoe shine kit, I found the draft of a letter Mom had written. It was addressed to Arsen Marsoobian, a married man and father of three who belonged to our church. Mom wrote that she had come to a decision. She wanted to break off their relationship before it got serious and the rumors spread beyond the committee members to the whole church community. It was clear from the letter that as a salve to his troubled marriage Arsen had relentlessly pursued Mom and she admitted that the years of loneliness made her an easy target. "I don't want to be the 'other woman' so we'll stop now, Arsen. I hope we can remain friends," the letter concluded.

Arsen Marsoobian? The city bureaucrat by day who preached the gospel of Amway and chain letters and pyramid schemes by night? The motivational tapes, Optimist Club, Bulldog Booster Club, future mayoral candidate Arsen?

I felt stupid and betrayed and stormed into the kitchen waving the letter in her face.

"What is this shit? So this is why you've been coming home late from those meetings. And we're the last ones to find out!"

"You've got no right going through my stuff. It's none of your business. That's the problem here. My life isn't my own. You kids think you own me."

"So you lie, huh? Who does this guy think he is anyway?"

"I wouldn't worry about it, Mark. It's over."

"Yeah. But not before the whole church knows about it. Just great. All those years they squawked about Dad. Now they're going to drag our name through the mud again because of this guy."

"No one knows about it. Your name's safe. I wouldn't worry."

"What do you mean? The members of that committee know."

"Just one or two."

"If one Armenian knows," I shouted, "they all know!"

The next day Arsen called and wanted to talk. We met at a coffee shop and he declared his love for Mom. If that's the case, I asked, why are you still living with your wife and kids? Why are you taking a chance with my mother's reputation? He said his marriage was a joke and that his wife had her own affair going. He pledged that he wouldn't see Mom until he had formally separated and filed for divorce—a promise he kept for two weeks. I packed my clothes and weights and moved in with Grandpa and Grandma Arax.

The consequences of murder took strange and remarkable forms—the relentless weight lifting, the sleeping in Mom's bed, the fear and dependence and melodramatic ruptures. But it also brought a fuller facing of who I was and what it meant to be second-generation Armenian-American.

None of my grandparents, not even preacher Hyreek, ever made me feel that I had to be Armenian, or that the Armenian I was was somehow not good enough. Not until college did this happen, not until I met Dickran Kouymjian in the fall of 1979. He was a short, bald, ferret of a man who headed the Armenian Studies Program at Cal State Fresno, a job that even in the Armenian-rich San Joaquin Valley demanded a certain amount of panhandling.

He believed that every Armenian on campus had a moral obligation to support the program and here I was, Armenian-American, editor of the college daily, and I hadn't signed up for a single Kouymjian course. He seemed to hold responsible my mentor, Professor Roger Tatarian, once the editor-in-chief of United Press International and certainly a Who's Who Armenian.

Late one afternoon Kouymjian barged into my office at the *Daily Colle-*

gian demanding to know what I was going to do about Vintage Days—a spring festival of arts and crafts, music, games and debauchery—opening on April 24th, the very anniversary of the 1915 Genocide.

"They're planning to parade right past our memorial in the free-speech area, Arax. This is Fresno State. Armenians built this campus."

"This is the first I've heard of it," I said. "The contrast is sure striking. A parade of revelers and a parade of mourners. 'The Forgotten Genocide.' Great photo."

Maybe I was being too cavalier. His voice grew shrill.

"Photo? It's a helluva lot more than that. If you were thinking like an Armenian you'd see it."

He continued to rail. "As editor of this paper, what have you done for Armenians? Admit it. There's nothing about you that's remotely Armenian. You're just another shish kebab."

It hung in the air: *Shish kebab Armenian.* I guess I knew what he meant. Before I could respond he was gone. I'm not sure what I would have told him. Maybe that he was right. So what was it that endured in me and acted like a powerful magnet to Sam Titus and my other non-Armenian friends seeking an ethnic experience? Maybe it was shish kebab but not in the way Kouymjian meant it.

I had felt it most keenly at family doings, all the aunts, uncles, cousins and grandparents in one place. It was the same in summer or winter. The women would be cooking pilaf and baking cheese booregs in the kitchen and the men would be gathered around a fire of grape stumps in the backyard. The meat had been cut into thick cubes and impaled by long steel skewers: lamb, tomato, lamb, bell pepper, lamb, eggplant, lamb, onion. You didn't dare leave the fire long or you risked missing the best part, the judging of the meat. The first samples were teasers, tiny fingers of lamb almost severed from the cube that flapped and dangled low over the fire and tasted of ash. These were followed by bigger and choicer pieces until sometimes a full hot skewer had been sampled by the men, furtive and panting *ha-ha's,* grumbling that the women couldn't time the pilaf right and the meat would again be cold on the table and overdone. Lamb tasted best pink through the middle, and when the mid-sized pieces had reached just shy of this state, Dad would call for the *peda* bread. He didn't slice the meat off the skewer or remove it piece by piece with a fork. Instead, holding the *peda* bread as insulation, he slid the kebab in one long procession slowly down the shaft of the skewer into a big bowl. Very little juice escaped this way and any that did got blotted up by the *peda*. This bread, too, was shared by the men.

I loved slurping the juice of red onions, tomatoes and vinegar that pooled in the salad bowl. I loved eating *jajuke,* sour yogurt mixed with fresh pressed garlic and cold Armenian cucumber. Armenian cucumber didn't give you gas like its English cousin and God knows the Armenian didn't need any more gas. I loved the heart of the watermelon fresh from the vine, slices of sharp cheddar to modulate its sweetness. I loved the jewel-like berries of pomegranates arrayed as only nature could inside waxy white catacomb. I loved Mom's *got-ah,* milk bread, hot from the oven, like Jewish *challah,* only lighter and sweeter.

As it turned out, Dr. Kouymjian didn't need my help. This was the 65th anniversary of the Genocide, a nice round number, and he had already roused a good many Armenians on and off the campus to protest the callous juxtaposition of the spring festival. His cry to rally was without incident until my mentor, Professor Tatarian, was confronted by one of my weight-lifting friends wearing a black armband snug around the bicep and carrying an extra one in hand. He barged in as Tatarian was meeting with a student in his office.

"Dr. Tatarian, I was wondering if you would put this on to memoralize the one and a half million Armenians who died in a massacre that began sixty-five years ago today."

Tatarian's lips quivered trying to restrain rage. He was a prudent man, not at all fond of armbands and placards. He didn't need a lecture on history and he didn't need to peacock his ethnicity.

"I have made it a policy throughout my journalistic career not to join in public displays for any cause," Tatarian told him. "I hope you understand."

My friend persisted. "But you're Armenian."

"Yes, I'm Armenian. And I'm proud of the fact. But I don't wear badges for anyone."

I marveled at my mentor's ability to detach himself in the name of journalistic objectivity, an exile that no matter how hard I tried at different points in my life I would never quite achieve. That day, I wore a black armband and read one of my grandfather's poems to the crowd of students and survivors in the free-speech area. As editor of the *Daily Collegian,* I had broken one of the principal tenets of journalism and made the transgression worse by assigning one of my reporters to cover the event.

Spring, Constantinople, 1915
News travels, mouth to mouth
Black, black shadows
With what adolescent dreams can one live
How can one look at the rosebud
At the butterflies of nubile almond trees
At the cherry's red earrings
How can afflicted hearts greet the return
Of swallows
The sun is blood
The sky is blood
I wish this morning of the dark night had never broken
Spring, Fresno, 1980
I am looking for a Turk
On this memorial day's vigil
With a bead of tear in his black eye
A young Turk, fearless, farseeing
His hand extended to the Armenian people
A tender shepherd
On the banks of a river
Feeding ladles of water to the Armenian lambs
On the dawn of this April day
I am looking for a Turk
A *Nazim Hikmet*
In our reborn motherland
On the plain of Ararat
Kneeling before the everlasting flame
Of the martyr's monument
A young Turk from the new generation
With the soot of genocide on his forehead

Aram Arax, April 24, 1980

I began to tell the story of the Genocide to area high school classes as part of a group of Armenian college students intent on teaching our history to the Fresno masses, whose complete ignorance of our culture struck me as a measure of how pitifully far we had gone to blend in.

I imagined I was taking on the mantle of my grandfathers, and yet they themselves rarely, if ever, talked about the Genocide. Instead, it got told obliquely, through their remoteness, through the ardor of their old-world politics, through verse and sermon.

Unlike my parents, who never found it necessary to ask their parents about life in Turkey during World War I, I no longer saw history as something I had to circumnavigate. My insides didn't gnaw with a hunger to blend in. The question for me was opposite, everything but a sprig of Armenia and Armenians lost, and I had no one but my parents to thank and blame. When it came time to name their first son, it wasn't Aram or Ara or Karnig or Serop but Mark. *Mark Randy.* When I came home that first week of school dumb to Armenian, there was no argument waged or disappointment registered. All but a few words—anatomical parts and bodily functions—were eventually lost to me. I cursed the inability to talk to my grandparents in their language and did nothing to remedy the situation. What remained of our homeland, one part now Turkey and another part Soviet Armenia, a source of friction between Dad and Mom's clan, didn't exactly stir me either. Still, deep down and unstated, my mother expected I would marry an Armenian and when I brought home Coby, my pretty blonde *o-dar* (the dismissive word we Armenians reserved for those outside the race), she found it difficult to display even a touch of the warmth she lavished on my male friends, Armenian and otherwise. When Coby's reception was decidedly warmer at Grandma and Grandpa Arax's house, Mom remarked, "You could have brought home anyone and your grandparents wouldn't have cared."

I had lost my father and I wasn't willing to lose that rest of him, and me, without a fight. One day not long after I declared independence from Mom, I called a meeting between my two grandfathers to ask the question my parents never needed to ask.

They were each fifteen years old when Talat Pasha, under the cry "Turkey for Moslems," ordered the razing of the Armenian homeland. Fifteen, the same age as I was when murder trenched my life. That day in the living room, my grandfathers began to will their irrevocable past to me. It took so little prodding—actually one small question—that I later wondered how it was possible that they had managed for so long not to poison with bitterness their children and grandchildren.

The man I called Pop, my father's father, had a contempt for the Turks that was hard to reconcile with his sweet nature and poetry, paeans to Lenin and Dr. King and Cesar Chávez. The Turks, he said, were cousins of the great bandits of the world, nomads who took from every culture they conquered. The original motley crew. They were great warriors, no doubt, capturing the Armenian saddleback of Anatolia and then Constantinople itself in 1453, a new empire that exceeded even the Roman in girth. But this tradition of plunder-and-run allowed so little opportunity for craft building that the sultan's first act was to summon Armenians to rebuild the city. For the next 500 years, shorn of country, the fate of the Armenians would rest in the hands of these Ottomans whose arrival they had preceded by 1,500 years.

"On one hand, the Turks said we were loyal subjects. On the other they barred us from government and banned us from carrying arms."

He mixed English, Armenian and a few words of Turkish, the swear words. His accent was not harsh: fawdr (father); vehdee (very); eeder (either); reech (rich). He shook his fist. "Our testimony in court meant nothing . . . We were *gavours,* infidels."

"What about these Armenian extremists who are now assassinating Turkish diplomats and bombing airports, killing innocents in the name of justice," I asked. "Can this be right?"

"These are vehdee bad things, Mark. But you know, you can only take so much. We must never condone these killers, but . . ."

The poet faded into silence, equivocation.

The priest thumbed his worry beads two-by-two.

"It was late in the day," my mother's father, Reverend Yegishe Mekhitarian, the man we called Hyreek, began. "The Turks came inside my house. My mother said, 'Son, your father and mother are going.' I hugged her. I was crying. And she handed me this Bible and told me to run, not look back. I ran.

"I saw with my own eyes. I saw everything. The babies still in their mother's wombs. The nipples cut off their breasts and strung around the soldiers' necks. I walked for three years pretending to be Turkish. I saw thousands and thousands of bodies. Systematic. The Turkish government, the Turkish people, the Turkish army. Because the Armenian people were reech people. We had our own homes, villages, schools, churches. Everything we owned in Turkey."

Hyreek had officially retired from the pulpit after 50 years of "dedicated service," words scrawled into gold plate and displayed on his dining table turned shrine. His wife had died a year earlier and he was lost without her and the routine of the church. He tried going to the Asbarez Hall where the old freedom fighters smoked cigars, drank Turkish coffee and cursed at the backgammon boards, but he could never be one of the boys. The collar made sure of that. They were polite and respectful—too polite and too respectful—and he must have felt their unease. Unshaven, swigging VO from a fifth he kept cold in the refrigerator, he had stopped dressing as priest and unveiled his neck. One hundred and seven degrees outside and he wore two frayed shirts under a brown wool cardigan.

I quoted the official Turkish line: "The deportation was necessary because the Armenians were revolting and joining forces with Russia, the enemy."

"Big lies, big liar. Not revolting. Not against the Turkish government. It was because we are Armenian and we have our causes. That country belong to us, for centuries and centuries. Forty-two people in my family. Vehdee big. Vehdee reech family. All gone. My father, Khoorshood Mekhitarian. His father, Baghdasar. My uncles, Garabed, Hagop and Sarkis. My mother, Atlas. My three brothers, Hovsep, who was nineteen with a wife and two children. Khonar who was twenty. Antranig who was younger than me, maybe eleven or twelve. My four sisters, Khatoon, who was married. Noyemi was nine. Verkin was seven or eight. Anakas was five or six. We lived in a big house. In the same family forty-two people. All of them gone. Turkish government. All of them killed. I don't know how, but God saved me. Only me."

Sixty-five years later and my grandfathers were still drudging for justice, still waiting for Turkey to acknowledge that its sire, the Ottoman Empire, had committed the crime of their youth. What they got instead was a perverse battle each year in the U.S. Congress over a bill to set aside April 24th as an official day of mourning—the day Armenia's greatest poets, musicians, painters and political leaders were herded for slaughter.

In this unholy fight, Armenians and Turks were going to great lengths to court the Jewish heart. Armenians portrayed the Genocide as a harbinger of the Holocaust, pointing out that Hitler had remarked on the eve of invading Poland: "Who talks nowadays of the extermination of the Armenians?" Turkish-American groups took out ads in Jewish weeklies accusing Armenians of debasing the oneness of the Holocaust with a phony precursor. When historical revision didn't work, the Turks tried extortion, warning American Jewish leaders that their sponsorship of Armenian genocide speeches would imperil the well-being of Jews in Turkey.

I myself never doubted that the mass slaughter was anything but genocide: genocide in premeditation, genocide in efficiency, genocide in cover-up. But we were not the lambs our own busy lobby in Washington wanted the world to believe. The Armenians of Ottoman Turkey were not casual observers. They were not patsies. Armenian political parties agitated for independence. Armenian irregulars existed in greater numbers than Armenian scholars were willing to admit. And many Armenians boldly rooted for Russia to defeat Turkey and liberate them.

Yet because the men who controlled the machinery of death were Turks, none of these things, alone or together, threatened the empire's existence. The pashas who oversaw the massacres were not responding to the imperatives of civil war. They made no attempt to distinguish villages of discontent from villages of calm. The decision to do away with the Armenians was general, sweeping and based on the single genus of race.

What they launched lacked the gas chambers and visual documentation of the Nazis. But this was quibbling over contrivances, the form and style of killers three decades apart. What got lost was that the Turks, using the means available to them at the time, wiped out the presence of Armenians from their ancient homeland. And never has modern Turkey come clean on this.

What happened to Armenia stood on its own, I thought. It needn't be linked to the Holocaust. It needn't matter that each year Congress sided with Turkey, that the importance of military bases outweighed any duty to history. In a perverse way Turkey's unrepentance had done us a favor. The Genocide was the one thing unassailable, the one thing resonant, the one thing Armenians could agree on.

At the same time, there was something in the accounts of both my grandfathers, particularly the priest, that bothered me. The hint of arrogance? Presumption? Naïveté? *We were Armenian. We were smart and educated. We demanded freedom because the land belonged to us. We were there first.*

Maybe the Armenian had let his contempt for the Turks' backwardness blind him to his power. How the Turk must have felt, a supplicant in a land he had conquered but could not manage, leaning on the Armenian merchant and banker to negotiate with the outside powers. How could Armenians instigate for equal rights and talk revolt at a time when Turkey was watching its empire crumble? They had lived side-by-side with the Turks, 800 years of bloody history. Could they not have forseen the consequences of these acts? Had the Turk not killed for less?

At some point it occurred to me: These were some of the same questions I was asking about my father. Did Dad provoke his murder by betraying the world around him and did this betrayal somehow reduce the crime? Didn't the Armenians see it coming? Didn't Dad see it coming? Why hadn't they bailed out in time? Why hadn't *he?* The Armenians were talking freedom, talking independence, willing to risk everything. That they even pressed their rights at all and some armed themselves and fought back was being used to discredit a genocide. Yes, they went about it stupidly. Yes, whatever Dad did, it was naïve and foolhardy. Restive Armenia. Restive Ara. Neither one quite knew how to gauge and navigate the dangers.

In those early years, I more or less honored my mother's request to leave the murder be. I set aside any focus on hitmen or perfidious business partners or dirty cops. Instead, I began constructing a family history through the accounts of my grandparents, great uncles and aunts and longtime family friends. None of them ever thought that my delving into their past had anything to do with Dad's murder, or if they did, they never let on. As far as I could tell, they simply chalked up my curiosity to a quirk of my nature. Markie, our inquisitor. Markie, our historian. Some were more eager to delight my interest than others. Maybe they sensed I was using history to compensate for my terrible loss. I couldn't take up a gun. I had no financial or political sway. No one was giving me a straight answer. No one I knew necessarily had a straight answer. I was Ara-boy's son armed with nothing more than a tape recorder and the endurance to listen for hours and hours, and they would oblige me the stories. I was hardly aware of the forces at work myself. There seemed to be no rhyme or reason to my mission. I simply trudged from living room to living room with no greater purpose than to preserve their voices before it was too late. Only years later, playing back the voices that now haunt me, did I recognize a purpose. I was searching for a meaning that would triumph over murder. In my early flailings to understand my father and myself—how he could so miserably fail at the one thing he owed us, to survive—I understood that the question of who we were and where we came from was no less important than who pulled the trigger and why.

That spring and summer living with my grandparents had a quality unlike any other, an urgency that if I didn't do certain things now they would never get done. This was especially true about Grandpa Arax. He was eighty years old and, unable to see enough to shave, had grown a Whitman-like beard that matched perfectly his shock of white mane.

He raged at blindness. He'd sit me down at the kitchen table and make me watch as he worked his way through a stack of playing cards. He'd hold each card a few inches from his face, call out the correct number and suit and slap it back down on the kitchen table, triumphantly. Grandma scoffed. "What improvement? He's just memorized the stack." He protested, demanded I reshuffle and then performed the stunt all over again, missing only a few.

We planted one last garden. Pop placed the spade in my hand and pointed to where he wanted me to turn the soil. To evade Grandma's constant chatter, we spent hours alone in the den. He, too, it seemed, was trying to make some order for himself and day by day, as his world grew darker and darker, he began to reveal more and more of himself.

It was a perfect collusion. He became my one witness, my spiritual connection to Dad, and I became his audience of one, the instrument to tap into his past. The cards he held were darker than I ever imagined, and he did not show all of them. Some things I would learn years later, from others, after his fall into senility and death.

There were four murders in our family, I discovered. Two of us killed. Two of us killers. Two murders in the old country. Two murders in the new one. In between was the murder of the Armenian nation. It all linked up in his stories, each crime bound to the other, each crime traced to the Turks. His grandfather had been killed in the tensions that led to the Genocide. The murdered man's son, Grandpa's uncle, watched the Turks butcher his wife and children and then escaped to Bulgaria, where he then killed a man. It was this murder that brought our clan to America and in the streets of America, in 1934, Grandpa's brother killed a forty-year-old police officer. Forty years later the word in the streets was that the police had something to do with the murder of his forty-year-old son.

He told me: "If we would have gone back to Armenia, we could have saved your fawder . . . but who knows those things." He was referring to the time in the early 1940s when he and Grandma contemplated repatriation to Soviet Armenia and went so far as to have passport photos taken of themselves and the children. "It turned out," Grandma explained, "that they (she couldn't quite bring herself to say "the Soviets") needed Grandpa more here than there."

Over time, I too would come to see a link between the tragedies of country and clan and father, only it wasn't the same link of communal fate and superstition my grandfather saw. There was a snag in our family, a flaw of grandiosity and self-deception and hot temper through the generations that extended to my father. This trait, as much as the implacable social forces Grandpa railed against—the Turks, the Genocide, the corruption deep in the bone of America and its little Fresno—explained our bloodshed. And there was another secret hidden in the family as well, one that I would discover at the end of my search, one that my grandfather and grandmother and uncle had been keeping from me for twenty years.

○ ○ ○

Grandpa Arax was born Jonig Hovsepian in 1900 in the Great New Village near Bursa, the first capital of the Ottomans. I cannot find the village on present-day maps, the Armenian names all obliterated. It sat about 40 miles southeast of Istanbul between the Sea of Marmara and Lake Nicaea in a fruitful valley beneath the Duman Dagh, the mountain of mist.

His father, Hovsep, fished and ran a coffee house where the menfolk smoked hashish and played backgammon and complained about taxes. Not only did the Armenian patriarch levy fees in the name of the sultan but villagers were forced to pay tribute to local Ottoman officials as well. These officials, by design, did not earn a lira in government salary; their sole income derived from the power to dun the minorities.

Most of these bagmen were Turkish. Grandpa's maternal grandfather, Jonig Demirjian, had been one of the few Armenians. He was known as Jonig Agha, a title of dubious merit given to functionaries. Many of the *aghas* were hated as instruments of Turkish repression and gouging. My great-great-grandfather, dressed all in white, must have done his job exceedingly well for in the year 1883 the Armenians of the region invited him to a banquet in his honor, a banquet from which he never returned.

A day or so later his wife found a burlap sack on the front porch. His body, hacked into a hundred pieces, was stuffed inside. In the funeral march from home to church the widow tramped behind the coffin, flinging dirt and shouting curses at the Armenians who lined the way. It was in honor of this murdered grandfather that my grandfather was christened Jonig.

I have heard the story told differently, with other killers and other motives. One version is that Turks, not Armenians, murdered a tenderhearted Jonig. Jonig's oldest son, Ervant, supposedly tracked down the Turkish killers and one by one exacted revenge. A sentence of death hanging over him, Ervant escaped to Bulgaria and finally America.

It is an attractive story, so perfectly rounded and sweet in its reprisal, especially in light of what the Turks would later do to the Armenians. But Ervant was not yet five years old when his father was killed. What seems more plausible is that Jonig Agha had been done in by his own ego, duped by Armenians who, to his utter surprise, had singled him out as an agent of Turkish tyranny. Years later, Ervant, the son, lost his wife and children in the 1915 Genocide and escaped to Bulgaria. One day, working in the coal mines, unable to control a hair-trigger temper, he killed a man and fled to America, where he would send for his nephew—my grandfather—and the rest of the family.

Grandpa grew up in a period of calm between these two murders. The 11,000 or so Armenians in the Great New Village ran the farms and shops and the few Turks toiled as domestics and cheap labor. "It was a Turkish way of life," he said. "Vehdee lazy. We had grapes. We had olive oil. We had silk from the mulberry. My fawdr would catch fish on Lake Nicaea. There was plenty to eat. I never saw anyone go begging for food. Our crops were vehdee reech crops."

What Grandpa never told me—what I learned later from other relatives—was that the "Turkish" languor of his village was underwritten by the best cash crop of all. Grandpa was nine years old when village elders began wrapping his body with opium and hashish and sending him on a half day's journey to Istanbul. By the time he reached the big city, his pores had opened up and absorbed the narcotic. He was high and smelled so rank that none of the passengers on the boat would sit next to him. He was met by a middleman who took him to a residence, removed the drugs and handed him an envelope to take back home.

None of my relatives ever told me who these "village elders" were. The assumption was that this was Turkey, a source of opium for the world, and it would be naïve to think that Armenians didn't capitalize on the trade from time to time. By the time I got around to wondering if my grandfather's father and mother were complicit in the scheme, the family members who told the original story were all dead or senile. My interest in the material wasn't that I thought it had specific implications for my father's actions a half century and world away. But it did bother me, this image of greedy hands strapping to the belly of a child a drug shipment for the far-off city.

The year my grandfather turned nine, the chimney fell down, a bad-bad omen his grandfather muttered. That spring the drought-weakened mulberry refused to bloom. Then a freakish summer hail storm destroyed the olive crop. Once exempt from hardship, the Great New Village could no longer sustain its own and whole families migrated to Istanbul. His mother, who had given birth to a fourth child, a boy named Ara, was forced to hire out as a wet nurse and cook for rich Istanbul Armenians. His father signed on with a ship ferrying olive oil to and from Italy.

It was agreed that the children would stay behind in the village with relatives until housing in Istanbul could be secured. By the time they were reunited almost a year later, baby Ara, robbed of mother's milk, had died of disease. To say that the family's move to a dank house in the city was propitious would be an understatement. Not a single adult who stayed behind in the village ever made it out alive. "If my mother had not taken that job in Istanbul," he told me, "none of us would be here today." Still, he never forgot Ara, the baby brother whose life had been sacrificed for the good of all.

His father's ship was leaving Italian waters freighted with olive oil in 1912 when war broke out between Turkey and Italy. The Italians detained the crew for several weeks until supplies ran low and they were suddenly released to a sea now hostile. The two-week voyage took two months. All his father would tell the family is that he and the others had been forced to drink sea water to survive. A day or two after their homecoming, the ship's captain fell ill and died. His father was attending the captain's funeral when he too collapsed. His fever never broke and he died two days later.

Although my grandfather never told me in so many words, Baby Ara's death followed so closely by the death of his father embittered him deeply and gave rise to the atheist and dissident-in-making. I began to notice in our talks that his earliest voice was mostly that of victim. The theme insinuated itself constantly and in fact was a source of competition between him and Grandma. Who was more afflicted? Who was the greater underdog? Who had more sympathy for the underdog? Who was going to die first? And yet my grandfather, unlike a lot of other genocide survivors, was no brooder. He could be a fun-loving man, sometimes too fun-loving for Grandma's taste.

One of his favorite stories recalled the time when he was twelve and had to take a part-time job managing the books for an Armenian shopkeeper. That first week, he was asked to carry two bags of produce to the shopkeeper's house several blocks away. They were walking across the Bridge of Galata that linked the Christian and Moslem halves of the great merchant city, Grandpa with the bags of onions and tomatoes and peppers in his arms and the Armenian boss unburdened three paces ahead. It was cold and windy and he wanted to quicken the pace but each time he pulled even with his boss he got a hand in the chest and a shove backward. *Hed dev us kaleh,* the boss glared: walk behind me.

Grandpa said he fancied dumping the vegetables right there into the waters of the Golden Horn but he kept on, three paces behind, until the delivery was made and he ran home, tears clouding his eyes. He grabbed a pen and paper and watched in detached awe as it tumbled out. He titled the prose piece "Walk Behind Me" and mailed it to the big Armenian daily. A few days later, like that, it appeared as a letter to the editor, his first published writing.

He quickly went to work for a cobbler named Donabedian, a grossly overweight man with a wife who bullied him. One Saturday, it was raining and a Turkish beggar girl not more than seven stumbled into the shop all wet. Effendi Donabedian, upset at the water dripping onto his floor, lifted the girl by the neck and dropped her outside, making sure to hand her the equivalent of a nickel before she hit the ground.

Grandpa said he didn't hide his disgust and Effendi, feeling bad, invited him to dinner the next night. In between the invitation and dinner, the afternoon paper came out with Grandpa's newest broadside, a story about Armenian merchants who "give a nickel and take a pint of blood in interest." It was titled *Vash-ka-rogh,* usurer, and he named his boss. Grandpa knocked on the door of the elegant apartment at six sharp and Mrs. Donabedian answered with a blow across his face. "*Vash-ka-rogh* is the name of my husband now," she shouted. He was stunned, thinking the story would appear that weekend, if at all. Effendi calmed his wife and after a fine dinner informed Grandpa that as of Monday his salary would be doubled.

Before the outbreak of the war, the Armenians of Istanbul had been lulled into a false sense of impregnability. They believed the port city didn't belong to Turkey so much as it belonged to the world, the breeze of four seas blowing in Europe's temperance. Then one night shortly after he turned fifteen, Grandpa heard a fierce drumbeat followed by a chant, the latest Turkish edict.

> Armenian Men Between the Ages of Sixteen and Sixty Report at Once to the Army Depot. Bring a Week's Supply of Food. No Excuses. Those Who Fail to Show Up Will Be Court-Martialed.

Thousands heeded the call only to be herded into labor battalions and sent to the interior where they were slaughtered. My grandfather and perhaps 20,000 other young Armenian men took to their attics in hiding, the *Tavan Tabouri,* the Army of the Attics.

"I stayed up there one year. My life was with the books. Lamartine, the French poet, and Verlaine and Baudelaire and Maupassant. All these lives, these flirtations, in this two-by-four room. My life was more romantic than any other time. I dreamed about Sorbonne University and I waited for the victory of the Allied nations."

He came down in 1917 to learn that the village where he was born and where the extended family still lived had been plundered, every church burned, every house demolished. Only three small starving cousins survived and they showed up one day at the doorstep, a pathetic package. "They came to live with us for awhile, three small children, bones. One of them later died. He ate so much he died."

With the defeat of Turkey and Germany, the streets of Istanbul were safe again. Grandpa got a job at Babigian's bookstore where his short story about classmates poking fun at his shabby overcoat caught the fancy of a group of Armenian writers. They argued about a pen name for their small, frail charge. Before the Genocide, Grandpa had called himself Vart Badrik, the rose priest, but roses no longer seemed appropriate. He began using Aram Aslan, Aram the Lion, until one day the great Armenian satirist, Yervant Oudian, proclaimed, "You look like a lot of things, Jonig, but a lion is not one of them. Why not Arax after our muddy river? Yes. Aram Arax."

He went to work on an anthem for the Armenian Boy Scouts who in the first postwar year had grown to 5,000 strong, many of them former attic-dwellers. A wealthy railroad magnate with no children read his poems and offered to pay his way to the Sorbonne. He was about to accept when a letter arrived from his mother's brother, Ervant, singing the virtues of America, California, the San Joaquin Valley, Fresno. His plan was to join his uncle, work a summer or two and then study literature at the University of California at Berkeley. He wanted to write for a newspaper. His mother, brother and sister would join him in a year.

His failure to take up the railroad man on his offer of the Sorbonne would become one of the true regrets of my grandfather's life; only years later, in senility, would he make the choice right.

The Boy Scout band played a rousing send off. It was May 1920. He was nineteen years old. "I was all alone except for an Armenian boy and two Syrian girls, vehdee pretty. We slept on the bottom of the boat. Just like catfish. On the Sea of Marmara it was moonlight. Family, good friends, all behind me. A sadness you could never describe."

The train chugged into Fresno and he took one look at the valley rolling out lush and vibrant to the Sierra Nevada and exclaimed, *Jisht yergri bes;* just like the old land. Here you could grow almost any fruit or vegetable in ground that froze only a few days a year, and it was just about the best place in the world to turn grapes into raisins. The 105 degree days of summer hastened ripening so that the bunches could be picked by August. This gave the berries a full month to cure on trays in the sun.

Armenian defiance had already begun to shape this valley, with new methods for growing and drying fruit and a challenge to the monopoly of Southern Pacific. Fed up with the railroad's ever-higher rates, the Seropian brothers hitched a span of mules to a pair of wagons and hauled the fruit themselves into San Francisco. Their revolt made the front pages, broke Southern Pacific's iron hold and paved the way for the Santa Fe.

At age forty-five, Uncle Ervant was starting over as a fieldhand. He was a good-sized Armenian with a clean open face and he did not pretend to hide his pride as he pulled up to the railroad station that day in his polished open-top Model T to pick up my newly arrived grandfather. They spent a day catching up and then drove south to Delano where Ervant had secured work on a muscat vineyard. The summer picking season was a month away and the bunches had to be thinned. My grandfather had never labored with his hands, and that first week his fingers swelled and blistered.

They moved from farm to farm, crop to crop, up and down the Great Central Valley. Fruit tramps. Apricots in spring, then peaches, then nectarines, then plums, then table grapes, wine grapes, raisin grapes, then late summer's watermelon and cantaloupe and finally winter's citrus. As soon as the navels had been picked, the calendar said January and time to prune the vines. It was a grind, twelve hours a day in the sun, and sleep came easy on a bed of raisin boxes and alfalfa in a paperboard shack.

The following summer, Grandpa's mother, brother, sister, and sister's husband arrived, and the whole clan found work and lodging at the Kerkorian ranch in Delano. Villa Kerkorian was one of the genuine characters, his first name a moniker on account of his drooping Pancho Villa mustache. He was a paper millionaire, one raisin bust from bankruptcy, and when it finally came a few years later he was in such a state of disbelief that he grabbed a hoe and severed the ear of the bank's auctioneer. He would never live to see compensation in the form of his youngest son, Kirk Kerkorian, the financier and MGM hotel builder who would become one of the world's wealthiest men.

Spring was a slack time in the fields, a time when the family, at least the women and children, had to move to the cannery towns of Isleton, Emeryville and Rio Vista to survive. Del Monte was paying forty cents an hour straight time, and caravans of Armenian ragheads—sunbaked migrants in bandannas—followed in cars, trucks and even a hearse up dusty 99 to the delta. It was precise labor, cutting fruit in perfect halves. That first week my great-grandmother, Azniv, and her daughter, Mariam, awoke to stiff hands and arms and gave them a good soak in hot vinegar water.

Mariam had been blessed with her mother's soprano and at night, in a beautiful bittersweet voice, she would sing the church songs and love songs of Armenia. The whole camp of canners, even the Portuguese, would be huddled around the fire. Her singing would just start to get a little sad when one of the camp veterans did her best imitation of the mirthful *oud,* the Arab's pregnant guitar. *Ning ning ning ning ning ning ning. Ning ning ning ning ning ning ning.* Soon the others joined in, mimicking the *oud,* clapping, stamping, imploring the young ones to dance. And they danced, legs kicking dust, pinkies twined, one big gyrating wheel under the moon and stars.

Uncle Ervant had paid everyone's way over. As benevolent patriarch he insisted on keeping the kitty. No one begrudged him this until he began donning a white shirt, necktie and straw hat and driving to downtown Fresno to play pinochle all week. One evening at the barn that housed them, Ervant was about to launch into one of his famous lectures when young Harry, my grandfather's brother, broke in.

"By the way, Uncle Ervant, how much money is in the family savings box?"

"Tell the little one to shut up!"

"It's a legitimate question, Uncle," my young grandfather said.

"I don't think a person should get paid for days not worked," Harry persisted.

All he had given this family, Ervant ranted. "That boat that brought you over . . . I would have been better off had it brought a sack of potatoes instead."

Ervant ran and grabbed the pistol and with a trembling hand raised it to his head. "I'm going to kill myself . . . then see how you ingrates will survive."

"No, brother!" Azniv pleaded.

Harry burst out laughing. "Let him kill himself, Momma. The son of a bitch ain't going to kill himself. He's a coward. It's just another of his ploys."

Ervant moaned, grabbed his face and ran out of the shack vowing never to return. My great-grandmother Azniv ran after him but it was too late, the dust from the tires of his Model T hanging in the heat.

The first time I heard the "sack of potatoes" story, I couldn't help laughing. The overblown language, the pathetic martyrdom, Ervant's trembling hand—it seemed to say so much about the clan. The relatives who told the story were quite certain that Ervant was bluffing, but to me it was only a matter of how badly he wanted to guilt my grandfather and his brother for their crime of disrespect. He had killed that Bulgarian. With his bare hands or with a gun, no one seemed to know, but he had gone that far; what he was threatening with his trembling hand in the barnhouse that day didn't seem a whole lot further to me.

The rift got so bad that Ervant would stand at the edge of his vineyard after a long day and spot his nephews, my grandfather and his brother, happening by—*toca, toca, toca*—in their beat-up 1916 Dodge they bought for $125. At the precise moment they crossed his plane, Ervant would turn his back, pull down his pants and grab both cheeks of his ass and rub. His big ventures always went south. Melons, cucumbers, it didn't matter. He sent for two cousins in the old country, confirmed bachelors in their late thirties, totally unpredictable, and they disappointed him as well. One year a bad frost sent the field into an early dormancy. The vines would have come back fine the next year but these cousins got the idea of leveling the land. So they pulled out forty acres of the best Thompson grapes and planted worthless soybeans. One cousin was killed in a car accident and the other sold the ranch and each year vacationed to a different brothel in France. He died a pauper.

In his mid forties, Ervant married a widow with five children and promptly fathered two more, a daughter and son whom he named after the daughter and son killed in the massacres. At the baptism of the daughter, christened Suvig-Nushig (little egg and almond) Great-grandma Anziv baked her brother a peace offering from the Arax clan, a forty-layer baklava drenched in honey.

Ervant accepted but never did he learn to control his temper. He got into an argument with a hired hand over the best way to bleach raisins and marched upstairs and loaded the shotgun. His wife and sister, fearing another Bulgaria episode, tackled him and all three came tumbling down the stairs. After that, they took to hiding the guns and knives whenever he got mad. Once they forgot the shotgun in the oven and heated it full blast and the shells exploded, spewing pellets everywhere.

Three years in America had yielded a used Chevy and $300 in a coffee can. To risk the money in a produce stand with brother Harry or keep it for college, that was my grandfather's quandary. On the sly he had gone to the University of California at Berkeley and taken the entrance examination in French and passed. Armenians there were willing to put him up for free. This had been his dream, to study literature and write for a newspaper. The decision was made easier by the steady presence of his sister's husband, Saghatel, who would look after his mother and brother while he was away.

A few weeks into the quarter, brother Harry borrowed $10 for gas and drove to Berkeley with a scheme to lease 320 acres of prime farmland. All he needed was my grandfather, who should have known better, to oversee things. Grandpa fell for it. He wanted me to believe that Harry talked such a good game that he talked him right out of his life's ambition: "I think fifty percent of it was lie," he conceded. "But Harry was so fluid, such a bullsheet artist."

There were other forces clearly at work—the guilt of the oldest son, the tug of family and certainly his own lack of direction bumping up against pure laziness. Maybe nothing hurt so much as shedding his dream of the Sorbonne, and all the other partings only got easier after that. I do know that when he had a chance to right things in the form of me, torn between a career in law and big-city journalism, he did not hesitate to intervene. I would not become another Armenian attorney in Fresno if he could help it. He would not let the tug of family kill his grandson's dreams.

Harry's farm venture was doomed, if not this year then next. With Uncle Ervant out of the picture, the only one willing to do the hard labor was Saghatel, Grandpa's brother-in-law. He was the mule. He did all the plowing himself. At the end of the year's lease, Grandpa and Saghatel split $7,000 and Harry, who had cavorted most of the year in San Francisco's red-light district, pocketed $900. Grandpa took his share and bought twenty acres west of town. Saghatel did the same. Harry went straight to the Ford dealership and paid cash for a 1924 Model T roadster.

They had gone from fruit tramps to the landed in four years.

Grandpa loved the soil. He loved tilling and irrigating and harvesting. He loved the smell of the farm late at night and the spine chill it gave him. He loved work without a boss, one man shoulder to shoulder with nature.

He talked about the humility that came with dirt under the fingernails and he would write about his brothers under the sun—Filipinos, Japanese and Mexicans.

There was only one problem. He loved not the sweat but the concept of these things. They existed for him as ideas. A worker he was not. Family members recalled his pocket always stuffed with *The New Masses,* his pocketbook empty.

"At harvest time, cousin Aram would always get sick. Mediterranean disease," one relative told me. "He stayed inside while us kids worked. He had no implements. No horses. Now his mother Azniv could work. She picked beans like nothing. She was a wonderful woman. And his brother, Harry, worked too if he was around. But Aram's stomach hurt. Politics is what he lived for."

Grandpa frittered away whole days at the Armenian club across from Courthouse Park. There, in a loft full of smoke and the idle hours of men, he kept America at bay. The news from the home front wasn't good. During the last months of the war, much of what remained of the Armenian race had huddled inside Russia and declared an independent nation. As the Allies carved up Turkey on paper and President Wilson pledged support for a grander Armenia, a Turkish rebel army led by Kemal Ataturk stormed across Anatolia. War-weary Europe stood by and watched new massacres and a final breach of Armenia by Kemal and Lenin. What was left of the hapless homeland became part of the U.S.S.R.

Grandpa never quite forgave America and Europe for deserting Armenia one last time. He was a nationalist and the republic had failed. Instead of continuing to long for independence, as so many other nationalists chose to do, he wasted no time declaring Soviet Armenia as his own. The way he saw it, only the supreme nationalist could love this sad, stinted, token, rocky, Mt. Ararat-less Armenia. It was a compromise, the best a nation buffeted on all sides could hope for. And if you loved Armenia, wasn't it right to love its protector, the Soviet Union, too?

Thus, his chauvinism became laced with practicality, the dreamer cloaked as realist. It also helped that he already leaned to the left and his sentiment was idealistic. The socialist rhetoric tapped into some of his childhood resentments. He was, after all, the son whose widowed mother was forced to feed her breast to the rich while his own baby brother suckled sugar water and died.

So began the compact—the quixotic marriage of communism and capitalism, the poet's idealism yielding to the immigrant's craving and vice-versa—that shaped the lives of my grandfather and grandmother and father and uncle and aunt and reached down and touched my life.

On a November morning in 1928, Aram Arax flagged down eighteen-year-old Alma Chakurian between classes at Fresno Normal College where she was studying art. He had fallen in love with the bowlegged neighbor girl with reddish hair and beautiful skin. He proffered a box of dried figs, read a poem he had composed the night before and then insisted she elope with him to San Francisco before the bell rang for class. In the event she demurred, he informed her, a letter had been sent to her cruel and disapproving uncles that disclosed their undying love and plans to marry.

Whether this was eleventh-hour extortion or a gentle nudge of an all-too-willing Alma, it has nourished a lifetime of squabbles between the Araxes and the Chakurians, squabbles that they did not hesitate to heap onto me with hopes of arbitration.

My grandfather had nothing to lose. He was twenty-eight and not exactly a dashing man going big places. As to the question of extortion or nudge, Grandma waffled depending on her mood. She protected Grandpa and yet she conceded that eloping to San Francisco changed everything.

In one reckless act she quit college, turned her back on the tradition of arranged marriage, broke a promise to herself never to marry a foreign-born Armenian, not to mention a man ten years her senior, and poisoned relations with her family. As soon as her uncles, the family breadwinners, read the letter, they renounced Alma and her good-for-nothing husband and made sure her father and mother did the same.

The Chakurians were a feisty bunch, long-lived and stubborn to the marrow. Grandma's father, Manoug, had to flee Turkey a wanted man after authorities caught him stockpiling weapons in the village cemetery. Grandma's mother, Mary Janjanian, came to America as a seventeen-year-old orphan. Her brothers were famous Armenian musicians and singers and when they learned of her impending marriage to Manoug Chakurian, who was fast approaching forty, they swore to stop it. Manoug got wind of their displeasure and arrived in New York City in disguise and accompanied by a priest. My great-grandparents were married right there at Ellis Island.

The Chakurians, like the Araxes, had no business farming. They bought a twenty-acre vineyard east of Fresno not knowing the soil was hardpan. They broke down two horses trying to break up the red clay and had to barter Persian carpets brought over from the old country for a new team.

Grandma said her two uncles ran the whole show while her stroke-weary father shuffled around trying to make himself useful. Mary managed a small market on a corner of the ranch and cooked, washed and ministered to the needs of her ailing husband and his two younger brothers. At night she rubbed olive oil onto her varicose veins.

Grandma took after her father. Everything made her nervous. She loved old Manoug and felt sorry for him but couldn't take being alone with him. She tried helping out in the market but the customers made her nervous, too. She wanted to go to college and study art, and, after much harangue, her uncles gave in. The last thing they expected was for Alma to quit school and elope with that *Bolsheviki* from down the block.

"Aram showed up at the college stretched out dead in the backseat of his Uncle Ervant's Model T," Grandma's sister Roxie recalled. "Ervant told Alma we have to take him to the hospital. 'He's having a breakdown.' I was the one who read the telegram sent to the family. It said: 'Aram and

I are going away to get married. That's my fate. Don't worry.' Alma didn't write that telegram. She told me years later she got tricked. Maybe it's true. Aram had done dirty."

Whenever Grandpa talked to me about his marriage, he recollected a gentle, sensuous courtship at Roeding Park sharing the works of Anatole France. Never did he mention any dirty tricks or arm twisting. He snickered: "Of course her family was against our marriage. They always thought that she should get a reech one. Her fawdr was a very nice man. Old man. Nobody paid him attention. One uncle, Sarkis, was no guud. That bastard came after me on the streets and called me a 'man without honor.' I think Sarkis had some kind of . . . well, I hate to say this, Mark, but I think he was with Alma's mother. You can't write anything like that, but this is what happened."

Grandpa assured his new bride that his twenty acres west of town was a producer. He boasted an average of three tons of raisins an acre, double most vineyards. What he failed to tell her or overlooked himself was that the raisin had a lousy future. What capital was loose in Fresno had gone into raisin production, and hundreds of out-of-town investors had bought up prairie land and planted Thompson seedless vines.

The Thompson was nothing if not versatile. It could be picked as table grapes, pummeled as wine, dried as raisins. Overplanting had been a problem even before Grandpa arrived in America. But it wasn't until Prohibition, all those wine grapes suddenly forced into raisins, that farmers like Grandpa began choking on the surplus.

Who ate raisins? Who even knew what they were? Fresno did what it could to educate the nation about the wizened berry, pushing the Sun Maid girl and raisin bread. But the fact remained that a lot of what the valley produced wasn't staple but nature's confectionery, and the raisin wasn't exactly what the sweet tooth lusted for.

The price for Grandpa's harvest in 1929 was $30 a ton, down from $300 a ton a few years earlier. It wasn't even enough to pay the Mexican and Filipino fieldhands, let alone the doctor who delivered Navo after the Crash.

Sun Maid went belly up and a host of doctors, lawyers, merchants and banks followed suit. The population of Fresno, essentially a one-crop town, plummeted from 80,000 to 50,000 in what seemed like overnight. Thousands of Armenians, their plight told in ditties, left for Los Angeles and San Francisco: *I am loss. You are loss. The banks are loss. We all find ourselves in loss Angeles.*

My grandparents earned enough money at the canneries each spring to hold on. The last thing they needed was a second child, and Azniv assured her daughter-in-law that as long as she kept one baby on the breast it was impossible to have another in the womb. So when Navo spurned the breast, Grandma decided to spurn Grandpa. Only it was too late.

She showed right away. By the sixth month, she was bigger than she had ever been with Navo. One night, already overdue, she slipped on a puddle of bathwater and began to bleed. The next morning, September 24, 1931, she went into labor. My father was a huge baby. His feet were square. His hands were square. Dr. Adams put something to Grandma's nose to make her dopey and then he tied a dishrag to the vegetable scale and it registered eleven pounds and some ounces, four pounds bigger than Navo. Azniv took one look at her new grandson and declared him hers: "He's *jermahg* (white) just like me." They named him Ara after King Ara the *Keghetzig,* Ara the Beautiful.

"Navo's nose was swollen and his eyes were this way," Grandma explained. "That's because they had to manipulate him to get him out. But Ara was perfect. His hair was beautiful and I let it grow long, English-style, like Little Lord Fauntleroy. He was so boyish, big hands and big feet, that you couldn't take him for a girl. But a lot of people would stop and say, 'What a pretty girl.' And he would say, 'No. I boy.' So wherever we went I used to say, 'This is Navo and this is Ara-boy,' so they knew that he was a boy."

Grandma was frying fish one afternoon when she heard one of the boys cry outside. She always checked the irrigation ditch that ran in front of the house first, water her greatest fear. By the time she found them safe, a piece of wallpaper dislodged by a rat had fallen into the frying pan. Grandpa and his mother were tying vines and saw smoke. It was too late to save the house.

Grandma blamed Grandpa's sloth.

"I always had the fear the boys were going to drown in the ditch. You would think Grandpa would have put up a fence but he never did. The house burned. It burned like someone poured kerosene. Azniv almost passed out in the field. She thought we were still in the house. We lost everything. Grandpa lost some beautiful poems. But I was happy in a way. It was full of rats and the rats died in there."

By the time my father was six, his father had lost three farms to a combination of bad timing, raisin glut, the Depression, vine hoppers, fungus and his own Mediterranean disease and indolence. They had lost two homes to fire. If Grandpa was dispirited, it's not likely he blamed himself. The fact that his brother-in-law, Saghatel, had been able to tough it out during that same decade and add to his acreage—the focus of much of Grandma's discontent—was not a consideration.

Grandpa was thirty-eight years old and had spent exactly half his life in the Central Valley. If he still looked upon Armenia as spiritual homeland, the dirt beneath his fingernails was the dirt of the San Joaquin. It wasn't easy wrenching himself from this valley and moving to San Francisco, but over time he came to love the city. The farm, he decided, had been an island.

There was nothing clean about family history. Old stories got spun into new ones at whim, and the pieces often did not assume a logic until years later, too late to check for confirmation. My approach was simply to jump in and let it stick where it stuck and sometimes the stories stuck on a particularly pivotal year. Like 1941. Everyone—Grandpa, Grandma, Uncle Navo and Aunt Jeanette—seemed to agree. In that year of Pearl Harbor and the end of America's isolation, all that was crazy and wrong with their lives suddenly came into focus. And with it came resignation about the future.

It was the year Jeanette was born; the year Grandpa was bedridden with stomach cramps and an extreme case of psoriasis that would plague him on and off the rest of his life; it was the year Grandma, thirty-two, her hands full with baby, had to manage the store alone; the year Navo, a fifth grader at the top of his class, began missing school to help out; it was the year doctors botched an operation to remove a tumor from Grandma's reproductive organs, inducing a menopause that would drive her to emotional breakdown; it was the year they turned to the Communist Party for coherence in their lives; the year the FBI, prompted by Grandpa's visit to a bookstore, listed him as a subversive and initiated a forty-two-year "national security" surveillance that would generate 1,130 pages of investigation before it finally ended with him blind and confused, eighty-three years old; it was the year Grandma, Uncle Navo and maybe even my father began to understand that this life of engagement and flight, this fitfulness, was not Grandpa taking a risk but Grandpa incapable of taking a stand.

Uncle Navo's maturity, his ability to tackle the adult world, underscored for Grandma all her husband's shortcomings. What it must have done to Navo to realize that his father wasn't up to the task, that he lacked the strength to buffer child from mother, that he, Navo, the eleven-year-old, was now her breadwinner and confidant. What a mixed-up time for my father to be a child and Jeanette to be an infant.

Years later, whenever Grandma needed to define one of her children, she would harken back to those early war years. Navo was forever the shrewd capable eleven-, twelve- and thirteen-year-old; my father the gullible, ethereal child and Jeanette the insufferable baby. It was as if each child had ceased to exist for her outside the prism of those years.

"They were very different boys. Ara depended on Navo for everything. Navo learned to tie his shoes real young. He would stick his tongue out and maneuver the lace until he got it. Ara would just stick out his shoe and say, 'Here, Ma.' Ara was more emotional. He didn't like it so much that we moved. When we started to back out the driveway, he'd say good-bye house, good-bye yard, good-bye tree. Navo just sat in the backseat. He never showed a thing. Navo was kind of a . . . I don't know. I can't figure out Navo too much. He was his own person. He knew what he was doing.

"Ara was a very dreamy boy. He loved to dance. He used to put the music on and do this. (She twirls like a ballerina.) He always had dreams of this and that. Grandpa used to get those Mediterranean sicknesses whenever there was too much to do. I don't know. It might have been in his head. I had to manage the store and Navo was very helpful. He did a lot of work for his father. Navo was the father. Just like you are the father. Grandpa always needed help. He just talks big, you know.

"Jeanette was a child who wanted lots of attention. She was always tempermental. She would pass out from anger. She would go *bllllll-laaaaaahhh!* She was a different personality. I never had any problems with Navo. Never. And Ara was a dreamer. He had lots of imagination. I never had any trouble with the boys. Ever. Only when they got older I got a little worried about it."

There were a half dozen moves during those first disjointed years uprooted from the farm. Grandpa traded in a small fruit stand in San Francisco's Panhandle for a bigger one on Geneva Avenue. He might not have been much of a worker but he had a keen smell for the right location. He was saving $25 a week—good enough to play the ponies and buy Navo violin lessons.

Grandma's youngest sister, Zep, and her husband, Sam, had settled in San Francisco. Sam had a quiet knack for making money and Grandpa took to him right off. Instead of opening another produce stand, Sam advised, why not buy a full-scale market. Sam pledged $1,000 to the cause. They found a perfect little market across the bay in Albany, close enough that Grandma and Zep had lots of Sunday dinners back and forth.

On Pearl Harbor Sunday, my father, who was nine, dialed Zep's house frantic and out of breath. "Auntie! Auntie! The Japs are on their way to our house. They're coming! They're coming!" That night the two families piled into Grandpa's station wagon and drove aimlessly up and down the San Francisco hillsides until dawn.

Grandpa had actually joined the Communist Party while on the farm during the Depression; he must have been an energetic foot soldier because the FBI has him listed in 1934 as a member of the party's state central committee. During the early years in the Bay Area, he would hush the crowd at weddings and motion his two young sons on stage to sing. "Rise you prisoners of salvation . . . rise!" He read *Das Kapital* to the winos buying their morning muscatel and displayed the *Daily Peoples World* in a stand next to the cash register.

Each Friday a group of Jewish and black intellectuals and disgruntled union men met in the rear of our Albany store. A Berkeley professor managed the clock and gave each member five minutes to say his piece. The meetings lasted one hour. Grandma admired that. Nothing like the gassy Armenians.

It was all innocent stuff, she said. How to make the unions stronger and landlords more responsive to the rights of the poor. Because the government saw it differently, each member took a party name. Grandpa became

"John Harris" and Grandma "Alma Harris." John was derived from his real first name, Jonig, and Harris sounded like a slurred anglicized version of Arax. Plugged into a new social set, they attended parties in the hills of Berkeley where the serpentine paths were lined in red lanterns and the dogs and cats were named Vladimir and Ilyich.

Already the FBI had opened a "Security Matter-C" file on Grandpa. Agents listed a string of aliases: Abram Arax, Aran Arax, Aram Araz, Janig Hopsepian, Bjanik Hoosepian. The funny thing was these weren't aliases at all but typos in Armenian-American newspapers and secretarial errors from the documents Grandpa had filled out to become a U.S. citizen. The one actual alias, John Harris, Hoover's men never uncovered.

My Uncle Navo may have known of this ruse, for when it became necessary to choose his own alias, he too picked the first name John. "My father was unreal about America," he told me. "He gave us these fucking names, Navasart and Ara. When Jeanette came along, he wanted to name her Babushka or something. I talked him out of it. When I was in the third or fourth grade, I'd tell the other kids my name is John. Call me John."

It may have been admirable, my grandparents' willingness to defy the grain, but it was hardly innocent stuff. Uncle Navo realized this at a young age but I wonder if my father ever did. My grandfather, it seemed, was doing the same things in his late thirties with a wife and three kids that my father did in his late thirties with a wife and three kids—a frantic and risky juggling of two contradictory worlds. Running a business, depending on a wife who was having a nervous breakdown and an oldest son not yet twelve, throwing full weight into The Party, Grandpa was playing with a kind of fire. It didn't burn him in quite the same way that it burned my father, but his behavior became a model for my father. That crazy life they had, we had.

Grandpa heard about fortunes in the making in nearby Richmond, a boom town stoked by war. Kaiser was building ships there for the navy and the promise of jobs beckoned thousands of Portuguese and Italians and southern whites and blacks. Grandpa followed his nose and bought a rundown market on San Pablo Street below the affluent Richmond Hills.

The Richmond market became a gold mine. He got tired of counting the money, he said. So much money that he bought a house for $3,000 and made the milkman a one-third partner. The milkman overhauled the store top to bottom; Grandpa checked in on his way to political powwows that lasted well into the night.

As busy as the store was, Grandpa's accountant, George Miller, felt it should have been busier. He pointed out that maybe politics was the reason. "Aram, what the hell are you trying to prove displaying these Bolshevik publications? All the neighborhood is talking. They say the grocer whose shelves are bare but whose counter is stocked with Soviet propaganda. This is a government town, for Christ's sakes. They're building ships for the navy."

Miller was Grandpa's first non-Armenian friend and he held him in high esteem. George was no reactionary. Although he hailed from fancy Hillcrest he spent much of the day embroiled in union matters at the shipyards. He went on to become a state senator and his son, George Miller Jr., a powerful liberal congressman from California.

Grandpa took down the display but refused to stop reading Marx to the morning winos. A short time later, the city informed him that the store stood in the path of a highway expansion, and they would have to move again. Grandma, for the first and only time in her life, began drinking. Jeanette found her one morning at the bus stop, a small suitcase in hand. Navo later found a letter she had written Grandpa hidden among her personal belongings. She didn't love him, it said. She had never loved him. Navo left the letter right where he found it, never knowing if his father read it.

Grandpa was looking for a way back to the farm and George Miller needed a tax shelter. That's pretty much how the Araxes and Millers ended up partners in 160 acres of grapes, melons and sunflowers in Manteca at the northern end of the San Joaquin Valley. Grandma finally had a kitchen big enough to contain her nervous energy.

Fifteen-year-old Navo, lips smacking cigarette, hauled the crop by truck over the mountain to San Francisco. Dad did the tractor work. Grandpa tried to raise hens as a sideline. He came home with 200 baby chicks and Grandma yelled at him. He kept them in a box outside. It got cold one night and in a stampede to find warmth half the chicks were crushed. Grandpa hired a Dutch man to build a pen where he placed the survivors. Out of those 200 chicks, Grandma said, one grew to see hen-hood.

The boys fit in remarkably well at Manteca Union High for being the only Armenians. Dad was a freshman and Uncle Navo a sophomore and both played varsity baseball, side-by-side on one knee in the team picture. Dad joined the Future Farmers of America and Uncle Navo dazzled the hicks with a worldly-wise wit. Then one of Grandpa's party comrades died in Los Angeles and he drove down to deliver the eulogy. He stayed three weeks. When he got back, Grandma had found a buyer for the Manteca ranch.

I could never get a straight answer why she put it up for sale and why he didn't put up more of a stink.

"That place became a vacation home for all of Grandpa's friends," she explained. "An Armenian mandolin player from Los Angeles came. Grandpa's committee members came. A woman brought her kids and they peed in our beds. See, Grandpa does things. He's a good, you know, finder. But on the way he gives up. Is that a restless soul?

"So Grandpa went to Los Angeles for a funeral and my eyes were closed from these allergies. When he came back, the ranch was sold. I don't know what happened to everything we owned. I don't know why or when. He should have kept it all. He did cuckoo things, you know. Gypsies. Don't you know we were gypsies?"

Grandpa was even more vague. "Manteca ranch was just like gold. But naturally we didn't keep that, either. I was in Los Angeles. One of our comrades died. I had to speak for the funeral. When I returned, the farm was gone. Your fawdr loved that place. He'd get on the tractor and drive like hell. I'd say, 'Ara, what are you doing?' He'd say, 'I am enjoying.' He loved farming."

Grandpa cleared forty grand in one year buying and selling the Manteca farm, and after nearly a decade away they returned to Fresno. Grandpa tried buying back the old ranches but he couldn't touch any of them for under a quarter of a million. He bought a house in an established neighborhood off limits to Armenians. Apparently the realtor didn't bother checking the surname Arax.

As soon as the neighbors learned the truth they took up a petition. The block bully marched up to little Jeanette and said Armenians weren't allowed on the sidewalk. Jeanette refused to budge and he bloodied her nose. Grandma didn't know what to do and slapped Jeanette for defying a neighbor. Not only did Grandpa decide to stay but he invited a Japanese-American student only a few years removed from the internment camps to live with them.

Coming from the Bay Area where everybody was something different and no one gave a damn, Dad and Uncle Navo didn't know what to make of Fresno. They attended Fresno High, an all-white school whose students came from the town's most prominent families. Some kid refused to shower with "those stinking Armenians" and Dad and Richard Choohajian, whose family owned a men's clothes shop, beat the kid silly with a wet towel.

Friends took note of how different the brothers reacted to their outsider status. Bob Kurtovich, a basketball star who grew up in a Slavic home, remembered that my father wasn't shy about his Armenian-ness or his father's politics. Navo was another matter.

"Ara was the first person I met on the first day of school. I was standing by the gym and he walked up and put his hand out and introduced himself. Kids just didn't do that in high school. Navo was harder to get to know. Darker. After graduation, the two brothers were running the ice cream and hamburger stand across the street from Fresno High. I thought, 'How can this be? These two guys are kids just like me and they're running a business. And their father is a Communist.' It was beyond me."

Armenian friends, well versed in the eccentricities of old-world politics, seemed to understand. "As far as Aram's communism was concerned, we never judged it," said Larry Momjian. "Our parents never told us don't hang around the Arax boys because of their father. Aram Arax was seen as a novelty item. One of a kind. Poet, farmer, businessman, Communist."

Uncle Navo made the all-state team, a scrappy third baseman who hit line drives to all fields. A drop back passer in the mold of Eddie LeBaron, he became the first quarterback at the new Fresno Junior College. He played pro baseball for a season in the Pirates organization.

Dad stood for hours in the mirror tinkering with his swing. One game he looked like DiMaggio, the next like Williams from the right side. He became an all-city catcher and a three-year letterman in football. His running style was so punishing that rival schools burned an effigy of him—a big-nosed Indian named "Poison Ara"—at pep rallies. Pasadena City College converted Dad from fullback to guard. His biography in the official game program read: "Ara Arax. No. 42 . . . guard . . . big and rough. A good man to have on your side."

For my father and uncle, sports unlocked the door to the Cambridge Club, one of the two fraternities on the Fresno High campus, but it couldn't buffer them from everything. The late forties and fifties were a time when Americans didn't question the faith and here was indiscreet Grandpa, a "revolutionary" in Navo's words, punching holes in the cold war conformity.

He responded to McCarthyism by turning up the volume of his anti-American, pro-Soviet rhetoric. He was a big wheel in the Armenian Progressive League of America, an organization that nurtured ties between Soviet and American Armenians. Each Labor Day the group threw a picnic south of Fresno that drew thousands of Armenians from all political walks. Grandpa, the master of ceremonies, would read one of his poems about "the fatherland" and launch into a harangue about the tyranny of corporate America and the need to emancipate the working class. This didn't sit well with the big grape growers. Some of Grandpa's own comrades cringed. If he felt that strongly, they wondered, why not repatriate?

He took the Armenian Progressive League further to the left and the group splintered. Grandpa's faction had been active in the Communist Party a decade earlier and continued to subscribe to the *People's World* and offer the family couch to young cadres traveling the state. They cursed the cold war and marched for peace, but in the end Grandpa and his comrades were moved less by class struggle than by devotion to Soviet Armenia. They were nationalists above all else. You had to wonder what their politics would have sounded like had Armenia gone the other way.

Where their group actually stood in the American political spectrum no longer mattered by May of 1951. That's when the House Un-American Activities Committee announced its list of subversive organizations. The

Armenian Progressive League of America was fourth on the list, sand-
wiched between the Appeal for Lawrence Simpson and the theatrical
group ARTEF.

That same month, Congress published a series titled "100 Things You
Should Know About Communism." Reading that manifesto for the first
time, I nearly convulsed in laughter. How different it must have read, I
thought, to my father and uncle in a time of loyalty oaths and the Rosen-
bergs and the enemy within.

Are the Communists just trying to get my church?
No. They're also out to get your job, to get your union, to get
your farm, to get your school, to get your property, to get your
Government. They're out to get YOU and make you a slave of
Communism from cradle to grave.

The Bay Area had lent some camouflage, at least. There was no place to
hide in a farm belt where Dust Bowl migrants shunned unions and the
bottom line was moving the crop from field to market. The ethnic en-
clave—the shelter that continued to protect Grandpa—could not harbor
his children. As he snickered at the flickering images of the cold war, his
son, my father, was being nicknamed "Junior Commie."

For young Jeanette, the late 1940s and early '50s were a time of vigilance and fear.

"The FBI would come calling, always in pairs. I'd run and get all of
Daddy's Tolstoy and Turgenev and Dostoyevsky and hide them under my
bed. I remember he was watching the Rosenberg execution with some
friends and one of them said, 'Aram, they could do that to us. You could
go.' There was this TV show called *I Led Three Lives* about a triple agent. It
portrayed these sneaky Communists pulling all these shenanigans, infil-
trating the PTA. And here were all these people around me like my father
and the Balakians who were kind and loving and intelligent. They were
nothing like the Communists on this show. So I lived in sort of a split
world.

"I remember being scared most of the time. We had a crazy life and it
came from Daddy's restlessness, wanting to make it big. Ara had pride in

the family. He'd always tell me how popular Daddy was, what a great public speaker he was. He tried to boost me up. Navo pushed it away. I mean here's Navo, an assimilating Armenian male, ambitious and smart and his father, during the height of McCarthyism, is an outspoken Communist. It's almost like living with a leper. Communist. Armenian. Navo was short and had a big nose and Grandma was obsessed with height and good looks."

At my father's high school graduation party, he got into a terrible fist fight with a best friend who popped off about Grandpa's politics. Navo refused to be engaged. Grandpa decided not to tell his two sons that federal agents had come to his market threatening to deport him if he didn't become an informant. He told the feds he would answer any questions about himself but he would not be a "stool pigeon." The government continued to threaten him even though its own files showed that he had joined the Communist Party years after becoming a U.S. citizen, which protected him from deportation.

Between 1950 and 1955, from Dad's high school graduation to his marriage, Grandpa moved the family six more times in search of the big hit. A vineyard in Caruthers would bankroll a hotel in Taft that grubstaked a market in Lamont, the heart of Okie country. Grandpa was operating for the first time without the benefit of Navo, who was playing baseball for the marines.

Replacing Navo on the farm was Dad's friend Tommy Bayless. Tommy grew exhausted watching Dad flit from one half-done job to the other. His farmwork and Grandma's housework shared an incoherence. Dad held off any big decisions, telling Tommy, "Let's wait for Navo to get back. Navo will know what to do." Uncle Navo loomed so large for Dad that when Tommy finally met him—marine corps tattoo and all—he came away a little disappointed.

USC was offering Dad a full athletic scholarship provided he could pass the entrance exam and get his application in order. A friend sneaked in and took the test for him and passed. In between classes at Pasadena City College, Dad wrote Uncle Navo a letter remarkable for the utter lack of responsibility it conveyed and the near complete reliance on his older brother.

Dear Navo,

How is everything? I am very busy at my mid-term exams. This place is not easy. They say it's as hard as S.C. I want you to do these things for me. You can't let Ma do them.

1. See if Stoney has written that letter of recommendation for me.

2. Get my transcripts from Fresno Junior College and Fresno High because USC requires original school.

Get these done. They are very important. I went and saw the USC–Stanford game. It was terrific but I think Cal will beat Stanford. Try and get tickets for that game. I will come home. I hope Ma, Jeanette and Daddy are O.K. Say hello to the boys for me. Don't work too hard. I hope you can help me because I need it. The deadline is not very far away. Thanks.

Your brother always, Ara

P.S. Take care of yourself.

Dad won a full ride to Southern Cal and finished that first semester with a C average. He brought quarterback Rudy Bukich home to Bakersfield to meet the family. He was enrolled in the summer session and appeared to be fitting in just fine when my grandparents drove down to Los Angeles for a visit. The three of them spent the longest time talking in the car, one of his roommates recalled. A week or so later, Dad inexplicably quit the team and came home.

I cannot think of a bigger decision in my father's life—had he decided to stay it might have changed everything. So fateful was his choice that family members, in the wake of his murder, pointed fingers at one another for his leaving.

"The biggest thing was when his parents drove to USC and took him out of school," said Uncle Mike. "Ara talked about that on many occasions. They came down there and told him someone has got to help run the ranch. He hung on to his SC jacket. He had that jacket for years and years in the closet."

Uncle Navo saw it differently. "There was an All-American playing in front of him and Ara was as good if not better. Ara has to put in his time.

But he's not willing to do that. Not on the field. Not in class. He was book dumb. He was poor with details.

"Grandma had let him skate by. I guess she felt sorry for him or something. Ara didn't have the patience for college. You know your Dad was a fuck-off. Then he got married and almost overnight he got serious. I never saw anybody work harder. But as a kid he was lazy. I was given the responsibility to look after him. 'Take care of your brother.'"

chapter 17

The Rainbow Ballroom in downtown Fresno is a place where each generation has brought its bands and music and dancing. It is the place where I met my wife listening to a local band cover The Guess Who in 1976, and the place where my parents twenty-five years earlier met between sets of Les Brown and his Band of Reknown. Ours was a deep kiss on the dance floor. Theirs was little more than a glance, an encounter soon forgotten if not for a second chance meeting a week later.

Mom was working as a teller at the Bank of America where Navo had climbed to supervisor. Dad had dropped out of Fresno State, this time no football coach or parental arm-twisting to blame. The army came calling, an eighteen-month hitch. Before leaving he presented Mom with a gold necklace in the tradition of *khos-gob: khos* meant verbal; *gob* meant tie. The promise before the promise to marry.

She had kept him guessing through a year-long courtship with practiced indifference. Whether this was apathy or the self-possession of one of the prettier Armenian girls in town, he couldn't be certain. She ended up accepting the necklace with her customary tepidness and he departed for the 6th Infantry Division at Fort Ord, more or less assured in his own mind she was his girl.

Then the unsigned letter from Fresno arrived. "You'd better come quick," it said. "Flora is dating an Italian and it's beginning to look serious."

Even before the letter, the United States Army had pegged Dad as high strung. The deprivations of military life brought out the worst in him. He suffered most of the better-known phobias, some that hadn't been coined yet. He dreaded the five-foot waters of the swimming pool, the fifteen-foot shin up the rope, the three-foot confines of the fox hole. He blanched at the trickle of blood, shredded his fish dinner searching for the tiniest bone. He ran through the barracks trying to quiet ringing ears. And yet in the hand-to-hand combat and bayonet drills, he feared no man. He starred on the Company George baseball team, a catcher. His intrepid play behind home plate risked his whole body. An opponent didn't score from second base on a single without hesitating, a stammer at third, at the hulk in iron mask and leather gear. Home plate belonged to Ara.

So did Flora. He went AWOL the day after he got the letter and caught Mom and the Italian parked in front of the red-brick church. The Italian recognized Dad from high school and rolled down the window. The poor guy didn't know about any *khos-gob*. Dad had him halfway out of the car and then offered a cigarette, a bow to female duplicity. "It's not your fault," he apologized. "How could you know. The bitch!" A moment later, he wanted to kill the guy again.

The whole neighborhood stood outside gawking at the spectacle of fury and contrition. The cops hauled them away and asked Mom which one she was with. "Neither," she said. The next morning, Uncle George walked into the kitchen and did a double take. There was his sister in her bathrobe seated at the table and Ara in army boots and olive fatigues standing over the oven. He was scrambling tomatoes and eggs. They were laughing like last night never happened.

Dad was discharged honorably a few months later thanks to an unspecified neurotic condition. The following May, he and Mom were engaged.

My mother's people were hard to please and nothing pleased them more than a good row. They hailed from the highlands of ancient Armenia, mountaineers born and bred to bicker.

Orphaned by the Genocide, my mother's father fled to Jerusalem in 1923 and was taken in by seminarians. The church became family. Hyreek was ordained and sent to the Armenian ghetto of Saint-Loup, a suburb of Marseilles, where he built a church and school and found a bride, Lucine.

She bore him four children, three girls and a boy, my mother the third child. Lucine, the daughter of school masters, vowed that each one would learn to play an instrument and she chose the violin for her first born, Jeanette. As priest's wife, she had so little time for herself, they said, that she often left the house with her hair wet and one day caught a cold deep in the lungs. The next thing they knew she was beckoning each child to her bedside. "Don't forget your violin," she told Jeanette. The children—ages nine, seven, five and two—were forbidden from the funeral. Jeanette sneaked in and saw her father collapse and ran.

Whatever warmth had remained in Hyreek after the Genocide ossified into something cold and impenetrable after the death of his wife. He distanced himself from the children and poured grief into work. It wasn't easy separating priest from politician, sermon from manifesto. The skinny bald man, jet-black goatee, transformed into something fierce and galvanic in the pulpit. The Bolsheviks even tried to recruit my mother's father as a spokesman for Soviet Armenia and he laughed in their face. They kidnapped him once and tried to assassinate him twice, the last bullet tearing through his derby as he bent down to unlock the front door.

He was a bagman of sorts during World War II, traversing Algeria, Morocco, Tunisia, Spain, Italy and Chile, collecting funds for new churches and the Dashnak party. Bolsheviks like Grandpa Arax alleged the trips were a cover, that Hyreek was collaborating with the German occupiers of France and delivering documents to Nazi outposts. It was a scandalous charge considering the Germans were allies of the Turks during the years they wiped out Hyreek's entire family.

Once the Nazis became entrenched in the Armenian quarter of Marseilles, it was important not to alarm them. How extensive his contacts were with the Germans, I cannot say for sure. I do know that German soldiers brought over food once or twice and Hyreek thanked them. My mother recalled seeing him come home in a German jeep once. And wherever his son, Georgie, went, he made sure to click his heels and shout "Heil Hitler!"

They arrived in America in 1946—Hyreek, the four children and a new wife, the woman I would call Grandma. He had taken a post with the Armenian church in Philadelphia, a job that also required him to tend to the flock in Washington, D.C., and Richmond, Armenian communities too small to have a pastor of their own. He gave them four good years, enough time to build an Armenian church in the nation's capital. My mother was seventeen when her father accepted the position at Holy Trinity in Fresno and immediately sparked a dispute that would make permanent the "two-flag" split in the Armenian church.

The mother church, behind the iron curtain in Soviet Armenia, directed Hyreek to declare November 29th a high holiday—the date in 1920 when independent Armenia was dissolved and the Soviet republic formed. These were fighting words to Hyreek, whose Dashnak comrades had killed Archbishop Tourian in New York thirteen years earlier for insisting upon the Soviet flag. Hyreek fired off a letter to superiors refusing to hallow the Soviet anniversary with a high mass. He knew full well this equated to treason and he knew the consequences. The mother church defrocked him, snatched collar and robe. He fired back a second letter even more defiant.

That Sunday, Holy Trinity filled to rafters, Hyreek dispensed with religious pretense and got right to it. He wasn't going anywhere and he wasn't taking orders from any Communist "fellow travelers." No one, save God himself, could remove the holy water that ordained him priest.

Heeding his call, parishioners boldly voted to sever their last tenuous ties to the mother church in Soviet Armenia and operate as an independent parish. Then, in 1956, under Hyreek's leadership, Holy Trinity and dozens of likeminded churches threw their support to a pro-Dashnak pope in Lebanon.

The Armenian Apostolic Church, thanks in large measure to my mother's father, had split into two formal camps, two holy fathers, two flags. It would remain that way even after the demise of the Soviet Union.

This was the backdrop to the improbable wedding of my parents in the spring of 1955. Hyreek, the red baiter, outgoing mail stamped "Help Save America, Outlaw Communism," giving the hand of his favorite daughter to the son of Aram Arax, the Bolshevik-capitalist whose mail was being monitored by the FBI. Fortunately, all but the two old titans themselves had forgotten that twenty years earlier Grandpa Arax's comrades would have killed Hyreek if not for poor aim.

The wedding album captured only smiles and expectations. Uncle Navo was the best man. Dad and Mom made a handsome pair. He with gap-toothed grin and sparkling brown eyes and still enough hair to offset those ample ears, and she with delicately arched eyebrows and tiny nose and heart-shaped face smiling fine and pretty.

Grandpa Arax counted on the newlyweds moving into a vacant shack on the Highway 41 land and my father resuming farming. Mom nixed the idea. "I'm not living in a farmhouse with a bunch of rats," she vowed. Twenty years later, those 160 acres sold for more than a million dollars.

Whenever the subject came up, my grandparents were sweet about it, only occasionally intimating that my mother was at fault. "Supposing I had that million dollars," Grandpa told me. "Do you think I would be happier than this?" Toward the end of his life, as he plunged deeper into senility, his accusation against my mother grew more shrill, even as he had forgotten her name and taken to calling her "the priest's daughter."

"The priest's daughter made the mistake. She had no business to get that ranch out because we had a beautiful thing over there." I got the sense that he and Grandma blamed my mother not only for a fortune lost but, through an absurd permutation of events, even for what happened to Dad.

○ ○ ○

In those first years after the murder, rummaging for clues into my father's character, seizing history from nook and cranny, nothing mattered to me but the knowing and knowing more. It was a spectacular banquet in which family and friends served up dish after dish and I stuffed my face and they waited for the first sign of surfeit. It never came. I did not allow my grandfather his silences. I did not stop at discomfort, mine or anyone else's. I couldn't afford to listen in that lazy way you listen to family. It seemed that each time I showed up at a home unprepared, quite certain I had picked the past clean, nothing in mind but a nice chat, they saved until then their best stories. Caught without recorder or paper and pen, I scrambled to turn their surprise narratives into mnemonic codes only too preposterous. When that failed, I cut short my visits, often indelicately, mumbling key words out their door and all the way home to the safekeeping of my notebook in the middle desk drawer.

My approach, my willingness to consider everything, sometimes caused me great pain. It wasn't easy learning that a silver-tongued Grandpa Arax took hard-earned cash from friends during the Depression, loans he never got around to repaying. Or glimpsing my father's reliance on his brother, hearing relative after relative portray him as a naïve "Joe Football." Or discovering that behind the smile in my mother's wedding day portrait, a smile that could not have seemed brighter or of more genuine delight, was the story of a remorse she had never mentioned.

A few years before meeting Dad, she had been a bridesmaid in the wedding of her sister Jeanette and Mike Mamigonian. In all the hullabalo, she fell in love with Mike's handsome younger brother, Abby. The prospect of a second daughter marrying into the Mamigonian clan—headed by a forbidding patriarch—irritated Hyreek to no end. He knew enough about my mother to understand that a confrontation would push his youngest daughter right into Abby's arms. So Hyreek sent in Rosette, the middle daughter, to do his spadework.

Aunt Rosette opened Mom's letters and scouted her movements and kept Hyreek abreast of everything. They tried dousing the romance with icy water. "You're only nineteen. Wait a few years." When that didn't work, Great-grandma Perouz, Big Momma, stepped forward chanting taboo and dangling amulet. "Two daughters cannot marry two sons," she pronounced. "Bad things will come to their offspring."

Abby moved to Oakland for a few months to sort things out. When he got back, it was over. "Your mother really didn't want to marry your father," Jessy Shahbazian, Mom's best friend, told me. "Somehow it became the thing to do after Abby married. She blamed her father and Rosette for the way her life turned out. Maybe she was right. Maybe it would have been different had she married Abby."

What made the story especially painful, beyond the obvious, was that it came at a time in 1979 when I had left home in a dispute with Mom over Arsen Marsoobian, the plugger of chain letters and pyramid schemes, who broke his word to me not to see Mom until after separating from his wife.

"My life is not my own!" my mother had screamed when I confronted her with the letter revealing their affair. It was only after I had moved in with Grandpa and Grandma Arax that spring and began to hunt down our history that I understood the full weight of my mother's comment. I was playing spoiler, begrudging her a chance at happiness, and it wasn't the first time. Hyreek and Aunt Rosette had played the same role with Abby.

So I moved back home that last semester at Fresno State, reconciled to a future with Arsen. I'd like to think I had come around, that Mom's happiness was more important than any animosity I still bore for what he had put us through. Truth be known, I needed Arsen to keep Mom company while I chased my own future.

I was headed to law school at the University of California at Davis, when the acceptance letter from Columbia University's Graduate School of Journalism arrived. Mom wanted me to pursue law. All this talk of becoming a journalist and writer was so much of Grandpa Arax's bohemian poppycock. Besides, Davis was only a short drive from home—not like New York City. My girlfriend, Coby, offered up the same reasons for my attending law school.

In those years that Pop stood in for Dad, he was careful to use a light hand when guiding me, so fine and delicate a touch that I often failed to detect its sway. This changed, however, in those months I vacillated between careers. He told me his greatest regret leaving Istanbul in 1920 wasn't being uprooted from homeland or kin but that his devotion to being a writer died in America. His pen fell silent for fifty years, he said, awakened only by my father's murder. "The truth is, Mark, I forgot I could write. That's why you must keep on writing. Don't buckle. Don't slave for two-bit jobs. Let nobody pressure your will of writing."

In the end I chose New York City and Columbia University, thinking I might get a law degree after the master's degree in journalism.

In those last weeks of my last summer at home in 1980, I was awakened from a nap one afternoon by a young kid with American-Indian features knocking softly at the back door, a shaggy dog in tow. Through the mesh curtain covering the half window, I could see a big white boat of an El Dorado, fins shimmering in the sun, trunk opened. A tiny, leathery man under a giant straw hat was lugging crates of beautiful bell peppers, red onions and grapes. I smiled and shook my head. Harry Arax, San Quentin lifer, Grandpa's only brother who had briefly illuminated my life a decade earlier and then vanished, was a comet back from the dead.

"Uncle Harry," I shouted, running past the Indian boy and mongrel sheepdog to hug him.

"Hello, son." He still talked out of the side of his mouth, puffing an un-filtered Camel.

He asked where my mother was and I wondered if he knew what hap-pened to Dad.

"I know, son, I know. I was in a bar in the desert, 1974 or '75, and two men were talking about an Arax who got killed in Fresno. I knew it was Ara-boy."

He examined my fingers. "Your wart. It's gone."

I didn't tell him his apple cider vinegar failed to do the trick. A few months after he disappeared, my planter's wart had to be frozen off by Dr. Gretzinger.

"This is Billy and Podgie," he said.

I don't recall when I first heard we had a murderer in the family, a cop killer at that. And what I did recall of his crime—that he was running whiskey during Prohibition and gunned down his partner, a dirty Long Beach policeman in self-defense—turned out to be pure myth.

In truth, it was a sensational, completely senseless crime that shadowed two generations of our clan and caused a permanent rift between those who continued to support Harry and those who turned their back, apparently shamed by the headlines: ARAX IS SOUGHT and ARAX IS FOUND. Pop talked very little about his younger brother, and the stories all seemed to take place in Istanbul and early Fresno, before 1934 and the dead cop. Grandma would end each story with the same words: "Harry was such a lively boy."

He was an athlete, a swimmer, champion soccer player and long-distance runner. Oh, what a runner. It began at age twelve, Grandpa said. Something upset Harry and he ran out the back door and into the streets of Istanbul and didn't come home for two months.

My mother had no interest in Harry's past other than to know that he was family and had driven eight hours from Coachella for a taste of her *kheyma,* the raw meat dish that was her specialty. Harry knew how to play Mom. She had one indelicate feature, her large hands, God's gift to *kheyma*-making, Harry called them.

Her thick fingers went straight to work, kneading and massaging and shaping the mixture of ground sirloin, tomato sauce and fine cracked wheat—first into little balls and then into oval patties, all the while pouring ice cold water to firm their shape. Uncle Harry liked it spicy and Mom added red pepper and a sprinkling of red and green onions and Armenian parsley. She served it with wet cracker bread and summer salad.

He ate slowly and tasted every mouthful. He was eating to outpace lung cancer, he explained. "Cancer kills, we say, three cells a day. So I am eating the equivalent of four cells to stay ahead."

Family history took on sudden and surprising twists, a gloss, when Harry was telling it. All the good stuff Grandpa left out. At the Del Monte cannery, it was Harry who made an instant impression. He taught the little ones origami. He filled the camp with paper chickens, paper boats, paper hats. He made the best paper kites. On a ten-dollar bet he plunged off the Rio Vista bridge into the icy waters of the Sacramento River and swam ashore to the delight of the crowd, which included a young Portuguese gal whom he deflowered that night.

Harry, it seemed, was the one who located the first farm and finagled the lease that allowed us to own property in America. He was the righter of wrongs, the common-sense one, the worker. In Harry's hands, Ervant wasn't the warm, generous, easy-to-hurt and easy-to-anger uncle who brought us to America but a lazy conniver who wanted only a workforce. Azniv wasn't the selfless, immaculate mother who cooked her children eggs drenched in olive oil and lemon, and if the yolk wasn't done just right they sent it back and she did it all over again. In Harry's hands, Azniv was the mother who held him back and never treated him like a man and, deep down, was the reason for his life of crime.

"She was a very cunning woman. Very cunning. She spoke for me. She wanted to keep me."

At the time, I thought of his talent for embroidering reality, his capacity to delude himself, as a flaw that was uniquely his. The more I examined his life—peppering him with questions, traveling to Long Beach to look up old newspaper accounts of his crime—the more I saw that it wasn't an uncommon trait to the family at all. A good bit of Harry lived in all of us. Later, I wondered why Harry, sitting in a bar overhearing a story about an Arax killed in Fresno, would automatically assume that the victim was Ara, my father. I wondered if there was some connection between his murdering a cop and my father being murdered and the two murders back in the old country, some shared character flaw that offered a key to it all.

By all accounts, Harry was the one born worker in the family. A Japanese man, the grape-picking champion, so overextended himself trying to keep up with Harry's 420 trays a day that he got a bloody nose. Grandpa tried to harness this energy, quicksilver busted free. He handed his brother a new pair of overalls and boots and pruning shears and put him to work with the understanding that all profits on the ranch would be split down the middle. An hour into the first day, Harry dropped the shears, overalls and boots in a neat little pile and drove off in his black roadster. He was gone two years, cabbie to bootleggers and pimps, leaving a trail of bad checks and swindled Armenians in towns and cities across America, debts Grandpa had to make good on.

"Bullshit!" Harry said. "He never bought me pruning shears. That's a bullshit story."

"How about the bad checks? Grandpa recalls bad checks amounting to thousands of dollars."

"It was more than that. I figured if I can get it, I'm going to get it."

By the time he returned home in 1927, Uncle Harry was speaking a wondrous nomad's dialect, everyday Armenian mixed with a touch of the midwestern and laced with the vernacular of Damon Runyon. The family didn't always comprehend him. When he took to jogging barefoot around the vineyard at the start and finish of each work day, eight miles a session, sixteen miles a day, they figured it was the restlessness stirring in him again. Any day now Harry would be taking off.

Sure enough, he called the family into the small farmhouse and told them of his plans to run across the country. Only this time he would do it by foot, without shoes, carrying the flag of Armenia. They'd read about it in the papers, the Barefoot Armenian. C. C. Pyle's Bunion Derby, Los Angeles to Chicago to New York, $25,000 to the winner.

They took off from Los Angeles, 275 runners from around the globe, several former Olympians in the pack. With Harry leading the way, they averaged forty-one miles a day, trailing a caravan that included promoter Pyle, football great Red Grange and sideshow acts that entertained the towns along Route 66. By the time they reached Needles, on the eighth day, half the runners had given up. Harry kept this promise, all the way to Seligman, Arizona, where on the twelfth day, running dog trot, he came down with a hernia and had to drop out.

He returned to the farm a local celebrity. Thanks to his bare feet, his face had made the papers.

Harry Arax, alias Harry Housepian, alias Harry Sarkisian, alias Harry Katz, alias Jack Herman, alias Jack Bernard, alias Sam Pappas, alias

Frenchy, checked into the Lincoln Hotel in Long Beach late afternoon December 11, 1934, alias Sam Giordano. He carried a small suitcase with two bottles of whiskey, the December issue of *American Magazine* from which he clipped several sports articles, a few toiletries and a .32-caliber handgun.

He was thirty years old and on the run again. He had shot his way to freedom in a gun battle with San Francisco police following a holdup there. A bullet grazed his shoulder. Utah wanted him for flooding Salt Lake City with hot paper. During his last visit to Long Beach, five months earlier, he passed a bogus $12.40 check at a drug store. The druggist hadn't forgotten the short, muscular man with the hard jaw and obsidian eyes.

He alerted traffic cop William J. MacLean to the same man getting his shoes shined on Ocean Boulevard. The officer approached and Uncle Harry bolted. There was no way MacLean was going to catch him, The Barefoot Armenian, shoes or no shoes. The officer fired two shots in the air but Uncle Harry didn't break stride. He sprinted back to the Lincoln Hotel and ran up the stairs to his room.

A minute later, MacLean burst through the hotel front door, breathless. "Where'd he go?"

"Upstairs to room eighteen," the woman clerk answered. "Watch out! He's got a gun!"

As the officer reached the door, Harry jerked it open and fired three shots point blank. MacLean rolled down the stairs. Harry fled through the back door and leaped onto the running board of a passing car. The woman driver, too frantic to stop, kept honking the horn. He jumped off a block later pursued by an angry mob screaming, "He shot a policeman!"

He dashed into the subway and emerged several blocks later at a small tailor shop where he donned a new coat, white shirt, suspenders and hat. Once across the Pacific Harbor bridge, he threw the gun into the ocean and hopped the rails to Los Angeles.

Officer MacLean, a single bullet to the heart, died before reaching the hospital. He was forty years old, a widower, survived by a twelve-year-old daughter.

Harry made the front page, only they were calling him Sam Giordano. Because he had never been charged with a crime, no agency of the law had his fingerprints or mug shot. It wasn't until the *Fresno Bee* discovered The

Barefoot Armenian photo in its files that the cops knew for sure it was Harry Arax they were after.

"The fugitive is a linguist," wrote the *Bee*. "He frequents coffee houses and shoe-shine stands."

The feds staked out the farm. Harry's sister, Mariam, wrote him off. Grandpa didn't want to talk about it. When it came to tending to the lowly and the sick, there was no one better than Grandma Alma. She hid her brother-in-law from authorities and scolded Mariam for turning her back on kin. A cousin spotted Harry in San Francisco tooting a horn and tossing confetti in a New Year's parade. He was featured in all the crime and detective magazines. One reader noticed a likeness between the photo and the bouncer at the Club Arabie in Cheyenne, Wyoming, and called the cops. Harry made a gallant run for it. It took the snow and a bullet in the calf to stop him.

Harry's girlfriend, an Armenian-Mormon taxi dancer, sought out Uncle Ervant for help, and he talked Aram Saroyan into taking the case for a small retainer. The Saroyans were a loud, crazy, bickering, brilliant bunch. And none of them was louder or crazier or more full of bombast than lawyer Aram. He was regarded as the finest orator and courtroom advocate the Armenian community had to offer. He was writer William Saroyan's uncle, his tormenter and benefactor and grist for so many of his short stories.

He made Harry dress all in white. He made two associates examine and crossexamine the witnesses and present all the mundane aspects of the defense. Aram Saroyan saved for himself the final argument.

Harry Arax was the psychological victim of genocide, he began. In Turkey, the gendarmes, the police, meant one thing to the Armenian and that was death. They had wiped out Harry's entire family with the exception of mother, brother, sister, and left the boy scarred for life. What judge and jury didn't learn was that Harry, having grown up in Istanbul proper, was hundreds of miles from any killing fields. He never saw a single Armenian slain by a Turk. This was vintage Saroyan—sands of truth blown into a bubble of fine glass with a lot of hot air. No one had yet coined post-traumatic stress syndrome but that's precisely what Saroyan was expounding.

The jury, several of its members reduced to tears by Saroyan histrionics, returned a guilty verdict to the charge of first-degree murder but did not sentence him to death. Harry's life was spared. The judge was not pleased.

"You are entitled to hang and the jury would have been entirely justified in bringing in a verdict with the death penalty. You came to this land of promise and freedom and had your opportunity at age sixteen to still form your character. Instead you became a scourge on your country, your adopted state."

Harry appeared near collapse. His mother, Azniv, who had been seated in the front row throughout the four-day trial, was absent for the verdict. The next day's *Long Beach Press Telegram* screamed: LIFE TERM GIVEN ARAX.

He spent the next fifteen years in San Quentin. When authorities made the mistake of assigning him to a camp detail in the foothills outside Fresno in 1950, Harry promptly busted free. He got word to his mother that she was to meet him next to a ditch where they swam that first summer in America. "Bring all the money you can," she was told.

My great-grandmother's entire life had been fractured by murder—first her father's gruesome hacking in Turkey when she was a month old, then her brother killing a man in Bulgaria and fleeing to America, and finally her youngest son, in the streets of Long Beach, gunning down a police officer. Thank goodness she was eight years dead by the time we buried my father, her favorite grandchild.

If misfortune turned her bitter, it was not something I saw as a child. My Great-grandmother Azniv was the most loving and hardworking woman I ever knew. I never left her house without a visit to her bedroom where she kept a stash of silver dollars in a box on her dresser. "Here, honey," she'd say, pressing three or four coins into my hand. "Buy yourself some chocolate."

It was with this same press of the hand that she delivered two thousand dollars collected from Grandpa and Grandma's pinochle cronies to a middleman who then delivered it to a fleeing Harry. He made the FBI's Ten Most Wanted List in 1950 and was featured on the radio show "Gangbusters." The law caught up with him three months later in Hutchinson, Kansas, where he had opened a hamburger stand and befriended the mayor and Boy Scouts under a new alias, Roy Hagger.

My father eventually found Uncle Harry at a halfway house in Oakland

and in 1969 got him paroled to Fresno and a job at Gallo Winery. "Ara was the only one who gave a shit," he muttered. "The rest of them you can have."

Twice a year until he died of cancer in 1982, Uncle Harry drove up in his big white El Dorado, its trunk brimming with grapes and vegetables ripened early in the desert sun. He was now Mike Simonian, the last alias, a half-Armenian, half-Mexican identity he stole from a dead man buried in the Coachella cemetery. He had a job as a foreman overseeing Mexican laborers outside Palm Springs. He went through three mongrels, each named Podgie, and several teenage sidekicks, most of them male, black-haired and American Indian.

We all wondered. Once, I asked him.

"Do you know what it means to be behind bars for thirty years without female companionship?" he protested. "But I am a woman lover. What is it on a man that you're going to like? Man is nothing but a goddamn piece of rock. How the hell can you be in love with a rock?" He laughed. "You know on my prison jacket one shrink classified me as a 'sexual psychopath.'"

It was Uncle Harry who made me understand that prison was a world apart, a nation with its own hierarchy, rules, economy, those who served and those who got served. In that world, he had risen to the top not simply because he wore the jacket of cop killer but because he was an Arax with the survival skills, charm and leadership of an Arax. He was the one with the most cigarettes, the one who sneaked in his girlfriend, Ruth, to the infirmary for quickies, the best and brightest, the king of cons.

He never stopped thinking the cops were after him, never stopped running. Once we were out driving and he spotted a police car a few blocks away. "Mark! Make a quick right here!"

In the clear he explained: "I'm still an imposter. When you get comfortable, that's when you get caught. My cover story has to jibe. I'm Mike Simonian. My wife died some twelve years ago. I have four children, one boy and three girls. I am here in Fresno to visit my daughter."

He had a real daughter from a brief, failed marriage in the thirties. I tried once to find this lost Arax, now a teacher with a family in Oregon, but her relatives refused to pass along my name and number. "She doesn't want to have anything to do with the Araxes. They're not so good people," one of them told me. "Harry was a killer. And there was another one murdered in Fresno."

The daughter, it seemed, no longer mattered to Harry. "I don't give her a thought. I'm not going to be sentimental that way. I don't regret about anything. I figured that . . . all these years . . . the philosophy that I developed. The whole thing is written. It's written."

Once, I asked him about the murder.

"It seems at odds with the old man sitting across from me," I said.

"It isn't the type. It's the time," he said. "You become practical because survival becomes the first order of the day. It's either he or you. See, son?"

"Did this cop leave behind any children?"

"Damn if I know. It didn't matter to me those things, Mark. There is no such thing as kindness between me and the cop anyway. That's the way human beings are. There's no more vicious animal than the so-called human. You kill each other."

"It's that simple?"

"If you face a situation like that, then all your thinking, all your morality, becomes centered on this one thing: to survive. How many Armenian women during the massacres refused to subdue? There were no Joan of Arcs who said, 'I'm not going to submit myself to this Turk.' No. They gave themselves to the Turk in order to survive. In order to save their children. See. Crime breeds only in poverty. And there's more than one kind of poverty. When I was seven in Turkey, I stole these tablets from my teacher's desk to write on. That was my first crime. Some poor people do without because they're scared. I had no fear. I figured if I can get it, I'm going to get it and I got it."

"From stealing paper to murder. In twenty short years."

"Not murder, see, son. I wasn't guilty of murder. Let me get up and illustrate. Here's my hotel room. Here's the corridor. I can hear the cop talking to the landlady. I come right to here and I shoot one and then I shoot two and before I shoot three—watch this so you understand—the man falls down. Now, they didn't find the gun on me. Shots one and two missed. They dug those two bullets out of the wall but the bullet that supposedly struck his heart they never produced. Right today I could get an acquittal if I wanted it."

I had made a choice—New York City and the journalism graduate school at Columbia University—that was going to equip me with the skills to one day find and face the truth of my father's murder. Was it a conscious choice? I still wonder.

One of my professors at Fresno State, George Diestel, would argue that it was and it wasn't. I had gone to Diestel in my senior year looking for career guidance. He was a scraggly-haired professor of speech whose sinuous lectures wove Aristotle and Aquinas with his own near death from alcohol, and he knew enough about me to sense that my dilemma—journalism or law—resulted in part from a desire to someday find the truth about my father.

After class he asked me to take a walk with him. "Mark, I can't make that career decision for you. My fear is that you're going to spend your life sucked up in the swirl of all these rumors and you'll never become what you want to become."

Diestel faced me squarely, a rail-thin figure swathed in torn jeans and Indian gauze shirt, and confessed that years earlier, after reading of the murder in the *Fresno Bee,* he sullied my father's name in a class lecture. He apologized for assuming that a bar owner killed under the circumstances in which he was killed had to be dirty, because he should have known better.

"Rosalie Lima sat in front of me in the second grade," he explained. "I pulled on her pigtails one day and the nun punished me and I wanted to get back at Rosalie so I told a fib about her. The nun got wind of the rumor and told me to bring a pillow from home the next day. She took me out on the roof of the school overlooking San Francisco and pulled out a scissor from her habit and cut the pillow in half and shook the feathers until the pillow was no more and then she said, 'Now go get them.' I couldn't pick them all up, the wind had caught the feathers and carried them all over the city. It was an impossible task and I started to cry. The lesson was about the irrevocability of a rumor. A lie about someone can never be completely erased. No matter how hard or long you try you can never pick up all the feathers, Mark. You can never completely vindicate your father's spirit. I'm concerned about your freedom and your right to do with your life what you damn please. Don't spend the rest of it trying to undo the damage."

On the eve of my New York City adventure, Grandpa Arax called to say that he had set up a meeting with William Saroyan, and I was to pick him up at two o'clock sharp. The stated purpose was to present the writer with a medal Grandpa had brought back from Soviet Armenia a few months earlier.

Saroyan was a friend of Pop's and no stranger to me. Once or twice I had driven him home after an evening of too much food and Russian vodka at my grandparents' house. One of these visits I managed to turn into a feature story for the college weekly, a quirky little piece filled with Saroyan's musings on spring. It was a story I wouldn't soon forget, my first showing on page one and one of the few times I've written without notes. Saroyan wouldn't let me take any.

"Notes are crutches," he explained. "If you're going to be a writer, you have to see things. And you can't very well see things if your face is stuck in some notebook."

Back then, sadly, I thought of Saroyan as a museum piece. All summer long, Pop bugged me about the medal and a poem he was dedicating to Saroyan titled "Crane," the bird of message and return in Armenian folklore. He could have gotten a dozen others to jump at the invitation but it seemed important that I be the one to accompany him to the writer's house. No other friend or grandchild would do. Although he was never one to play favorites—quite the opposite of Grandma—it was clear that I had become his second chance, a realization of everything he dreamed of and left behind in the fields, everything my father and uncle weren't. I was his English-speaking grandson and potential writer, and with New York City beckoning, I would benefit from a visit with Saroyan, the first-generation Armenian-American, the link between Pop's world and mine. If a torch was going to be passed, I, his eldest grandson, was going to be the one to receive it.

Saroyan divided his year between a flat in Paris and two stucco houses side by side in a modest tract off Highway 99 in Fresno. He wrote in one house and the other sat cluttered with the oddments of decades: two player pianos and hundreds of musical scrolls, pebbles and shards of glass, nails, feathers and twine collected during furious bike rides through town.

The front lawn wasn't so much grass but a waist-high thicket of milk weed, puncture vines, wild flowers, dandelions and the mint Saroyan harvested and ate raw with yogurt. Piled high in the garage were newspapers and magazines from the thirties and forties that chronicled his soaring flight into fame and his rejection of the Pulitzer Prize for Drama because his play, *The Time of Your Life,* was "no more great than anything else I have ever written."

He saw us through the screen window. "Come on in, fellow Armenians, writers." The voice boomed and bellowed and in softer moments betrayed a slight whistle lisp. "I'm just finishing lunch."

He looked like a vision from the grape fields—chinos and wrinkled cotton shirt stained with sweat, food and drink, the Armenian peasant farmer. We had a name for such shabbiness, *ped e shan.* A remnant of chili stuck to his chin below the great gray walrus mustache, and I could see he had lost considerable weight since our last visit.

It was 105 degrees outside and the den where he wrote, on an old Royal typewriter, felt like a blast furnace. He said he liked to perspire when he worked and feel the cool of air conditioning only at night, in bed.

"I am alive and that is something. I have no more vices. I gave up the race track and the roulette tables and I've given up drinking, too. There is nothing left but writing. So I write, day and night."

A big Formica-topped desk stood in the center of the room surrounded by piles of books, letters, free-form art he had drawn in crayon and pen, treasures from yesterday's bike ride and several pairs of shoes lined in a corner and burnished in French polish. He said he collected the pebbles and rocks to remind himself that art should be simple. He liked to shine his shoes to unwind. He was seventy-one years old, long past the days when he was one of the most talked about writers in the world.

"Villiam, I know you are a busy man and Mark and I don't want to take up too much of your time," Grandpa said, his tone suddenly official. "I have brought with me a medal from Soviet Armenia in honor of you. A great writer and a great humanitarian."

Grandpa reached into his pants and handed Saroyan a small plastic box. Saroyan opened the box and lifted a medal ribboned in the red and blue of the Soviet-Armenian flag. In the dusty light he turned it this way and that.

"This is a great honor, Aram. Spiritually, I am part of Soviet Armenia. It doesn't matter that I live here. Armenia is in me as it is in you and your fine grandson. Thank you."

He got up and opened the window to the dead heat of midday and stood there a moment, silent, squinting into a backyard of plums, apricots, peaches, pomegranates and seedless grapes. On the window ledge he had placed a recorder with which he taped the sounds of night—hours and hours of nothing punctuated by the buzz of a fly, the chirp of a robin. I interrupted his reverie by telling him if he ever needed blank cassettes, I had a supply at the college paper.

A tea kettle sang in the kitchen. He said he drank as many as thirty cups a day, no sugar. He offered us a cup and then we talked, first about my plans to study journalism at Columbia University, then my ambivalence about leading the life of a writer, at least in the style of a Saroyan.

He laughed, a big belly laugh. "Please don't judge a writer by these surroundings. There is no formula for being a writer. It's what you are and what you're going to be and what's going to happen."

"But the way you live seems important."

"It's only important to find what works for you. You must be alone and have a place to write. So it's lonely sometimes but it isn't abject loneliness. Rather a kind of majestic one, a kinship with larger things."

Did being a writer, a real writer, mean there would be no time for marriage or children?

He was too kind to laugh again.

"Not if it's the right marriage. Not any more than any other intensely felt profession. Maybe less. I was married to the same woman twice. Walter Matthau has her now, thank God. She had crazy excesses and I couldn't live with her. Only it took me two marriages to realize it. She wanted Hollywood and all its trappings. I felt stifled when I lived with her. The atmosphere wasn't for writing. It was for entertaining and I couldn't have that neatness again."

Never in those previous visits had Saroyan touched on things so personal, and I tried to steer it back to writing by asking him what American authors I should be reading.

On the back side of an opened envelope from his publisher, he scribbled wildly in pencil: Mark Twain, "our best." Edgar Lee Masters for the *Spoon River Anthology*. Sherwood Anderson for *Winesburg, Ohio*. Faulkner, Hemingway, Fitzgerald, even himself, though he seemed almost apologetic. "Let's include Saroyan, *Sons Come and Go, Mothers Hang in There Forever,* even though that's not the title I wanted," he said.

He finished the list with Thomas Wolfe's *Look Homeward, Angel*. "He was a swift, intense, lyrical writer but they criticized him for being too autobiographical. I guess they have accused me of the same thing. Of writing about the small man, about Armenians and Fresno and my crazy family and everyone else I have encountered along the way. But what does a writer write if not what he has lived, what he has seen and smelled and tasted? You must write about what you know in the language that you know it."

Saroyan opened a desk drawer filled with family photos and gently placed the medal inside. He thanked Grandpa again.

"We should be going, Mark."

Saroyan showed us to the front door. "When you get a chance, would you mind bringing over some blank tapes? I've run out."

"Sure," I said.

Then, from behind his back, like a magician, he produced a copy of his latest book, *Obituaries*.

"Here," he said, "this is for you. For New York. Don't be put off by the title. It's not about death at all. It's about living."

When I got in the car, I opened the book and on the first blank page, to my surprise and delight, Saroyan had penned a note. I read it to Pop:

"For Aram Arax, grandfather, and to Mark Arax, grandson. Fellow Armenians. Fellow writers. It is a track. It is a profession. But most of all writing is being alive. Continued good luck, Bill Saroyan."

Pop nodded his head and smiled. Then he laughed. "You would have thought the *esh* (jackass) could have turned on the air conditioning a while."

That was the last time I saw Saroyan. Eight months later, prostate cancer riddling his body, he called the AP office in Fresno and issued a final statement. "Everybody has got to die, but I have always believed an exception would be made in my case. Now, what?"

The young female reporter said the comma between the last two words seemed awkward and suggested he remove it. Saroyan, who had fought all his writing life against "the big literary editor's pencil," conceded the point.

A few days later, the pain too much, he forced down a handful of pills with a dish of ice cream. The newspapers reported that he had collapsed from the ravages of cancer and been taken to the hospital. What they didn't know is that Bill Saroyan, who had told me he respected Hemingway more for his courage to end life than the courage of his work, had tried to kill himself, too. He died a month later at the Veteran's Hospital in Fresno. Pop broke the news to me over the phone. "We have lost our crane," he said.

I moved into an apartment on 27th Street near Third Avenue, a forty-five-minute subway ride to Columbia each morning, and each night I worked myself into exhaustion. On weekends, I walked to Little Italy and ordered proscuitto and provolone sandwiches and watched the Chinese encroach on Mafia turf.

I wrote letters of longing to Coby and letters of love and reproach to a brother who was failing to stand in my stead and to a mother who was behaving like some silly schoolgirl, one week certain of marriage to Arsen and the next week refusing to see him. She fired back a letter of her own, a declaration of liberation.

"Mark, the burden you are carrying on your shoulders is very heavy and many times I felt I was adding to that burden. But whatever mistakes I make in my life from now on should have no reflection on you. THANKS FOR BEING MY SON. I LOVE YOU VERY MUCH. I AM VERY PROUD OF YOU. Mom."

Determined to show that Fresno State had prepared me for the rigors of Columbia, I finished that first semester at the top of the class. One rainy afternoon, riding high, guard down, I stood in a professor's office with three other students, all Ivy Leaguers, discussing a story in the *New York*

Times that was actually four stories, or vignettes, woven into one. In my excitement to describe the technique, I mispronounced the word vignette. I pronounced it "vigenette" with a hard "g."

There was a pause, a few chuckles, an attempt by the professor to cover up the gaffe. (Those damn French words, he muttered.) I had taken language from books and the newspaper, and my vocabulary list contained hundreds of words I had never heard enunciated, certainly not at home and not in the classrooms at Fresno State. I found myself constrained by the spoken word. So many words came to mind in conversation, so many rich and felicitous words. But I dared not utter them.

I signed up for Mel Mencher's investigative reporting course, one of the most demanding and popular in the program. He was a bully of a man, scarcely five feet tall. Word spread that the class had filled and he would be handpicking students. I decided to state my case in person, firing off a list of college accolades that included a summer stint at the *Fresno Bee*.

"So you're a Fresno boy," he glared.

Unknown to me, Mencher had worked at the *Fresno Bee* from 1954 to 1958. The *Bee* belonged to a chain of respected valley newspapers headquartered in Sacramento and owned and operated by the McClatchy family. One branch of the clan, which had been engaged in the newspaper business since the Gold Rush days, grew up in Fresno and took a special interest in the local product. When it faded into a journalistic torpor, management summoned reporter Mencher, who had just completed a Nieman Fellowship at Harvard, to shake things up.

Mencher said he found a wide-open Fresno, its residents complacent, politicians complicit. He was astonished at the *Bee*'s tolerance of the corruption. Fresno was known by truckers throughout the nation as a mecca of prostitution. The same with gambling. Mencher discovered that Police Chief Hank Morton and a small group of henchmen were monitoring the whorehouses, all right, but not for purposes of law enforcement. They were making sure the madams weren't shortchanging them on the customer count. Mencher said he spotted a state senator and Morton's deputy chief leaving the same cathouse.

"The whole thing was well organized, well protected," Mencher told me. "The whole damn government was involved. The newspaper gave me absolutely no support. It was run by a bunch of terrified little hacks. The city editor was frightened to death because I was upsetting the tranquility of Fresno. At one point they killed the stories on Chief Morton and I had to appeal to the editors in Sacramento, who said 'Run it!'"

I shared with Mencher my own story: My father, a nightclub owner, had been murdered days after he met with high-ranking members of the Fresno Police Department. Morton was police chief. There was no official record of the visits.

"What year was that?"

"1972."

"You're talking about only fourteen years after I left town," Mencher said. "You might want to look up those old stories. They'd be a good place to begin. And I'd start with one assumption. Nothing had changed in those fourteen years."

I left Mencher's office shaking my head. Here I was, 3,000 miles from home, a world away, and the murder had tracked me down again. It would not let go.

On the strength of my final number-four placement in the class, I wrote to twenty newspapers of all sizes and reputations across the country. Nineteen rejected me outright. The only offer came from the *Baltimore Evening Sun,* once home of H. L. Mencken, and I accepted.

The newsroom on Calvert Street housed two competing staffs separated not only by morning and evening deadlines but by journalistic mission as well. One side belonged to the venerable *Baltimore Sun.* The other side, my side, belonged to the *Evening Sun* where the sartorial preference leaned to polyester and the staff held a yearly funky tie contest in honor of the drunken rewrite man, decked in inimitable neckware, who died of a massive stroke on deadline.

Baltimore evinced this same split personality. The city had the warm embrace of a small town. In a matter of twenty minutes, I made the drive from Anne Arundel County, where two rednecks in a flatbed nearly ran me off the road because my passenger was a black woman, to the city schools department where the superintendent herself was black.

The *Evening Sun* clanged and clamored with the eccentricities of an afternoon paper. Jim "Dawg" Day, the weekend editor, hailed from the backwoods of Glen Burnie and every Saturday morning at 6:15 came his twangy wake-up call. "Arax. This is Dawg Day. You're fifteen minutes late and counting but I'm willing to forget it as long as you get in here by seven and produce me an eleven-alarm fire."

Tragedies became my forte, the way I rose from county bureau to city staff to special projects. Survivors never turned me away. Into my notebook I scribbled the most intimate details of their lives and pain, and when I sat down to write, some of my own anguish seemed to creep into their stories.

The entire time back East, one year in New York and three in Baltimore, I was concerned about my mother's health. She had launched a career in real estate only to see interest rates skyrocket to 16 percent and kill the market.

My sister, Michelle, married her first boyfriend, an Armenian grape grower like my father. It was only after Coby joined me in Baltimore and we married that my mother finally felt free to wed Arsen Marsoobian. By this time, things were no longer right between them. She demanded that he sign a prenuptial agreement forswearing any claim to our house. Driving to Las Vegas she informed him that she wouldn't be taking his last name. The marriage lasted a year.

I mailed home a few hundred dollars each month and tried to pep talk my mother out of depression. She shut me up with Armenian proverbs steeped in fatalism, destinies carved into foreheads.

She had undergone several tests in the spring of 1984 to determine the cause of bronchial pain laboring her breath. I stayed home from work awaiting her phone call with the results. There was no pretense of calm on her part or mine. Once before I had heard this voice.

"Mark! I've got lung cancer. Inoperable lung cancer."

"I knew it, Mom," I shouted. "I knew it! I'm coming home. I'll be there tomorrow."

Coby stayed behind with my relatives in Virginia for a final month of college. I wanted to quit the *Evening Sun,* but my editors insisted on a leave of absence. They were genuinely perplexed over my certainty that I would not be back. How could I explain the sacrifices made by my mother, the strength she mustered to raise three children, to withstand all the rumors and fears and money problems and never once miss our games or fail to put a home-cooked meal on the table. I shared some of the blame for her second marriage not working, and now that she was alone and dying, there was no question what I would do.

She had lost thirteen pounds, now a few pounds shy of 100, and her eyeglasses kept sliding off her sunken face. She used an oral inhaler five times a day in the false hope that bronchitis caused the short breaths and pain.

The first oncologist, a forbidding German, told her we are all dying. We sought a second opinion and the doctors at Stanford diagnosed adenocarcinoma of the lungs. This cancer had nothing to do with smoking. Ironically, smoker's lung cancer, the so-called oat cell, responded much better to chemotherapy. She would never get better, they said, and the best hope was to arrest the disease for a time.

We were referred to an oncologist in Fresno named Peter Wittlinger. He was soft-spoken and pleasant enough, citing all the statistics on chemotherapy's effectiveness and carefully avoiding the particular: How long did Mom have? Even if he had ventured a guess, I'm not sure we would have heard him. Mom confided to a girlfriend that Wittlinger was cute but that "Mark and I haven't decided yet on chemotherapy."

I pored over the periodicals at the main library and called friends at newspapers hoping to learn of an experimental treatment. I was given the name and phone number of a man in Arkansas who claimed to have the cure for cancer. At my mother's prodding, I called.

"This isn't some Laetrile," the man insisted. "And we're not profiting off people's desperation. It's free."

He said the drug, Cancell, was being tested by the head of oncological research at a New York medical college. It was derived from a plant substance used in certain dyes. After years of trying to impede its underground distribution, the FDA had finally agreed to consider the drug's efficacy. There were no side effects. Just mix two teaspoons into a pint of water or juice and drink the pint over the course of a day.

The New York cancer doctor confirmed that Cancell had been 100 percent effective on tumors in mice and would be the subject of human trials. "I think it has a major potential beyond chemotherapy," he said. "But until we do the human trials, I can't say for sure what that potential is."

The UPS package arrived from Arkansas three days later, muddy water inside a plastic bottle. She drank the mix of Cancell and apple juice throughout the day. At night we prayed together and I massaged Lourdes water into her back. Sometimes the pain took a while to go away and I fell asleep in my old spot.

By the time Coby graduated and flew out, my mother and I were a team again, Mark and Flora, thwarting the odds. She gained three pounds and resumed housework. The Cancell folks advised against chemotherapy, arguing that it would impair her immune system and slow down recovery. I decided to hedge our bets and go with both.

Uncle Navo visited each afternoon. I found out that Mom's first phone call after hearing the diagnosis wasn't to me but to him. I had a harder time forgetting the years he had neglected us. Every summer, he rented a big beach house in Santa Cruz and invited family and friends. Somehow my sister, brother, mother and I never made the list. One summer, Grandma and Grandpa Arax rented a small, musty shack near the same beach—just to bring us along. Grandma blamed Navo's second wife, Josette, for the oversight.

Then a few years later, out of the blue, Uncle Navo came through with tickets to the 49ers championship series, the one where they beat the New York Giants and Dallas Cowboys to finally reach the Super Bowl. We had a wonderful time—he and cousin Brian and Donny and I, laughing so hard on the way to San Francisco that he had to pull over near Los Baños to keep from crashing. Driving home, in the darkness of the Pacheco Pass, we told ghost stories.

I will never forget his story. Our stories were fiction, made up on the spot. His story evidently was real.

"I was visiting your father's grave one day. Never a problem in all the visits before. But this time, as I was walking back from the headstone, the wind began to howl. 'Navo,' it said. 'Navo. Don't come back! Don't come back!' I used to go to the grave all the time. But I've never been back, and I won't ever go back. I heard Ara's voice in the wind. Was it the wind?"

Was the voice angry? Generous? He never said. I assumed the voice was somehow aggrieved, and he had been banished from the graveyard. But it was Brian's impression that my father was letting his father know that he had suffered enough and there was nothing to be gained out there; he was set free.

ooo

After seven weeks of Cancell and two chemotherapy treatments, my mother went in for her first checkup. The X rays showed a reduction in the lung tumors between 80 and 90 percent. Dr. Wittlinger walked back from the X ray lights wearing a bewildered grin. He called it a "near complete response." She gave him a big hug and confessed her use of Cancell. Wittlinger listened, not saying much. His skepticism seemed tempered by the knowledge that two treatments of chemotherapy couldn't fully explain what he would later describe in his notes as a "miraculous" recovery. He asked how he could contact the Cancell people.

"You're my miracle worker, Mark," she gushed. "Let's call up everybody."

Uncle Navo treated the whole family to a victory dinner at the Basque restaurant. We made up a ballad, "Cancell, Cancell," to the tune of "New York, New York." ("Those cancer cell blues . . . are melting away.") We sat late into the night devising strategies to make riches off the drug.

Mom lost her hair after the two rounds of chemotherapy and decided to forego any more treatment in favor of Cancell. We were told the second bottle of the drug had come from a different batch but not to worry. She was doing so well that I took a job with the *Los Angeles Times* and worked out a way to spend Friday through early Monday morning in Fresno and the rest of the week in Los Angeles.

For the next several weeks, she got no better and no worse. The Cancell people were stumped. Then her phone call awakened me at three in the morning.

"I'm dying, Mark!"

"No you're not, Mom. Just calm down."

She said her eye and sternum had swelled to grotesque proportions, the pain unbearable. She saw Dr. Wittlinger the next day and he pressed the case for more chemotherapy.

"I think we should, Mark. Let's go with both. It worked the first time."

She endured two more rounds of chemotherapy and continued to slip. The lungs remained 90 percent clear but the cancer had spread to her bones. I had kept a diary of the treatment and went back and retraced every step. It was impossible to pin down the variables. In the first weeks of Cancell, when she hadn't yet started chemotherapy, her recovery was evident. No one could tell me different. Yet Dr. Wittlinger was equally adamant that the remission was the work of chemotherapy. I would never know for sure. I had poisoned the well by pursuing both treatments.

My mother didn't seem to care that I was spending less of each work week in Los Angeles, a risky proposition since my status at the *Times* was still probationary. She had the uncanny knack of needing a glass of ice water or a back rub every time Coby and I were about to get intimate.

I began to resent the frantic pace, the late-night marathons between Los Angeles and Fresno, the disappointment in her face whenever we left the house for a few minutes. But I didn't need to hear it from my wife.

"That women is ruining our lives!" Coby announced.

"That woman?" I shouted. "That woman?"

Before I knew it, my wife was confronting my mother in her bedroom. "You know, Flora, I'm really sorry that you lost your husband, but Mark is my husband."

Mom struck right back. "This wouldn't be an issue if my son had married an Armenian."

I ran back and forth, mother to wife, imploring them to stop before one said something that could not be forgotten. They kept arguing whether I was a son or a husband, as if I couldn't be both.

That night, I watched my mother fall asleep on the sofa. "Ara, wait. I'm coming, Ara."

Friends overwhelmed us with jars of fresh carrot juice, stories of Armenian farmers who destroyed cancer cells by eating crates of raw purple onions, books extolling the virtues of coffee enemas and a patient's own urine.

We rejected none of these outright. One book chronicled a physician's conquest of prostate cancer through a strict diet of brown rice, whole grains, seaweed and miso soup. I had always believed in the regenerative powers of the Eastern diet. Mom was willing to give it a try while we waited for an original batch of Cancell.

The macrobiotics movement was centered in Los Angeles and I had no trouble finding a healer. She agreed to come at the cost of $75-a-day plus plane fare, food and lodging. She whirled right past Mom, electric hair and organic cotton outfit, throwing open every window and sliding glass door to the crisp November night.

"This house smells like cancer! Like disease! Out! Out with it! In! In with the fresh air! To produce healthy red blood cells you need to breathe pure air."

The next morning, she swallowed a cup of coffee and muffin and took us through the diet that would produce healthy red blood cells. She exhorted my mother to chew every mouthful fifty to a hundred times and caught a flight to LA.

At the East-West Center for Macrobiotic Studies, I found Cecile Levin, the genuine article. She would come to Fresno on the condition that she could fly in and out the same day. Her fee, not including plane fare, was $400. "Everything I teach you, I practice," she said in an obvious reference to her predecessor. "Otherwise, I have no credibility."

Levin had seen the Godhead and did not suffer Philistines lightly. There was a precise way to clean and cut and cook every vegetable according to the universal dual forces of yin (expansion) and yang (contraction). "Fire and water," she kept saying. "The alchemy of these two forces can create magic."

With great care, she prepared a colorful lunch and served Mom small portions on a TV tray in the living room. "As long as she tastes a little, it's a good beginning."

My mother lost parts of herself imperceptible to us. One day we turned around and she was no longer making it to the bedroom. "Let me sleep on the couch." Constipation swelled her abdomen, and Coby and I learned to inject suppositories and squeeze disposable enemas, peek into the toilet and applaud. The walk to the bathroom became too much so we made space in the family room for a portable potty and hospital bed with eggshell mattress. A bed sore festered anyway, stubborn on the tail bone, and I fought to keep it the size of a dime, a quarter, a half dollar. Keep it dry, the nurse told me. Use a blow dryer. When I finished dressing the wound, I shot the hot electric air over her goosebumpy skin.

"That feels so good."

She sprouted new hair. "Do you think I'll be around to see it grow all the way back?"

"Sure, Birdwoman."

She never lost her sense of humor—she was never funnier—talking about the German air raids over Marseilles, Big Momma superstitiously making the girls drink little Georgie's urine to stave off fright, Hyreek sheltering an American reporter in the basement but also accepting a jeep ride home from the Third Reich, collaborators paraded through the streets, heads shaven in shame, Mom getting caught behind the gate of the witch's house, her eyes crisscrossing from fear.

For those who visited every few weeks, the changes must have been ghastly. We didn't see it. My mother cloistered in the family room without mirrors didn't see it, not until the day Coby wheeled her up to the hospital for X rays. She stared straight ahead at her reflection in a mirrored wall. Bones swaddled in diaper.

"I look like one of those cancer patients. All dried up. I've got to put on some weight."

Her teeth grew bigger. Her eyes grew bigger. They crisscrossed again, glasses magnifying the terror. I will never forget the eyes.

"Take me to the pool. Please, Mark. Stick my head under the water. Drown me."

I had waited too long to administer the morphine. When it finally took hold, her apologies were profuse and she explained.

"It's a pain unlike any pain I've ever had. In some ways it's like you're in labor but you never end up giving birth. It feels like there's a war going on inside. Like the cancer cells are shooting all the good ones. It's like a smelly pain. If you opened me up I bet it would stink. The cancer would smell very bad."

Her legs and underarms had gone unshaven and she wanted to feel like a lady again. She couldn't walk or stand so I placed a plastic chair in the shower and carried her to it. I took off the nightgown and tried not to stare at what cancer had done to my mother. Focus on the feet, plump and unchanged. I soaped her legs and underarms and shaved the stubble.

"You're the most wonderful son a mother could ask for."

Coby walked into the bathroom.

"Your husband's giving me a shower. He's worth a million bucks." *Your husband.*

We dried her off and Coby rubbed lotion into her arms and legs, clipped and polished her toenails and dressed her in a new sweatsuit.

"How do you feel, Flora?"

"I feel like a human again."

○ ○ ○

She stopped taking chemotherapy while we waited for a new batch of Cancell. A massive infection related to the chemotherapy took root. Instead of cancer in her lungs, she had the equivalent of AIDS-related pneumonia. Her mouth and tongue were white with thrush and she talked in a cute lisp, voice high from the lack of oxygen.

The citrus trees ripened in the backyard and she wanted a taste, forbidden by The Diet.

"Please, Mark. Just one orange. One small orange."

"I can't, Mom. Cecile says no fruit."

"Just one slice, then. One tiny slice of tangerine?"

"I'm sorry. It's for your own good. You've been pain free for three days now. Something must be working."

Aunt Rosette cornered me in the kitchen.

"What are you doing, Marrrrrkkk? Can't you see this macrobiotics is killing her? Four weeks of this diet and she's wasted away to nothing. This is craaaaazy."

All her life, Rosette had been the sanctimonious one, standing there in judgment, stone-blind to hypocrisy. "Goddamm it, you've got no right to second guess!" I screamed. "It's not this diet that's wasting her. Can't you see? It's the disease."

I began to sob, not so much for my mother as for myself, exposed in the glare of my aunt's accusation.

I had once sent a tape-recorded message of hope to a childhood friend frozen in coma, believing that the sound of my voice, the magic of my shared pain, the power of my exhortation—Wake up, Brian! Wake up, Brian!—could rouse him from the sleepy dead. This absurdly inflated idea of myself, of what goodness and sincerity could achieve, may or may not have been a by-product of overcoming murder, though at times I did almost convince myself that it was me who took those five bullets and walked on. My aunt was right about this much: I was no shaman. My mother wasn't indestructible by virtue of her eldest son, robbed of father, needing her so. There was no exemption that parceled out suffering. No pardon. My mother was dying and there wasn't a damn thing I could do, and now I was denying her one stinking orange.

I gave her one orange. The next morning she awoke with a shooting pain in her neck. I couldn't get her to lift her head high enough to take the morphine.

"Please, let's do something now. I can't take this pain anymore. I've lived my years, Mark. I've done what I had to do. Please . . . let me go."

I called Cecile Levin in LA. "I think the cancer has spread to her neck."

"Don't project your conclusions to me," she snapped. "Just describe the pain and I'll tell you what to do."

"She can't raise her neck from a flat position."

"Is she thirsty?"

"Yes, she's been asking for water."

"Okay. The neck pain and the thirst come from the same thing. You're putting too much salt in her diet. She's too yang. This is not a correct thing. Give her a boiled radish and tea made of grated daikon."

"That's it?"

"That's it."

That wasn't it. "Anytime you call seeking information for Flora, I need to be paid for that. The fee is fifty dollars."

We got the morphine down Mom and she apologized. Then, for the first time since I had returned home six months before, she called the next move by herself.

"Mark, I'm going to stop this diet and go just with the Cancell. We know we've got the real stuff now. It worked once, right?"

Two weeks before Christmas my mother slipped into a semicoma and was taken to St. Agnes. Every few hours we sneaked into her room in intensive care, pulled down the oxygen mask and fed her drops of Cancell. The doctors asked about heroic measures and we agreed there would be no life support. On the third morning, four members of the hospital staff led us into Mom's room.

"Tell her it's all right to let go. Tell her she can give up now. Let her have some peace."

They had removed the oxygen mask and she was heaving for air. She throbbed like the baby bird I once picked from the tree and tried to possess in a nest made of egg carton and cotton.

"Put that mask on her face," I shrieked. "Can't you see she's trying to breathe! What's the level? Fifty percent? Can't you increase to pure oxygen until she recovers her breathing?"

"You told us you didn't want any extraordinary measures," the doctor replied. "We asked about life support and you said no."

"Is an oxygen mask life support?"

"No, it isn't."

"Then why can't you put the son of a bitch back on?"

The nurse adjusted the straps, reset the calibration. "Come on, Mom. You can do it. Don't stop. Don't stop. Don't stop. Don't stop. Don't stop."

It was no longer in her power. In six months of endless nights, we never talked about dying. There were no neat stages of protest, despair and acquiescence. She didn't stop heaving until the last crazed breath. She went deeply surprised, nothing peaceful about it.

We didn't linger in the room. One by one we kissed her cheek and I wiped the muddy stains of Cancell from her lips. My parents had died thirteen years apart in this same hospital. Mom was fifty-one. Outside, Donny said he never wanted to see St. Agnes again, not until a baby had been born there. I began to think of her death only in the context of murder. My mother became for me the killers' second victim; cancer the sixth bullet that had missed him.

I once thought nothing could be crueler than to behold a father, at his absolute prime, stricken in an instant dead. I once thought cancer's bit-by-bit waste at least gave warning, the chance for a prolonged farewell and kiss. But I will always remember my father at his absolute best and my mother as an emaciated figure completely defenseless on a chair in the shower.

It seems strange, then, to say that her death also freed me. Not only from the despair of her life and the hell of her dying but from the uncertainty of what must be done next. The way I figured it, I was no longer bound by my promise to her to leave the murder be. What had the last thirteen years been if not preparation for this book. It was never far away: the taped recollections of family; the decision to become a journalist; the kind of journalist I became. So I would resurrect the old questions, pursue the old rumors, hunt down the old names. I would find what I would find.

We sold the adobe house and divided up my mother's modest estate. Coby and I returned to Pasadena and in one twenty-four-hour period, in the whirl of the Rose Bowl parade, she gave birth to our first child, a girl, and I moved us into our first house.

My brother, who was nineteen and didn't know the first thing about living on his own, moved in with a group of college friends in Fresno. He counted on me to manage his life from afar.

Over the next four years, as I poked around the edges of my father's murder, I buried myself in work at the *Los Angeles Times,* writing almost exclusively on the Asian immigrant community. A number of the stories appeared on page one and a profile of a lost generation of Vietnamese youth made the cover of the Sunday Magazine. I was promoted to the Metro staff, nominated by the paper for a Pulitzer and given the freedom to pursue the big stories I wanted. Everything seemed to be opening up at once.

Gary Taubes, a classmate from Columbia, heard the good news and asked me to lunch. He had recently published his first book and wondered why I was moving so tentatively on mine. "I can understand your hesitation," he said. "But you've already lost your mother."

The way Gary saw it, here were all these novels imagining murder as dramatic thrust, all these true-crime stories written secondhand, and here was my life, without invention or hype, hemmed in by a murder I knew almost nothing about, and the trail was only getting colder.

"Have you seen the murder report?"

"No."

"Then why not start there?"

That afternoon, my wife was tending to our baby daughter in the kitchen, her back turned to me, when I came home early from work and abruptly announced my desire. I wanted to return to Fresno and finally write the book about my family and the murder.

She did not look up from her nimble hands at gentle work, and I tried to explain the dangers involved: that the killers, or at least the men who hired them, probably still lived in the Fresno area. I told her the passage of time had surely dimmed many memories and obscured many trails. I had already lost my mother to cancer, and if I waited much longer I might lose the others who knew him best and could shed a light on what happened.

Another wife might have reminded me of everything we had to lose, the blossoming career and Tudor house she had remolded with her own hands, the caring neighbors and glorious view of the San Gabriel mountains clean after a hard rain. But ever since we met when I was eighteen and she was fifteen, Coby had watched, baffled and amused, as I secretly recorded conversations with the cops and collected the stories from family. When it came time to choose a career for myself, the career I chose, investigative reporter, was no accident. I chose it knowing that the past persisted and someday I would have to return to Fresno to face again—this time more directly—the one event that so marked my life.

My wife knew this. She knew that we had each rehearsed this conversation too many times in our minds to pretend that it was a surprise. Besides, Fresno was her home, too, her parents were there and she was a new mother. If she wanted to resume her teaching career, the prospects would be better back home.

"I think it's a great idea," she said, with a big grin.

She had no idea that this journey back in time would change our lives forever. How could I tell her? I didn't know myself.

○ ○ ○

The *Fresno Bee* happened to be doing a story on unsolved murders when I telephoned reporter Royal Calkins in the spring of 1988 asking for help. A week later, he had the homicide investigation in hand.

"I'll put it in the overnight mail but I have to warn you," he said. "There are some parts that are going to get you down. It describes your father's last minutes."

At lunch the next day, the newsroom empty, I peeled back the envelope and pulled out the contents, not at all sure this was the time or place. After sixteen years, after trying once myself to obtain the file directly and being told by Fresno police that it was off limits to family, I finally had the object in hand. I counted fewer than 100 pages typewritten front and back. I had expected more. I peeked inside and noticed right off the words that caused my friend at the *Bee* to pause. They were hard to miss, each one in bold letters. I felt for a moment an eerie transcendence, as if I was contemplating myself from above, a grand vista that took in present and future, the *Los Angeles Times,* my wife and baby up the road in Pasadena, the empty chairs of colleagues who shared their space but knew almost nothing about me, the past I now held irresolutely in my hands. I could see myself stepping backwards.

There were descriptions of the two young gunmen—brown hair and brown eyes, medium height and weight, neatly groomed and very good looking—and a detailed accounting of the crime, autopsy findings and investigation. From the placement of wounds and the location of bullet slugs and casings, I could trace a mental image of the actual shooting.

Gunman number one stood over my father in his office chair and lifted a 7.65 mm German Mauser to his forehead. Dad somehow dipped just enough so that this first bullet—a .32 caliber fired at such close range that gunpowder singed the wisps of his brown hair—missed the mark. It skimmed the top of the skull bone, barely penetrating the scalp, and exited through the back office wall and into the parking lot. Dad must have been crouching or attempting to rise from his chair when the second bullet, fired at a downward angle, split the breast bone and exited clean at the left hip. He fought his assailant into the hallway and the third bullet, shot from a distance of ten feet, cracked his right wrist. My father charged and managed to twist away the weapon despite the exhortations of the second gunman, who kept shouting, "Shoot the motherfucker." Before Dad could return a shot, this second gunman stepped up and fired three times from a .38-caliber Charter Arms revolver. One bullet missed, one bullet tore through the left thigh and one bullet, the fatal bullet, pierced the abdomen and punctured the vena cava, the great vein that gorges the heart. Both shooters ran and Dad followed for about twenty feet, stopped and fired a single shot from the German Mauser. He may have hit one of the gunmen because the slug from this shot was never found. Then he turned back in the direction of his office, stumbled twenty feet, knocked over a barstool and collapsed to the carpet, the gun at his side.

That night I sat in bed and read the report cover to cover. It was as if all the years that separated us had never existed. I was a child again, only I wasn't the child in the emergency waiting room, Bible in hand. This time I was beside my father in the bar as he rested on both knees, turned a half circle toward the first police officer to arrive and lifted his shirt to show the belly wound. His face began to blanch and perspire and the officer told him to lie back, and he lay back, blood seeping into the booze-stained carpet. In the emergency room, I saw movements I had never seen before, heard words I had never heard: I WAS JUST SITTING THERE DOING THE BOOKS AND TWO GUYS CAME IN AND STARTED SHOOTING. I TOOK THE GUN AWAY FROM ONE OF THEM AND SHOT BACK. AREN'T YOU GUYS GOING TO SEW ME UP? LET'S TAKE CARE OF THIS LITTLE PROBLEM AND I'LL BUY YOU ALL A DRINK. LET'S GET THE SHOW ON THE ROAD! I'M BLEEDING PRETTY GOOD HERE. WHAT'S GOING ON? DOC, GIVE ME SOMETHING FOR THE PAIN. I'M PRETTY TOUGH. I'M PRETTY TOUGH. My father was dying a second time, this time right before me, and there was not one thing I could do to help. Four of the wounds were manageable. The head surgeon misread the extent of the stomach wound and delayed surgery for nearly an hour. He let him bleed to death.

It took me four hours to finish the report. Afterward, I felt nauseous and rubbery, as if I had taken a blow to the head. My mind raced with questions, bowels jerked and lost control. *Mark, why touch it now? Why take a chance when you really don't need to? There was a natural process back then that took its course, allowed you to carry on. Why upset all that? What if the man I find is not the man I imagine? What will that make him? What will that make me?*

I stayed up that night, my wife and child asleep, and questioned the wisdom of this project and what moved me toward it? I carried little animus for the men who shot my father. By my reckoning, they were mere instruments. My hatred, if that's what it was after so many years, was directed instead at the men who presumably engineered the murder, who met, debated and traded to end my father's life.

And yet I lacked the anger that nourished revenge. I was a healthy, relatively happy person. I no longer dwelled on their deaths. Time was a great, indiscriminate painkiller. All the while it inured me to sorrow—and I was thankful for that—it slowly, just perceptibly, swept away everything else: the sting of his hand; the heave of his voice; the warmth of his eyes.

I asked myself, was this a hunt for justice? Or was there something more base that stirred me? The murder and my fight with it had elevated my life, drawn attention to me, marked me different from the rest. My brother and sister would say the same. What we endured must not be profaned to satisfy some lust in me. It was not mine alone to do what I saw fit, not mine to turn into some peepshow.

○○○

The next morning I retraced the steps of detectives and broke down their investigation into categories of theories.

Their work was made difficult by a number of factors outside their control. For one, the prominence of the case meant that every hype and thief who needed to curry favor with the cops passed along some two-bit street rumor. The detectives hopped from one outlandish theory to the next. One theory had my mother and a lover in Lake Tahoe getting rid of their obstacle. Another had my father hiding thirty grand for a big drug dealer and never giving it back.

The *Fresno Bee*'s Secret Witness reward only multiplied the number of bogus tips. When the composite of one of the gunmen appeared in the *Bee*, readers deluged the paper and police with the names of hundreds of look-alikes:

Check out the orderly at my mother's nursing home, a guy named Christianson.

A repo man named Rogers is a dead ringer.

The gunman is my neighbor's son who likes to throw bricks through the window when he's high. If anything comes of this, please split the $2,000 between the Cancer Fund and the Heart Fund.

With only twenty murders a year, and most of those escalations of passion or drunkenness, the police department didn't need a separate homicide division. The detectives assigned to my father's murder had to juggle robberies, rapes and beatings throughout the year and a half they actively worked the case.

The report was replete with instances of sloppy and indolent police work. The first officer on the scene failed to accompany my father in the ambulance. My father's strength and mental acuity had apparently lulled the cop into believing that the wounds were not mortal. Even if my father had wanted to make a dying declaration, or had some idea of the men responsible, there wasn't a cop within earshot.

The first twenty-four hours are the most crucial in a murder investigation. That's when the evidence is fresh and untrampled and the killers vulnerable to errors of judgment and inconsistency. It is not uncommon in these first hours, especially with a big murder case in a small town, to canvass the city with teams of officers knocking on doors and questioning family, friends and suspects. Detectives investigating my father's murder talked only to the emergency room staff, Uncle Navo, bartender Linda Lewis and bar manager Mike Garvey in the first day. A full week elapsed before several of the more obvious suspects were even contacted to schedule interviews.

The report raises numerous plausible scenarios and names people close to my father as possible conspirators. So much of their behavior preceding and following the murder is bizarre and inexplicable. Whether these are the movements of accomplices or merely the movements of grotesques is not clear. Since the first shooter allowed my father to take his gun and return fire, the competency of the killers must be questioned. If they were pros, they barely got the job done.

The profile that emerges is a gullible Ara. He carries a soft spot for hard luck stories and is always slipping $50 or $100 to someone in a pinch. He writes letters to the county probation department attesting to the good character of a customer and offers jobs to a couple of guys right out of jail.

He has a vision of what people can be. If they play along, he helps them all he can. If they cross him, as it often happened, he reacts with great indignation and occasional violence.

The report mentions four such confrontations in the six months leading up to the murder:

• In the summer of 1971, Dad hired Van Keyes to book rock bands for The Forum. Keyes came from a well-to-do Fresno family with a history of drinking problems. In his mid-twenties, he was already battling the bottle. One Sunday Dad and Keyes and another man sat around our kitchen table discussing a local prep star who had chosen to play football for the University of Alabama rather than Fresno State. Dad suggested that the youth wasn't big enough for the pros and since he planned to return to Fresno anyway it might have been wiser to play at State and build local contacts. Keyes chuckled and pointed out an inconsistency in Dad's argument from a previous discussion.

Dad rose from the chair, did his lower-lip-biting routine and unloaded a backhand that knocked Keyes out of his chair: "No one calls me a liar in my house." Then he grabbed him by the hair and dragged him facedown across the cold Spanish tile out the back door. Keyes had no way home except on foot. I followed him outside and apologized as he teetered down the block, every few feet shedding another clump of stringy blond hair. "Your old man . . . he's fucking nuts."

• Five weeks before the murder, my father and mother took Uncle Navo, his future wife, Josette Romano, and Josette's parents out to dinner. During the meal Gary Prestidge, Fresno's number one pimp and bookie, walked up and introduced a date. A tipsy Josette whispered too loud, "I wonder if she's one of his whores." An offended Prestidge grabbed Uncle Navo by the tie and Josette's father took a swing at him and missed, fracturing Josette's cheek. Dad was able to free Uncle Navo by lifting Prestidge by the neck and shoving him facedown into a plate of lobster thermidor. Mom later told me that Prestidge, calm as could be, left without saying a word.

• Four weeks before the murder, Dad was told that a golf hustler and drug smuggler named Frank Nunez was badmouthing him around town.

Nunez was a friend of Dan Hornig, Dad's partner in The Forum. One of the comments got back to Dad and he pretended to laugh it off at first. Then, out of nowhere, he struck Nunez in the face.

• The final quarrel took place a week before the murder at The Apartments' front door. Frankie Photopoulos, a champion weight lifter and hype who had served time in San Quentin for armed robbery, walked past Dad with a sixteen-year-old girl on his arm.

"Frankie, we're facing a two-week shutdown for serving minors. I can't let your girlfriend in here."

"No one cares."

"I care. She has to leave."

Mike Garvey and another bartender pushed Photopoulos and his girlfriend back outside. He tried to shove Dad. Dad spat in his face.

"Next time Ara," Photopoulos growled, "I'm going to kill you."

Police pursued the theory that any one of these incidents could have escalated into murder. They didn't rule out robbery either, even though no money was taken. Among the motives was a possible falling out with Mike Garvey in The Apartments or with Hornig in The Forum. Both partnerships, like an earlier one with my mother's brother, George, were hidden from state authorities.

Police also speculated about a marijuana smuggling ring, one of the nation's largest, centered in Fresno. Several prominent citizens who frequented the bar were involved in moving the dope from Mexico to Fresno. Police speculated that my father may have helped finance the loads and was killed in a dispute over money. They also pursued the theory that Dad, loudly opposed to drugs, threatened to expose the involvement of patrons, employees or partners as a way to buy favor with law enforcement.

Of the big three motives (money, revenge, sex), sex was notably absent. The only mention of affairs of the heart was someone telling police that my father had almost left my mother several years back for a redhead named Carol, something I dimly recalled.

Finally, there was Linda Lewis's account of my father's actions before the gunmen arrived. It made me wonder if he had sensed death's approach.

First, Dad came out of the office and ordered a grapefruit juice. Then he reappeared a few minutes later asking for a shot of Canadian Club. He seemed agitated and complained about having to work on a Sunday evening. Sweat poured off his brow even though the bar was cold enough that Lewis wore a jacket. This must have been right before the shooting broke out, for the shot glass was found the next day on the desk, brimming whiskey.

o o o

I had secured an agent, a publishing house willing to underwrite my venture and a handshake deal from my editors at the *Times* that however long the book took me—two, three or four years—I would be welcomed back. The day I cleared out my desk, several colleagues came up to wish me well and confess their envy. Pete King, who sat across from me, knew better. He, too, had grown up in Fresno and we played in the same Babe Ruth League and attended the same high school. He graduated two years ahead of me and forever, it seemed, I played catch up.

He had talked about returning home one day and maybe buying a vineyard. The longer he was away, he confided, the more he grew to love and hate Fresno. Pete understood the town and he understood me. He knew I wouldn't be satisfied with anything less than solving the murder and naming the names in a book. This, he thought, was a mistake.

"Remember, Mark," he admonished. "This is not about solving a crime. It's about solving a life."

Pete had watched my father coach in the youth football league. He recalled that Dad was big-hearted but hard-nosed and he didn't take guff— traits that may have led to his murder, traits passed down to his son.

"You don't want your daughter growing up with the same bitterness, the same hard edge, as you did," he said. "You don't want her to ask, 'Why didn't my father learn the lesson passed down from his father?' "

"I'm not sure I can accept anything less on this story. I'm not sure I can ever let go without knowing all the answers."

"As maudlin as it sounds," he said, "I guess you have to have a long conversation with your old man. Ask him, 'What does it take to make it right by you?' If I understand what you're doing, this is about an Armenian family, the vineyards, hometown. I wouldn't judge success or failure on finding the killers."

I appreciated what Pete was telling me, but I couldn't help adding up all the neglected leads and forgotten questions of the official investigation and feeling confident about my chances of finding the missing evidence that would force police to reopen the case and bring the killers to justice. The more I read the file, the more convinced I became that my father's murder wasn't so much unsolved as it was uninvestigated.

As I said good-bye to Los Angeles and the newsroom that day, I was certain about one thing: The traditional journalistic detachment I had learned as a reporter would have to be set aside. To find my father's killers and at the same time protect myself, I couldn't be constrained by newsroom convention.

My first task was to hire a private investigator who once worked for the FBI to help me with the do's and don'ts of moving back to Fresno and living underground. First, he counseled, only the most trusted family and friends could know that we had moved back home and why. Everyone else would get a standard cover story I concocted: I had left the *Times* and was visiting Fresno to gather information for a book on Southeast Asian refugees who had settled by the tens of thousands in the San Joaquin Valley. While in town, I was looking up a few people who might tell me what kind of man my father was.

I had to be prepared to pose in different guises and talk in different voices, he said. I had to be willing to play law enforcement off the bad guys and the bad guys off law enforcement and secretly record both onto hidden cassettes.

"And make damn sure the recorder isn't the kind that beeps when the tape is finished," he said, laughing.

The other experts who counseled me those first weeks were less kind, each one pointing out the same shortcomings. You lack the immediacy of the crime. You lack the necessary detachment to draw painful judgments. Piecing together a murder, especially a murder-for-hire, is not the province of a journalist and certainly not the province of a son. And a seventeen-year-old unsolved murder falls to the domain of fools.

I was the first to admit that I knew practically nothing about the science of homicide investigation, and the only murders I had followed had been from a newspaperman's safe distance. But journalism does furnish a framework, I protested, a methodology to extract some approximation of the truth. At the very least, my interviewing skills equaled those of the detectives assigned to Dad's case. Sure they had the advantage of immediacy, but where did it get them? They frittered it away by waiting weeks and months to confront prime suspects.

I promised myself I would not go into this with preconceived notions. I would remain skeptical and distrust even my own theories. Think of every conceivable reason why it could not be so. "Others will tell you to try to prove you are right," the great chemist Pasteur had said. "I tell you to try to prove you are wrong." The truth of the murder, I told myself, will emerge a dozen different ways, from a dozen different angles. At the same time, I would operate from a base of assumptions:

1) My father's death was not a random event. He had placed himself, wittingly or unwittingly, in a position where someone wanted him dead.

2) The murder was somehow tied to his business. Follow the dollar.

3) Someone close to Dad, someone aware of his movements, betrayed him. This betrayer could be one of his business partners, Mike Garvey or Dan Hornig, bartender Linda Lewis or another employee or patron.

4) The murder was precipitated by a change in Dad's relationship with someone at the bar, either a partner, employee or patron.

5) The best evidence would be found in Dad's movements during the six months or so prior to the murder.

One of the first rules of investigative reporting was that you never busted down a door without first trying to find the key to unlock it. This meant postponing certain critical interviews until you learned all you could from other sources. You never knew what missing links could be found in court and business records, and it did little good to find these nuggets if you had already revealed yourself to your target. Only the stupid ones gave you a second unguarded shot.

I compiled an initial list of 150 sources and ranked them according to the danger posed. On the outside circle, what I called the "safe perimeter," I arrayed family members and close friends. The middle circles contained Fresno politicians, developers, cops, drug dealers, bookies, whores and madams. On the inside circles were the suspected gunmen and conspirators. By working my way slowly toward the center, I hoped to retain an element of surprise and diminish the chance that one source would contaminate another.

The passage of years, while a serious obstacle, could work in my favor. Someone close to Dad who seemed an unlikely suspect in 1972 might have revealed a criminal nature over time. And people bound by love or common cause at the time of the murder might have severed their relationships in the years since. My best hope rested with finding a former wife, girlfriend or associate who kept silent out of a love or loyalty long ago extinguished.

My investigative manner would be that of Ara's young son who knew next to nothing. I would talk in generalities and never betray a deeper knowledge no matter how far into the search. To keep myself in a subordinate role, I would address people as Mr. and Mrs. This wide-eyed innocence would be my sharpest tool.

I decided to begin right where the cops began—with Linda Lewis. She was the sole witness to the shooting, and the shooting is where I had to start, then work back.

Lewis had grown up on the beaches of Orange County and moved to Fresno in 1970 to be with a boyfriend who played in one of the bands. Dad hired her as a cocktail waitress and a year later began training her to tend bar. It was one of his wrinkles, to be the first nightclub owner in the San Joaquin Valley with female bartenders. Lewis had worked only a few Sunday shifts before the day of the shooting.

Nobody knew her whereabouts, and mention of her name stirred old suspicions. Why did the shooters spare Lewis? Why did she disappear shortly after the murder? Several sources had heard that she moved back to Orange County and died of a drug overdose.

With the help of a state investigator, I learned that she had used three different names and was well traveled, hopping from fleabag motel to halfway house in between arrests for drunken driving. I tracked her to one motel near Disneyland, only to discover that she had checked out six weeks earlier with no forwarding address. The Department of Motor Vehicles reported that her license had been suspended. As a last resort, I gave her social security number to the private investigator who once worked for the FBI. A few phone calls later he had found her.

"Well, she's alive and you shouldn't have a problem getting to her," he said. "She's at the James Musick Orange County Branch Jail. It's a minimum-security prison farm. Drunks, hypes and thieves. She's been there for several months but due for release any day."

I arrived at the jail farm early the next morning and a guard led me to an interview room where the female prisoners were marched in, single file.

Linda Lewis looked nothing like the beauty I envisioned. She was tall and stout, hair speckled gray, ratted too many times. Surveying me, her one visitor, her hazel eyes registered confusion. The guard had neglected to tell her my last name.

"Oh my God . . . you're Markie?" She reached over and hugged me. "Wow . . . freaky."

She started to cry and I apologized.

"You do look like him . . . it's been so long."

"It's been seventeen years."

I launched into a lengthy explanation of why I was there, but it was hardly necessary. "You came," she interrupted, "because I was the one who saw it." Yes, I nodded. She recalled that it was a dreary day with few customers. My father had come in to prepare the quarterly report for the bookkeeper. It was unusual for him to be there early Sunday evening, she said, and he was complaining about "taxes, taxes." She remembered it being so cold inside that she had to wear a coat. She remembered that my father was sweating.

"It was a dead day. Dead. And then these two white guys came in and ordered a couple beers. They had gloves on."

"Had you ever seen them before?"

"No, never. In fact, it didn't look like they were from Fresno the way they dressed. But that doesn't mean anything. They went back and played a game or two of pool. Your dad was sitting in the office with the door opened and if he bothered to look up he had to see them. They definitely saw him. They came back out, set their drinks on the bar and left."

She said they weren't gone long, maybe ten or fifteen minutes, before they returned. The bar was empty and she asked if they wanted another beer. One of them stopped and replied "Yeah," while the other walked straight to the office and started shooting. It was the same account she had given police the night of the murder, right down to the time frame and some of the phrasing. I had expected to find a memory dulled by years of drinking and hard drugs. Not only was her memory near-perfect but she was obviously bright, something I wasn't prepared for in one of the bar's employees. She told me she read some 200 mystery books a year, a compulsion passed down from her mother, a librarian. She had worked her way through too many murder plots to know that this wasn't robbery but a hit, albeit an amateur hit. She heard no demand for money or words exchanged. Before she knew it, my father had backed the first gunman out of the office and into the hallway, in full view.

"This guy is walking backwards. He's shooting your dad and your dad is saying, 'Why? What are you doing?' Your father had his hands out like this, his palms skyward. 'Why? Why?' He just was amazed. These guys were kids, twenty-three or twenty-four. I guess the first guy ran out of bullets. That's when the other guy holding a gun on me starts yelling, 'Kill the motherfucker! Kill the motherfucker!' And your dad kept coming forward. 'Why? Why? Why?' Then the second guy starts shooting Ara."

Much of this was familiar, too, but to hear it from Linda's own mouth and to see how it anguished her, the memory fresh and resonant, filled some recess deep inside me. I couldn't get enough. Linda was shivering, not sure she could go on. Why not a better time, Markie? A better place? I'm out of this joint in two weeks. Let's do it then. I forged ahead, pretending not to hear.

She said she dove under the bar and hid. If she hadn't, she said by way of apology, they would have killed her, too. She waited until it was quiet and then she ran over to check on my father. He was trying to get up.

"I said, 'Why Ara? Why?' He said, 'I don't know. I don't know.' I said, 'Ara, who were those guys?' He said, 'I don't know. I never saw them before.' He had no idea. I had no idea. It happened so quick, Mark. So quick. He was talking with all these bullets in him. He was up on his knees. He really wanted to get up. He really wanted to think he was going to be okay."

Five bullet wounds, I thought, not enough to steal his optimism. He grabbed a barstool and tried to pull himself up. The barstool fell over on its side and he tried another.

"I said, 'Ara, just let go of the stool. Sit, sit. Relax. I'm going to call somebody.' I could see he had a good one in the stomach. He kept saying, 'I'm going to be all right, Linda. I'm going to be all right.' At the end, just before the ambulance came, he told me he was going to die."

The police, she said, insisted it was a robbery and that angered her. "Every single penny was in that register and they're telling me it was a robbery. I never heard a word from those two about money. They were there to kill him."

"You never heard that Dad was involved in drugs?"

"No, I never heard that. The only thing I ever thought was that maybe your father had money where he shouldn't of had money. If someone came to your dad with a proposition that he could double his money, I could see him maybe putting money into something to get money out. My way of thinking, nobody would have put it to your dad that it was for drugs. They would have put it another way."

A drug deal that wasn't a drug deal? It sounded too wishy-washy. My father may have been eager to believe the best about people. He might have been naïve and erratic, but he was no dummy. As for the love of money driving him to do wrong, the notion would have made my mother shriek. "What? Your father was a social service agency onto himself." If he did take a short cut, I reasoned, if he did get involved in a deal that ran counter to his stated hatred of drugs, it wasn't greed but desperation. He would have to be facing financial ruin to take such a step. Nothing short of. And Linda Lewis was too far removed from him to have known anything about that.

"Those were some crazy, sweet times, Mark. I miss them. But I don't know if I'd want to relive them. I wished Ara had lived. All of our lives might have been different. Who knows."

She said she even recalled the song that was playing on the jukebox that day. Then she began to sing it, pauses and all.

"'Bye, bye, Miss American Pie. Drove my Chevy to the levee but the levee was dry. Them good old boys were drinking whiskey and rye, singing this will be the day that I die.' Don McLean wasn't one of my favorites. But for some reason, all that day, I kept playing that song."

Our time was up. I promised to visit again as soon as she was freed. On the way out I was stopped by a guard who wanted to know why she had broken down. Had I delivered sad news about a family member? Should she be placed on a suicide watch? "No. We're just old friends who haven't seen each other in a long time." I turned to wave good-bye, but Linda couldn't see me. She sat slumped on a chair in the corner, head cradled in hands, sobbing again.

I walked away feeling confident that Linda Lewis had no role in the murder except as terrified eyewitness. They were there to kill my father and why Linda's life was spared—because she happened to duck under the bar at the right time, because my father's tenacity complicated things—was not a question I needed to consider anymore.

On the way home, though, I played the tape once, twice, making sure there wasn't a pause or stutter that might indicate she was hiding something. I tried to blot out the sorry image of my father walking toward his killers, outstretched hands, each step forward met by another shot, each shot eliciting another soft plea. "Why me? Why are you doing this to me?" I pounded the steering wheel and cursed myself for going about it all wrong. Here I was preparing to write a book, vowing not to cross the line, assuring everyone who had a stake in it—wife, sister, brother—that all the ugly business of vengeance was behind me. I'm not stalking killers, I told them. I'm seeking the truth . . . what bullshit. What absolute bullshit. I was whoring after abstractions and these bastards had killed my father. My God, he had been butchered!

That night I dreamed my cousin Michael and I were poring over the murder file when he came across a series of black and white photographs taken before and after the shooting. They were arrayed on a single proof sheet. The first showed Dad in the back billiard room sitting on a stool, cigarette in hand. Beside him were two Armenian priests, bearded and bald, tied together and slumped dead like so many photos of the Armenian massacres. My father sat pensively and waited his turn. The second photo was a close up of Dad's frightened face and inside the eyes I could see the reflection of his killers, mocking him. The last photo again showed only Dad, face blasted away, propped up against the office door. None of this was even faintly true. Not even the cigarette, which he had given up years before. But there he was, alive and dead again, this time an innocent, someone's scapegoat, a new generation's martyr.

○○○

I called Pop and Grandma and the rest of the family to tell them the good news: We had sold our Pasadena home and I was beginning a book on Southeast Asians that would put me in Fresno for long stretches. Grandma was especially happy. "I've missed you so much, Marcus Aurelius. Have you told your uncle yet?"

Four years earlier, after burying my mother, Uncle Navo and I sat alone in the back bedroom, and he fought to keep back tears. "Flora was like a sister to me. I've never known anyone who got dealt a more rotten hand." He gave me his leather jacket, told me to stay in touch, and if I ever needed anything, just ask. We talked maybe two or three times in the years since and this pained my grandmother, the idea that her first-born son and first-born grandson, her two favorites, were lukewarm to each other.

That day, preparing to move my wife and two-year-old daughter back to Fresno to renew my search, I gave in and called my uncle at his property management company. He sounded happy to hear from me and we chatted for a few minutes, small talk about the San Francisco 49ers and the four Super Bowls my father, a long suffering fan, had missed.

"It's hard to believe he never got a chance to see Joe Montana," he said.

"One of these days," I said, "I'd like to sit down and talk about him, if you wouldn't mind." There was a small pause and I knew what would come next. Through the highs and lows of our relationship, the one constant was his advice that I should put the matter behind me.

"Mark, it's going to destroy you. It almost destroyed me. I carried around all kinds of things for years. You have to know that you may never find what you're looking for."

"Maybe I'm just looking for him."

"You may not find that either. I loved him and he was my brother but he was a complicated son of a bitch. He could be so gentle coaching those kids during the day and then at night he surrounded himself with all those fucking assholes, filthy, loud music. I made a statement to Pa. I said it in Armenian. I said, 'Pa, Ara better be careful of the company he keeps because if he doesn't watch out, he's going to get shot.' I said this not six months before your dad was killed."

"I'd like to come back. Clear his name."

"What name? I don't think your dad has a bad name among the people that count. And most of the others don't even remember. I mean some people even call me Ara. They've forgotten, Mark."

Murder heeds no clock, I assured him, a crime without statutory limit. Even though the detectives had retired and no one in the Fresno Police Department had touched the file for more than a decade, it was hardly forgotten. Our murder had become a part of Fresno folklore.

"Ara Arax? Oh yeah," one police lieutenant told my friend at the *Bee*. "One of the most sensational murders in this town. I'd hate to think where the answer leads."

Part Two

T h e T o w n

In all the years I lived there, protected from the outside world, I never took measure of Fresno. I didn't question how the crops got picked, the feudal arrangement between grower and migrant. I saw duster planes swoop low over country roads but never stopped to wonder what was being dumped on the cotton and alfalfa below. Irrigation canals latticed the city but like the railroad tracks that could stop you three times in the same crosstown trip, they blended into the landscape. Even when a child or two drowned, a tragedy that marked each summer, no one bothered to question why the canals were unfenced and completely accessible. I did watch in awe whenever Cesar Chávez and his campesinos trudged through town, noise and fury, raised fists and raised Aztec eagle flag. "Viva La Causa! Viva La Raza!" But I felt no stirrings. It was just another parade to me. Maybe it was asking too much of a kid surrounded by wide sky and brightness, awakened only to possibility, to discern the darker chambers of his landscape. And yet even later, as a big-city journalist home to visit and then to care for Mom, I failed to comprehend Fresno—the imported water that made a few men rich, the four out of every ten children who lived in poverty. I'm not sure if this complacency was me or a function of Fresno, its detached geography, its narrow people, its familiar face. I just know that my eye got blurry the closer I got to home.

Oh, how I ached to return there. My wife once remarked that I never connected to the places we were living because I was too busy contriving a way to get back. When I finally made it back, it seemed so long ago and naïve, this pining for Fresno, the joy I felt as the perfect geometry of its fields came into focus from the air. For almost nothing of my Fresno remained. Not the town I remembered. Not the history I took as faith.

When my grandfather arrived here in 1920, the Sierra snow melt flooded riparian stands of cottonwood, oak and willow and transformed the lowest land into marsh teeming with honkers, gray and Canadian geese, tule elk and antelope. He could hear salmon splashing in the San Joaquin River at night. The higher ground, staked out by the farmer, bubbled with artesian wells. This well water came from an underground lake, replenished with each spring melt and critical to our survival because the valley qualified as desert, not even ten inches of rain a year. Along some rows in Grandpa's first vineyard, the water table brimmed so high that no irrigation was needed. The vines actually fed themselves.

By the time word reached the old country, it was an exultation. *Grapes like jade goose eggs! Watermelons as big as boats!* Another wave of Swedes, Danes, Russians, Japanese, Armenians, Slavs, Dust Bowl Okies, Arkies and a special breed of Germans from the Volga in Russia came to work the land.

The overtaxed water table plummeted hundreds of feet, the ground itself sinking as a consequence. The Bureau of Reclamation, summoned by panicky boosters, took one look at the disparity between rain-drenched northern California and arid central and southern and dubbed the problem "misplaced rain." In an extraordinary feat of engineering played out over four decades, the bureau constructed a labryinth of dams, reservoirs, canals and pumping stations that harnessed every river flowing out of the Sierra. They moved the rain.

Like so much else, this plumbing job was unremarkable to me, and I grew up believing the San Joaquin Valley was safe from change, that the mountains acted as great walls. For a half century, the Tehachapis to the south had served as California's Mason-Dixon line, separating the sprawl of Los Angeles from the fruit and cotton fields of the valley. It was one thing to be born on our side of the mountain, I thought, to not have a choice. But who would actually move to this place where it took the August sun just eighteen days to blister a grape into a raisin?

By the time Coby and I returned home after almost a decade away, demographers were calling the San Joaquin Valley the most profoundly changed landscape in America. Every fourth resident was a newcomer. What had appeared benignly to me on visits home during the 1980s—a minimall here, a faux Mediterranean housing tract there—was actually Los Angeles marching up and over the mountain.

Even the municipal water district—LA's guzzling Hydra—had crossed the divide, dangling its huge treasury to entice farmers to fallow their land and sell their water to a Southern California still hell-bent on expansion.

Sadly, the land being gobbled up wasn't the alkaline scrub on the valley's vast west side. Rather, it was fine loam along Highway 99, almost twenty square miles of it vanishing each year. That the near future promised one long suburban blur seemed ungodly to me. The San Joaquin and Sacramento valleys, two contiguous farm belts that form the Great Central Valley, stretch like a trough more than 450 miles long and 60 miles wide.

It is a land without equal in the breadth of its bounty, the richest farm belt in the world. There are cattle spreads and fruit orchards and vegetable gardens where acreage is counted in the tens of thousands. The biggest farmer in the world, cotton king J. G. Boswell, is here. So are Dole and SunWorld and Gallo.

These are not the bucolic farms of the Midwest. The land is too flat, vistas too few, to appreciate its actual lushness. Instead, the image is roadside—corrugated metal sheds, rusty tractors, raisin trays, old tires, tumbleweeds, dry grass, spent oleanders, railroad tracks, packing houses. Here, they coined the word "agribusiness."

The big growers prided themselves as rugged individualists, the hardy stock who made the desert bloom and had no use for Washington's hand. In truth, there was little that was rugged or individualistic about it. The zip code in fancy northwest Fresno where I grew up—far from the cotton fields—was home to more wealthy farmers collecting federal crop subsidy checks than any other zip code in America. And that didn't count the cheap irrigation water that Uncle Sam also furnished as a kind of endowment in perpetuity.

The land has paid a heavy price for this munificence. The San Joaquin River, once plied by passenger boats, is now a ghost. Dammed two dozen times in its upper reaches, 98 percent of its flow has been diverted to distant farms. The leftover trickle is nothing more than a public sewer, a drain for farming and municipal waste. What ground isn't set aside for gravel mining in the old river bottom has been given over to golf courses.

FRESNO, FASTEST GROWING BIG CITY IN THE COUNTRY, the headlines shouted. 400,000 AND COUNTING. And my wife, daughter and I were part of the great migration, moving into an apartment complex north of town called Heron Pointe. It had been built a few years earlier on what the manager called "reclaimed" fig orchard land, and each morning the air filled with the din and dust of huge tractors leveling the thick, gnarled trunks of the implacable tree. An entire orchard vanquished in two days.

The whole town seemed delirious, a frenzy of uprooting and building. The Fresno of my youth had been a quiet place, save for crickets' rasp. This Fresno was filled with the hum of deal making and the whir of circular saws, an incessant noise that seemed to come from nowhere and everywhere, just like the crickets.

I imagined a great beast unleashed. It paid no heed to the fact that Fresno had the nation's third-worst air and a topography far worse than Los Angeles for smog. It didn't concern itself with a lack of water, or residents in new tracts complaining that they couldn't even summon enough pressure to rinse the shampoo from their hair. It was oblivious to everything but appetite.

Naturally, there was a long, sordid history and it could be glimpsed in the way Fresno sprouted from a railroad stop in the 1870s. Downtown had been built in a grid that logically followed the northwesterly direction of the railroad. Then the boomers who controlled the land north figured out that they could squeeze more profits by subdividing their property in a different pattern. So Fresno literally changed course midstream, its downtown forever in discord with the rest of the city.

In the mad dash north, the city now sprawled 100 square miles to the river bottom itself, a monotonous, treeless, asphalt torpor. In a gesture of surrender, the bureaucrats at city hall changed their name. They were no longer the Planning Department, something to be scorned, but now the Development Department, a perfect template to the city's bullishness.

The local paper didn't think it necessary to assign a reporter to cover growth and planning—the biggest story in town. So Fresnans were never told that their elected officials were selling votes to a dozen developers for laundered campaign contributions and a surcharge passed in envelopes at the golf course. The old mayor and a major developer were inseparable all the while the mayor voted on zoning changes that made the developer millions. The developer had given the mayor's wife a two-bit job answering phones. When the mayor's daughter got married, the developer sprang for her wedding dress.

While other cities were charging hefty fees for new parks and libraries, sewer lines, major streets and even water cleanup, Fresno was failing to collect tens of millions of dollars from developers.

"Fresno is like the ugly girl who never gets invited to the prom," a local attorney explained to me over lunch. "When she's finally asked, she's willing to do just about anything."

Some hubris from the boomers could be excused—comeuppance for all those years of Johnny Carson jokes and travel guides that jilted Fresno. "Almost classic in its ugliness," one stated. The town had never quite gotten over one survey that ranked Fresno number 277 among U.S. cities, dead last.

The math of all this sprawl was simple. Fresno was replacing farmland that produced something real and brought in hard cash with a minimall and cheap housing economy that exchanged only soft dollars. The unemployment rate still hovered at 15 percent, and the sprawl didn't even generate enough taxes to pay for itself. Like a giant Ponzi scheme, each new subdivision had to subsidize the losing subdivision before it. Fresno was growing itself right into bankruptcy.

That first spring home, the orchards bursting pink and white and the vineyards translucent green, I went looking for familiar landmarks, only to be disappointed. Downtown had been practically abandoned. The dozen or so buildings that made up its meager skyline were either boarded up, padlocked or three-quarters empty. The fancy hotel where my parents held their wedding reception was a roost for pigeons and winos. So was the shoe store where we shopped, and the clothier.

I drove the breadth of the new north end, its population swollen by white flight, and glimpsed not a black, Latino or Asian face, in a city that was 51 percent black, Latino and Asian. My father, I reckoned, wouldn't know this place. Only in the distance beyond the new tracts was the sky still wide, if not blue, and the empty space as flat and far ranging as he would remember.

If Fresno had taken on the lineaments of a big city, it remained, in its true heart, a backwater of aching conservatism and hatred, a truck driver's town. My own people, the Armenians, had triumphed over a history of blackball here only to become someone else's oppressor. The slumlord who warehoused Hmong refugees from Laos was the son of an Armenian refugee. So was the town's biggest developer, the man most responsible for perverting the plan for orderly growth.

I once listened to Los Angeles natives not yet fifty years old recall the Southern California of their youth—orange and lemon and avocado groves—and thought how quickly it had happened and yet how carping they sounded. I had been away from Fresno not even a decade and now I too was a churlish old-timer.

Every time I tried to find the bright side, it seemed, I found another study that ranked Fresno the worst in this and the worst in that. The arson capital of America. The auto theft capital of the West. One study deemed the city the nation's skinflint, rock bottom when it came to giving to charity. The same city in which the Fresno State boosters club, for five years running, collected more millions than any other similar organization in the country. More than USC or Notre Dame or Nebraska.

The growth boom had managed to exaggerate the space between rich and poor so that Fresno and the entire San Joaquin Valley resembled some banana republic with its potentates and peasants. As a kind of game, I challenged friends to come up with another city or region where such incredible wealth was concentrated in the hands of so few farmers and developers, while every fourth person collected a welfare check.

My wife likened me to a tent show revivalist who night after night drew the same audience of deaf mutes but delivered his burning refrain just the same. It wasn't always easy suffering the evangelist come home. My outrage seemed outdated, if not cheap, and I didn't always pick my spots well. At a fancy restaurant, I cornered and nagged a childhood friend and she stared back as if it were the law of gravitation I was defying. "Growth is good. Growth is inevitable," she snapped. "And if it gets as bad as you're saying, we'll just move somewhere else."

Strange as it sounds, I counted on the town's growth to protect me. My presence, I figured, would hardly make a splash. In this Fresno, there were places to hide. As extra precaution, I improved on the advice of the ex-FBI man, took it one step further. We would live underground, I decided, for however long it took to finish the book, and I'd keep my day-to-day movements a secret from even family and friends, as much for their protection as mine.

We moved into Heron Pointe under an assumed name, Norris. I checked the list of tenants on the outside gate to make sure no name was familiar. I loaded the .38 with special flesh-shredding bullets that flowered on impact. We conducted all our affairs in cash. Credit cards were forbidden, purchases easily traced by a private detective. Mail from Pasadena was forwarded to my in-law's house. All new mail under our alias came to the apartment.

Coby thought the whole notion silly, the idea that I could live underground back home and confront people from my father's past and not expect them to talk, to compare their own notes. "Who do you think you're fooling?" she asked.

I dismissed her logic, accused her of crumbling to pressure before the project even began. I would confront former cops and prosecutors and bar employees and patrons, and if they suspected something more than a son wanting to know his father, I'd use my earnestness to turn them into friendly conspirators in my search.

What I didn't figure on, at least not sufficiently, was that my father's murder still echoed loudly two decades later, and it echoed with Rich, the man who lived in the apartment next to us.

I had told him that I was a writer from Los Angeles working on a book about Hmong refugees from the highlands of Laos. Mark Norris. For reasons of verisimilitude. He began cornering me in the garage on nights I worked out with the weights. He said he was making big money selling safety devices for trucks but he wasn't satisfied. He wanted out of Fresno.

"I should have never come back to this frigging town. I can't figure out how these frigging people have been able to operate for so long."

"What do you mean?" I asked.

"I mean dope and gambling. It's wide open."

He told me to go back to the newspaper files and pull the names of three unsolved murders. "Look up the Arax murder in the 1970s," he said. "It involved the same stuff."

I stood there speechless, trying my best not to show it. Here I was, a few weeks home, hiding my whereabouts from family and friends and my identity from neighbors, and the man next door is telling me to look up the Arax murder. For a second I wondered if I had given myself away. I pressed on, figuring I had just tripped over the first coincidence.

"What happened to Arax?" I asked, trying to sound nonchalant.

"All this dope was being flown here from Mexico by the Lambes and Simones, two Italian fig ranchers. When they were busted, these politicians and bigwigs who used to gamble and screw whores at the Italian Dante Club came to their defense. They got off real light. Arax had a bar where the Lambes and Simones hung out. He was involved, probably didn't pay some debt and was murdered."

I wanted so badly to say something. *You SOB! You don't know the first thing about Ara Arax. He was my father. I'm his oldest son.* It took all the restraint I could muster to muzzle myself. If I was going to pull this off, I had to remember that there were a hundred Riches out there, little guys on the bent fringe who squirreled away the stories but knew nothing really. And as much as I detested his cold logic, in one way he was only stating casually what I already believed: My father's death did not come by way of gratuitous shooting. Someone wanted him, needed him dead.

I tried to stall Grandpa Arax's slow slide into senility with the same omnipresence I brought to bear on my mother's cancer. His daughter, Jeanette, was the first to notice his decline. She had accompanied him to Armenia six years earlier to dedicate a shrine to Saroyan and found him that first night about to urinate in the hotel closet. The next day he gave a speech that was excessive even by Soviet standards. Jeanette chalked it up to jet lag and blindness, but there were more slips.

He could no longer hunt and peck on his typewriter and wondered if a tape recorder might do for one last stab at an epic poem about early Fresno. I bought him a nice compact Sony but he kept pushing the wrong buttons. Frustrated, he just let the tape run end to end, one free flowing verse of shower arias and socialist rant and love songs to Daisy the dog.

I took him everywhere with me. Driving to Modesto to visit a reporter who had come across a State Department of Justice report on Dad's murder, we got on the subject of a poet's muse and he told me about a woman whose urgings and scoldings were the reason he took up writing again in the 1960s, after decades of silence.

"I have loved this woman for twenty-five years," he said calmly, an admission that could not have found a more eager and willing audience.

I tried to strike a note of indifference but my voice revealed me. "Love?"

"Maybe it was Platonic inspiration. Maybe indebtedness. She was the one who told me, 'Aram, you are spending all your time in the coffee houses playing pinochle. You must write everyday. Everyday a poem.'

"She has all my poems. In case you want my writings after I die. . . . Maybe we will visit her one day."

The next day I helped him into the car and we said good-bye to Grandma under pretenses now forgotten. He had the map of Fresno memorized and called out the streets in a bouncy, giddy voice.

"You know, Mark, I haven't bought her anything for four or five years. Maybe that's why she's angry with me."

He made me stop at a drugstore where he picked out a box of Whitman's chocolates, the nutty kind because she detested the soft ones. His pace quickened, and I began to feel a little funny about the whole thing. He explained that she had four sisters who were killed along with their father and mother in the massacres. She came to America an orphan. Her husband, a tyrant, died when she was fifty-seven and she has lived alone ever since.

Her name is Mushkanetz in Turkish and Shahd Naz in Armenian. It means much/little, the ambivalence that was their relationship. Friends call her Mary but he called her Mush. Grandma called her the woman with the flesh hanging from her arms.

Mary greeted us at the front steps and took us around to the back, pointing to a spot where Grandpa planted a row of camelias that died in a frost many years ago. She was a big-boned woman, all around sturdy, thick hands, ankles and feet. She had pretty blue eyes and a pleasant face painted in red lipstick and rouge. Her hair was dyed dark brown, eyebrows a shade lighter.

Grandpa and I sat down on the couch. Mary hurried into the kitchen and came out with a tray of walnuts, almonds, raisins and 7-Up.

"Come sit by me," he said sweetly. "I want to see your face."

She pretended not to hear him and took a seat across the room.

"I don't like it," she gestured to his beard. "I don't like it at all."

"How about a rendezvous in Armenia?" He was playing with her and she played back, a little nasty.

"What comrades do you have anymore?" she asked, knowing full well that all but two of them had died. "Assadurian in Pasadena maybe?"

"Assadurian died last week. Heart attack."

"You had someone else in Pasadena? Varich? Varich die, too?"

"No, he's still alive."

She wanted him to know that however bad he had it, she had it worse. "You've got people over all the time, Aram. You've got Alma."

"She likes to talk too much. Her ears are fine but they don't hear too well."

There was silence. This small talk did not please him. He gestured as if leaving.

"Why are you going?"

"Because you don't like me anymore. . . . What do I have to do over here, America," he said. "Mark is over here. I enjoy it. You're here. I enjoy that. But what else? That is my country. I have been back seven times and it is not enough."

She scowled and began to court me: "He goes with the big shots in Armenia. He goes to operas and dinner meetings. But my relatives back there say life is very hard. Aram comes back here and says there is no place like Armenia. I see another Armenia."

"So many loves without body," he muttered twice.

She scolded him, gently at first. "You went to Armenia seven times and there is not a book still! You go there, you come together and drink and talk. You never wrote your book!"

"What is it good for if I am the only one who reads it?"

"It has to come into the world, generation to generation. The book is never lost. You were lazy about your work. You promised me you were going to write a book. What happened, Aram?"

She excused herself and brought out two grocery bags filled with his letters, cards and poems kept in a closet for twenty years. There was a tacky card with a young couple naked in soft focus and the words, "The Pleasures of Love."

She grabbed a poem and held it up as exhibit. "I am the reason Aram is famous. Before he met me, he was living in the Armenian coffee houses, gambling his life away. I told him to stop frequenting. 'This is the beginning of your new life.' I made him the writer. He became famous and I became the talk of the Armenian community. He was famous. I was gossip."

Pop didn't know what to say. "Yes, she was my inspiration. I can admit that. But she was an orphan and she had the martyrs' syndrome. She could not live with my love. So our relationship became this."

She couldn't turn him away, she said. There was always something. She began to count the somethings. "His mother's death. Ara-boy's death. His sicknesses. How could I close the door? I pitied him. He was at the back door, tears falling on the ground. 'My Ara-boy.'"

I waited for Pop to interrupt, to say that she was exaggerating her importance in his life, that he was too proud for pity. He said nothing.

She went on, telling the story of a rich Armenian in Los Angeles who wanted to marry her and she was about to say yes until he invited her to dinner. "His eating impressed me so badly. When I saw the difference between your grandfather and him, I said, 'I can't live with that millionaire one minute.'"

"Money is the main thing for her. Why? I don't know. Being an orphan or something. She never said don't come to this house. She cried with me several days. She loved Ara so much."

She sat beside him now, the poems spread out before her, and began to read them out loud, sunlight through the kitchen window dancing across their faces. They were eye-to-eye for the first time, no more nasty jabs and scoring points through me, and suddenly I felt like an interloper. He smiled and showed teeth, cheeks tightened, pink with blood.

"Twenty years of my life," she said. "Not knowing what to do. It was difficult but it was not tragic. He is my *ungar* now. My comrade. Nothing more."

"Mark, on summer nights I came here and we sit out late on the porch. I tried to kiss her. I kissed her. She said, 'No, please Aram. The moon will see it.'"

"I was scared, Aram. I worried. All the time someone going to see us."

"We did the right thing," he said.

"Everybody start to talk. I feel shamed."

"Careless you asked? I don't feel guilty. I feel proud that I loved you. If you didn't feel proud, that's your business."

"I didn't feel free. You think too much free. I'm not your type, Aram. I'm still old-country type. Don't put my name in people's mouth . . ."

She lifted the poem to her nose and sniffed the years.

"Markie, I wrote him letter from San Francisco. I sent it to the bar. I told him when he reads it, tear it and throw it away. He kept it in the office desk and she found it. Your grandma couldn't share literary love. So I wrote him this letter encouraging him to write and she found it."

"I couldn't tear it," he said. "She found it."

"Your grandmother spoiled my name. What can I do now? It's too late. My character went down. Still today people talk about me. . . . Your grandfather is too much free-minded."

"I am not the slave of those bastards. I don't care what they think. There is nothing wrong. There is nothing right in this world. If I love you and you love me, forget everyone else. Forget the world."

"When I love, I want free love. Love that I'm not scared. I want to live with the man I love. I don't want to live with closed windows. Behind shades. Knock on the door and he runs in the closet. I couldn't live with you. I want real love, not dreaming love. Do you know how many men I returned because of him, Markie? It's too late. The damage to my character is done."

There was silence again. It was time to go.

"Can I visit you sometime?" he asked.

"No. Just when Markie's here."

We got up to leave and he leaned over to kiss her. She turned away, offering her sturdy hand. In the car, back home to Grandma, I asked if he was all right.

"She's practically dead anyhow. She smells like hell. Like all those old women. I am alive. But I am dead every way else, too. Sometimes I feel like I'm living in a desert. I don't mean the weather, Mark. There is nothing to satisfy me. There is nothing left for me here."

Late that afternoon, while Pop napped and Grandma busied herself in the kitchen, I rummaged through the contents of those two grocery bags now entrusted to me. There were poems and fragments of poems and what appeared to be the outline of a two-act play written on scraps of paper and Ara's Apartments cocktail napkins. Much of it was indecipherable, penned in Armenian. One poem, half completed, leaped out from the rest. It was titled "Green Stem Broken," composed in English in his meticulous arabesque. As I read it a second time, I began to wonder what my grandfather had known once and forgotten to tell me.

> January second, 1972
> At the doorsteps of the New Year
> Two criminals, insidious,
> Kill my 40-year-old Ara
> Be a father and endure this
> Be a mother and endure this
> I never want my enemy to have such evil misfortune
> The heart and the beloved
> The loss of a son
> Innocent offspring
> What do I say?
> How can I look into your eyes when I see the protest
> Against the killers of this society?
> Against drug dealers
> Do not kill, my beloved offspring
> Do not seek vengeance
> This is the will of my sunset

My wife went along with most of my contrivances aimed at securing ourselves in Fresno, humoring me until I began taking sudden turns onto side roads whenever a car seemed to be trailing us for too long. I was Uncle Harry all over again, only in reverse— the "good guy" on the run. Coby tried to get me to see the folly of thinking that my small evasions would confound anyone with half a brain. Sure, Fresno had doubled, but at the core it remained a suffocatingly small place with a few resounding murders, my father's high among them. If nothing else, the fluky encounter with Rich, the stranger next door who spouted off about "the Arax murder," proved that some crimes enter a realm of legend, and legends die hard.

"If the right people want to find you," she said assuredly, "they'll find you."

This was ground I believed we had covered thoroughly, and it annoyed me to have to go over it again. My goal, I explained, was to delay the inevitable discovery of why I had come back to town, to proceed in a manner that reserved some element of surprise until it came time to confront the men responsible. Don't give these guys too much credit. They have their own lives, their own unresolved problems. By the time the old Apartments crowd got to buzzing, if ever, the book would be out, names and all, and the killers would be stupid to attempt to find and harm us. They'd only be pointing a finger at themselves, confirmation of evil deeds two decades apart.

Coby could have responded that the criminal mind was more elusive than that, but I didn't give her a chance. I proudly trotted out my chart, the elaborate one filled with names and circles, and recited the precautions I would take to keep one source from tipping off the other.

"If being circumspect means taking six months to accomplish what another disinterested journalist could finish in one month, so be it," I told her. "The peace of mind alone is worth it."

Coby said nothing but she might as well have laughed in my face, so precise and wounding was her facial gesture: If you want to delude yourself, go ahead, but don't expect me to be an adherent to your silly faith.

It was a week or so later, in the early summer of 1989, that I found myself talking again to neighbor Rich, this time near the gated entrance of our apartment complex.

He was telling me about his young girlfriend, a stunning redhead who graduated with honors from Berkeley and did some work for the FBI and CIA, when our attention was deflected to a shiny black Corvette, top down. The security guard nodded knowingly at the driver, a corpulent and haughty man, peroxide wings flowing from bald crown, sun shimmering off bad-dude sunglasses. I immediately recognized the sunburned face as that belonging to a suspect in my father's murder. The old rumor was that my father was holding thirty grand for this guy while he was on the run from a drug charge. Dad snitched off the guy's whereabouts in hopes of keeping the money and the guy had him killed from prison.

Rich, who still knew me as Mark Norris, said the man, an unrepentent gangster now sixty years old, resided a few pods down from us with his girlfriend, who was also quite familiar to me. Both had taken the precaution, like I had, to register under an alias. A few weeks later, I learned that another man rumored to be a key suspect had moved back to town after a decade in prison for a series of drug crimes.

I couldn't wipe the image of these men floating free in Fresno from my mind. Big men behind sunglasses began to haunt my dreams again, only they looked different from the ones who visited me as a child. These dreams accommodated the physiognomy I imagined these men had taken on over two decades—the packed-on flesh and double chins and hair wraps. I dreamed they found me and my gun malfunctioned, super bullets dribbling out. They laughed at me, at the feebleness of my weapon. I dreamed a different outcome to my search each night. One night I dreamed my father was a good man caught in an impossible situation; the next night that he was a participant in something illicit that fell back on him. Then I dreamed what maybe I dreaded most, that I could neither damn nor vindicate him, that it was some weak messy truth in between.

I was trying to put my hands on another image the day I returned to our old neighborhood in northwest Fresno, whose quiet and fastidious streets, once a sedative to our noisy lives, I had avoided since my mother's death. It was here, not far from the bluffs of the river, that my father chose to build a custom Spanish-style house in 1968. The way he softened up Ethel Wertheimer, the sullen doctor's widow who lived next door, was a piece of work to behold. He dismissed most of the other neighbors as stuffed shirts not worthy of his ministrations, calling them "plastic fantastics" after a song by the Jefferson Airplane. Only the Stephan family down the block and Burr and Ginger Frye across the street did he regard as real people.

The Fryes, third-generation cotton merchants, grew up in Memphis and New Orleans and boasted that the family tree took in Andrew Jackson, the last chief of the Cherokee Nation and the last Confederate general to surrender. They were southern aristocrats who knew how to let their hair down and wouldn't mind a visitor from the past.

I arrived unannounced, the cold call now my MO.

"By golly!" Mrs. Frye exclaimed, "Mark Arax."

We hugged and I handed her a book she had loaned me years earlier about the history of one Mississippi plantation.

"Let me fix you a drink. It's not everyday that a newspaperman comes calling."

"I can't believe what they've done to our old house," I said, staring out the big window to what used to be ours. "Painting the adobe brick white and the beams blue. They're trying to turn Spanish into Colonial."

"Two shrinks from Santa Cruz bought it. Whaddya expect?"

We sat for an hour sipping cranberry and vodka and talking about the old and new South, her husband's cancer, crime in Fresno—everything but the one thing that had brought me there. It would be nearly the same whenever I called on someone from the past, the murder like a third person in the room, passed over, waiting to be bowed to. I finally did the honors.

I asked if she remembered the time shortly after the murder when I ran to their house in a panic, convinced that a strange car parked out front was laden with dynamite?

She paused to light a cigarette and before she could answer, Mr. Frye, home from work, doddered in. "Burr," she said his name sweetly, "we were just talking about the time Mark's father was killed. About the mystery car."

He was a small man with a dense southern drawl and a sense of humor so deadpan you couldn't be sure you weren't missing a joke. You laughed to cover the margin of error.

"I'll never forget that," he said. "The car belonged to this boy who was dating your cousin. We didn't know that at the time, of course. They were in the orchard behind your house necking. You came home and saw this car parked out front with an alarm clock ticking inside."

"An alarm clock? I don't remember an alarm clock."

"Yeah. There was this Big Ben ticking inside."

"You mean my fear wasn't so crazy?"

"Hell, your father had just been murdered. And then this car is parked out front with a clock inside. You ran over to our house and I was loose as a goose. 'Mr. Frye, they're going to blow up our house!' So I put your family in the back of your house and I put Ginger and the dog in the back of our house and I walked up and took a look inside. Sure enough, it was ticking."

"Who called the cops?"

"I did. They didn't know what to do. They were a joke. That's about the time your cousin and her boyfriend showed up. Turned out your cousin's boyfriend always came home late, so his mother put a battery-operated clock in the front seat."

Mrs. Frye's tone suddenly turned confessional. She had more to say about Dad's murder. She heard stories. She heard the lady bartender was involved. She heard the hitmen were from LA. That the Mafia had sent for them. She recalled a local judge telling her that my father was involved in the drug trade and "got what was coming to him."

"I told him to shove it," she said. "That judge didn't see your father in the front yard with every kid on the block. He didn't see the games of catch. Hours and hours. The games of basketball."

"It seemed like the judge had a pipeline to the police department," Mr. Frye added. "I don't know how to bring it all to you."

We talked another hour, about Fresno's tradition of corruption, about the madam who ran whores out of a house next door to the Fryes' old house. This madam ended up marrying Hank Morton, the man who was police chief at the time of my father's murder.

"In the front window," Mrs. Frye said, "she displayed a ceramic parrot. When she was open for business this parrot's pecker faced the street. And when she was closed his pecker faced the other way."

The Fryes also knew that a number of prominent businessmen and farmers in the early 1970s turned to drug smuggling as a way out of the recession. They mentioned the Lambes and Simones, the same Italian fig ranchers my neighbor Rich had talked about. "You had these great big farms with landing strips and airplanes flying in dope night and day from Mexico," she said. "You had these car dealers involved."

The more old-timers I met, the more I would come to realize that Fresno's sordid past, a blank spot in the pages of the local newspaper, was not a story unchronicled. The Fyres and other longtime Fresnans were more than able to fill in the gap.

I waved good-bye that afternoon and drove to the end of the block, to the house where the Stephan family used to live, and killed the engine. I thought how the Fryes had carted the past with them in their trunk full of Civil War letters and Jim Crow proclamations, from Memphis to Fresno. And how I had carried with me from Fresno to New York to Baltimore to Los Angeles the first notebook of my search, written in a child's penmanship. I kept my own trunk stuffed with memories—Dad's shaving kit and hair brush, his wallet and coach's whistle.

I gazed back to the house my father built, the one enduring shrine of him having made good, and tried to recollect those endless games of catch and one-on-one when I wanted nothing more than to defeat him, and each victory was tarnished by the deep-down knowledge that he had thrown the game in a way he hoped I wouldn't detect. "You lost on purpose," I kicked and shouted, and he smiled rather than issue a denial, perhaps wanting me to know he was still king. As I sat in my car waiting for the familiar view to inspire a moment of communion I had forgotten or forgotten to remember, I recollected instead that January night when I ran down the street shouting the news.

"I heard this noise coming up the block," Craig Stephan had told me. "I thought an animal had been hit and was wailing. Then it sounded like a fight. All of a sudden there was this pounding at the front door and I opened it and you fell in my arms."

All I remembered was running, running out of breath in a fog that muffled sound. I could see now that it measured only the length of four familiar houses, not even half a block. It was a sprint, trifling. Wouldn't it be something, I thought, if I could close my eyes right here and reverse that run, and when my grown-up strides had swallowed the distance I would open them again and the adobe house wouldn't be white and the beams wouldn't be blue and I was a kid again and it was all a fantastic dream? Like a movie? Like *The Wizard of Oz?*

○ ○ ○

What the Fryes and others told me about Fresno in those first months back home came as no surprise. Even as a kid, I sensed that all was not right with my town, the shenanigans at the Italian Dante club, the cops working the front door at Dad's bar, Dad telling me the D.A. had married a paraplegic and adopted children as an elaborate front to hide his homosexuality. But like so much else of Fresno, I just assumed this was the way towns ran and my town was no better or no worse. Why cavil?

It wasn't until I visited the local newspaper morgue, sifting through old files, that I began to sense that there was a good deal more to Fresno's shady past than even the old-timers knew, or I suspected. Inside those files, I found a federal report dated 1922 that listed the opium dens of Chinatown as one of the busiest in the nation. Twenty years later, famed Washington columnist Drew Pearson was depicting Fresno as one of the most venal cities in the country. A national magazine, under the headline, ANYTHING GOES, could only marvel at the bald-faced beauty of it all, comparing the town's freewheeling tenderloin to New Orleans. The exposés written in 1957 by Melvin Mencher, my professor at Columbia, were there too, detailing a vast network of prostitution houses operating without the slightest hint of police interference. The city physician was proud doctor to the whores.

What I found in those files was an astonishing tolerance for corruption passed from one generation to the next, Fresno's patrimony. And unlike Philly or Chicago or New Orleans or Birmingham, my hometown had succeeded in hiding its evil, or at least not owning up to it. It certainly wasn't the world told to me by Saroyan, that sweet mythical village of Ithaca, California, "East-West—Home is Best, Welcome Stranger."

From the very start, in 1872, the town heeded its own code. Not only did the valley's geography impose a kind of banishment, but many of the early inhabitants were outcasts from the Old World—unbowed Confederates fleeing the carpetbagger South and refugees escaping pogroms in Russia, Turkey and Asia.

They carried dark memories of death marches and despots; a strong, central government equaled genocide to many. The best rule was the least rule. Besides, they had come to this desolate place to make money and didn't necessarily plan on staying. Civics was someone else's burden. What evolved was this crazy patchwork where each group—Chinese, Italian, Armenian, Volga German—controlled a piece of the action.

The Chinese had been drawn to California by the Gold Rush and the steady wages of railroad and levee work. They farmed vegetables on the west side and built a Chinatown of underground passages and iron gates that sheltered dens of opium, lottery games and prostitution.

White businessmen and farmers raised powerful voices on behalf of this vice, arguing that gambling and prostitution lured dollars downtown and kept the migrant farmworkers docile. The town's first mayor, L. O.

Stephens, refused to curb the prostitutes who arrived each Friday by train from all parts of the state. They worked out of a "crib," which resembled a horse stable, only flimsier. It was mattress and plywood, and if you looked closely between the cracks you could make out the tryst right there from the street.

The murder rate was higher than in Chicago. The cops were drunk. Everybody packed a gun. Fire alarms were seen as government intrusion so the custom developed that whoever saw the flames first pulled out his six-shooter and fired five times in the air. The next man closer to the fire station would then discharge his weapon and so and so on until it finally reached the firemen, who, if sober, would hear the shots and respond, usually too late to save the house or store.

"Fresno is known all over California as the wickedest spot in the state," bemoaned newspaperman Chester Rowell, a relentless reformer who tried to shame Fresnans out of their considerable acquiescence. "Gambling houses running wide open all night and day without even the pretense of concealment. A whole criminal reservation given over to public prostitution. A tenderloin population equal to that of an Eastern city ten times our size."

But even Rowell, more often than not, acquitted Fresno law enforcement of culpability. His newspaper, the *Fresno Republican,* which later merged with the *Bee,* pinned the blame instead on the wily Chinese.

"The Chinese gambling house owners are playing a foxy game," read one typical news story. "The Celestials are trying to antagonize the police into making raids so that they can then file an injunction. They are keeping the dens ablaze with an array of electric lights on the inside, where a slant-eyed son of the land of dragons is perched high on a little stool keeping close watch. As soon as the officer gets within a few feet of the entrance, the watchman pulls a string and the large iron doors close with a clang."

In 1905, Mayor Stephens, an undertaker, gave way to W. Parker Lyon, a millionaire who sold lead-lined coffins and proved equally soft on the question of vice. It wasn't until 1917, during the regime of Police Chief John Goehring, the reputed brother or cousin of future Nazi Field Marshal Hermann Goering, that federal agents began taking note of Fresno.

Raiding Ku Klux Klan headquarters in Los Angeles, they seized a statewide membership list that named seven Fresno police officers. The new mayor fired the men, only to be overturned by the civil service board.

During Prohibition, federal agents considered Fresno County the wettest spot in the state and mounted an undercover investigation that led to bootlegging indictments of three immigrants from Italy. The Italians outlined an incredible syndicate that extended from west side farms to a downtown strip called Whiskey Row. Farmers facing another year of fickle raisin and fig prices were full partners in the scheme.

The Italians had operated without restraint for four years and cleared an average of $120,000 a year. Half the profit, $5,000 a month, was handed over to the Fresno Police Department. More than a quarter of the seventy-member force, the chief included, had taken bribes to look the other way. The previous chief and a captain had bagged enough cash to retire on vineyards north of town.

"The police department is at the center of a gigantic web of corruption and graft and God knows where it ends," said the federal agent who headed the case. "It is enough to say that the effects of the investigation reach beyond the wildest dreams of corruption among officials of a city as small as Fresno."

The evidence presented at trial was overwhelming but only one of the thirteen officers was convicted—and for a minor offense. The Italian kingpin went into the ice cream business. The whole affair was quickly forgotten.

Twenty-five years later, nothing had changed. Abe Davidian, trying to worm his way out of a heroin trafficking charge, spilled his guts to the feds, implicating local and state law enforcement every step of the way. The twenty-eight-year-old former boxer told a federal grand jury that whorehouses up and down the San Joaquin Valley were moving dope for Joe and Fred Sica, two Fresno boys who now lived in LA and were enlisted with Mickey Cohen's mob.

On January 18, 1950, the Sicas and fourteen others were indicted for operating a million-dollar-a-year heroin ring—the largest ever uncovered on the West Coast.

Davidian was betraying the wrong people at the worst time. Cohen's mob had been paying off California Attorney General Frederick N.

Howser since his days as a prosecutor in Los Angeles. Howser was so thoroughly corrupted that Governor Earl Warren had taken the extraordinary step of forming a state crime commission with the sole purpose of unmasking the attorney general.

Howser had reason to be nervous about Davidian, who not only possessed intricate knowledge about the Sica heroin ring but could name names in a statewide system of graft that linked the attorney general to Fresno vice lords.

After the federal grand jury finished with Davidian, Governor Warren's crime commission debriefed him. Davidian revealed that the Fresno Police Department ran at least one house of prostitution by itself and collected protection money from thirty-six others. Each house paid a franchise fee of $5,000 and an operating fee of $175-a-month per girl. Police Chief Ray Wallace, in the spirit of his predecessors, had used the money to amass more than 1,700 acres of ranch and other lands in two counties.

Soon after Howser assumed office, Davidian testified, the attorney general put the bite into Fresno politicians for $25,000. This was the price to keep his state agents from investigating the town. As soon as the money was delivered, Howser declared Fresno "free from rackets."

"Law enforcement there is of a very high order," he stated.

The feds must have surmised how Howser and the Sicas would react to the specter of Abraham Davidian on the witness stand. And yet they decided against keeping their prize informant under protective custody. Davidian moved back to Fresno, to the family's small house next to the red brick church in Armenian town, and slept in a different room each night, a rifle and tear gas kit at the ready. He did not bother to make himself invisible, carousing each night with the patrons of the Swing Club, a downtown establishment owned by Joe Sica's good friend.

Six weeks before the trial, on a February afternoon in 1950, Davidian's mother returned home early from work and noticed that her eldest son hadn't moved from the chesterfield in the den where he had fallen asleep after a long night selling dope and whores in Chinatown. From afar she could see something dark streaming from his nostrils that had congealed about the lips and chin. She moved close enough to see that the eyelids were purple and puffy and a neat little hole had been bored just above the right ear straight through to the other side. It was a perfect job, one .32-caliber bullet to the brain of a man sound asleep. Powder burns indicated a shot from three feet away. On the lace window curtain next to the sofa were a few specks of bloodspray. Otherwise, no mess. The slug had come to rest in the folds of his pillow. She ran down the streets of Armenian town screaming the news in her native tongue: "Someone killed my big boy!"

The Davidian murder went down in federal archives as one of the most sensational Mafia hits of a generation, right up there with Bugsy Siegel. Their main witness silenced, federal prosecutors had no choice but to dismiss all charges against Joe Sica and his heroin ring. Governor Warren's crime commission all but accused Howser of complicity in the hit, implying that the attorney general had leaked Davidian's secret role as witness to Sica. The feds also pursued the theory that Fresno police—several high-ranking officers were friendly with Sica—betrayed Davidian.

One woman, apparently overlooked by investigators, had a clear view of the alley behind Davidian's house that day. She would tell me, nearly four decades later, that she too saw a green Buick sighted by neighbors only moments before the shooting. The driver, she said, was a state narcotic agent working for Attorney General Howser. The passengers were a Fresno County investigator close to Sica and a former cop named Rusty Doan, who had been indicted as part of the heroin ring.

"I was so shocked because the state agent, a close friend of mine, had been assigned to the San Francisco office," she said. "I later told him, 'I know who killed Davidian. Rusty Doan was in the car with you. He pulled the trigger.' He told me I was crazy. But there they were."

Twenty years later, one of the cops suspected of giving away Davidian's movements, Fresno Lieutenant John Orndoff, would possess inside information in another sensational murder, my father's. Orndoff was one of the officers my father had visited at police headquarters in the days before he was killed.

The murder file that landed on my
desk at the *Times* more than a year earlier was an insult to good police
work. One hundred pages of gaping holes, leads never pursued, polygraph
tests never administered, key people close to my father never questioned. I
might have smelled a cover-up if I hadn't soon learned that state investigators had helped Fresno police diagram the murder in 1980 and the entire file ran several hundred pages. After weeks of hounding Royal
Calkins, the *Fresno Bee* reporter, he called with good news. The city attorney had agreed to let us see the rest of the file.

"I told them I'm bringing along an assistant," he said. "We'll make up
some name for you."

In the batch of reports already in my possession, only once did detectives
mention my father's visits to the Fresno Police Department. "The reason
for these visits have (sic) not become clear at this time," they wrote. Even
as a kid scribbling notes to myself, I had wondered about his contacts with
police and if they played some part in the murder. At the time, I had little
to go on.

A family friend, Wayne Saghatelian, had seen my father bounding down the second floor stairs at police headquarters only a week before the murder. He was totally upbeat.

"He hugged me and asked what I was doing down there and I told him I had found some merchandise fallen off a delivery truck. I was trying to find the rightful owner. He said, 'Good for you, Wayne. This city would be a helluva lot better if we had more civic-minded people.'"

This was the same do-gooder Ara this friend had always known. "He seemed to be on top of things. The smile, the demeanor. He was buoyant. A week later he was dead." Saghatelian had a theory: "The way he complimented me and the fact that he was coming down from the offices of police higher-ups, I've always thought Ara was working with them. I think he was cooperating and that's why he was killed."

Then, when I was eighteen, Janice Bletcher, Big Armond's wife, got drunk at our house and let it slip that she knew a possible motive. I pleaded and pleaded but she wouldn't elaborate. The most she would tell me was that a police lieutenant named John Orndoff had seen Dad visiting the department, not once but several times in the weeks before his death. Orndoff, who headed the vice and detective divisions, had retired and moved to the Central Coast.

The next day I sneaked into the bathroom while my mother was shopping and dialed his number and pressed the tape recorder to the receiver. I didn't know at the time that Orndoff had been a suspect in the Abe Davidian murder.

"I probably know as much as anybody but that ain't too much," he said. "You just go ahead and ask and if I can answer, I'll tell you."

"I've been told that my father was down at the police department in the month before he was killed."

"That's correct. Several times. At that time, he didn't have any idea that he was going to be killed."

"Is there a record of his visits?"

"Well, no. I think he had an idea that we were watching the place, had it under surveillance for drug traffickers and he came down to the department to find out. But his coming down had nothing to do with what had actually taken place at the end, you know."

"Was my father providing information to you guys?"

"Absolutely not. Absolutely not. He was concerned about the people who were hanging around his place of business and I don't blame him. But some of the people he was real buddy-buddy with were involved in drug trafficking."

"Who was he meeting?"

"He would meet with me and then he would go in the back and I guess it was Coke Keeney he was visiting. And Eddie Heizenrader. . . . He was head of the intelligence division at the time."

The names didn't mean much to me. Heizenrader was a lieutenant whose unit was responsible for organized crime investigations. Keeney was an officer in the unit. I could only speculate on what my father might have told them.

Orndoff insisted there was no mystery to it at all. My father wasn't a "stool pigeon," he said. "He was concerned about his business and about the racketeers hanging around there. He didn't get killed because he was squealing. Because he wasn't. He was killed because somebody thought he was giving us some information."

I never asked Orndoff how Dad's visits to the police department got back to these unnamed racketeers. He seemed to imply that Fresno was a small town and word got around fast.

I had no problem believing my father was killed because he posed a threat to the Fresno mob. Once his contacts with police were discovered, they had no choice but to silence him. But if Orndoff was telling the truth, the bad guys had blundered. There was no reason to kill him. My father had given the police nothing. I believed Orndoff's explanation, at least back then. As for why a cop would use the words "stool pigeon" and "squealer" for an informant, I didn't question that either.

I stood in the entrance of police headquarters while Royal Calkins of the *Bee* checked us in at the front counter. On the wall of the foyer hung a photo of the motorcycle squadron circa the 1960s with Hank Morton, the police chief who married the town's biggest madam, at the apex, and Coke Keeney, one of the cops my father visited in his last week, to Morton's side. I studied each face for clues. Morton looked soft and delicate. Nothing like advertised. Keeney was clearly the greenhorn of the bunch, tall and thin with a clear-eyed gaze to the future.

Through the plate glass, I could see the stairs leading up to the second floor administrative offices, the same stairs my father bounded down the last week of his life. *He was bouyant. The smile. The demeanor. A week later he was dead.*

We were led to a small room on the second floor by the city attorney who thought I was just another reporter assisting Calkins. "This is it. The Arax murder file."

He pointed to a small box and I could feel my legs tremble. Last second jitters, I told myself, a silly fear that I had come all this way only for the city attorney to demand my ID or for some cop I knew to stumble by and holler "Arax." Ever so close, I'd be booted out and the file forever lost to me. That's what I thought at the time. But I think now my dread was this other apprehension.

I had never thought of my father dissolving into dust in a box in the ground. Rather, the picture I couldn't erase was what I imagined took place before his body ever reached the funeral home, and one day confronted with these autopsy photos, a head-to-toe bloody mess, I wouldn't be able to muster the decency to turn away. I had asked Calkins to cleanse the file of any photos of my father at the scene or the morgue, but as he and the city attorney talked over the ground rules—"You have two days to finish and request any copies you want"—I could feel the pull of the box urging me its way.

They were still negotiating the copying fee when I tore open the lid. The next two days were at once an amorphous daze and a microscopic focus for me.

Stuffed inside were tips to the *Bee*'s secret witness program, lie detector tests, notes recovered from my father's briefcase and a list of the long-distance calls made by him and several of the key suspects—all missing from the first packet sent me.

There were the last words he jotted before he found himself in a struggle for his life: MAP OR PLOT PLAN. There were teletypes to Wisconsin, Missouri and Arizona. Rap sheets and mug shots and fingerprints of more than a hundred would-be hitmen. A handsome kid nicknamed "Preacher" from South San Francisco. Two bony longhairs from Winnemucca, Nevada, a supposed mecca for triggermen out west. Abe Davidian's nephew with a half dozen aliases of his own. All the debris that rolled ashore in a big murder investigation, pages and pages of names and towns and faces I would have to sort through to decide who needed to be followed and who was better left behind.

The file had already been purged for us. There were no autopsy photos, which made me thankful, and no hint of the taped interviews with key suspects, which made me wonder who in the police department had gone through the box and what else they had lifted, and why.

More than a year earlier, piecing together those sketchy reports, I had outlined several murder theories. Nothing in the expanded file before me offered a definite answer. Nothing changed my overall impression that this was a listless investigation marred by the failure to question my father's closest friends, associates, bookkeeper, accountant. But even with these flaws there was enough new to narrow my hunt for killers, if not my deeper search, and to raise more questions about my father's visits to the police department.

Of the seven or eight theories involving scores of bad guys inside those pages, only a few made any sense and just one made my heart race.

It began with my father's partnership with Dan Hornig in The Forum nightclub. One of the documents found inside Dad's briefcase the night of the murder detailed his interest in The Forum. He would give Hornig $30,000 in exchange for a 40 percent stake. He would pay $18,000 up front with the remaining $12,000 secured by a promissory note.

The Forum partnership agreement had been drafted in June, 1971, seven months before the murder. It was standard in every way except one: It had never been signed by Dad and Hornig. And this wasn't the only puzzling aspect. My father and Hornig had met with state alcohol regulators after Dad invested the $18,000. Each stated in a signed affidavit on file with the state agency that my father was to become manager of The Forum, not partner, and that no money had changed hands.

Why lie? My father didn't have a criminal record like Garvey. Nothing compelled him to hide his investment in The Forum. At the time of the agreement, Hornig tottered on the brink of personal bankruptcy. He hardly commanded the leverage to dictate terms that left my father without contractual protection. Sure, it was well known that my father conducted business on a hunch, but handing over $18,000 without any paper?

One likely reason for lying on the state affidavit was that Hornig re-fused to name my father as a partner and place him on The Forum liquor license until the full $30,000 had been received. But that still didn't ex-plain why the partnership agreement, a document seen only by Dad and Hornig, wasn't signed.

The cops could think of two reasons why my father didn't sign the con-tract. He and Hornig had a falling out right after the money had been given and Dad had second thoughts about the partnership. Or, he feared leaving behind any signed documents linking him to the money.

In late August, a few weeks after he handed over the $18,000 to Hornig, state and local authorities confiscated a white and gold Cessna be-longing to drug smuggler Frank Nunez at the Madera Airport, twenty miles north of Fresno. Stuffed inside the seatless cabin were 800 pounds of high-grade marijuana from Mexico.

Hornig and Nunez were golfing pals. Police surmised that a broke Hornig had used a portion of my father's money to finance this bungled shipment. Other prominent Fresnans were involved as investors in the ring, including Hornig's realtor buddy, Leonard Maselli. A pilot, copilot and a driver had been arrested and were keeping mum about these fi-nanciers. They faced a January 17, 1972 trial in Madera County Superior Court.

The timing of the $18,000 transaction raised all sorts of intriguing questions: Did my father believe that Hornig handed over a portion of his money to Nunez to finance a drug shipment? If so, was my father expect-ing to double his money, too? Was this the reason he lied to state alcohol regulators about his investment in Hornig's bar, because he knew the money was destined for a dope buy? Or did he conclude what Hornig had done with his money only after the plane, loaded down with marijuana, was seized in Madera? If Hornig had used the money without my father's knowledge to smuggle drugs and now the heat was coming down, noth-ing would upset my father more. Maybe this was why he refused to sign the partnership papers, knowing that it would link him to a drug ring he played no part in?

The Madera trial was pending and Hornig, Nunez and Maselli had so far eluded authorities. Could my father have been angry enough to threaten exposure? Both The Apartments and The Forum were in trouble with state alcohol regulators for under-age drinking. Might he have tried to broker some kind of deal? The information he possessed, the money trail, was certainly damning.

And what about my father striking Nunez a month before the murder? Hornig, for one, made light of the fight. He told police that Nunez had referred to Ara as a cheap Armenian whose idea of betting on the golf course was a $1 wager. The comment apparently got back to Dad. The next time he caught sight of Nunez inside The Forum, he rested a big friendly arm across his back and steered him to the billiard room. By the time Nunez realized my father's intentions and grabbed a pool cue, he was wiping the sting from his mouth and dusting off his rear end.

Was I to believe Hornig? Could the fight have involved something more, like Dad threatening to expose the drug ring? Might Nunez have then taken care of the grudge and Dad's loose mouth with the same bullet?

As much as I distrusted Hornig, I had a hard time conceiving of him as a conspirator in a murder. He might have torched one of his failing bars, as authorities suspected, and invested in drugs to crawl out of a financial hole. But concealing a crime with homicide seemed a realm beyond. This was a guy I knew, a guy I saw playing catch in his front yard with his son, Daniel Hornig Jr., a redhaired and freckle-faced kid whom he nicknamed "Tiger."

The detectives questioned Hornig twice, once with the assistant district attorney present. He denied ever speaking to Nunez about drug smuggling. He denied knowing anything about the murder, either before or after the fact. "He said he had no idea who might have shot Ara," the report read. "But he believes that it was just a holdup." Then this caught my eye: Hornig had been the other person who called our house and talked to Dad on the afternoon of the murder. He told police he had called to talk about a sound system they were renting at the nightclub.

The problem with conspiracies, I told my friend that day at police headquarters, was that once put to work they kept on accumulating, spilling everywhere and nowhere, an anarchy of affiliation. Journalistic training had taught me to question chance and coincidence and heed the pattern of conforming events. But it also imparted a healthy mistrust of conspiracies.

This much was clear: My father had been killed by two gunmen. All but a robbery theory presupposed that the shooters had been hired by a third party. And depending on the motives of that third party (revenge, silencing a loose mouth, greed) the conspiracy ranged from run-of-the-mill to something more remarkable. Then, deep in the file, I found four more pieces to the puzzle, revelations that provided some insight into my father's last movements, if not his motive for going to the police.

• In late November, one month before the murder, Dad placed a phone call to Dick Walley, a veteran agent with the state Bureau of Narcotic Enforcement. From a reconstruction of the notes, part of their conversation went something like this:

"Dick, I want you to know that some of my employees are dealing drugs and I'm dead set against it. My manager, Mike Garvey, and another bartender are smuggling reds. Last week, they brought a bunch of pills into town and are selling them."

"Are they dealing by themselves or through another group?"

"I'm not sure. I think they're getting the stuff from Mexico. There's a lot of shit going down here. I'd like to clean it up. But I don't know what to do."

• Three weeks before the murder, my father placed a call to the county building in Madera, California, where the drug trial involving Frank Nunez and Dan Hornig's three associates was being held. The county building housed the district attorney's office and the superior court but because the number my father dialed was a general switchboard number, it was impossible to tell who he talked to and for how long. As far as I knew, he had nothing going in Madera County. No lawsuits. No traffic tickets.

The timing of the call—five weeks before the trial of the men in the Nunez–Hornig drug ring—introduced a number of possibilities, most of them pointing to my father as an informant. The homicide team did contact Madera authorities to ask if anyone had received a phone call from Ara Arax about the upcoming trial. The answer came back negative, and the matter was dropped.

• Twelve days before the murder, Dad placed a call to the state Attorney General's office in Sacramento—the last long distance call on our phone records before the murder. Again, this was a general switchboard number. Whatever nagged at him, I reasoned, he didn't stop with state agent Walley or Heizenrader, Orndoff and Keeney at the Fresno Police Department. The matter that bothered him, he pursued with the state's highest law enforcement authority as well.

• About this same time, Dad went to see Butch Turner, a private eye who had quietly opened his business with the help of the intelligence unit, specifically Lieutenant Heizenrader and Officer Ivan "Moose" Nyberg. The two cops were more or less hidden partners, and Turner didn't hesitate to trade on this association. If he needed access to state crime computers, the intelligence unit would punch it in for him. Turner was allowed to accompany Heizenrader on police investigations, question witnesses, collect evidence and even confiscate property.

In return, Turner passed along secrets gleaned from clients—the juicy stuff finding its way into police dossiers used to bend politicians, bureaucrats and businessmen. Turner might have lacked a badge but he boasted something even better: a relationship with Police Chief Hank Morton that was as dear as father and son. "Butch Turner's closer to me than my own," Morton told friends.

According to the report, my father apparently went to Turner with questions about Dan Hornig and Mike Garvey and a drug smuggler tied to Frank Nunez. Whatever he told Turner—their conversations were not revealed in the reports—I had to assume it got back to the police department, to Morton and Heizenrader.

"You can sure smell something deadly in the air," said Royal Calkins, flipping through the last of the file. "I mean, if your father's talking to Eddie Heizenrader, he's talking to the wrong guy. If he's talking to Coke Keeney or Butch Turner, he's talking to the wrong guy."

Then he turned to the back of the binder. "You'll be interested in this . . . Coke Keeney is the subject of the last entry, dated 3-5-79. It says that a television reporter came into headquarters and asked to see the Ara Arax file. The reporter said he heard Ara had given Coke Keeney some information about narcotics before his death. Keeney is then questioned by his captain.

"What does he say?"

"Keeney says he met your father in 1968 at The Apartments during a routine check of drug-dealing hangouts. He stated that this was the one and only time he ever met or saw Arax. And that's the end of the file."

"That's hard to believe. Bartenders remember my father comping Keeney drinks. The intelligence unit lived inside bars. You mean the captain bought that explanation?"

"It's the last entry."

On my way down the stairs that day, I recalled what a former madam had told me: "Coke Keeney is the quiet, humble guy who made you believe you could trust him with your deepest secrets." Now that sounded like a policeman my father would have sought out in a time of trouble. "But I wouldn't trust Coke for one moment. He and Eddie (Heizenrader) and Hank (Morton) were up to their eyeballs in corruption."

In bed that night, I told myself if my father had to be murdered, I wanted it to be like this. No mere payback or everyday robbery. If he had to be murdered, why not murder as a metaphor for a time and place. I wanted to believe the best as his son. I knew none of this meant a thing unless I pursued my best instincts as a journalist.

This was the tension that I told myself would lead to a final discovery: a son trying to clear his father's name. A journalist digging past the silence and rumor, myth and deceit. It was the accumulations of twenty years that separated me from my father, and that night, like each night that followed, I sifted its layers, and tried to find sleep, wondering if what I had unearthed would not kill me.

Hank Morton ran the Fresno Police Department for twenty-two years, accountable to no one. Exposés written by Professor Mencher in the 1950s placed him at the center of a network of gambling and prostitution houses in the city's tenderloin. Fresnans greeted the Mencher series with a wide yawn, for it was no news at all to them. There were no letters to the editor, no pretenses of soul searching, no calls for heads to roll. The stories came early in Morton's reign and he survived them, moving on to become the most powerful man in the San Joaquin Valley.

If part of my answer lay hidden in the city and its police force, as part of me suspected all along, I had to go back and assemble the main characters. I had to know how bad Hank Morton and Eddie Heizenrader and John Orndoff and the others were. What, if anything, had changed from the fifties to 1972? What was the legacy of the Fresno Police Department? Were these men capable of murder?

Hank Morton was a local boy, a truck driver who joined the police force in 1939 and patrolled Chinatown, a beat that required a certain amount of mingling with madams and grifters. He forged such trust that before long he was mediating disputes between the department and the tenderloin and siphoning payoffs to Police Chief Ray Wallace.

Before Wallace went to prison for trying to buy a side business with $10,000 in whorehouse five and tens, he rewarded Morton with a promotion to sergeant. Morton divorced his first wife, a paraplegic, and married Bessie Wong, a Chinatown waitress. They were a study in the attraction of opposites: slender, bright, sedate Bessie; paunchy, foul-tempered, besotted Hank.

He became the city's eighth police chief when no other candidate could pass the exam. Early on, he did well to hide his vices but as he grew into the job, his conduct became more insolent—the work days spent fishing and hunting, the long nights drinking and whoring and sneaking back into the police property room to filch pistols and shotguns.

In fine Fresno tradition, Morton bought a big spread north of town where he stashed the weapons and raised race horses. He made it known that promotions hinged on working off-duty gratis at his ranch. Officers mended fences and barns and built a mock Dodge City complete with a saloon, jailhouse and boot hill.

Under Morton's tutelage, even the police yearbooks took on the patina of the Old West. The articles had almost nothing to do with policing or community issues. Instead, page after page was devoted to yarns about Rattlesnake Dick and Pegleg Smith, Jesse James and Sheet Iron Jack and Mexican desperados Joaquin Murieta and Tiburcio Vasquez.

It was Morton's way of celebrating the hazy line between the good guys and the bad guys, and he surrounded himself with a cadre of officers who embodied this ambiguity. One barely finished the fifth grade. Another was grossly overweight, couldn't pass the physical and knocked up the baby-sitter. Another liked to bludgeon black men on the west side and he bludgeoned more than one to death. Each one farmed his beat, sucked out every bit he could.

It wasn't until 1964, well into Morton's second decade as police chief, that someone came along with the cheek to question his leadership. He was Henry Hunter, the new city manager from Riverside, a six foot four, slow-talking Tennessean who had taken the Fresno post knowing full well the city's reputation. Even so, that first week on the job Hunter was struck dumb by the nonchalance of city hall secretaries and department heads setting fire to documents and chucking them down a big cast-iron chute that deposited only ashes. It was a peculiar way to do housekeeping, he thought.

Then he learned that federal agents raiding a $2.2 million Fresno bookmaking ring had made a point of keeping Chief Morton in the dark. Hunter pulled up past police budgets and was astonished to learn that the city never audited tens of thousands of dollars in vice funds. The money, intended to pay informants, had been used by Morton to conduct dirty tricks on anyone who dared stand in his way.

On February 26, 1965, City Manager Hunter did the unthinkable: He fired Hank Morton. The long list of charges included failure to suppress bookmaking and prostitution, misuse of vice funds and failure to destroy guns as required by law.

It would prove to be a monstrous miscalculation by a man who had been in Fresno barely a year.

First, Morton feigned one of his fourteen reported heart attacks, a favorite trick to buy time. Then his friends threw a big testimonial dinner at Holy Trinity Armenian Church. Nearly 1,000 people packed the large hall—judges, the mayor, city councilmen, the sheriff, prominent farmers and church leaders. Governor Edmund G. "Pat" Brown sent a telegram gushing praise. The backslapping Irish pol and Morton were longtime friends. A few years earlier, as attorney general, Brown had not pursued two state probes into Fresno police corruption. Not surprisingly, Morton and his Police Relief Association were key political allies.

Morton had good reason to be cocky about his prospects of overturning the firing. He had civil service protection, and the body that would hear his appeal consisted of several men he had handpicked. Indeed, the head of the board, attorney Bill McPike, had accepted a gift from Chief Morton— one of the guns purloined from the police property room. McPike was apparently afraid that the gift would be revealed and the civil service proceedings thrown into disarray. On the eve of the hearings, a nervous McPike telephoned Deputy Chief Bill Mortland, who privately despised Morton.

Mortland had a vivid memory of the call twenty-five years later. "McPike was frantic. He said Chief Morton had given him a gun out of the property room as a gift. Well, this was one of the charges against Morton. And McPike, as board chairman, was going to judge this charge. 'What in the hell am I going to do?' he asked. 'If that gun comes out, I'm a dead man.' Well, the matter never came up. That was Morton's luck. And McPike's luck. McPike then wrote the opinion clearing Morton of all wrongdoing."

Morton was reinstated with full back pay and an apology. City Manager Hunter was promptly sent packing by the city council. The police chief could hardly contain himself. He invited a few friends to celebrate his victory at his horse ranch. On the mock boot hill built by off-duty police officers, Morton embedded a gravestone with an epitaph that can still be read today: "Here lies H. K. Hunter. Died 6-3-65 in a gun duel with H. R. Morton."

Chief Morton culled an important lesson from his showdown with City Manager Hunter, telling close friends he would never again find himself at the mercy of bureaucrats and politicians. From the first day he patrolled the west side, he had been enthralled with the rituals of Chinatown, its tongs and vice lords and opium dens. And his appreciation of this world only grew after his marriage to Bessie Wong.

Morton responded to the Hunter affair by elevating a half dozen officers to positions of implicit trust, men with whom he formed his own tong. In a secret ceremony, he presented each one with a jade-on-gold ring.

Several of these men hailed from Volga German homes. They were known as "Rooshians," descendants of a hardy band of German wheat farmers lured to Russia's Volga River in the eighteenth century by Catherine the Great, herself a German. Tens of thousands of Volga Germans, unwilling to give up their language and strict ways, were eventually forced out by Czarist and then Soviet persecution. A large colony took root on Fresno's west side beginning in the 1890s. Their houses were easy to spot—a fresh coat of paint and immaculate walkway and a separate backhouse for cooking. These Volga Germans didn't care much for the Armenians, who lived just across the tracks, an ill will that supposedly stemmed from the Armenian penchant for negotiating prices. And they cared even less for blacks, who took over their neighborhood after they prospered and moved north toward the river. The Volga Germans controlled patronage. City hall was their machine.

Morton assigned two boys from the neighborhood—Eddie Heizenrader and Hal Britton—to the investigative and intelligence units. This was window dressing because they answered to no one but Morton and roamed completely free of the organizational structure. Heizenrader's job was two-fold: to serve as Morton's bagman and to gather the intelligence that would make up Morton's files on prominent citizens.

The jade ring gang would pick out a target and indulge his fancy, capturing the vice on still and moving film. Judges, ministers, politicians, prosecutors, city employees, developers and union heads were invited to big blowouts at the Dante Club, the Italian social hall on the city's west side. The all-night "smokers" were replete with naked dancers, prostitutes and casino gambling. It didn't seem possible that Hank Morton and Eddie Heizenrader, who were as drunk and compromised as the rest, were engaging in blackmail.

County District Attorney William Daly liked teenage boys. His wife, like Morton's first wife, was a paraplegic. Morton dangled the threat of exposure over Daly and extended his grip into the district attorney's office. For seven years, Daly truckled to Morton's will until finally a California Highway Patrol officer observed the district attorney and a teenage boy naked in a county car parked in an orchard. Daly resigned in the swirl of a state investigation and never recovered. His was one of the saddest stories I came across in Fresno, and he was quite determined to die with it.

"I don't have clear memories," Daly said with a chuckle, deflecting my questions about Morton and the jade ring gang.

"You laugh," I persisted. "But you were one of their victims."

"I was a victim. You're right. But I don't think it's ever going to come out. The story of Fresno will never be told."

I found only one local official targeted for blackmail who was willing to talk on the record. Bruce Reiss, the city manager in the early 1970s, said his troubles began innocently enough, with a phone call from a city councilman who was one of Morton's bootlickers.

"They were having a big lunch for the chief of police from our sister city in Mexico. Morton was there. Heizenrader was there. So I go to this party in the mountains and have a barbecue."

As the party was winding down, he recalled, Chief Morton invited him to a more intimate affair back in Fresno at the Ramada Inn. "For just a few of my close friends," Morton whispered. The hotel room was cramped with city councilmen and a number of high-ranking police officers. A bar was set up and everyone was drinking bourbon and water. Morton and Heizenrader served as hosts.

"I mentioned something about dinner and this cop takes me to the bedroom and says, 'Hey, I'll show you what you're going to have for dinner.' He opens the door and there's this policeman on the bed naked and this gal naked sucking his dick. The cop turns to me and says, 'Since you're the city manager, you're next.'"

Reiss and an assistant panicked and left in a hurry. The next day he got a call from the Ramada Inn manager asking if the city was going to cover the damage to the rooms. "Damage? What damage?" he asked.

"Well, there's a hole at the top of the ceiling above the bed and it goes clear through to the room above it. Sheet rock cut through and through."

Then Reiss learned that Morton and the boys had installed a movie camera in the room above and were going to film him with the prostitute.

"That was the whole plan for me being there," he said. "I was going to be set up pitifully. And once Hank Morton got his hooks in you, you were his all the way."

Morton's secret police may have earned a reputation for omniscience that was undeserved; the extent of the dossiers I could never confirm. But the mere hint of espionage or a secret file often proved enough to keep both politician and bureaucrat in line.

In this way Morton defanged the local watchdogs and took over the vice rackets without fear, doling out prostitution and gambling franchises to friends and relatives and keeping a few houses for himself. It was better than the Abe Davidian era, more structured and lucrative. And every week, Morton sent one of his boys down to Los Angeles to deliver a cut of the gambling spoils to Joe Sica, the prime suspect in the Davidian murder.

"Hank Morton was basically a pimp," said Marion Phillips, the former intelligence head for the state attorney general's organized crime division. "The Sicas owned a restaurant in Los Angeles and once a week a captain from the Fresno Police Department would drive down and meet with them. I'd say the Sicas and the police department were partners in organized crime all the way through the 1960s."

Morton knew he didn't have much to fear from federal or state law en-

forcement. Even if J. Edgar Hoover had been interested in police corruption, it's unlikely that local FBI agents would have pursued Morton, their
drinking and fishing buddy. Treasury agents in San Francisco and state
agents in Sacramento were well aware of the rot in Fresno, but the town
was a long hot drive down Highway 99. For those foolhardy feds inclined
to make the three-hour trek, there was the "Fresno factor" to weigh.

"We had these major bookmaking busts in the early 1960s and there
was virtually no community response. No pressure brought down on law
enforcement or the politicians," said Larry Miller, an IRS special agent.
"Fresnans didn't give a fiddler's fuck for anything. The indifference was
practically suffocating. They deserved what they got. It was a rotten town
with a rotten police force."

Unlike his mentor, Ray Wallace, Hank Morton rarely dirtied his own
hands. He functioned instead through Lieutenant Eddie Heizenrader, who
wasn't content to simply oversee the traditional crime rackets on behalf of
his boss. From his second floor office at police headquarters, Heizenrader
controlled land-use matters as well.

"Morton and Heizenrader were involved in the total political process,"
said a former Fresno County prosecutor who is now a judge. "Zoning decisions were bought by paying the right city councilmen and planning com-
missioners. And you couldn't get to the politicians and bureaucrats
without going through Morton and Heizenrader first."

Eddie Heizenrader had his own deep roots in Fresno. His father had been
something of a power broker on the west side. In the twenties, thirties and
forties, a steady stream of supplicants paid homage to the old man at a
blacksmith shop converted into a German political club. In return for delivering the Volga German vote, politicians afforded him considerable
voice in patronage and he saw to it that four of his sons secured spots in
the city hall trough. Two others became bookmakers.

Eddie was the backslapper of the bunch. The first thing you noticed
about him wasn't his size—six-foot-two, 210 pounds—or athletic
prowess, but a wonderful smile that showed off the gaps in his teeth.

As head of the intelligence division, Heizenrader was supposed to be
keeping tabs on organized crime. His peculiar work style consisted of entire days spent lolling inside bars and whorehouses with his sidekick,

Moose Nyberg. Heizenrader couldn't fight a lick when drinking and yet that's the first thing booze made him do. Nyberg, a six-foot-three, 240-pound bulwark, all jaw and pride, would step in with these killer eyes and rescue Heizenrader, who would then claim his injuries were sustained in the course of duty and take weeks off on disability.

Heizenrader made little attempt to disguise his meetings with local mobsters at bars and on the golf course. The wife of pimp Gary Prestidge recalled meetings with Heizenrader and his two underlings at a well-known Fresno nightclub in the early 1970s—meetings at which the pimp would hand over $5,000 to Heizenrader.

"Gary and I had regular meetings with Eddie and Ivan Nyberg and Coke Keeney. I always thought of the money as payoffs in return for protecting Gary's gambling and prostitution business. But when I look back, it seems the cops and Gary were actually partners. They helped him run the whores and the crap games. Eddie pretty much ran things. Nyberg was this big dense strongarm and Keeney the nice, quiet one who gave you every reason to trust him except for the company he kept. Gary had tapes of attorneys, politicians and cops in bed with his girls. He recorded their afternoon delights. But he never dared get anything on Chief Morton. He called Morton a stone-cold killer."

The second floor of the police department itself had become a gathering place for all sorts of scoundrels, a cast of characters that included private eye Butch Turner (Morton's surrogate son) and one of the main suspects in my father's murder—strongarm Armond Bletcher. And in late December 1971, my father himself was twice spotted there.

Bletcher would park his Harley chopper in a space reserved for the brass. During student and farmworker protests led by Cesar Chávez, Bletcher accompanied Heizenrader to police briefings and manned the vanguard of the police rampart. At one point, Heizenrader talked openly about making Armond a cop but the big guy couldn't stay out of trouble. He got into a shootout in front of his house, wounding two men with a gun Heizenrader had loaned him.

In December 1971, after twenty-one years at the top, Morton was making plans to retire. "I don't want to be another J. Edgar Hoover," he told the *Bee*. Cantankerous and defiant, he now betrayed megalomania, too. He divorced Bessie Wong and went public, marrying his longtime sweetheart, Jeannie Lucien, the Fresno madam whose cathouses and call girl operations were legendary. Morton's only acknowledgment of her past life was to chastise friends who made the mistake of calling her Jeannie: "Her name's Jannene now."

As to the question of Morton's successor, Ted Wills, the bow-tied mayor of Fresno, a Volga German himself, engineered a drive on behalf of Lieutenant Heizenrader. His back door campaign to secure Heizenrader the top job was taking place at the precise time my father, through the front door, was visiting the police department and talking to private eye Turner and making noise to at least one friend that Heizenrader was dirty beyond belief, and he was going to do something about it.

Time. It hadn't stood still for the men and women who shared my father's world as it had for me. What was sensational in 1972 seemed almost prosaic in the 1990s, an era swirling with drugs and murder. No one needed to tell me how violent a place my own town had become. The parade of dead included many of my father's own employees and customers.

There was Donnie Edwards, one of the felons Dad tried to reform by giving him a day job. So brazen was Edwards that state narcotic agents found him crawling in the garage below their offices photographing the license plates on their unmarked cars. He was later busted at the airport with a stash of heroin and on the eve of his trial, asleep on the couch, he was executed with a single shot above the right ear—the same way old Abe Davidian went. The Edwards slaying, too, was never solved. One of the key suspects was the fat, tanned drug smuggler who resided a few pods away from us at Heron Pointe. He was the same gangster rumored to have killed my father over $30,000 in disputed drug profits.

Then there was the passing of Big Armond Bletcher himself. A few months after Dad's murder, he showed up at our house in a tizzy. Mom wasn't home and he asked to use the phone and the next thing I knew he was belching death threats to the man on the other end. This man, a fellow weight lifter, apparently had the audacity to tell friends at the YMCA that he had taken Armond in wrist wrestling. "You're the number one shit on my list." His mouth salivated like a hungry man and between sick laughs he had to suck back the froth to talk on. "Sonbitch. When I finish beating the fuck out of you, I'm going to beat the fuck out of your old lady."

Four years later, the FBI received a tip that Armond was impersonating an agent. Two agents tracked him down and read him the riot act in the backseat of their sedan. A third agent stood outside braced for a wrath that never came. Instead, Armond began to sob, and it was no act, "I'm sorry for what I did—I didn't mean anything by it. It's just that all my life I've wanted to be an FBI agent."

The next day Armond telephoned two brothers, his distant cousins, and asked if the FBI had contacted them. He wanted Dave and Tim Pashayan to lie for him and tell the agents that he worked at their custom wheel shop downtown. Dave Pashayan told Armond he wouldn't cover for him and slammed down the phone.

A few minutes later Armond pulled up in a 1936 Ford pickup, his chest twice its normal size, puffed up like a pouter pigeon. Dave Pashayan grabbed a three-foot wooden ax handle and steeled himself.

"Hi, cousin," Armond sneered, a sardonic laugh.

"Stay back. Don't come any closer," Pashayan shouted.

The Pashayans each stood under five-feet-seven inches and weighed less than 170 pounds. Dave Pashayan wound up and swung the ax handle like a baseball bat, whacking Armond twice on the head. The brothers said he simply shrugged off the blows and growled. Tim Pashayan grabbed a 9mm handgun from the counter and fired two warning shots into the cement at Armond's feet. Armond lunged forward and Pashayan fired three more times at a target impossible to miss. The big man, mortally wounded, staggered and dropped to the floor.

Police found Armond facedown in a pool of congealed blood, blue feral eyes wide open. He was 33—the same age as Christ, his mother told me. Tim Pashayan told police that Armond often bragged of his Mafia contacts and that he knew who killed Ara Arax. Armond never mentioned any names though. Police released the Pashayans, saying the shooting had been in self-defense. What jury would find otherwise?

The autopsy report later revealed that Armond had been struck not twice by the ax handle but at least five times to the stomach, chest and head. One of the blows ripped open the scalp and fractured the base of the skull, producing a massive hemorrhage. Not even a man of Armond's legend could have sustained a blow of that magnitude and pressed forward in the manner the Pashayans described to police.

Tim Pashayan said Armond was facing him when he fired the fatal shots, but the autopsy showed that all three slugs entered from the right side of Armond's back. Big Armond, who traveled through life back to the wall, had realized his greatest fear. One prosecutor argued that it was an execution, and the Pashayans deserved to be charged with murder. Knocked unconscious from the head blows, Armond was reeling downward when Pashayan pumped the coup de grace into his back. But the district attorney concurred with police and decided against prosecution.

It took only the customary six men, not twelve as Armond had boasted at my father's funeral, to bear the casket to the grave. More than 300 people, 200 of them bikers riding hogs, escorted the hearse to Belmont Memorial Park. His widow donated some of his weights to our gym. The myth grew. The county coroner confirmed that Armond's bulk had absorbed the entire force of the bullets. There was not a single exit wound. It was also noted that after thirteen years of anabolic steroid abuse, Armond had the heart of a sixty-five-year-old fat man. He would have never lived past the age of forty anyway.

Crime statistics in the 1990s showed Fresno to be one of the two or three most violent cities in the state for its 400,000 population. Nearly ninety people were being murdered each year. This was quadruple the number of homicides in 1972, while the population had only doubled.

I wondered how a town hardened to violence would react to me knocking at its door, especially the bar people who had seen more than their share of murder and mayhem in the years between. One of the first people I looked up, Dr. Fitzalbert Marius, the black surgeon who was our next-door neighbor in the 1950s, wondered about this, too.

We hadn't talked in years and I explained that I was home for a visit and wanted to ask a few questions about my father. Knowing me and knowing the profession I had chosen, Dr. Marius didn't question my curiosity, though he did question where it might lead me and what I might find in a place gone numb to guns and shooting.

"Markie, with the depth of mayhem committed today, it makes what happened to your dad pale," he said. "Gosh, these cats are going around giving Colombian neckties, killing out whole families over this drug issue. People have gotten callous."

I wasn't so sure he wasn't talking about himself and what I did next was something cruel. I made him recollect that Sunday night at the emergency room at St. Agnes, from the moment he got the call at church that my father had been shot to the last hopeless attempt at reviving him. His account was so vivid in spite of the years, so much a protest against the diminution of murder, that it spoke as much about his regard for my father as it did about my father's incredible will to live and how close he had come to saving him.

"I had just arrived at our evening service when Dr. Torre called. 'Ara's been shot and he's asking for you.' Markie, his fate at that point had already been sealed. The ambulance taking him to St. Agnes was a fatal decision. St. Agnes wasn't equipped to handle a person in that condition."

He was bleeding and he needed to go into surgery but there was no blood. The hospital had failed to type and match his blood. All the time, Dad was chattering, chattering very rapidly. He kept asking if he was going to be all right, if he was going to make it, and he kept asking for Bertie Marius. When his good friend finally strode into the room, he was so hopeful he raised himself off the gurney and shook his hand, and he shook it firm.

"He seemed to be relatively stable. I was concerned about the wound to the gut. I noticed he didn't have sufficient intravenous lines. I mean the first thing you do is put in big lines that deliver lots of fluid. And you stick a tube into the stomach immediately. This tells you if there's bleeding in the stomach and it empties the stomach. None of these things had been done. So I put two big lines in his legs. I was screaming and hollering: 'Get some blood! Go up and type and cross match and get me some blood quickly!' Someone told me it's going to take forty-five minutes. Heck, he'd already been there an hour."

The thing that amazed the doctors and nurses was, as he was going into shock, Dad remained lucid. People who go into shock get less profusion in the brain and they start babbling. My father was as white as a sheet, and no one in that room could understand how he could be talking and recognizing everyone. His blood pressure was zero and he was still talking.

"I think that's what fooled us, Markie. He had such determination. He should have been up in surgery and his abdomen opened a long time ago. He knew this. I saw in his face. I saw . . . concern. I saw a man who had intended to see his kids grow up and be a grandfather. Yes, I saw that there came a time in that room at that moment that those things flashed through his mind: 'This is never going to happen. I'm not going to be around here tomorrow.' There was a look of disbelief: 'No. This is not for real. This is not really happening.'"

I had once read that gunshot to the gut was the most painful way to go, stomach acid spilling into blood, an incredible burning. An animal deserved better. Now I had this knowledge, its cruelty, to live with. It was a mocking, enough time to think he was going to make it, enough time to consider all the things he was about to miss.

"The anesthesiologist showed up and he was in the process of putting a tube down the trachea for surgery when all of a sudden Ara raised off the gurney and gushed vomit all over the place. We turned him over so he wouldn't aspirate but he was already dead. It wasn't the aspiration that killed him, Markie. He had lost so much blood that there was nothing left for the heart to pump. I tried cardiac massage and I got a long needle and injected some adrenalin into his heart. But those things don't work if you don't have something for the heart to pump. There was nothing wrong with his heart. In fact, he had an incredibly strong heart. He just didn't have enough fluid to circulate. He died of cardiac arrest."

He died facedown. The autopsy revealed that he had suffered a perforation of the inferior vena cava, which meant that the fluid they were pumping in from below was lost. Much of it was going out the hole and filling up his stomach instead of getting up to the heart.

"But that was correctable at surgery. I was that close, Markie. The timing was off just a little. I stomped around and kicked the walls for weeks.

That was my good buddy. I have to tell you that one of the skills blacks from my era have is you know the difference between sincerity and insincerity. Nobody can come up and fool you with a bunch of jive. I liked Ara right off. Many people you meet, you have to cut through the veneer to find out what they are. Not Ara. I never thought of your dad as white.

"When we moved next door, you were only a few years old but already he was your hero. That wasn't just a relationship some boys have with their father. And it came out in you. It came out full blast. I mean, you didn't believe it. Months afterward, you still weren't accepting. As far as you were concerned he was alive and he was going to come back. By some hook or crook or magic or miracle, one day your dad was going to open the door and walk back in. 'See, I told you people.' You went stark raving mad. Like someone cut off your arm or leg or gouged out your eyes. You were going to find the men who did this if it took the rest of your life."

He had come full circle, to what he assumed was the point of my visit. But this wise man who had stood up to the racists in our old neighborhood, my father at his side, thought it best that I forget the murder, at least the search for killers, and focus only on my father and me.

"Markie, people just aren't going to hand you the answer because they feel bad or sorry for you. And even if you found the killers, you wouldn't be able to resurrect him. His end doesn't change. What you need to answer isn't who killed your father and why but a real understanding of who he was. That's the end point. Who your Dad was in relationship to you, not who your Dad was in relationship to society. You need to find him in *you*."

Like Linda Lewis, Dr. Marius had made it all real again. He took me to a place I had not been and now he was asking me to leave it there, to do something which he felt was much harder and more important than turning myself into a stalker of killers. I told him it was too early in the game to drop one quest for the other. Actually, it was too late. I had to find the men responsible. Their identities and motives were questions that had defined the whole of my life since age fifteen, and only after I had answered the whos and whys of murder could I pursue what Dr. Marius considered my real mission: to find that part of my father in me.

I didn't expect anyone to simply drop answers in my lap. Sure, some people made cynical by the violent times would greet my questions with indifference. But I never doubted for a minute that I would connect emotionally with most of them. It was my gift, this willingness to maneuver my tragedy, the knack to relate to other people and their own pain. I first noticed it in high school when a classmate selected me to confide her pregnancy and abortion and boyfriend's foot fetish, all in the same confessional. And not one word about my tragedy had to be uttered. It was an understanding, one of those equations in which the premise was implicit.

Over the years, I honed this gift so that family and friends chose me to carry their stories. I became a receptacle for the dreams and defeats of those around me, and I bore their hope and pain not as weight but as ballast. Only later would I question the debasement of this gift, whether in the game of journalism it had become alloyed with the false earnestness of a con man.

Even so, I didn't question its fruit. I was the first journalist to interview the Hinkleys after their son John tried to kill President Reagan. I found them walking out of Fort Meade army hospital a few days after he tried to kill himself. The father hesitated and I talked fast. There was the military man in suburban Maryland whose wife and three children were killed by a drunk driver as they headed to church to perform the parts of Mary and Jesus in the Christmas play. My colleague and I knocked on that taciturn man's front door and he invited us inside and took us to each of their bedrooms and stayed strong until he reached the living room and caught sight of the Christmas tree. I scribbled furiously. Later, I crossed the cultural and linguistic divide of LA's Asian community by befriending the children first. They were caught in between, an age-old flux. Honor and obey your parents. Hurry and find your way in America. I hung out at coffeehouses and restaurants, pool halls and motels. "FBI, FBI," they'd whisper as I entered the room. It took months of gambling, drinking and death threats before they asked me home. "This is the white ghost," they'd tell their parents. "*Nee ha ma,*" I would greet them, bowing.

And so it became with family and friends and the people who shared Dad's world, only I wasn't a journalist anymore but "Markie," the son they had never stopped feeling sorry for.

Mike Garvey, the bar manager, recalled the time he and one of the regulars tried to get Dad to smoke a joint in the car.

"We passed it back and forth and then we passed it to Ara. 'Come on, Ara. Just give it a try.' He wasn't the least bit curious. We had a cocktail waitress named Tina who came to work stumbling on downers. Your dad turned to me all upset and said, 'Go talk to Tina. She's loaded on uppers again.' Ara didn't know a red from a white from a blue. He'd have an occasional drink but I can't say I ever saw him drunk. . . . Yeah, he had a fling or two. But he was no chaser."

Judy Morley, a cocktail waitress, remembered the cleanliness that drove some employees crazy.

"When I first went to work for your father, everybody told me when you clean the tables make sure you check underneath for gum. And I said, 'Gum?' They said, 'Oh, yeah, Ara will come around and check.' I thought, 'Oh, they must be kidding.' And sure enough he did. He'd come in and the first thing he'd do is put his hands under the tables to see if there was gum."

Stan Paramore, another bartender, said it was like two generations talking past each other.

"He took that chicken shit little place and made it into the most happening and classy nightclub in the valley. Then the drug dealing burglars came. Ara contributed to it. First the jukebox. Then the go-go girls. Then live music. Get high and screw. That's all we lived for. Ara couldn't understand it. 'Ara, it feels good, man. How about you and Flora?' He said, 'Look, once a week we have an appointment. Sometimes when I go to the appointment she's got a headache. I say, 'What the hell. Next week we've got another appointment.'"

Marc Chenault, a music promoter, felt that my father, bored of his spot in the safe, soft middle, tingled at life on the raw and perilous edge. Armond Bletcher and the others must have seemed a safe ship there.

"The Apartments was a fucking zoo, man. There was a trendy group and then a group of hoods who were kind of celebrities. It was kind of mixing different people up. Your dad kept it stirred up. He was gregarious. Very funny. And he took care of the rascals on some level. He hired me to book Chuck Berry. This is before "My Ding-a-Ling" became a hit. The place was packed. Berry was pretty strung out but he was good. I remember going into the back room to get the $1,000 to pay him. And Mike Garvey told me he'd get the money back if I wanted. He and his buddies would roll Chuck Berry in the parking lot. All I had to do was give him the nod."

Richard Dillon, a patron who smuggled drugs in the 1960s, recalled a man who stood his ground.

"Ara's Apartments. Moths to flame. Fast cats, $100 bills, women, guns. Ara was tough. That stuff didn't shake his shit. We'd meet our connection at Ara's. Your father didn't respect that. He resented the money we were making and how we were making it. In his own way, he was taking the money back from us and putting it into Little League."

This is what counted for another friend. Russ Pulliam—Ara the family man, Ara the Little-League coach and Pop Warner football sponsor.

"I remember the day we bought new helmets and jerseys and he got in trouble with the city because we had the best equipment. They tried to ban the helmets and Ara got pissed. 'Why not outfit all the kids with new gear? This old crap is dangerous.' He'd bring home these vagabonds from the bar and your mom would look at me and say, 'Who in the hell is this one?' Ara had no color. Everyone was the same. I don't think he ever changed."

Tracy Stockwell, a cocktail waitress, was embarrassed to see me when I finally tracked her down in Orange County. She told me she had spent the past eighteen years trying not to feel anything, medicating her brain and body with heroin, numbed against love and pain. She was a huge woman, tall and still carrying the weight of a recent pregnancy. Her swollen hands and feet bore the brunt of her disfigurement. Dr. Scholl's medicated powder, her cutting agent, had eaten away at her flesh.

I wanted to know why my father thrived on the praise and dependence of people who so often were weak, broken and so young. How he could surround himself with hoods like Armond Bletcher and Donnie Edwards and believe he wouldn't get hurt. Not hurt his family.

"Your dad saw potential in all these guys. He saw what they could be if they weren't throwing away their lives. You've got to remember, this was twenty years ago. Nobody knew just what a hold drugs could get on people. And your dad thought that, well, if you can just give people some hope, give them some money to start them off in a little business or whatever, that they'll change."

"What you're saying is that he was stupid enough, gullible enough, to believe he could impose his morality on people who had a completely different ethic?"

"Because he was right. He ended up very dead right. He had his convictions and he had the courage of his convictions and he just didn't realize how stupid and treacherous and petty people can be. Your dad was a man. And it was a lesser man that undoubtedly was the reason he was killed."

I sat in her tiny, filthy apartment for three hours trying to keep myself from drowning in the whirlpool of her memories. I didn't know what to make of her. She couldn't sit still. She asked me five times if I wanted something to drink. She picked up and dropped the phone twice. The baby was fussing and it seemed to me a simple matter of a dirty diaper. Tracy got nowhere with her bounces and lullaby. This was Southern California, it was the nineties, but the ease with which she spilled the most private details embarrassed even me. She had a dozen different stories of lovers and betrayers, and heroin and cocaine were their own separate sagas. By the time she had finished and was ready to return to the subject of my father, she was sopping wet from sweat. Was it drugs? Was it some knowledge of my father's murder she was hiding?

"I know. It almost would have been better for him to be an asshole, then you wouldn't have much reason to miss him. A slime creature that you're better off he's dead. But he wasn't. Your father didn't approve of drugs. And he didn't keep his mouth shut. He talked about it too much. He was a moral man. Way too much for the world he was in."

I wondered out loud if her words weren't too kind, and she bristled.

"I had enough respect for Ara not to bullshit his son. No reason to whitewash him. Your dad didn't need to be whitewashed."

She said she had failed my father, failed his vision of what she could be. If he were alive today, he'd be disappointed in her, in all of them.

"I left Orange County in 1970 and moved to Fresno because I couldn't stand my father. Your dad was my friend. The guy was real. He didn't pull punches. He became my role model for what a father should be. I'm going to put it this way: I replaced my gutless father with your gutsy father. Your father had balls. Too many. He stepped on somebody's toes and they caused him to lose all of his. I loved Ara. There was nothing sexual, nothing illicit about it. Your dad was just a fucking giant. He was a giant in my life."

The praise of the wounded. I took it as his legacy, a salve for my own battered soul. I no longer bothered to question it, separate it from the desolate woman recalling with fantasy and possibility her own youth. This song was a gift, and I embraced it, sang it, as I walked out her door.

Their stories shared the basic theme of innocence amid treachery. They recalled the time he fired the band, a bunch of longhairs, for smoking grass during rehearsal. They said he refused to believe that employees and patrons were dealing dope—until the evidence stared him straight in the eye.

"Ara was absolutely the most optimistic person I have ever known," said cocktail waitress Judy Morley. "He always had the feeling that it was going to turn out right. Everything was going to be fine."

"We used to smoke this parsley dipped in elephant tranquilizer," said Digby Sanders, another regular. "It didn't smell like marijuana and we'd smoke it in The Apartments all the time. We knew Ara worked at nights and came in around eight. Someone would yell from behind the bar that Ara had left home and was on his way to the bar. We had to put out our cigarettes before he got there."

Even police and prosecutors, state and federal drug agents were willing to give him the benefit of the doubt. Don't be so harsh. This was the sixties. It all went down fast. How could one man gauge the danger or know that two decades later people would be killed everyday in the crossfire of drugs. Don't imbue him with your perfect knowledge.

"Every few weeks, I'd get a call from Ara late at night," George Carter, the defense attorney, confided over drinks. "He'd awaken me from a sound sleep with the same plea. 'George, what are we going to do about the drugs and corruption in this town?'"

This time I interrupted the story. Please, no more Ara as moralistic prattler, babbling antidrug slogans to the heavies. No more naïve Ara. Virtuous Ara. It was too easy in the face of imponderables.

"Cut the bullshit, George," I said. "I want a father. Not some fucking saint."

He shook his head and grinned. "I don't get you, Arax. You push and push and push. Why can't you believe your old man was a helluva guy. That he died on the right side. He cared about this town and wanted to clean it up. Why are you so sure we're all lying? What's wrong with you?"

Others, more forthright perhaps, felt obliged to reconcile the dark rumors with the good man they knew. If he did get involved in the narcotics trade, they reasoned, it was with great reluctance and in the face of financial pressure and a past in which bankruptcy had broken him.

"I always had the feeling that Ara was an incredibly savvy person," said Van Keyes, another bartender. "He may have been involved on a financial level. 'Here's some money. I don't care what you do with it but I want this much back.' Now there was nothing I ever saw to validate that. But at the very least, he turned away."

"There was a struggle inside Ara," said Marc Chenault. "Demons of bankruptcy. Demons of family. Demons of self-control. He talked a lot about the Peacock Markets, losing it all at a young age and having a nervous breakdown. He overcame a lot. He had his own system and it worked out all right. But maybe when he made his comeback, he vowed that that's not going to happen to me again. And maybe he did whatever he had to do to not let it happen."

Some of those closest to my father detected a change toward the end, though I wondered if this wasn't the hindsight of tragedy talking. There wasn't that easy smile or laugh when he walked in the room. He finally realized, it seemed, that whatever he gave to these people, and he gave a lot, it was never going to be enough. As his misgivings grew, so did his frustration and outbursts.

"There was a fight at the bar and Ara ran everybody outside and closed the door," Linda Iskendarian, Dad's younger cousin, recalled. "He was yelling and screaming. 'You're not going to fight in my place.' He was right in their faces. We all got the hell out of there. It was a wild time and I'd be afraid to walk into a place like that today. But I felt safe because Ara was around and he didn't put up with nobody's crap. These were heavy people and they listened to him."

If all this caused some deeper questioning, my father did not change course substantively. Yes, he went to a more mellow band. Yes, he wasn't afraid to make his displeasure known and some patrons, out of respect, took to doing their dope smoking and dealing behind his back. But no one could recall my father at any point seriously contemplating selling the bars and moving on. Moreover, it seemed to me that any concerns he expressed about "drugs and corruption"—concerns that may have gotten him killed—came very late in the game and without much thought to fallout. To be a hero, I told myself, it wasn't enough to be a victim.

This was not the impression of Jess Ortiz, a retired narcotics officer with the Fresno Police Department whose beat took in The Apartments. As early as 1969, he said, my father had grown sufficiently frustrated over his inability to control the bar that he began meeting with Ortiz's partner, Gene Bain. He didn't bother hiding the meetings. They met right there at the bar.

"Your father would ask us to come into the back office, the one where he was killed. 'Bring the boys a drink.' Your dad and Gene talked. About what I don't know because Gene always asked me to step out. 'Hey partner, would you excuse us a minute?' They'd talk for forty-five minutes and I'd have four or five scotch and waters. Later, after Gene was killed in a plane crash, I saw your father at headquarters. Who he was seeing and why, I don't know."

Whenever I found myself torn between conflicting images of my father, doubting the instincts that made me a good reporter, I turned to Danny Melnick, the English professor and writer who married my father's sister. During summers away from Berkeley in the late 1960s and early seventies, he was kept busy doing odd jobs for Dad at the bar. He was trying to make sense of this family he had married into, and he didn't know at first what to make of my father. He watched him mixing drinks behind the bar, clearly enjoying the effect his energy had on people, his ability to make them feel loved and important. He was wired in a way that made you think of the finest in a politician. That ability to project trust to a group and getting their trust in return, it's what he seemed to live for. And he didn't discriminate. It wasn't in his nature. He wanted to be liked and accepted so badly, that he let himself be flattered by people who weren't always worthy of his attention.

Danny began to see a kind of Gatsby, at once a man of great integrity and energy and a big fake. One Christmas, Danny excused himself from the dinner table and went into my parents' bedroom to watch a rare televised concert of two famous Soviet classical musicians. No one thought of peeking in on Danny. No one except my father. He stood in the bedroom only a few seconds watching this strange concert. If I could, he told Danny, this would be the kind of life I'd lead. All of us living together in a kind of communal setting with music and art. All of us appreciating each other and learning from one another's different interests.

"Was he putting me on? Was he serious? I'm not sure it mattered," Danny said. "He had built a world of illusion out of a desire to please other people. He stayed in the room with me no more than twenty or thirty seconds. What? Was he going to sit there and listen to a Beethoven sonata? No, no, no. That was part of Ara's integrity. He was giving me a gift. That he appreciated the life these artists had to offer. And that he could connect with me, however fleeting. And I felt that gift.

"I've always believed that it was this quality, this sense of community, that got Ara into a situation beyond his controlling. His basic good-naturedness shaped his vision but it also got him into a lot of arguments. I can imagine a combination of blowing up and fear."

Danny said he would always wonder what kind of spirit my father might have been had he taught himself a greater grace and greater control without losing that energy and vitality. Instead, all that wonderful life, all that appreciation for life, went for nothing, spilled out in an empty bar room.

○ ○ ○

Why did my father, a grape grower and grocer, a man with ostensible options, feel himself tethered to the bar business, so that at a time of doubt and disillusionment, rather than cut himself free, he tied the rope even tighter with a second nightclub, The Forum?

We were gypsies, my grandmother said, farm to city and back again. In one five-year span, Uncle Navo, in the spirit of Grandpa, bounded from grocer to notions seller to private eye to a salesman of roofs and aluminum siding and, finally, vacuum cleaners. My uncle never looked back. My father couldn't so easily let go.

My mother knew well his insecurity and neediness, the ego caress he got from the bar, and she tried in her impetuous way to break its hold on him. "Your name in lights," she mocked him. "Mentor to all the creeps and whores." His distaste for starting over was certainly colored by the grocery store years, as Marc Chenault and others surmised. His mental breakdown as he tried to save the markets must have been a descent into a melancholy he had not known, and his recovery a soaring rebirth. The beginning, middle and end of that passage were reduced to four disjunct images for me: my father, naked and standing over my mother in bed, begging her to wake up because his heart had skipped a beat; the butcher picking him up each morning and dropping him off each night; his exercise program in boxer shorts that shook the whole house; all of us piling into the car Tuesdays after dinner and driving him to a dark wooden house and picking him up an hour later. "He's visiting a friend," Mom explained.

I don't know at what age I put two and two together and figured out it was a shrink my father was seeing. When one of my aunts told me his name was Donn Beedle and he was still alive, I wasted no time tracking him down and getting him to agree to an interview.

He knew our family well, and from a number of different vantages, having first counseled my father's sister, Jeanette, during a troubled childhood and then Navo during a troubled marriage. My father started seeing him in 1961, a year or so before the Peacocks went belly up. He determined right off that the usual couch and hypnotherapy weren't needed. Unlike Navo, whose sessions went nowhere, my father was easy to work with. Any troubles he had, he was eager to face.

At first, his complaints focused on my mother's ambitions. She was pushing him—to make more money, to raise the standard of their life. And then he focused on Navo and the Peacocks.

"Ara loved giving to people. Naturally they took advantage of him. He'd take it and take it and then he'd blow up. It was real quick. He didn't hold a grudge. But he did have an intense need to be someone. To make it. To keep up with his brother. Navo was the frontman. Your grandmother's favorite. He could do a lot of bullshitting and that wasn't your dad's style. He felt very strongly that Navo wasn't working as hard as he was. Along with this resentment came pressure from your mother. So Ara felt pretty inadequate. And his anxieties became disabling: 'My heart is skipping.'; 'I can't drive anymore.' He was in a situation where he felt he didn't have control over anything in his life. So literally, psychologically, he began the process of dying because he couldn't be what he wanted to be. The boss. His own man."

For eight years on and off, he visited Beedle. He'd feel fine for a long stretch and then something would bug him and he'd call and say, "I need to talk." In 1968, the anxiety attacks and driving phobias no more, his equilibrium more or less restored, he stopped seeing Beedle professionally. They remained good friends.

"He blossomed in the bar business. And what's the first thing he does? He goes out and gets a Little League team. He told me the baseball world was the best possible world because there are rules that everybody has to live by. Straight lines.

"I was a sounding board for Ara and over time most of his symptoms disappeared. Seeing him through that misery and seeing him blossom, God, that's your whole purpose for being in this profession. 'Cause the rest is crap. And then the shocker. You hear that your flower has been *whooooosssshhed*—cut down. I don't remember anything that affected me more in my private practice."

"You said most of his symptoms disappeared?"

"I give a test early in the visits to measure how a person views himself and the world. If he manipulates the world or if the world manipulates him. Ara felt the world was impinging on him. That he was being manipulated. I'm not sure that ever changed, even though he became his own boss."

I asked him about the rumors of drug involvement, if he ever tried to reconcile them with the Little League coach who kept the diamond in mint condition.

"The question whether he was involved or not is not a question I dealt with."

"Why not?"

"To say yes or no, I just didn't think about it. If you're asking me now, I don't honestly know. He was clean through and through. What he said was it. But there were pressures. He wanted the bar to succeed. To show Navo. To show himself that he could do it on his own."

I told Beedle about my father's visits to the police department and my struggle to understand his motives. Was he there to expose wrongdoing or cover up for his own wrongdoing and strike a deal. Either way, he was seeing the wrong cops.

"Something just flashed through my mind," he said, a little startled at the memory. "I wondered that same thing once. I thought it to myself. Your father going to authorities, risking himself for the community. I told you he felt the world was impinging on him. But he also had a strong sense of outrage.

"That combination," he said. "It can be a dangerous one."

○ ○ ○

No one ever came right out and said it but the implication was plain on their lips. If your father took a short cut, if he betrayed his ideals, it was to please your mother, to keep up with her growing needs and wants. Her coworkers at Bank of America, the job she held before she met Dad, recalled the clotheshorse who blew her paycheck at Fresno's fanciest dress shops.

Her best friend remembered how she kept my father guessing through their year-long courtship. Others recalled how my father went AWOL when he found out Flora was dating the Italian boy. Their roller coaster relationship became my childhood, the drop between high and low ever more precipitous once Dad bought the bar. Even the way they fought was different. These weren't the bridled arguments of the grocery store years, but vile and violent confrontations over someone I knew only as "the redhead."

"It's not red anymore," she said. "A little gray and blonde and brown now."

She had driven up in a shiny new black Cadillac Coupe de Ville laced in gold. She shimmered, too. All black and purple. Everything color-coordinated right down to her sunglasses and lipstick, shoulder scarf and nail polish. There was enough retained to suggest the beauty she had been. She was built like Mom, short and slim. The skin of her face was tight and shiny, her teeth a little gray. She had a pinched nose, long but not exceedingly so, and the most beautiful blue eyes. I knew what Mom would have said. Too much makeup. Too much hair. Too much gold and diamonds. Somehow she carried it off, just shy of garish. She was pretty and sweet and on her fourth marriage.

They met in 1966, a few months after my father bought the bar. She was working cosmetics at Thrifty Drug Store and one of her customers was this blonde bombshell named Patsy. One night, she accompanied Patsy to The Apartments and my father bought them a drink. They returned the next weekend and Dad asked Carole to dance.

"We danced the whole night and then he asked if he could see me again. I said, 'I thought you were interested in Patsy.' He laughed. 'That's way too much woman for me.' We fell in love that night on the dance floor. I mean, it was just like that with us."

She was ten years younger but she wanted me to know he was no sugar daddy. Except for one nice dress on her birthday and covering a few months rent for her and a child, he didn't lavish gifts or expensive dinners. They mostly took long drives into the foothills and talked until three or four in the morning—the mornings my mother chained the door in protest and Dad would knock on my window and I'd tiptoe down the hall to let him in.

"I'm curious. . . . How was—"

"He was wonderful. He was wonderful. I'll be honest. We went to motels. It was funny, Mark, because he never registered. The key was always under the mat. A friend of his owned the motel. When we got ready to leave, he would always put money on the dresser. 'Why are you leaving money there?' I'd ask. 'For the maid who cleans up this room.' I mean, who does that?"

She said they weren't together long when my mother, clutching her proof, confronted Dad. "Is this some little whore on the side?" Dad told her he was in love. "Do you think you can afford a divorce? You better realize what it will cost you. The business? The kids?"

"Never once did your mother say, 'I love you, Ara. Don't leave me, Ara.' She wanted nice things and she wanted him to make lots of money. But big money didn't matter to him. That's why when I heard those rumors about drugs, it was very hard for me to believe."

One night, my mother feigned a suicide attempt, swishing her mouth with whiskey and setting a vial of pills on the kitchen table. She telephoned a girlfriend who called Dad at work.

"Your mother didn't drink but there was a bottle of booze out and she had taken some sips and maybe some pills. It scared us both to death. To think that it had come to this. We were sitting at our table and he said, 'I don't know what to do. You're young. You don't need all this hassle with me. I don't want to deceive you. I can't leave my family.' There was no fighting. There was no yelling. There were tears, both of us. He wiped his eyes."

Their physical relationship ended that night, she said, a year after it began. A few months later, Dad set her up with one of his bartenders, a clean-cut guy closer to her age. Six months later, they announced their engagement at the bar.

"Ara kept staring at me and we both, I know, were still in love. He said, 'I'm so happy for you.' He bought a round of champagne and came up and hugged me and kissed me and said, 'I want you to be happy.'"

He called her at work and sent flowers on her birthday. When her marriage broke up, Dad asked if he could see her again. This was a few years before he was killed and she met him at the bar and they drove all night in the rain.

"He took me by the house he built. I said, 'It's really pretty, Ara.' And he said, 'It's okay. The old house was fine. But this is what she wanted.' . . . I'm not blaming your mother, yet in a way, I am. If he had walked away from her, I just think he'd be here today. I know that sounds harsh. But he wanted to go back to the grocery business. I was in retail and we used to laugh about that. Starting over. The two of us."

I asked her why she was so sure she could have made it work with him, considering her track record.

"The men I married after your father were, I don't know, abusive. Ara was the most kind and gentle man I ever knew."

I began to recite my father's explosive, brutal side but it didn't go very far. This was not a man she recognized. After all, they had known each other intimately only a year and it was long before the bar became violent. I didn't bother to correct her, to tell her that it was my father who instigated for a new house, and when driving people by it for the first time, he took the long way down Van Ness Extension—a route paved with a wealth that could not be mistaken. She excused herself to go to the restroom and I thought how easy I was letting her off. Here was the woman who defined so much of my childhood, who caused untold grief and nearly sundered us for good and I was laughing and sighing with her, a conspirator to her sweeter, gentler Ara. She had charmed the hour with her sentimental speculations. She had captivated me not unlike the way she had captivated my father that night on the dance floor. Oh, what would my mother think?

"You said you were nervous about today. Well, I have to tell you that I was nervous, too. Nervous about what I might find. 'The other woman.' Maybe you couldn't put a sentence together. Maybe my father meant nothing to you after all these years."

"Mark, I can remember the first night I met him. It's right here in my eyes. He came and sat down and our eyes met and I thought, 'What beautiful brown eyes and long, curly eyelashes.' I hope you put this all down and get this all clear in your mind. How many people can love someone and split up with someone and all these years later say, 'Yeah, I love that person. I will always love that person.' He's in my heart. He will always have a place there. The compassion I see in your face, it's the same that your father had. Exactly. And the tears you have in your eyes, I've seen in his. You have a lot of love. You have that of his.

"I owe you an apology for bringing so much heartache to your family and your mother. I didn't do it to your mother deliberately. I fell in love with your father. Your mother happened to be married to your father at the time. It's not a morally wonderful thing, but you know what Mark, I wouldn't change it if I had to do it all over again.

"I will always remember his face. It was kind, very kind. It was like he could put his arms around you and protect you from the whole world and nothing could hurt you. That's how I felt with Ara. Nothing or no one could hurt me. He made me feel very secure. He made me feel very protected. And I loved him very much."

1 devoted nearly a year alone to under-
standing three major drug conspiracies in full swing at the time of the
murder: Nunez–Hornig, Lambe–Simone and Buddy Barnard. I dia-
grammed the day-to-day movements of the ringleaders and their pilots
and mules—from the phone numbers they called to the planes, cars and
hotels they rented. I constructed two charts, one outlining the general
events in the last six months of my father's life and the other breaking
down the movements of Dad and the major suspects in the twenty-four
hours before and after the shooting.

Even as shapes began to emerge I wondered if the whole exercise wasn't
a ritual in what writer Don DeLillo called the religion of coincidence.
Many patterns weren't patterns at all but appeared so only by the dint of
examination. The critical eye was a cohering eye. And then there was my
memory, a merciful timekeeper. Events I swore took place a year or two
prior to the murder actually happened in the final months and weeks. It
was as if my mind had elongated the hourglass, distorted the clock to give
us more time.

Beclouding the picture was my father—his outbursts and rantings and
half-baked business deals. His hair-trigger temper thumbed its nose at

fear and prudence. A sensible man, a man keen to survival, never would have spat in the face of a thug and world champion weight lifter (Photopoulos). A sensible man never would have pilloried the town's biggest pimp (Prestidge) and a drug smuggler (Nunez) on successive weekends. A sensible man never would have entered into two partnerships hidden from state regulators, never would have catered to a drug crowd while loudly protesting their behavior and then firing and incriminating employees involved in drugs.

My father understood that Police Chief Hank Morton and Lieutenant Eddie Heizenrader weren't cartoon bad guys. You took care of them—free booze and a paid advertisement in Morton's police annual—and they took care of you. They could fix any little problem.

"Ara was always feeding free drinks to the cops," Mike Garvey, the manager of The Apartments, told me. Once, my father even fired Garvey at the behest of two narcotic officers who threatened to put heat on the bar if he didn't. Then, in typical fashion, trying to make both sides happy, he hired Garvey back and then hired two cops to work the front door.

Fresnans were content as long as the black community was kept west of the railroad tracks and vice was contained downtown. My father knew this. He knew that anyone who bucked the system, anyone who stood up and shouted the truth, was a damn fool. He knew that bar owners saw and heard plenty and the smart ones filed and forgot.

He knew, or should have known, that Dan Hornig was a sandbagger whose failing nightclub was ravaged in an arson fire in which he was the only suspect. Around town, they called him The Torch. He knew, too, that you didn't shame a man before his friends, especially a big-time Mexican drug smuggler like Frank Nunez whose entire life—from his white wife to his white golfing buddies—was one of cultural effacement.

How then do I explain my indiscreet father? How do I account for his hidden partnership with Hornig and his rage at the end, the explosion that caused him to knock down Nunez with a single devastating blow, call the attorney general's office, call agent Walley and visit the police intelligence unit?

And what if he was divulging something dangerous to police about major drug activity. From where did his knowledge come? Did it come from men who trusted him and discussed their business openly? From business partners involved against his wishes? Or from his own complicity that impelled a last minute, foolhardy expiation? It was no small difference. It was the difference between the father I had ennobled and a snitch trying to save his own ass.

I took my questions to a county investigator with whom I had become friendly, a former cop whose file cabinet, like mine, told the story of Fresno all the way back to Davidian. He sat me down in his office and pulled out a copy of the police investigation into my father's murder and began reading to himself the notes made when he was a rookie. Every now and then he shook his head.

"What is it?" I asked.

"You know I'd forgotten the climate of fear in Fresno around the time of your father's murder. The Lambe–Simone ring had just come down and people were running scared. . . . It was a nervous time. A frightening time."

The Lambe and Simone families, related by marriage, were prominent in Fresno's Italian community. They had been fig ranchers for years, so successful that Tony Simone Sr. was known throughout the valley as Mr. Fig. Less well-known were the illicit roots of their empire.

During Prohibition, immigrant Mauro Simone had been convicted of operating a still on his west side ranch as part of Fresno's great liquor scandal. Bootlegging enabled the old man to ride out hard times. Four decades later, federal agents concluded that his son, Tony, and daughter, Antoinette Lambe, and son-in-law Frank Lambe and two grandsons were smuggling marijuana and cocaine to weather another recession.

Their planes (Frank Lambe owned the busiest Piper aircraft dealership in the country) hauled kilo bricks from Mexico to Fresno for distribution over a wide area of California. The conspirators included a powerful state senator from San Mateo, Richard Dolwig, and a Fresno attorney and fixer named Vince Todisco who was suspected of laundering the profits through a local chain of pizza parlors. They were so far ahead of the game, controlling every phase of the operation but street sales, that even the U.S. Justice Department's organized crime strike force in San Francisco took notice. One 2,400 pound load of marijuana belonging to the group was found in the scrub outside Phoenix, the largest seizure ever made in the U.S. at the

time. A special drug conspiracy unit was formed and Lambe–Simone became its number one target.

Flatland fortified by mountains, the San Joaquin Valley was the perfect
hub, sustaining the dope smuggler with three requisites: a ready source of
crop duster pilots, any number of desolate places to land and the outright
complicity of Hank Morton's police department and Melvin Willmirth's
sheriff's office.

Crop dusters earning $10,000 for an entire season of farmwork took
home nearly that much in one furtive run to Mexico. Mules made anywhere from $1,000 to $2,000 to ferry a load to the San Francisco Bay
Area. The money flowed so plentiful that it often came stapled in stacks.

The cash registers at Ara's Apartments rang with these perforated dollars. In fact, it was in the back billiard room of our bar where Garvin Dale
White, a former bartender, helped put together the Lambe–Simone ring
in the summer of 1969.

My friend at the D.A.'s office naturally wondered about this. Was my
father aware that White and other employees and patrons were involved in
a major drug conspiracy? Did he approve? Disapprove? Did he make his
disapproval known? Might he have put in five to make ten?

White's rap sheet ran some twenty pages; he had escaped two maximum-
security prisons and was now behind bars in U.S.P. Marion, the most
heavily guarded federal pen in America. His young son, a brilliant student
who barely knew him, had gone into training with some survivalists and
attacked Marion a few years earlier, coming within a whisker of breaking
his father out. The boy was never caught but, out of a sort of kinship with
his dad, turned himself in and was now locked away in a federal prison in
Mississippi.

"Why not write the father?" a mutual friend suggested. "He'd love to
hear from you."

Three weeks later, a letter from P.O. Box 1000, Marion, Illinois, arrived
at the *Los Angeles Times*.

Hello Mark Arax,

You've got guts to write a stranger in prison and want the truth
about your father not knowing what I might tell you. I remember

you well, Mark. Ara would sit you at the end of the bar on hot summer afternoons after the baseball park and introduce you (so proud) to all of us as you had a soda. You never stayed too long. I don't think your mother approved.

Ara had a zest for life that made him unique among some of the toughest rogues that ever came down the pike. I only wish that you were here in front of me, eye-to-eye, for me to tell you that your father never had any involvement in what we did that was illegal! Oh, he was asked by several that I know of but he would never even loan money for such things. And anyone who knew his principles wouldn't ask.

Those were great golden times—the sixties, The Apartments, go-go dancers—and Ara was some kind of special guy. No one could, or ever did, do it better. I live in a world now where a man lives or dies by his honesty. U.S.P. Marion, the nation's most max, has been locked down now for five years. We get an hour and a half out of our cells a day for shower and rec.

I envied your father's family-man attitude. His love for you, his whole family and your mother. Need I say more!

Venceremos,

G. Dale White

The first axiom of a homicide investigation is that everybody lies. So I wrote back and thanked White for his kind words and kept looking for a connection between my father and the Lambe–Simone ring. I found a DEA agent in Washington who worked the bar in 1971 as part of the Lambe–Simone case. "We developed a lot of snitches, Big Armond Bletcher included," David Wilson told me. "And none of them ever said your father was involved in this ring. His nightclub a meeting place? Yes. He himself involved? No."

In the summer of 1971, the federal strike force assembled enough evidence to charge Frank Lambe and his son, Anthony, and nephew Anthony Simone Jr. and twelve others in three separate indictments. Dale White was doing time on a minor drug crime when agents caught up with him, and he agreed to testify against the group in exchange for conjugal visits.

It was conceivable, with just the right combination of carrot and stick, that federal prosecutors would get those indicted to cough up other, bigger conspirators and maybe even the Fresno cops shielding the enterprise.

Sadly, the Lambe–Simone case finished with a whimper. Prosecutors not only neglected to test the waters of cooperation with pilots and mules, but they cut a deal with the kingpins to get those beneath them to plead guilty. Prosecutors reasoned that even if the case went to trial and even if the jury believed Dale White's testimony—barriers not easily scaled—they still faced U.S. District Court Judge Myron Crocker as sentencer.

It was Crocker who a decade earlier had imposed such ridiculously light sentences on Fresno's bookmakers that they had no incentive to turn government witness against their protectors in local law enforcement. They paid their small fines—a paltry tax on earnings—and went right back to work or graduated to drug smuggling. In the Lambe case, federal prosecutors argued that it was better to bargain a certain plea from the Lambes than to gamble with a judge like Crocker.

True to form, Crocker sentenced Frank Lambe and his son to three years in prison with parole after one year. That one year would be spent at Lompoc, the country-club facility where Nixon's aides would do their Watergate time. Nephew Anthony Simone Jr. got six months at a conservation camp.

As if the sentence wasn't light enough, Crocker agreed to delay imposition of the term seven months so Frank Lambe could harvest his fig and prune crop. Lambe kept pushing until he got U.S. Attorney Dwayne Keyes to agree not to seek criminal tax penalties or assess a $100-an-ounce marijuana excise. This alone saved Lambe hundreds of thousands of dollars.

It was during this time of plea bargaining and uncertainty over whether others would be indicted that my father was seeing a number of police officials, including Lieutenant Orndoff. If my father used those visits to reveal any aspect of the Lambe–Simone ring, he was gambling in a way he could not have known because it was Orndoff and another member of Morton's jade ring crew, Sergeant Sam Renna, who had tipped off the Lambes to impending busts.

I was slipping away, harder to reach. My wife was pregnant with our second child and the baby was kicking, but it all seemed unreal to me. I sat in my cluttered office, the past imported wall to wall, and wrote furiously to all hours of the morning. Notes on crime and punishment, I called it, my punishment, 600 pages and counting, much of it crazed.

What is necessary and what is indulgence? I was unable to decide. All those words and my father remained frustratingly indistinct. I tried to measure how deeply the murder had changed me. I had forgotten the depth of my protest. It was relatives and friends who carried a vision of me, not the thirty-five-year-old adult but the child beset, shoulders slumped, weary slog. I had done a neat job of concealing the past with straight-A report cards and writing awards, triumphs won by destroying parts of myself. What bothers me today is not that I have forgotten the child but that I am unable to determine what is me truly and what became of me on account of murder. We, the murder and me, twined a long time ago. I once thought if I found my answer, I would be free of it. But we are a perfect working team, parts indistinguishable. The murder has served as goad to whatever I have achieved in life. My reason for loving the way I do. My excuse for hating the way I do. I could not be free of it any more than I could be free of them. Or them of me. I am your handiwork. Look at me. My mother, my father and then you. What do you think of your offspring?

I read and re-read the murder report, a tedium broken only by my visits to the superior court downtown to look up old criminal files. I paid particular attention to the five men whose long-distance phone records the detectives had pulled: Bletcher, Garvey, Nunez, Hornig and Hornig's realtor buddy, Leonard Maselli.

These printouts, in addition to my father's toll calls from home and work, were the one perfectly preserved record of associations and contacts in the days before and after the murder. I couldn't have imagined going forward without them and yet that is precisely what the detectives did, not bothering to examine the relationships in 90 percent of the calls.

Had they charted the calls with more care, they would have immediately deduced two things: Nunez, Hornig and Maselli maintained close contact right up to the night of January 2; my father, on the other hand, was searching, desperately it seemed, for someone in law enforcement to talk to.

There was the phone call to state narcotics agent Dick Walley, who had died of lung cancer years ago, and the phone calls to the state attorney general's office and to the Madera courthouse where the pilot and mules in the Nunez–Hornig drug ring were facing trial, and visits with Lieutenant Heizenrader, Lieutenant Orndoff and Officer Keeney.

The homicide team passed off my father's concerns as paranoia. Sergeant Dominic Estilarte, the head investigator, surmised that Dad's contacts with state and local law enforcement on the eve of his death had little, if anything, to do with information he may have been providing. Rather, he had likely called the attorney general's office to complain about harassment from undercover state agents and to plead the case that he wasn't such a bad bar owner.

Instead of exposing drug activity, the cops reasoned, my father was likely attempting to gain information and ingratiate himself to agencies he feared were investigating The Forum for drug activity. His fear was heightened by the fact that The Apartments was already facing a two-week shutdown for serving two teens.

I recalled my father's concern about state regulators closing down one or both bars, but to conclude that this was the sole motive behind his conversations with law enforcement seemed too pat. For one, such a conclusion ignored the people and events surrounding him at the time.

Dick Walley wasn't just any state narcotic agent but one of the four investigators who unraveled the Lambe–Simone drug operation, whose principals were negotiating plea bargains at the time of the murder. There was talk that the Nunez–Hornig group was an offshoot of Lambe–Simone, and any information from my father linking the two rings would have surely upset things.

My father had given the last of his $18,000 to Hornig on August 10, 1971. Two weeks later, the planeload of marijuana belonging to Nunez, Hornig and Maselli was confiscated by authorities in Madera.

If I could trace the money and movements behind that load—when and where the meetings took place, when the plane was rented and by whom—I might be able to determine if my father was one of the businessmen financing Nunez's drug operation. Only then might I know what went down between Dad and Hornig and why he was trying to contact authorities.

The $18,000 was the only transaction that stood out in my father's checking and savings accounts. The biggest payment came in a $10,000 check he wrote to Hornig on July 1. The following day, Hornig cashed the check at a Bank of America branch in Fresno. I knew this from the canceled check itself, which I had kept for years in Dad's wallet in a box in my room.

Uncle Mike had told me that as far as Dad was concerned, the $18,000 was strictly a down payment on a 40 percent partnership with Hornig. He also believed that Hornig, without Dad's knowledge, had diverted at least some of the money to Nunez. He could only speculate about my father's reaction once he found out. "Ara wouldn't have kept quiet. Knowing how much he hated drugs, that was a big betrayal."

My buddy at the district attorney's office smelled the possibility of something devious. "What makes you so sure the partnership with Hornig wasn't a ruse to hide your father's investment in drugs."

"So why would he write a check?" I snapped. "That's certainly not hiding your tracks."

"Exactly my point," he countered. "The money had to come from somewhere. Your father didn't have a coffee can stuffed with cash in the backyard. Writing the check actually gives him more protection. If the whole drug thing goes awry and Hornig takes a fall, your father can always point to the check. 'See, it was meant for the partnership. Why else would I write a check?' "

I wanted to tell him he had it all wrong but I wasn't exactly in the best position. I was trying to persuade him—and every other law enforcement official with whom I crossed paths—that I was willing to weigh the tough questions and do the hard work of a journalist, even if it meant doubting what I believed to be true as a son. So I kept quiet, thanked him for playing devil's advocate and waited until I got home to pour out my defense in the diary I kept.

If my father truly intended the money to finance one or more smuggling missions, why the pretense of a partnership in The Forum? For deniability's sake? Dad wasn't that artful. He operated seat of the pants. For me to conclude that he fronted the money and then used the partnership as a ruse to cover up illicit intentions was to assume a level of guile and artifice he never before displayed in business dealings. Hidden partnership was my father's M.O. First Uncle George, then Mike Garvey and finally Dan Hornig. It was the old-country way, a deal sealed with a handshake. Later, when he had time, he'd make it all kosher with the lawyers and state regulators. If he wanted to double his money in a dope deal, there were far easier and safer ways. Maybe he didn't have a coffee can buried in the backyard, but he could have skimmed ten grand from The Apartments with hardly a trace and handed it to Nunez on the fifteenth fairway of any golf course in Fresno, just the two of them.

I drove to Madera hoping to find some answers in court files, only to learn that the entire drug case had been shipped to state archives in Sacramento. There, a resourceful clerk found several volumes of testimony hidden under a pile of old documents headed for the paper shredder. One month later and the official record of the Madera bust and trial would have been lost to me.

What I learned in those volumes encouraged my belief that my father wasn't financing Nunez's drug operation and that fear over the impending Madera trial and his loose mouth touched off the murder.

Shortly after midnight on August 25, 1971, a plane landed at the Madera Airport outside Fresno. The night watchman said it came down heavy, a *clump, clump, clump* across the mats. The tires were low, the interior gutted except for the pilot's seat. Dozens of white cloth sacks bearing the words *Azúcar Gránulo* (Granulated Sugar) were stacked bottom to top, side to side.

The pilot, Charles William Johnson, a tall, beefy man with a crew cut, was supposed to have landed fifty miles west of Fresno in a cotton and sugar beet town called Los Baños. A tank of bad Mexican gasoline had brought him down in Madera. It was the first time he had smuggled drugs across the border and it showed. "He was nervous as hell," the night watchman testified.

Johnson took a cab to Los Baños; the night watchman called authorities. "Something isn't legal with this airplane. I can see objects sticking out like bricks inside the sacks."

A briefcase inside the cabin tied pilot Johnson to the load. Fingerprints and a tool kit bearing the initials RLM led to the arrest of Richard Lee Morgan, Nunez's right-hand man.

At first, Johnson and Morgan refused to cooperate with authorities, keeping secret the role of Nunez, Hornig, Maselli and others. Then, as the trial began, Johnson tried to strike a deal with prosecutors. In return for leniency, he would tell all.

With Nunez glowering in the audience, Johnson testified that he feared for himself and his family. Not only had Morgan threatened to kill him if he named names but so had Morgan's good friend, drug smuggler Anthony Simone Jr. The night before his testimony, Johnson told the court, someone called his house and threatened to kill his ten-year-old son.

"Do you feel intimidated by the presence of Frank Nunez here?" his attorney asked.

"It bothers me," he replied.

Johnson testified that he was working as a car salesman in early August, 1971 when friend and golfing mate, Dan Hornig, approached him with an offer. For every load of marijuana he could fly from Culiacán, Mexico, to Fresno, Johnson would be paid $5,000.

Before agreeing to the deal, Johnson attended two more meetings at The Forum nightclub with Hornig, Frank Nunez and Leonard Maselli. Hornig and Maselli had been close friends for years. Like Hornig, Maselli had fallen on hard times in his real estate business, and he was looking to double what money he had left.

Nunez was clearly the organizer, the broker between the older business-men who financed the deals and the young dopers who flew the stuff over the border and transported it by truck to Oakland. There, it was sold to the Hell's Angels and distributed through a vast network of street ped-dlers. It was like a real estate deal, Johnson explained. Nunez, the devel-oper, lined up the Mexican supplier and the financiers willing to gamble five for ten, and he stacked things in such a way that he held a 50 percent share in each load without risking a dime of his own money. If the load was ripped off or seized—always a risk—Nunez had secured enough up-front financing to still pocket a few grand. Nunez was careful to let flunkies do the dirty work. He bought a small clothing store in east Fresno through which he laundered his drug profits.

Johnson testified that two days before his flight, he and Nunez met a final time in the parking lot at The Forum. Nunez told him not to worry. Should he be caught, the group would bail him out of jail and cover all legal expenses. The next day, Maselli handed Morgan $5,000 in cash and a machine gun as payment to the Mexican supplier.

"The farther I went into it, the bigger it looked," Johnson told the court. "It began to look like a big organization."

Despite Johnson's confession, the judge sentenced him to five years in prison, the same sentences handed down to an unrepentant Morgan. John-son was so upset that he refused to cooperate in a separate state and federal investigation of Nunez, Hornig and Maselli. Thus, the three men alleged to be at the center of the drug conspiracy never answered to charges on the Madera load. As a result, I was unable to determine exactly how much money Hornig and Maselli invested with Nunez and how much of that in-vestment was diverted from my father.

Dad's name never appeared in the thick file, not when Johnson identified the men who attended the meetings at The Forum, not when the matter of financing came up. But the murder did seem to lurk in the background.

In his closing argument, Johnson's attorney, Bill Smith, dropped a bombshell. The ring was far bigger than indicated during the trial. One name never surfaced, he said, the name of a millionaire businessman in Fresno who superseded even Nunez in the organization's hierarchy. This "Mr. Big" was tied directly to Dan Hornig. The only reason his client, Charles Johnson, hadn't been killed yet was because he had given the name of Mr. Big to the Fresno detectives. Mr. Big was nervous.

"These people are dangerous. These people are afraid," Smith exclaimed. "We have had shootings. We have had murders."

Bill Smith was still defending criminals out of a shabby downtown highrise when I looked him up. He recalled only flashes of the Madera trial and a feeling of deep regret for allowing Charles Johnson to take the stand and confess his role.

Mr. Big, he told me, was a Fresno car dealer named Herman Theroff, a close friend of Hornig and Maselli, not to mention a drinking pal of Chief Morton and Lieutenant Heizenrader. Smith said he was probably thinking of my father when he spoke of "shootings and murders" connected to the ring.

"That was a bit of overstatement, son. I never directly connected the Madera case with your father's murder."

Then he remembered that a note had been left on his car the foggy morning after the murder. He said he was on his way to the Madera courthouse for a pretrial hearing in the case when he noticed the soggy note beneath the windshield wiper. It read: "Ara Arax killed last night. Armond Bletcher had the contract. Be careful."

A soggy note implicating Bletcher? Did he believe it? Did he take it to the police? Smith said he took the note as a warning to Johnson and himself. What happened to Ara Arax can happen to you and your client if you don't keep your mouths shut. Smith said he drove to a gun store and bought a $75 Smith and Wesson.

"I took the note seriously. I took it to mean that some of the same people involved in the Madera case happened to be involved in your father's murder as well.

"But I didn't think the Madera load itself was tied to the murder. If Ara was killed because he was involved with these guys or threatening to expose them, that never emerged."

It was one of those explanations that made perfect sense but for which I could muster only scorn. It fell far short of what I sensed he was on the verge of telling me, only to shrug his shoulders and say it was a long time ago. Nothing quite deflected me like the alibi of time. Smith offered his file in the case as consolation, a skimpy envelope that contained almost nothing of consequence except for the receipt on the $75 gun and letters from Johnson in prison. These letters were the ventings of a family man who had clearly gone against his grain by agreeing to pilot a single load of dope at a time of desperate need. They were full of contrition and self-blame for allowing a friend, Hornig, to tempt and then abandon him.

If my father had his own role in the Nunez–Hornig operation and paid for it with his life, Charles Johnson, the other victim, was the one I needed to see. I found his elderly mother in a trailer park outside town and she told me he had moved the family to a golf and fishing resort in the Arizona mountains. I reached his wife on the phone and she said he was away on a business trip.

"Do you know The Word?"

She caught me off balance and I muttered some malarky.

"I want you to believe that it really does ease the pain. There is a day of reckoning for the ones who are evil, Mark. They will pay a price."

I sold Coby on the idea of an Arizona vacation and drove 800 miles through saguaro desert and salt canyon and Apache reservations to meet Charles Johnson face-to-face.

He walked into the town's main café with steps that didn't become his giant frame, and he was careful not to make eye contact with what must have been any number of familiar faces. I could see in his manner a man who had taken great pains to keep one life from contaminating the other. He was a small dealer of used cars trying to scratch out a living with a wife who sometimes let her well-meaning light shine a little too brightly. Now, seated in the corner booth, beyond the twitching of his eyes adjusting to the darkness, was a bit of the past he had surely left behind. From afar, his face looked flush as if he had just finished a brisk run. Only his stomach had gone to seed. Up close, the years were less kind. A thousand broken veins crisscrossed the pallid nose and cheeks. The rims of his eyes were pink, insides wary.

"Your dad was never involved, pal. He was a real man. He was against it. He fought this. That might have been what killed him. I can't prove it, but I've got my thoughts. You should be proud of your heritage."

"What thoughts?"

He glanced right and left, checking his flanks. "He slapped the shit out of some dope dealer one night."

"Nunez?"

"Yeah, Nunez."

"And he was killed over that?"

"It doesn't make sense. I know. Your dad had a sense of fair play. He was an athlete. Who knows what happened? Maybe he was in the wrong place at the wrong time. The good die young and all that bullshit. I don't know. I was just a pilot recruited at the last minute because their other pilot had been busted."

"My father handed over eighteen grand to Hornig just before your drug flight. Part of the deal?"

"No. Absolutely not. Not Arax. No way."

"Okay. Then how about the other way. My father gave the money to Hornig for a business deal and Hornig diverted it to Nunez. When my father found out, it became necessary to kill him."

He paused for a moment, playing over in his mind his long-ago friendship with Hornig.

"Hornig's done some funny things. He was fat city one day and busted the next. He was a hustler and a gambler. Yeah, the money he turned over to Nunez might have very well come from your father. He was broke at the time. But Hornig's no killer."

He said he didn't know about my father's visits to the police department or his calls to the state narcotics agent in the days before. He said he wasn't even aware of the note left on his attorney's car the morning after the murder that implied the same end for him if he testified what he knew.

"These guys were playing for keeps," I reminded him. "And it was my father they feared. Remember, you didn't decide to talk until five months after the murder, on the eve of the trial."

He said the threats on his life didn't come from Hornig or Maselli but from Nunez's right-hand man, Morgan, and Morgan's good friend, Anthony Simone Jr. Why Simone, he didn't know.

"They told me if anyone gives anyone up, they're going to hurt. Cement shoes. I had no intention of talking. Not until they called my house the night before I testified. They told my son they were going to kill him. That's what convinced me to name names. I became unglued. I said, 'Fuck it. If that's the way they want to play, that's the way I'm going to play.' I began carrying a gun. And had I seen one of those son of a bitches from a distance or from up close, I would have shot 'em."

He had listened to my murder theory and I had listened again as he recounted his trial testimony. In the end, what connected the two was only supposition—more mine than his. I thanked him for his kind words about my father and he assured me he had no reason to sugarcoat the truth. The disappointment that registered on my face as we shook hands must have seemed an insinuation because he insisted on driving me back to the motel and, once there, he began to apologize.

"I'm sorry I got involved. I really truly am sorry. I thought it was a little deal. Honest to goodness, Mark, I thought it was an adventure. Sky king for a day. I know that sounds stupid. But I really didn't associate Ara getting killed with this thing. I'm sorry you have to go through this. But I can't point a finger at anybody. All I can do is speculate and that won't do you any good."

Then he told me what he would do if circumstance was reversed.

"You're a down-to-earth kid and I don't want to see any harm to you. But if I was doing this thing, I'd scorch the earth. If Nunez had your father killed over the drug ring, I don't think Hornig or Maselli would have known about it until after. I'd talk to Hornig and I'd talk to Maselli and then when I found my answer I'd take the appropriate action. I hope you take care of it."

I told him I owed something to my father and to myself, to find the answer, and if I was alone in this world I would have no problem carrying out something graver. But I had a wife and child waiting for me in the motel lobby and I owed them something too, to not repeat the mistakes of my father, to not have my daughter wondering about her father the same way I wondered about mine.

I smiled. "Your wife told me on the phone that justice always prevails. We just don't always see it. I wish I shared her faith. But I can't help but think that vengeance is mine. I borrowed a gun. Yet I am unable to move."

"I wish I shared her faith, too." He smiled tightly. "But it's guys like me, the pissants, who end up paying . . . I hope you find your middle ground."

"I always knew you'd come to see me one day. I've never been able to put it away." He held his thumb and index finger an inch apart. "I came this close to solving it. This close and this far."

I had gone to see Dominic Estilarte, the retired police sergeant, because he was the man who headed the investigation, an honest cop, I was told, who may not have had the wits or fervor to solve a complex murder case but whose heart was right.

"I've thought a lot about you and your mother over the years," he said. "She was a beautiful woman, a real lady. I read in the obituaries. I'm sorry."

We sat in the living room and his wife brought out a tray of iced tea followed a few minutes later by a scrapbook opened to a page with the first *Bee* article: FRESNO TAVERN OWNER IS SHOT, KILLED; PAIR SOUGHT, and the photograph of my father in his wedding tuxedo, smiling sweetly. Slowly, as her husband and I stood over her, Mrs. Estilarte flipped through the pages, exhibiting each follow-up article as if it were an unveiling. She had put it together with obvious pride, a wife's touch. It was all there in one bound volume, her husband's important work, her quiet support, their lives together. It was one of those moments I had gotten used to by now, another discovery of the little and not so little ways our tragedy had spilled over into other lives. I had once thought I was the only one who cut and pasted those articles, keeper of the flame, the scrapbook Dad and I shared, his athletic feats taking up the first fifty pages and mine all used up in fifteen, the murder a chapter in between. Mrs. Estilarte dawdled at each page, waiting for a response. I didn't know what to say. I nodded my head and smiled. She closed the book, smiled and left the room.

He waited until he could no longer see her and then he began to talk in detail about the Madera case. The Madera load was the first of many loads Hornig, Maselli and other businessmen helped finance before and after the killing, he said. He, too, believed the key to the murder was the $18,000 Dad handed Hornig. In the beginning, he surmised that the money was intended by Dad to buy a stake in the Nunez operation. When the first load was confiscated by authorities in Madera, Nunez and Dad had a falling out and Dad threatened to go to authorities. But Estilarte also considered the equal possibility that my father had no part in their business and raged upon discovering how his $18,000 had been used.

"We could never say for sure if that $18,000 was for drugs or business. Did your dad cross the line and regret and try to make amends? Or was he upset that Hornig had given his money to a drug smuggler he hated?"

His reaction, though, was unmistakably Ara. He cornered Nunez, knocked him to the ground with a single blow and threatened to expose his drug enterprise. These threats, Estilarte said, could not have come at a more perilous time, with the trial in the Madera bust imminent.

"They were vulnerable and Ara was the one they feared," he said. "The three men arrested in the Madera case, the two pilots and the mule, weren't talking at the time. But Ara's money was a direct link to that load and others.

"This is what your father was struggling with the last weeks of his life: How much to expose. Whether or not to expose it. How much would it endanger his family and business? He was under a great deal of stress trying to decide which way to go."

He assured me that my father in the end did the right thing, deciding to expose the drug operation. But before he got a chance to talk to the right authorities, he took a wrong step and was killed. Estilarte then confirmed what I had suspected ever since I resumed my search, that my father had tried to contact state narcotics Agent Walley a second time—two days before the murder. Walley was supposed to get back to him but never did.

"That's why Walley was so active in our investigation. He felt that whatever your father was going to tell him ended up getting him killed."

I described the patterns that had emerged from my charts at home, the names and intricate events and myriad affiliations. It seemed to uncork his memory and he launched into a conspiracy theory of his own, one of scary proportions.

Hornig and Maselli, he said, had recruited a number of prominent Fresnans to finance Nunez. Among those suspected were car dealer Herman Theroff and attorney Vince Todisco, who had also come under scrutiny in the Lambe–Simone drug probe. Indeed, he surmised, remnants of Lambe–Simone had joined forces with Nunez, including wealthy fig rancher Tony Simone and his son Anthony Jr. There were also persistent rumors linking both rings to a second prominent state legislator, this one from the valley.

Estilarte believed that Nunez was the prime mover behind the murder. He made the call and bought the contract. He had two motives, to hush Dad's loose mouth and to pay him back for the knockdown he received in front of his friends. He didn't know what role, if any, Hornig and Maselli played in the murder plot, but he believed they knew after the fact and lied to police about Nunez. As for Armond Bletcher, Estilarte had lots of rumors and nothing solid. The note that attorney Smith found on his car tying Armond to the murder may have been nothing more than a Nunez smokescreen.

"Your father didn't understand how bad an egg Nunez was. He was very, very big. He was making hundreds of thousands of dollars flying in marijuana and cocaine and some heroin. He had a place in Lake Tahoe, a place in the Bay Area, a place in Arizona. He had a clothing store in east Fresno and he and Maselli and Hornig were buying race horses.

"And here comes this bar owner who hauls off and decks him in public.

And what does he do? He gets up and dusts himself off. That's the best he could do. He didn't dare swing back because your dad would have cleaned his plow.

"Your dad made this one trip and possibly more to the police department. I think it was that trip that got him killed. These guys had an operation in full swing with planes and trucks and stash houses. They weren't going to let Ara Arax upset the apple cart. So they kill him and send a message to Johnson and the others before the trial."

I appreciated his candor but it seemed about twenty years too late. I mean, why was none of this in the murder report? Why leave this impression that my father was dirty? Why were his visits to the police department glossed over? Who was he visiting and how did the bad guys find out? Was there a leak inside the department?

Estilarte didn't have the answers. "We did the best we could. You have to understand—your father didn't make it easy on us. He was a very unusual man. He loved sports and kids and did a lot for this community. But he was playing with some big-time people. I don't think your dad personally was a drug dealer. I think possibly they conned him out of this money. 'Make an investment. We'll pay you back triple.' Pretty soon he's involved and he realizes. 'Hey, I don't want to play this game.' But he's already in. It's too late."

He followed me outside into the heat of a blistering July day and wondered what became of Hornig, Maselli and Nunez. Hornig had moved to the Bay Area and was involved in construction. Maselli had made a fortune developing real estate in the Santa Cruz area. Nunez, after more than a decade in prison for drug smuggling, had recently moved back to town.

"Be careful, Mark. Nunez has got a cocaine deal going down not five minutes after his release. Remember. The first murder is the hardest. If he feels you are any threat, he'll have you done without blinking an eye."

That night, I read my daughter a bedtime story and she ran her toes through my hair, her goodnight ritual. She had never seen a photo of my father and each time I reached into the album drawer for his high school and wedding portraits, I stopped myself short. What difference would it make, Mark? How could anything I show or tell her mean a thing when she has a flesh and blood Grandpa who lives five minutes away and cooks her waffles every Saturday? I finished reading the story and her leg fell limp and I thought, next time.

My son was born that week, ten pounds and seven ounces, almost twenty-two inches, a giant baby with lots of beautiful brown hair. The nurse assured me his legs weren't abnormally crooked and his feet had a good arch. We named him Joseph Ara—Joseph because our real last name was Hovsepian, son of Joseph, and Ara in honor of my father. Uncle Navo couldn't believe his hands. "Look at this kid!" he shouted. "Look at this kid! His hands are mitts!"

We took a drive, just the two of us. "I hope I'm alive when Joe's sixteen or seventeen to watch him play ball," he said. "He's going to be a fullback, Mark. Just like your dad. You know he weighed twelve pounds when he was born. No kidding."

It pleased me to think of my father's grandson on the football field wearing his old number, 44, and his brother cheering in the stands as surrogate grandpa. Driving to a yogurt shop that evening to celebrate our first boy in the next generation's Arax, I felt closer to my uncle than I had in years. I had no idea that our hit-and-miss relationship, two decades of love trying to fend off distrust, was about to undergo its sternest test.

So much seemed clearer now. Funny how the names of the men I believed involved had not changed over two decades. I thought as a child, as I did now with some corroboration, that it was my father's threats to a drug ring headed by Frank Nunez and involving Hornig, Maselli and Bletcher and the Simones, father and son, that got him killed. I didn't know where the theory came from. Was it supposition by Mom or Uncle Mike that remained with me, unsubstantiated until now? Or was it something I picked up in the streets during those frantic, disordered years?

Part of me, embarking on this quest, refused to believe it. In fact, out of necessity, I forgot this theory until it kept coming back in one clue and another. None of the other theories made as much sense. Still, I had trouble believing that what I clutched as a child—untested and arrived at for reasons unknown—was the same answer that emerged now after three years of hard work. I wondered. Was it too tidy? Had I cast off everything contrary? Seized the familiar?

That day at police headquarters, rummaging through the complete file, my friend at the *Fresno Bee* came across a letter that sounded too good to be true. It was written to the *Bee*'s secret witness program in July, 1972. He handed the letter to me and I immediately recognized the large, whorling letters—a child's self-conscious penmanship masquerading as adult. It was a letter I had written and sent anonymously to the detectives six months after the crime.

Ara Arax

(murder)

Arax and Dan Hornig were partners at a bar in Fresno. Arax knew much about the dope traffic in Fresno. Hornig and a friend by the name of Frank Nunez were and are involved in this traffic. Arax knew about this and was going to tell the police about it. Nunez found out and got to Arax before he could get to the police. He hired two men to do the job for him.

This is what I believed as a fifteen-year-old and yet I was astonished to see the evidence to support it actually come into focus all these years later. Spread out on the bed before me were the long distance telephone calls made by my father, Nunez, Hornig, Maselli and Bletcher before and after the murder. I had reviewed these calls maybe eight to ten times over the past year. Now, with the dates of the Madera trial before me, I was suddenly struck by their timing.

Three weeks before the murder, Maselli in Santa Cruz calls attorney Vince Todisco in Fresno. A few days later, Maselli calls Nunez and Hornig. On the night of the murder, two hours after Dad is pronounced dead, Hornig's first call is to Maselli in Santa Cruz. There were no long-distance calls between my father and any of the suspects. There were, however, two calls from Maselli to the residence of Josette Romano, Uncle Navo's girlfriend at the time and soon to be his wife.

I didn't know what to make of these calls. Maselli had known Aunt Josette's family for years. Her father and uncles, products of the Italian west side, were original members of the Dante Social Club. Mobster Joe Sica, the prime suspect in the Davidian murder, was a house guest.

My impulse was to disregard Maselli's calls to Aunt Josette's residence and ignore, too, the most disturbing association on my chart: Maselli,

Hornig and attorney Todisco were Uncle Navo's close friends. They palled around, gambled at golf, gambled at gin.

I wanted to attribute this to a coincidence of proximity. Fresno was a small town. My father and Hornig became partners. He played golf with Hornig and Nunez. My mother chose Hornig to be a pallbearer. Why couldn't Uncle Navo have his own prior and separate relationship with these men?

But after seeing the complete murder report and realizing the extent of Maselli and Hornig's involvement with Nunez, I had to wonder what my uncle knew and why he no longer kept these friendships. Why, in fact, did he sever his ties to these men the moment his brother was killed?

Part Three

An Act of Decency

"I didn't know what it was all about, Mark. I still don't know what it was all about. I went through a period where I'd black out. I had a feeling of awful things, like my mind leaving my body. My doctor said, 'Navo, you're just coming unglued. There's this new stuff called Valium.' I was driving over curbs and sidewalks but Valium did serve a purpose. It numbed me through this episode."

Uncle Navo sat small in a huge leather chair in his office, dressed in crisp khakis and saddle Oxfords and sporting a golfer's tan. We were discussing my father and the murder for the first time. For a man who had locked away so much of his past, my uncle had turned his office into a curious celebration of the bygone, cluttered with collectibles and old magazine ads and photos of early-day Fresno, its Victorian downtown and grim-faced police force.

This homage to local history even extended to the building in which he housed his successful property management firm, the old Stillman Drug Store. Across the street stood Fresno High School, his alma mater, and catty-corner was the old Sugar Bowl soda fountain Grandpa and Grandma ran in the late 1940s.

Over the years, Uncle Navo liked to tell stories about his fallen younger brother. There was the time Ara dragged eight tacklers into the end zone, the time he broke a guy's arm at the drive-in for calling him a "dirty Armenian," the time he absorbed Navo's best shot and kept coming. "He was sixteen and I knew then that we had reached a new place in our relationship," he said. "That's when I learned to negotiate."

He passed down each story at holiday gatherings as if passing down some fable. Each one limned Dad's toughness and fearlessness. Each seemed directed not at the assembly of family and friends but at one person, me. He even fixed his gaze my way as he told it, as if to say, "You are the one I need to win over." Only once or twice did a phrase or intonation betray him and I glimpsed for a moment something deeper between brothers, my uncle's frustration perhaps that my father lacked the rudimentary skills (the brains?) for survival. He couldn't understand Dad's fascination with the Armond Bletchers of the world—dull, blunt, boring instruments of death. They possessed none of the charm of the bookies and golf hustlers Uncle Navo chose to hang around.

The one story most familiar to me concerned a last conversation between my uncle and father a day or two before the murder. Dad talked a little crazy and Uncle Navo detected a little fear. Dad didn't volunteer any details; Uncle Navo didn't ask.

"Tell me about that last conversation," I began.

"We went to a coffee shop on Blackstone. We were talking in general and then he said something like, 'You know this business is a crazy business. It's a dangerous business. There's crazy people out there.' For the first time in his whole life I noticed a little fear in his voice. But I don't know what the hell he was talking about."

"Did he mention anything specific?"

"They used to have fights in those places, you know. There was nothing specific, no specific incident. Well, he threw out, he threw out this guy Frank Nunez, this guy who I never did trust anyhow. I think he was involved in dope, that guy. Of course, his name wasn't discussed at the time. Then Hornig walked in and your dad said those things with Hornig being there."

"Hornig walked in? Hornig was at this last meeting?"

"Yeah. And your dad repeated those statements. It was almost like he had been threatened. But he didn't say he had been threatened. He never told me anything. Ara was very close-mouthed."

My father close-mouthed? I thought to myself. What had his life been if not the inability to keep his words and emotions to himself? It was my uncle whom everyone considered tight-lipped.

"I heard afterward that he had gone down to the police department and was talking to the police," he said. "I didn't know about anything like that."

My father had even failed to consult with him about buying an interest in The Forum, even though Navo and Hornig were longtime friends. If Dad had approached him, my uncle said, he would have told him to steer clear of Hornig. This, by itself, seemed a remarkable admission.

"Hornig wasn't a very good guy, Mark. They were Nazis. Hornig belonged to the German Youth Movement and his father belonged to the German-American Bund. They loved Hitler."

"If you had a theory about what happened to Dad, what would it be, Unc?"

"Mark, I just don't know. I just don't know."

"How about the rumors you heard?"

"I didn't really hear any. Somebody once said. 'Was your brother mixed up in anything?' What the hell was he mixed up in? He hated dope . . . I feel that Hornig . . . I know once that Hornig had been involved in stuff. Since then or before then, I can't remember. He had an episode of greed. But I don't think he would . . . I see no reason why he would want to have Ara killed."

Then, in a casual, offhand way, he recalled visiting Hornig at his bar one day only to stumble upon a strange gathering in the back office. There was Hornig and Maselli, a pilot named Charles Johnson and some others he could not recall. He said he later figured out, after a planeload of marijuana was found in Madera and Johnson testified that Hornig and Maselli had financed the deal, that this meeting concerned drugs.

"Was Nunez there?" I asked.

"I, I don't know. I, I don't know."

"What year are we talking about?"

"Oh, Mark. Gosh. It was a couple of years before your dad and Hornig became partners."

Uncle Navo's timing was off, so much so that he placed this meeting and the Madera drug trial in the mid-sixties—years before Dad and

Hornig became partners in The Forum, years before smuggling by air-plane even became fashionable. He described Maselli and Hornig's in-volvement in drugs as an "episode of greed" and a "one-time thing." And yet I knew that both of them were involved in Nunez's drug ring from the summer of 1971 to spring of 1972, and I strongly suspected that he knew, too. It seemed to me that my uncle was doing all he could to distance Nunez, Hornig and Maselli from the drug ring that surrounded Dad.

Here was my opening, a chance to ask the question that begged to be asked: Why did your friendship with Hornig and Maselli end that day? But I let it pass, telling myself there would be another day. Maybe I wanted to see how far he would take his dissembling. Maybe I wasn't pre-pared to defy him, our relationship still so bruised. My uncle had one of the best poker faces around. Maybe I halfway believed him. Maybe his memory, like mine, was a merciful timekeeper.

"I think Nunez . . . I've always had a very strong suspicion about that guy," he said. "Mostly because your dad knocked him on his ass in public and it was that, you know."

Wounded pride, he called it. Goddamn Mexican machismo. He wanted to believe, he wanted me to believe, it was nothing more than that. What I found more surprising was his revelation that Hornig had been present at that last meeting. I was inclined to chalk it up to another coincidence, the collision of friendships and Fresno. Then I met up with Uncle Navo's first wife, Carroll, and suddenly the direction of my search changed again, this time back to the family, to the relationship between brothers.

"Ara was onto something bloody big," Aunt Carroll began. She sipped a scotch and water and talked in an Aussie's voice lifted from the Cook Is-lands, the last stop in a lifetime of wanderlust. "Whatever drug cartel he got word of, Markie, he told Navo and this is what Navo told me.

"Ara said, 'I'm going to blow the whistle on them. And you're going to hear it as far away as Sacramento.' What he was onto involved up in the up, up, up. Big money. Big connections. Some of the politicians were in it. Your Uncle Navo was damn right scared.

"Navo told me, 'Ara was onto something very big. Be careful. These people are crazy.'"

The wonder in my eyes she could not have mistaken. Before I could respond with a question, she excused herself and went into the kitchen. Was this a pause for dramatic effect? Did my eagerness give her a second thought? Surely, she must have understood this wasn't a chat for old times' sake. My intentions were made clear in my resolve, if not in the phone call setting up our meeting. Her revelation, or something just like it, was the reason I was there. What expectations did she bring? What purpose? She was a bright, if insincere, woman who had traveled the world and successfully courted men of vastly different cultures and countries. She had to understand the consequences of what she was telling me: how it might damage her former husband and compel their only son to question his father; how it might help free her former nephew, whom she still considered a boy, or only lead to further no good. Was she weighing any of this as she stood in the kitchen, casually dropping ice cubes into another drink?

She sat back down in the living room and recalled a visit from my uncle a few days after the murder. He came into the restaurant where she waited tables to warn her of possible danger, she said. In his rear pocket he carried a .32-caliber gun.

"The gun was in his back pocket under his jacket. He said, 'I've got a gun,' and I reached in and felt it. We were all scared, Markie.

"Your father was a stubborn man. He didn't realize that they were as bad as they were. He told Navo, 'I've got proof of all this big drug activity and I'm going to blow the whistle and it's going to be heard from here to Sacramento.' And Uncle Navo told him. 'Ara, back out of this. Get away from it. Ara, please. Just leave these people alone.' It was making a lot of people rich. And they weren't going to let Ara put them in jail."

"Are you sure?" I interrupted. "Are you absolutely sure? Maybe Uncle Navo was embellishing the murder to you? Trying to make it sound like his life was in danger, too. As a way to get you to feel concerned about him. He hadn't married Josette just yet."

"Navo came to me in a very serious way, trying to protect me and tell me the gravity of this. He was a very frightened man."

"Did he mention any names?"

"No. He just said it was big. I don't think Ara provided anyone with any information yet. He didn't have the chance."

"Why lie to me? He knows the questions I have. He knows the doubt."

"You don't understand your uncle, Markie. He is different than your father. Your father was too open, too kind, too gentle, too trusting. Terribly trusting. Then when somebody shit on him, he was devastated. He would just explode like a big bear. To survive, you have to be like Navo. You have to be cynical. You have to be tough. You have to be calculating."

She told me to be careful, to not let pain become an indulgence. Then she left me with a question: "Has it occurred to you that there still might be a danger to Navo? That there is still some threat out there?"

How do I explain my uncle? The day before the murder, he sat and listened to his brother ramble incoherently, betraying obvious fear, and he never once tried to determine the source of that fear? The little brother left to his care since they were children? I might have found his story plausible, but then his first wife comes along with a completely different version of this last meeting.

Why would my uncle lie to me? Who was he trying to protect? Like Hornig and Maselli, he faced financial hardship in the summer of 1971, having just divorced my aunt. Was it really an accident, his walking in on that drug meeting? Might his good buddies have offered him a piece of the action? Might he have accepted? Was this the secret he concealed, the guilt he carried? His dalliance with the Nunez drug ring that ended up killing his pig-headed brother?

Even as I posed the questions to myself, I felt no desire to pursue them. Chasing my father's complicity in a drug ring was one thing. He was my father and the question was already there. But to raise such a specter about my uncle, a specter wholly of my own imagination, seemed the worst kind of greed. Maybe I was trying to find an easy answer to his elusiveness. Uncle Navo brought together the extremes of both his parents, Grandpa's detachment and Grandma's fears. He was more mysterious to me than either of them, for I could explain my distance from grandparents as the distance between worlds. If my father evoked the big-hearted, hot-blooded Armenian peasant, my uncle conjured up the shrewd, crafty rug dealer. The Armenian of the earth. The Armenian of the bazaar. It was such a tempting way to see them, the two faces of our caricature. And like all caricature, it held at least some truth.

To glimpse them in the same room, you would have never guessed they were brothers. My father was light and hot, my uncle dark and cool. My father was tall enough and big enough to play the line at USC. My uncle was the first quarterback at Fresno City College, his quick thinking and love of strategy compensation for his five-foot-six frame. My father didn't like his nose and tried a mustache. My uncle drove to Southern California at age nineteen and got his fixed. My father married the daughter of an Armenian priest, albeit one from the "other" church. My uncle married a non-Armenian, a divorcée with two children, the first one conceived when she was fifteen. My father considered gambling on golf games a perversion of the sport. My uncle sucked on a fat cigar and flashed a diamond pinky ring and a thick wad of golf hustlings.

And yet my uncle defined himself less by material goods than my father and for the longest time he drove a used car and took on the extra burden of raising two sons who weren't even his own. And my father could jettison virtue when it suited him. I learned that he supplemented the taxable liquor from the wholesaler with unreported booze trucked in at night from friendly liquor stores. He sold four and five grand in drinks at The Apartments each week, more than enough to support the family. In fact, the volume stunned state liquor auditors. But Dad still found it necessary to skim the cover charge money collected at the door, an average of $350 a week. Pure cream. This was the cash we lived on, the cash he used to buy two new cars (a Firebird and Gremlin) in the same week, the cash that built our swimming pool and provided him with a wardrobe that was the envy of his entourage.

My grandmother's sister Roxie recalled her two nephews this way: "Navo was the little smart one and Ara-boy was outgoing, all heart. We had this plank across the ditch so we could walk from one side of the ranch to the other. One day I go outside to gather the eggs and I see the two brothers close to the ditch bank and I yell. 'Wait until I get there!' Pretty soon, I see this little blond head bobbing on the board. It's Ara-boy and he's crawling across. And Navo is standing there, behind him, saying in Armenian, 'Little one, you go ahead first, you go across and I'll be following. I'll come.' I ran and grabbed Ara-boy and turned to Navo and said, 'If he would have fallen in, he would have drowned.' Navo said. 'No, I was there. I was protecting him.'"

The story said almost too much about my father and uncle. I once told myself I would not fall prey to gullibility when considering my father and uncle. I would reach past the myth. Why should one brother be sanctified simply because he was snuffed out? Why should one brother be disgraced for no other reason than he survived?

Yet here was more than one relative using the Armenian word *me-ah-meed* to describe my father, an innocence not of this world, an ingenuousness that was endearing in a child but hard to take seriously in the adult. And here were these same relatives describing my uncle, by way of contrast, as *dag-en;* sly, clever, underhanded.

"Navo would take something and absolutely dissect it before moving," Aunt Carroll had told me. "Ara barged right into it. Right now. He went by his hunches right or wrong. Ara never saw the bad. You had to be the biggest no-good crook for Ara not to like you. Navo didn't believe anyone."

Even Grandma, in her stippled way, crafted a line between her two sons. And yet she talked about these differences only in the context of them as children, repeating the same stories almost word-for-word.

"They were very different boys. Ara depended on Navo for everything. Then Navo would let Ara on his own and Ara would get mad. Ara was a dreamy boy. I can't figure out Navo too much. He knew what he was doing. Ara was more emotional. He didn't like it so much that we moved."

As the boys got older, my father's erratic, sometimes incoherent side became a point of ridicule inside the family.

"I hate to say this," said sister Jeanette, "but we drew pictures of Ara— 'Typical Ara Arax'—like a cartoon character, and Navo laughed about it. Navo and I were coloring it together. Grandma would say isn't it a shame that Navo wasn't able to go to college. In her eyes, Navo was the smartest. I was good in art. Ara had certain other virtues. He wasn't dumb but he had certain difficulties. It was hard to sit and have a conversation with him although he was more than willing. He was a little hyper, a little flighty. And he was extremely excitable. When the earthquake hit Bakersfield, he ran through the house screaming. 'The Russians are coming! The Russians are coming!'"

My grandparents had one of those Super-8 movie cameras with the big floodlights that knitted brows and melted ice cream. It seized a few blinding moments of every holiday and birthday for one decade, from cousin Brian's baptism in 1958 to Christmas 1968, and then it was put away.

Before I approached my uncle a second time about the murder and the role of his good friends, I ran that film again looking for anything that might illuminate his relationship with Dad. I already knew that my father as a young man idealized his brother; indeed, refused to make a decision without him. His letters home from college reflected a level of dependence I found hard to accept. So why did I remember it so differently growing up? What had taken place during the 1960s, when I began taking note of father and uncle, to change their relationship? The old family films only confirmed my feeling of something uneasy between them. Why in all those hours of hot lights was there always ten feet of coolness separating them?

Uncle Navo had said in our first conversation that it was not surprising, a once-dependent younger brother rebelling and finding his own way in the world. Others, however, recalled a separation that began with Uncle

Navo's decision to marry Carroll Libby and grew wider during the Peacock Market years.

By the time my parents married, Uncle Navo had been dating Carroll several months. No one knew how serious he was and his friends weren't about to ask. They had stopped calling him "The Nose," a cruel high school moniker. He was now "The Rock," a salute to his aloofness. "You couldn't break him," one friend explained. "And maybe he could break you." His wit attracted a group of toadies who considered him a "man's man." So what if his sarcasm betrayed a little man's cruelty, they said. He told a great joke, honed deprecation into a punishing foil, and he kept you guessing. Just when you thought you had him pegged and he was your best friend, Navo found another group to dazzle.

There was a pretty good chance my father lost his virginity in marriage. Uncle Navo was another story. Dark complexioned with pale blue eyes, he knew how to dress and radiated a cocksure air. He had several teenage conquests and there was a scandalous affair with an attractive Okie married to an Italian farmer in Bakersfield. The couple had been friendly with Grandpa and Grandma and watched over Jeanette, who sensed something strange and powerful between her brother and her caretaker. The affair destroyed the friendship and was one of the reasons the Araxes left Bakersfield.

The first time Navo brought Carroll home she reminded Grandma of the farmer's wife. A tall brunette with slim shoulders and long slender legs, Carroll flashed a big, horsetooth smile. The Libbys had come from Alabama; booze and divorce tore apart the whole clan. Carroll was coming off a divorce from a hard-drinking motorcycle nut. She did her damndest to flatter my grandparents and her efforts met with considerable success. My father, putting aside his position as worshipful younger brother for a change, tried to dissuade Navo with a hasty recital of Carroll's infidelities past. "Navo didn't give a damn what Ara or anyone else thought," one of my uncle's longtime friends said. "His marriage to Carroll was a real 'Screw you!'"

The best man who accompanied them to Las Vegas was not my father, and when Brian was born a few years later, Navo chose a cousin to stand in as baptismal godfather, an honor traditionally reserved for brother.

Carroll eventually won over the family. She learned a few words of Armenian and doted on Brian. She accompanied Grandma to Soviet Armenia and Grandpa to the Soviet consulate in San Francisco. She succeeded in ways she never imagined. Her freshness and zest for the chase enchanted them all, especially Grandpa. My father never quite bought the suburban housewife bit, and time would prove him right. She had a number of affairs during the marriage, one right under Grandma's nose in Soviet Armenia, and finally left Navo for another man, who, like her first husband, cherished motorcycles and beat women.

Since the Richmond market days when Grandpa dumped bags of money on the floor and the boys scrambled to count it, Uncle Navo had shown a special dexterity with numbers. Building their chain of Peacock Markets, it only made sense that he would handle the buying and meet the salesmen. My father took care of the produce and notions. Maybe it was the claustrophobic in him but Dad had an appreciation for space. He quickly visualized where things belonged and how to tie in different exhibits. Employees marveled at the designs he conceived, the perfect flow from one display to the next, his fury finally harnessed, and they never got enough of seeing him charm the old ladies.

"I know the family saw it as Navo the brains and Ara the brawn," said Ron Manuto, a speech professor who worked at Peacock in his youth. "But I found it different. Ara had a special way of dealing with the customers, especially the old ethnic women. He was vibrant. He would kid them. He knew a little bit about all their cultures. He made it a point to know about things going on in their families. Navo would sit in the room with the big guys and think business. Ara would sit in that same room and laugh and kid. He wasn't good with the figures. He responded to people, not money."

At some point, my father began to resent his position, the fact that Navo had exclusive rights to the salesmen, and he didn't always hide his frustration.

"Meeting the salesmen meant a lot of under-the-table deals," said Kirk Chutini, who worked for Arden Dairy. "Cash unseen. And Navo would get that cash. He was too smart for his own good, always belittling people.

And he belittled your father. 'You dumb shit!' I've got news for you. Ara was a very sharp man. But the other guy just squashed him. Like an ant. With his foot on his head all the time."

Others recalled the same tensions but said the two brothers rarely fought in the open. They respected the fact that they were family.

"Navo would come to me and say, 'Well, Ara's not too sharp when it comes to that,'" recalled Lou Dyer, who managed the main Peacock. "But he backed him up, too. Navo was the type who honestly felt that every man had his price. And Ara felt quite idealistic about certain things. By the time I left, Ara had more on the ball. He knew what the score was. Navo was taking money. He gave Ara a cut."

As the numbers man, Uncle Navo was the first to sense they were in big trouble. He approached my father a full year before they had to declare bankruptcy. He wanted to skim cash before the creditors lowered the boom. My father thought the stores could be saved.

"We can walk away with thousands," Navo told him. "All we have to do is start now and when they jerk on us we file Chapter Eleven."

"Let's give it six more months," my father said. "Things will turn around."

"You jackass! We don't have six months."

Carroll said it was a horrible time and Grandpa refused to intercede.

"Ara in his beautiful optimism said we can make it. And Navo couldn't convince him otherwise and they got into some terrible fights . . . I think we buried three or four thousand in the cellar. It should have been lots more. And Grandpa was wrong. He should have said, 'Ara . . .' But Grandpa is wishy-washy. It was sad because they worked so damn hard. They deserved that much."

My mother nagged at my father to grab his share before it was too late. He grabbed a few grand. The day before the creditors took over, he filled our garage with sugar, flour, canned goods, cereals and pasta. He crammed the eight-foot horizontal freezer with every cut of beef, pork, lamb and chicken imaginable.

"They're not going to starve us," he told a neighbor.

We left town for a week and when we got back the whole house reeked of death. The freezer had broken; the meats had rotted.

My father saved the last Peacock by finding investors willing to pour in capital and make him partner. My uncle spent the next fifteen years job-hopping. The breach between the two brothers never fully repaired itself.

I found no shortage of people willing to share their unflattering portraits of my uncle, tales of his ruthlessness in business and the empty-pocketed partners he left in his wake. I didn't question the motive behind their easy characterizations or why they saw in me, his nephew, a ready dumping ground. I didn't ask myself what clues I must have given that telegraphed my grudge. The wrong brother was killed, one of them told me. Your uncle, be careful, warned another. He has such a sweet tongue, he takes you in by giving you a piece of candy and all the while he's holding a club behind his back. I was so busy being grateful for any information that chimed with my own emerging thesis about my father and uncle that I didn't examine why my father was so easy to like and why my uncle inspired such spite. I didn't stop to think that the traits that endeared my father to people were traits that carried a personal risk. And the traits that set people against my uncle were traits that kept opponents guessing and enemies at bay. Grandma's sister, Zep, put it this way: "Too bad Ara was naïve. I appreciate the cunningness in Navo. He realizes that you just can't stick your chin out. That little larceny makes him interesting. Self-preservation."

Only once in a decade of collecting family stories did I ask my grandfather about my father and uncle, and never did I ask about the murder. We sat alone in a park, far from Grandma's disruptions. I was in college and he was eighty-two years old, and the difficulty back then wasn't his memory—he never repeated a story twice—but his silences. Each time I pressed for more he blocked me, gently. I remember going home frustrated. It was only years later, knowing what I would know, that I saw the answer he had given me.

"The boys were vehdee different boys. Your fawdr had a little temper of course, but we understand that vehdee easy. Because you see Navo was the first one. In Armenian family the first one always gets the best sometimes, you see."

"How were they different?"

"Your fawdr believed that working hard by hand is vehdee important.

And Navo thought that he could do without using his hands. When we had the markets, Navo managed pretty guud. The vegetable display was Ara-boy's. You should see those vegetables. Picture perfect.

"Ara was not crazy for money. He never had any money on him. Everytime we went somewhere he says, 'Give me five dollar. Give me ten dollar.' *'Baa bom,'* I say, 'You are just like beggar.' He used to laugh when I said that. . . . Okay, Mark, thank you. Yeah, in my memoirs, you will read everything. I will write one day."

"Just a few more questions, Pop."

"Okay."

"People describe them as 'Navo the brains' and 'Ara-boy the brawn.'"

"I wouldn't say that. Ara-boy had a vehdee brilliant mind. But something . . . if he wanted to do something, it was impossible for us to change his mind. He'd say, 'I'm going to do it.' Several times we questioned him. 'Ara-boy, don't do this.' Two incidents I will tell you. We had eighty acres and Ara was riding the tractor discing the ground and the tractor fell over, almost crushed him. But he was all right. I ran out and said, 'Ara, don't touch this tractor. I'm going to get a few wrenches and a jack so we'll raise it.' I come back and he is lying on the ditch bank hurt. He had tried to lift the tractor. Then we had 160 acres on Highway 41. Above the river. We pulled out the fig trees and Ara was piling them up. 'Ara, don't ever burn these fig trees. It's too windy. It's vehdee dangerous.' But he decided already that he's going to burn. When we arrived home the telephone came that he burned himself. He was at hospeetil. . . You see? . . . He wanted . . . when he got it in his mind, he had to do it. He had to conquer. He liked to conquer. To be hero. He's like that. He was vehdee, vehdee wonderful boy and, eh, really was tragedy. The biggest tragedy in my life."

"I've never talked to Grandma about this."

"It affected her *shad kesh,* vehdee bad. We became more warmer a little bit. But that didn't last vehdee long. Maybe a year. She wanted to talk about it. I said I never wanted to talk about it. I started at least a hundred poems. I couldn't finish. I've got all of them. Half written. . . Mark, I will write. I've got everything and I will put it together someday. I will do it. I will write. I'm not going. . ."

He fell silent.

"One thing I'm going to do, the book that I'm going to publish, it's going to be dedicated to your fawdr. It's going to be to him, my son, and to all the sons who have died from bullets. You see, Mark, parents never forget those things. Of course, children don't forget eeder. There is no question. I never wanted to come into your house after that day. Never. Years and years. But I had to."

He paused again.

"And I have another dream. I'd like to build a fountain in the memory of your fawdr and again all the sons who died in their youth. Along the Etchmiadzin-Sevan Highway in Armenia. I know the place. There are two big trees just off the road. Under there. I'd like to build a fountain . . . yeah. . . . That's all. . . Let's finish it, my son."

I met my uncle for breakfast at his
country club, the San Joaquin, in the old river bottom. He gave me a
quick tour of the clubhouse and introduced me to the boys huddled in the
back of the coffee shop awaiting tee times and gin games. The carpet store
owner was in the middle of a riff on women. "Cunts," he moaned. "If we
sewed up their holes there'd be a bounty on 'em. We'd shoot 'em down
like buffalo."

My uncle had long ago severed his relationship with Dan Hornig and
Leonard Maselli and their small-town circle of bookies, money launderers,
embezzlers and crooked builders, that was true. But he had found himself
a new cluster that looked and sounded very much like the old. In fact, this
new cluster was descended from the old one, the friends and relatives of
those he had broken off from after my father's murder. I saw no reason not
to lump both groups together. My uncle was able to draw the necessary
distinctions so that each Thanksgiving, he could seat my sister, brother
and me at the same table with the man who was Hornig's best friend, or
invite me to lunch and ask the friend who golfed and gambled with Frank
Nunez to join us. What was I to read, what did he intend me to read, if
anything, in his disregard for these associations? Not even when I began

to question him about the past, conjecture based on little more than associations, did he attempt to distance these friendships from me.

I had come to his turf, his world, to decide his involvement in the drug ring that likely led to my father's murder. My uncle had a hawklike eye for opportunity and danger. Unlike my father, he knew when to look and when to look away. Did his greed allow him to be seduced? Or did his fear keep him a safe distance away?

Seated at a panoramic window, we could almost glimpse the 160 acres across the river that Grandpa sold in the 1950s for less than $100,000. Twenty years later, the asking price was more than a million dollars—the lost fortune that my grandparents pinned at the feet of my mother, who had refused to live there.

"Grandma says if we would have held onto the Highway 41 land, all our lives would have been easier," I told my uncle.

"You listen to Grandma and you'll go fucking nuts."

We ordered breakfast and he seemed more preoccupied than usual, and a little nervous. He kept sucking on his teeth as if a string of meat was stuck there and he was having no luck vacuuming it out. There was no mistaking my game, I thought. Calling him "Unc," laughing at the pussy joke as hard as he laughed, fussing over the story of the seventy-five-foot putt he sank a week ago for a cool grand—none of it could disguise what to him, from across the table, looked predatory. I didn't trust him. He had no reason to trust me. I was dragging him back to a spot he had spent a lifetime dodging, not just the death of my father but the relationship between brothers in which so much more was required of him.

I barely mentioned my father when he interrupted and warned me again of the risks. He didn't ask if I was writing a book but for the first time let me know he suspected it.

"I tell you. If I knew the answer 100 percent, I seek justice the only way I know how. And that's not by advertising it."

"I think you already know."

"I think it was probably the Mexican," he said. "Your dad throwing him out of the bar, bodily."

"It's no secret Nunez was the prime suspect. But I think you've got the motive wrong."

I told him I had researched the Madera court case top to bottom. The drug meeting between Hornig and Maselli he stumbled on didn't happen in 1966, as he insisted, but in the summer of 1971, after my father and Hornig became partners. This wasn't any old smuggling venture. It was headed by Nunez and took in some of Fresno's most prominent citizens. My father, his motive unclear, was threatening to expose it all.

He was not impressed. He shook his head. "I really think it was more for that fight, Mark."

Had he been anyone else, my usual prey, I would have sprung on him right then the secret from his first wife: My father had gone to you in the days before the murder with plans to expose a drug ring involving your friends and golfing mates. For months after, you were afraid. You carried a gun. But when it came to my uncle, I lacked the killer instinct. I think I feared his reaction, and this obviously wasn't the place or the time, a table down from his partners hyping the big game a few minutes away. Not now, I told myself.

Breakfast arrived and he used the diversion to whisper how he finagled handicap strokes from golfers of equal skill, money in his pocket. "They call me Navo Crime," he teased a car dealer whose hundreds he held up in a thick wad for all to see. "And Crime doesn't pay."

They called his foursome over the loudspeaker. I handed him the business agreement between my father and Hornig that neither of them signed. "How do you think Dad would have reacted discovering what Hornig did with his money?" I asked.

"I think he might have told Hornig to shape up. Probably. I don't know. I don't know. How do I know what he would have done?"

"You told me Maselli knew why Dad was killed and who did it. He confided something to Josette before you guys got married."

"Yeah, he gave that indication to her."

"So why didn't you ever approach him?"

"Mark, let me tell you something, son. Nobody in his right mind is going to admit something like that to the brother. You don't think that thought crossed my mind? You don't think all that has crossed my mind? The difference between you and me is that I dwelled on this stuff as long as I could and then I dropped it. Because I could see no way."

His silence afforded me nothing. His silence smacked of complicity. How could something so obvious to me, the rudiments of which I grasped as a child, be a source of bewilderment to him, the keen one? If he had been even marginally involved in his brother's life, asked a question here or there or simply taken the time all these years later to think it through logically, he should have surmised the same. His insistence that his brother was killed because he couldn't check his temper, couldn't keep his hands to himself, struck me as convenient and selfish and another way to negate the complexities of my father. Surely, he knew more than this. Even if my uncle wasn't involved in the Nunez drug ring—and I had absolutely no proof he was—my father did confide in him about "blowing open the town."

Perhaps my uncle failed to take him seriously. My father was certainly capable of overreaction. He had a habit of excited, disjointed talk: The little boy screaming "The Japs are coming!" The young man mistaking the Bakersfield temblor for a Soviet nuclear attack. "Stop running, stupid," Navo had told him. "It's an earthquake." It wasn't always easy living with my father's hysteria. I remember him blurting out to a friend that Charles Manson was a harbinger: "There will be bodies piled up everywhere before this thing is over." Some of his old army habits never died. He shredded our fish dinner in search of the tiniest bone and whenever my little brother gagged on food, my father covered his ears and ran. Donny once choked on some Ju Ju Bees and by the time my mother extracted the hard candies, Dad and I were halfway down the block. I remember roughhousing in the kitchen and accidentally stabbing him in the arm with a pencil and blood trickling out. He grabbed several grapefruits from a bowl and started hurling them at me. Smash, one hit the door frame. Smash, one hit my head. I was laughing as I ran down the hallway trying to duck the onslaught. For an instant I thought he was playing until I heard his yelps follow me to the bedroom. I locked the door behind me and began to shudder. So who could blame my uncle if he dismissed my father's rantings about drugs and unmasking the town and putting important people behind bars? "Calm down, Ara. You're getting too excited, Ara."

I asked myself again and again: Was my uncle lying to me or lying to himself? Was this the dissembling of a Machiavellian or the self-evasion that allowed one brother to live on? I leaned toward the latter view even as I continued to record our conversations onto a hidden cassette. He must have calculated back then the likelihood that the drug ring hatched in the office of The Forum bar, the one involving his friends and golfing mates, somehow imploded and took with it his little brother. Why else would he have severed ties to Hornig and Maselli? But over the years he drew solace from what could not be proven. He returned to that emotionally safe ground, the irresolution that lightened the guilt he took on as a father fig-ure to my own father. If the cops couldn't nail down a motive, how could he be so sure it wasn't the fight with Nunez? *The difference between you and me, Mark, is that I dwelled on this stuff for as long as I could and then I dropped it.*

Leonard Maselli died before I could ask him about his long-distance phone conversation with Hornig an hour after my father was pronounced dead. He wouldn't have told me anything I would have believed anyway.

His funeral was an intimate affair. They brought the body back from Santa Cruz where he had lived the past twenty years and made a small for-tune in construction and real estate. I cautioned myself not to read too much into the choice of pallbearers, remembering the men who carried my father to the grave. Even so, it was exhilarating to see the connections in my file cabinet come to full life in mourning. Pallbearer Americo Papa-leo was a short, widebodied sheriff's captain named in state and federal probes as a bagman for the Fresno mob. The organized crime strike force stopped sharing information with Papaleo when agents discovered his close ties to the drug smugglers they were pursuing. The pallbearer stand-ing next to Papaleo was Herman Theroff, the car dealer reputed to be the "Mr. Big" backing Frank Nunez.

I spotted Dan Hornig in the middle of the sanctuary. I hadn't seen him since my father's funeral. Those dreams in which I conceived him in older age, the packed-on flesh and hair wrap, weren't too far off. The face, while fatter, had the same complacent and unmovable quality. He had brought with him a new wife, a stout woman with pouffed hair who seemed too matronly for the Hornig I remembered. I kept staring at him with this strange, detached thrall, as if it was *his* body preserved and *his* funeral I was attending. I fancied marching straight up to him and spitting in his stone face, or worse. I tried working myself into a rage but it was no use. I had waited too many years. He was dead already. From the side door of the funeral home, out of view, I scanned the pews for my uncle. He had known Maselli some forty years but was nowhere to be found. Maybe this was only fitting, given the way he and Maselli had parted. Then my eye caught a familiar figure two rows in back of Hornig, a woman draped in black dress and black hat and veiled behind big sunglasses. It was my uncle's second wife, my Aunt Josette.

We all thought she looked like Suzanne Pleshette the first time he brought her over. She was twelve years younger than my uncle and loved kids, and I took to her right off, an affinity that fast turned into trust. It was her streak of loyalty, though, that made me pause. Her family, the Romanos, were original members of the Dante Club; the Romanos and the Masellis went way back. I found a yellowed newspaper clipping from the 1920s about a bootlegging ring inside the Maselli olive oil company. One of the runners was a Romano. I knew that Josette was dating Leonard Maselli as well as my uncle in the months before my father's death.

Misgivings aside, I needed Josette not only for what she could tell me about my uncle but for what she might have discovered on her own about Maselli's involvement with Nunez. I picked a time when Uncle Navo was out playing golf. She poured us coffee and got to the heart of the matter quickly.

"Was your father involved? Was your uncle involved? I asked myself all those questions, Mark. Over and over again. Who is this man I married? All these guys were friends. I felt there was a chance they were all in this together. But I never knew for sure. So I just forgot about it. And yes, I knew the right people and I could have asked the right questions. That doesn't mean they would have told me."

A few months before the murder, she recalled, Maselli asked her to hold $5,000 for him. He told her he had sold some race horses and wanted to hide the money from his wife, whom he was divorcing. He never mentioned a word about investing in any drug shipments from Mexico, she said. After the murder, Josette called him and asked, "What is going on here, Leonard? What in the world is going on?" He said he couldn't tell her. "You don't understand." Or, "You can't understand." She was sure he knew who killed my father.

"The only thing your uncle has ever said about Leonard or Hornig was, 'Those assholes were involved in dope.' He thought from day one that the police department was involved in the murder but he's never said why. He was very afraid. He thought the phone was tapped and people were watching us. Ara's death laid very heavy on him. . . . It was no way to begin a marriage."

She too had assumed that Frank Nunez joined forces with members of the disbanded Lambe–Simone operation, including fig rancher Tony Simone and his son, Anthony. There were simply too many cross-links between the two groups. She recalled Navo's story about walking into The Forum and interrupting a drug meeting between Hornig, Maselli and others. Only he told her one thing that he failed to tell me—that his friends had asked him to join the venture, and he refused.

"Maybe the danger you pose to your uncle isn't that he was involved in this ring and that you might expose and embarrass him. Maybe what he really fears is that he's worked so hard to put this behind him and you and your questions are forcing him to deal with it all again. Maybe it's guilt not of being involved, but that he was unable to protect his brother from his own friends. I don't know what the answer is, Mark. All I know is that you're going to have to sit down with your uncle and ask him to come clean. And if he doesn't, please understand why."

○ ○ ○

My wife never stopped trying to get me to see the absurdity of living underground in Fresno. She was sure that most of the family, and a few people outside who bothered to think twice, knew that our address in Sacramento and my book on Southeast Asians were part of the same silly ruse.

Late one night, after another family get-together punctuated by my lies and evasions, she got up from bed and faced me in the kitchen where I was fixing a cup of tea. "Who do you think you're fooling? How do you think your uncles and aunts are going to react when they discover the truth."

"They'll understand."

"When are you going to tell them?"

"When it's safe."

"When's that? I mean if all this cloak-and-dagger stuff is on account of the bad guys, don't you think they can find you if they want to find you?"

I didn't want to get into this, not in the middle of the night, not in the middle of my work.

"So what are you proposing? That I make it easy on them? These guys have their own gigs going. They don't want to know about me. Not unless I make it obvious."

"All I'm asking is how much longer do we have to lie? The rest of our lives?"

"No. Not the rest of our lives," I mimicked. "But this is a book about Fresno. You know the connections. We have to be careful."

I took my tea into the office and she followed right behind. "It's gone way beyond careful, Mark. This thing is making you paranoid. It's making you sick. Three years and you're still hiding out like some criminal in a witness protection program."

"Listen, you agreed that we had to take certain precautions and it would complicate our lives, right? Keeping certain people in the dark is one of them."

"But family?"

"Yeah, family. This is a book about family."

"This book. This book. You've put yourself on some pedestal, high and mighty. You've designated yourself judge. It'll never be over. What is the truth, Mark? You tell me. The truth is that you're breaking apart this family. The truth is that you're destroying us with your truth, your vengeance."

She stomped out before I could tell her that Frank Nunez had been released from federal prison and was back in Fresno, living in the same house he lived in twenty years ago. His parole officer told my friend at the district attorney's office that he had no visible means of support. When asked to account for his high rolling, Nunez explained that he and his father were partners in a San Bernardino horse breeding ranch. When the parole officer asked him to document the enterprise, Nunez chuckled. "You don't understand the thoroughbred business. It's all cash."

He had come out of prison more connected than ever and gone right back into the drug business. Like the Nunez of old, he rarely put his hands on the cocaine or heroin or meth. He was the broker, the middleman between the Mexican producers and the American mules, peddlers and money launderers. He had two separate lives—a simple one in Fresno and a high-rolling one in Texas with a toupee and El Dorado and girlfriends.

A friendly state narcotics agent set his sights on Nunez. "His shit's looking a little ragged right now," he assured me. "We might not be able to nail him in your dad's murder. But one more conviction and he'll be a lifer just the same."

Two decades later and so much and so little has changed. I return to Fresno. Nunez returns a few months later. He lives in the same house and uses the same horse breeding front to hide a new drug venture. It's me, not my father, who keeps abreast of his movements and talks to state narcotics agents. Like 1971, he is feeling the heat. Only now he has four convictions behind him and twelve years in prison to know he's not going back. My father owned a couple bars and his choices were few. My weapons are different but I fear they are no better, not when it comes to putting second thoughts in a desperate man. I open and close the shutters, peeking out into the night with my .38, the lamppost illuminating just one sliver of my front yard, and I take aim at the shadows.

○ ○ ○

Navo's son, Brian, wanted an answer, too.

"This book you're doing, Mark. It's not about the Hmong, is it?"

We had once been like brothers, teammates in youth and soulmates in college. From opposite ends of the country, we shared long letters of brooding and awareness that no one in the family quite understood us like we understood each other. Now, in the five years since my mother's death, we had barely spoken. She had helped raise Brian and those last months he stayed away. We chose him as pallbearer and the morning of the funeral he told his father to tell us he had a stomachache and couldn't make it. He didn't bother with attending the church service either, the one that marked the end of the official forty-day mourning period. I wrote him a nasty letter about the wide space between his words and deeds. He wrote back saying he couldn't help but run from pain.

"This book, Mark. You don't have to answer. It's really none of my business."

"I wish that were true. But it's about my father and your father. Why not I come by and we take a drive."

He was an attorney at one of Fresno's most prestigious law firms, a bulwark of right-wing Christians whose clients included some of the biggest growers and insurance carriers in the state. This career choice was a little surprising considering that Brian was a liberal wavering on God. As a kid, he wrote poems about war and the Indy 500, and Grandpa entered a batch of them in a local contest and they took first prize. In college, he had studied history and talked about teaching at a university. At law school at USC, he contemplated a future in environmental law, then began interning summers at McCormick, Barstow—the Fresno insurance law firm that ended up hiring him.

On the letterhead he sent us, there wasn't a black or Latino or Italian or Armenian or Jew or woman in the long list of names above him. And Brian was hardly a concession to ethnic diversity. He had no ties to the Armenian community and looked almost completely like his mother's Anglo side.

His father was justifiably proud that he had landed at such a weighty place, though he feared Brian didn't have enough shark in him. Grandpa, who started telling snide lawyer jokes, wondered the same. He had a tough first year, misplacing case files and battling a bad stomach later diagnosed as colitis. In the years that followed, I watched his manner become more clipped and his opinions less certain. The times I did try to engage him, he retreated behind equivocation. He made partner, joined the Rotary Club and learned to ease his way into any crowd. My passions and fixed beliefs made him uneasy.

As we drove north toward the river that day, I explained how his father and mother each recalled a different version of the past. Uncle Navo wanted me to know that my father was "very close-mouthed." The only hint of disquiet were those rambling, almost incoherent statements the morning before the murder. No names. No threats. Just the sense that my father was scared. Aunt Carroll insisted Dad was onto something big. A drug ring. "Up in the up, up, up," she had said. He confided in Navo not only the dimensions of this ring but his plans to expose it.

Brian said he had no knowledge either way but he doubted that his mother would make up something like that. He recalled one comment in particular from his father that seemed to support Carroll's version of events: "My dad once told me that Uncle Ara said to him, 'Navo, no matter what happens to me, I love you.'"

"When did my father say that?"

"Shortly before he was killed. Maybe a day or two before."

"See, I've never heard that. Your father's never told me that."

"Mark, my father is quite capable, with a straight face, of hiding something. He's a survivor. That's the first thing you have to know about him. Never assume he's naïve. You won't get into trouble that way."

I had Brian at a disadvantage. He had grown up trying to please me, to live up to my big cousin example in sports and school, and he succeeded. Our love and rivalry weren't so much different from that of my father and his brother. I had lost both my parents at a young age, and he had grown up with a mother who blew in and out of his life like an erratic wind and a father who held back emotionally but gave him everything else in spades. There came a time between us, perhaps inevitable, of resentment and parting. Now he was feeling the need to make us whole again, to make me near whole again, even if it meant laying open the father he loved and feared more than anyone. I let him feel the obligation he was feeling.

"Your mom says after the murder he carried a gun," I said.

"I saw that gun. And I freaked out. He told me, 'You don't know what's going to happen here. Maybe they're after me. Maybe they got the wrong guy.' Something like that."

I told him how hard it was to get his father to even acknowledge that growing up Armenian and the son of a Bolshevik in Fresno pained him in any way. Yet their Sugar Bowl ice cream shop was known as the "Nose Bowl," and as soon as he finished high school he got a nose job.

"Nose job? I never knew my dad had a nose job."

"Well it wasn't exactly a pug they gave him."

"See, he's a riddle to me, too. He didn't seem to care if anything Armenian got passed onto me. He has the outward appearance of dominance, control, cockiness. But under all that, I'm afraid, he's basically weak. He tries to cover up by refusing to show what he regards as weakness. Except for that one moment at the end of your father's funeral, I've never seen him express grief. And the silence destroys him."

I laid out the police theory—supported by my own investigation—that Frank Nunez had my father killed to keep him from exposing a drug operation and to get back for knocking him down in front of his Anglo golfing buddies. Prominent businessmen, several of whom were Uncle Navo's good friends, were involved in the smuggling venture. I still had lingering suspicions about the financial involvement of both our fathers, though I didn't think it probable that my father would move to expose something in which he or his brother were involved. I told him that Dan Hornig's presence at that last meeting between our fathers had always bothered me. What if that meeting was an attempt to dissuade my father from talking? He was mad at Hornig for diverting his money to Nunez and wanted the eighteen grand back and out of the business partnership. What if Uncle Navo tried to mediate and failed? *Navo, I don't give a shit. I want my money back and I want out.* The fact that older brother couldn't protect younger brother from his friends—it explained so much. The guilt. The silence. The lies.

"I've always wondered, Mark, how my dad could associate with all these underworld figures and still keep his moral integrity. I don't think he ever crossed the line but he played right up to it."

"How well did your dad know Nunez?" I asked.

"Real well. Through Hornig. Then my dad got pissed off or something happened. He said Nunez was a bad, bad apple."

I didn't know how long we had been driving; I couldn't recall the route, so full of zigzags and meanderings. We were several miles past the river in the middle of a rolling vineyard. I stopped the car and looked at Brian. He was completely absorbed, head down. I thought of him writing or reading one of those letters we traded back in grad school. Each of us trying out something new on the other. Too honest. Too much.

I broke the silence. "Your dad must have known his friends posed a danger to my father. And that awareness had a price. A whole set of presumed responsibility came with it. 'Damn stupid Ara. How could he trust these guys? I never did and they were my friends. Why didn't he listen?'"

Brian, without an ounce of equivocation, agreed. "My dad knows when to dance in and dance out with these guys. He decides to take them for a few grand on the golf course. And when he wants to back out, he backs out. When he wants to play again, he plays. Your dad lacked that cunning. The one thing my dad says over and over is that your dad didn't know fear. He says this with the insinuation, 'How could Ara have been so stupid?'"

I turned the car around and headed back home. I asked Brian to keep the details of our conversation, and the real nature of my book, to himself.

He would spend the next two years lying to his parents to oblige me. I dropped him off in front of his house and we exchanged pats on the back and a promise to get together soon. He lingered in the car, a pained look on his face.

"This is not my crusade, Mark. I love my father but he's one of the most enigmatic characters. And it's not all good. Some of it could be disillusioning. But whatever you find, it won't change my love for him. You could tell me he fucked a donkey on the Fulton Mall and I wouldn't love him any less. Maybe it wasn't the smartest thing, getting married thirteen days after the murder. But that didn't give anyone the right to question his love for his brother. The one thing I'll never understand is that he turned his back on you and Michelle and Donny. Especially you. I have never forgiven him for that. But the last thing I want is to add to his pain. 'Cause he has carried this cross since the murder. He was a fraction of his old self for years and years. And there's still a part of him missing. Even when he laughs, there is something sad or ironic or not all there about it. That I know. There's an immense sadness in him. I want to do something to help but there's nothing I can do about his pain. It doesn't matter that I love him and I love him now more than ever. It doesn't matter that I convey that because nothing makes a difference."

"**I** was dying, you know, this morning. Yes. I am in vehdee bad condition."

Physically, my grandfather looked fine except for a missing tooth he had swallowed with last night's steak sandwich. Grandma, darting here and there, was another matter.

"Every day he gets up and says, 'Today is the day I'm going to die.' I say, 'Why do you say that? You've been saying that for fifty years. Don't be afraid to die. Death, if it comes easy, is not that bad.'"

"Are you afraid of dying, Pop?"

"Why should I? If I die, I die. That's all. Heaven is gone. *Tot trrrrrr rah tot, tot trrrrrr rah tot, tot trrrrrr rah tot. TOT.*"

Even as I was finding my father, I was losing my grandfather, each visit another piece of his mind vanished. He used to swear in Turkish. He now sang in Turkish, and he talked straight from his dreams, about legs of lamb growing on palm trees and a house with collapsible walls to accommodate the many dignitaries who would come for dinner. "A thousand guests," he beamed.

Most of his stories dealt with the regrets of his life, failures made good by senility. He recalled his first day at Sorbonne University, walking into the classroom of an esteemed professor and greeting him with the words, "You are my master." The professor looked up and smiled, "No, Aram Arax. You are *my* master." Armenian priests were continually inviting him to speak before their large parishes, the faithful rising in unison and chanting his name.

I challenged him. "So you think you were a great man?"

"No. Greatness really didn't interest me. I lived. I lived for Armenia."

We had attempted for several months to get him into a nursing home but Uncle Navo, who had the final word, was dragging his feet. Some of the family, Grandma included, commented that Navo was too busy playing golf to care. Others felt he probably cared too much and feared that a nursing home would be the final push. To get Pop into a home, Grandma needed a psychologist's referral; she picked the first Jewish shrink she could find in the phone book. She spent half the time telling him about her Jewish son-in-law, Danny Melnick, and Grandpa's poetry.

"In Soviet Armenia they published some of his work," she explained. "He didn't want to take the money but they said, 'No. No. We pay for everything.' To appreciate, you know."

"Where were you born, Aram?" the psychologist asked.

"Bursa, Turkey. I am sick. I am vehdee sick man. Everything is coming out now. Black things come out from my body."

He turned to me, his rheumy eyes straining to make out my outline. "I love your face. You come to Fresno and I'll give you my writing and we'll work together. Can we do that?"

"Sure, Pop."

He clapped.

"Pretty good one, isn't it," he said, pointing to his beret. "I am Bolshevik, yes. I am vehdee proud to be Bolshevik. . . I am pathetic, *tsahkis.* Sit by me. Take care of me. After all, I am the son of an Armenian."

The psychologist stepped back from the patient and addressed me. "Usually when the mind regresses this far, they become very belligerent. But he's social and pleasant and that's unusual."

"Grandma has some bruises on her arms. He's still very strong. He pulls her hair."

"He's been doing that for three or four months. Never in his life did he touch me. Ever. Until just lately."

"We'll give him something to soften the moods. I'm almost positive that he's suffering from small strokes."

I waited outside for them to finish. My grandfather, who had passed to me his hoe and his garden, who introduced me to steak and eggs at Sambo's and the poems of Siamento and Charents, to the "sunbaked taste of Armenian words, their lament like ancient lutes," was slipping away. The deterioration in the past few months was astounding. Grandma refused to believe it, still posing questions to him about the past and long-dead relatives. I refused to believe it. And just when he raised my hopes, when he was about to give me some piece of my father or uncle or our history, out of nowhere a word or vision swept him to another decade, generation, world, dream.

Back home, sitting in the kitchen like old times, he got up and walked out the door. Through the window I could see the lemon tree in the backyard shaking. I stood up and there was the little man, tearing at the branches. He always loved to prune, I thought. He moved over to the rose bush and started tugging at its leaves.

"Yesterday, he told me not to get too close to that tree," Grandma said. "He said, 'There's a treasure buried here and we don't want to alert the neighbors.' See, Mark. He's picking those leaves for you. He's got nothing to give you so he brings in the tender ones as gifts."

She laughed, that nervous, suppressed laugh. "Grandpa's really a kind man. He's gentle. It's only in the last year, he's started to hit me."

He walked in smelling of citrus. With a furtive tug he slipped me a few orange, lemon and rose leaves, his hands bloodied from the thorns.

"Look what happened," he said. "All my eyes gone to the wind." Then he pointed at Grandma and cried. "Please, Alma, don't take me to the *Der El Zor.*"

The Der El Zor was the desert Armenians were made to cross on their death marches.

"No one's taking you to Turkey, Pop."

"I can organize at least a hundred people in Soviet Armenia and attack those bastards," he shouted. "The Turks never put a finger on me. 'You cocksucker,' I said. 'You killed so many Armenians. Fifty-one in my family. That's enough.' I was not brave or strong man. But I did fight the Turk. I lived. I lived and before I died I wrote my poetry."

For a moment his mind had snapped back. And then he was gone again.

I want to say that it was just before my second encounter with Linda Lewis, the eyewitness to the shooting, that I crossed the line of reason and sanity, but my wife says no, that I cracked up months before that.

Convinced that my father's killers had tracked our whereabouts in Fresno, I had changed my sleep pattern so that I was awake and standing guard through the night and fighting to find sleep during the day. I suspected the phone had been tapped and a bug placed in our apartment, and whenever my best friend came over to discuss my findings, I turned on the television full blast and whispered. Each time we left the house, I placed at the entrance a ballpoint pen with the clip turned at a precise angle, not realizing that gravity itself could move it.

For our cars, I purchased a $1,000 alarm system with a mechanism that started the engine from a distance of 200 feet away. The salesman boasted that Walter Payton, the Chicago Bears running back, had this same system to warm his Mercedes on icy midwestern mornings. I didn't tell him I had another purpose in mind—to detonate any bombs connected to the engine. The thing worked beautifully until I neglected to put the car in neutral, pressed the magic button and it lurched forward into the weights and through the wall of the garage.

In moments of rationality, I reasoned, "We've been careful in our movements and all the neighbors still know us as Norris. How can the bad guys be so ubiquitous?" But these were fleeting moments. If Dad's killers didn't get me, disease would. The mole on my face was changing. Under a lightbulb, it looked as if a pimple had grown next to it. In sunlight, the red spot appeared to be an extension of the mole. In a fit of panic, I called the dermatologist but he couldn't see me for another week. "If this is melanoma," I admonished his secretary, "eight days could be the difference between living and dying."

I felt heavy in the chest, my breathing labored. My back ached and I found a lump in the groin. Dizziness, weight loss, 105 degree fevers. I was certain the past six years had finally caught up with me. Leaving Baltimore, trying to save my mother's life, back and forth between Los Angeles and Fresno, sinking mind and heart into my reporting career at the *Times*, having children, buying our first house, working late nights so Coby could get her teaching credential and now back in Fresno and living under an assumed name and tackling this project that had hung over me so long.

I went down the long list of likely causes—glaucoma, testicular cancer, lung cancer, melanoma, leukemia, brain tumor, heart virus, vertigo and Kaposi's sarcoma. I imagined the Kaposi's came from a razor I borrowed eight years earlier from a colleague who I later found out was gay. I kept checking the paper to make sure his byline was still there. Since I didn't smoke, I began to suspect that our old house sat on a vein of uranium, which produced radon gas, the second leading cause of lung cancer. I visited a different doctor every few months but the only diagnosis to date was that I suffered a sensitivity to elastic. I couldn't wear underwear anymore.

"You're going to break us in doctor bills alone," Coby screamed.

I didn't know who to trust, trapped the same way my father was trapped. So the discovery of an apparent link between Frank Nunez and Linda Lewis set my head spinning.

The week of the murder, Nunez, who was twenty-eight, dispatched a crew of pilots and mules to Scottsdale, Arizona, for a series of smuggling runs while he stayed behind in Fresno to work out logistics. The crew checked into room 206 at the Doubletree Inn in Scottsdale and over the next several days there were dozens of phone calls between Arizona and Fresno. Most of the calls appeared to deal with the dope hauls but some I could not explain. It was these calls that raised again my suspicion that Linda Lewis, Dad's bartender and the sole witness, helped the shooters carry out the execution.

• December 29, four days before the murder: Two long-distance calls from the farmhouse Lewis was renting in Fresno to the hotel room in Scottsdale where the Nunez crew was staying.

• January 1, twenty-four hours before the murder: One call from the hotel room to the Lewis residence; one call from the room to The Apartments bar. My father was not at work.

• January 2, three hours before Lewis reports to work and seven hours before the shooting: One call from the room to the Lewis residence.

• January 3, twenty-four hours after the murder: One call from the Lewis residence to the hotel room.

• January 4: Six calls between the Nunez crew and the Lewis residence.

So there it was, a link between Frank Nunez and Linda Lewis, a link the homicide team had glossed over and one that caught my eye only after I had charted all the long-distance phone records. Had I been gullible or what? One meeting inside a jailhouse interview room, one meeting bracketed by Linda's tears, and I had dismissed totally her role in the murder.

Fortunately, I had stayed in contact with Lewis or, more correctly, she had stayed in contact with me. Every few months after our meeting, she called the *Los Angeles Times* in a drunken stupor and left a message on my answering machine. "Mark, this is Linda. *Ummmmmmmmmmm.* Sure would like to talk to you. *Ummmmmmmmm.* 'Cause we have some unsettled business. I don't know how we're going to figure it out cause I don't know how to figure it out. But *ummmmmmmmmm.* I don't know, Mark." Twice she called on the anniversary of the murder and left a message saying she "just wanted to chat."

I headed for Huntington Beach to see Lewis again, this time driving a rented car instead of my own, in the event she was trying to get a bead on me for the killers.

"I'm so glad to see you, Mark. My mind's been racing all day. So many things to say to you."

We were eating dinner at a Chinese restaurant, and Lewis was behaving in an odd, nervous manner. She kept going to the bathroom with her purse. Every thirty minutes, she came up with a new excuse to leave the table. Every thirty minutes, I calculated, the length of one side of a tape.

"She's recording the whole damn thing," I whispered into the tape recorder beneath my shirt. "Be careful."

"I got a new tattoo," she said, returning to the table.

"Where?"

"On my ass. A dragon. I've got three others. I got a butterfly when I was working for your dad. Then one tattoo 'Vinnie' and another initialed 'RJC.' If you ever want a boyfriend to leave town, tattoo his name on your ass."

In the car I faced her. "How come you keep disappearing every thirty minutes?"

She clutched her purse.

"What's in the purse, Linda?"

"Nothing," she said meekly.

"Open it!"

She pulled back the fake leather flap and there it was, staring me right in the face . . . a gleaming pint of vodka.

"I'm a drunk," she cried. "You know that day you visited me in jail? Well, I was there because I'm a drunk. I thought I had one more high coming to me."

You jackass, Mark. She's been using the bathroom to sneak a shot of Smirnoff's and a quick spray of Binaca. "Linda, you don't have to hide from me. Hell, if you want a drink, let's go to the bar and have one straight up."

She ordered a kamikaze and toasted her dead mother and my dead father and then explained that the phone calls between Arizona and Fresno had nothing to do with her. It was her roommate, Tracy Stockwell, Dad's other female bartender, who placed and received the calls. Stockwell was talking to her boyfriend, Steve Rutledge, a member of the Nunez crew in room 206.

"They had a conversation the morning of the murder," she said. "Tracy was talking to Steve and then she put the receiver to her chest and asked me if I would work for her. She said, 'Linda, will you go in for me today?' And I said, 'Yeah.'"

"My God, Linda! Rutledge warned her of the murder and you went to work in her stead."

"I don't think so, Mark. She didn't twist my arm. We were always trading shifts. Tracy doesn't know anything. I guarantee it."

"I think you were set up."

"I wasn't set up. I guarantee it. Your dad was set up. We don't know why."

We stopped off at another bar where she was a regular and she wouldn't leave until the piano man played her favorite, "Greensleeves." At two in the morning, I drove her home and helped her out of the car.

"Fuck you, old man!" she yelled.

"Do you think he's waiting up for you?"

"I give you permission, Mark. To say 'Fuck you, old man!' to my father because he's still alive. Say it!"

"I don't even know him, Linda."

"Do it! Do it! I give you permission. Fuck you, old man! He's a pain in the ass. Say it!"

"I can't."

She took a few steps in the direction of the front door and stumbled.

"You hate my guts, don't you? . . . Seven fucking bullets. I'm telling you. They fucked up. I thought it was a joke. I didn't even know it was happening. I didn't even hear it. I didn't hear it. I didn't hear it. I was playing 'Bye, Bye, Miss American Pie.' . . . I don't know what to tell you, Mark."

I hoped Tracy Stockwell could lead me to Rutledge and whatever else I might discover about those phone calls between Fresno and Arizona. She was the hype who cut her dope with Dr. Scholl's medicated powder and sang my father's virtues and didn't once mention Frank Nunez or her old boyfriend, Steve Rutledge, in our visit a few years earlier. This time I had no luck finding her. She had moved out of her old apartment and none of her neighbors or relatives knew exactly where.

I thought of driving again to Arizona, this time to look up the federal drug agent and prosecutor who brought down Nunez's operation in Phoenix a week after the murder. A grand jury had indicted Nunez, Rutledge and six others.

Before making any trip, I decided to telephone the federal prosecutor in the case, Patricia Whitehead, who was now a municipal judge in Phoenix. I told her I was a newspaper reporter interested in Frank Nunez, who was in circulation again after several years behind bars. Did she know anything about a murder in Nunez's background?

"When we were interviewing some of our witnesses a murder came up. Some guy in a bar in Fresno. A rival drug dealer."

"He was my father. And he was no rival drug dealer."

"I'm sorry. I was never told that per se. I just assumed it, knowing the people we were dealing with."

"How did it come up?"

"These witnesses, in giving us details about the drug conspiracy, mentioned a murder in Fresno and that Nunez was behind it. You have to understand. These witnesses were afraid. They said they wouldn't talk to police in Fresno. They didn't trust them. I couldn't risk getting them killed. So I decided not to pursue it."

"But my father's murder was connected to the drug ring you were prosecuting."

"I didn't know that. I didn't know that. One of our witnesses had what amounted to street talk and the other had what I considered solid information. But for me to pursue the homicide, I would have had to go to the very law enforcement agency I suspected was corrupt. Fresno was not a town to be trusted."

"Let me just ask you this: Was the witness who had solid information a guy named Steve Rutledge?"

There was a long pause. "I won't tell you no."

I didn't think I'd find Steve Rutledge alive, not after reading in court records that he was strung out on heroin and hyping prostitutes in $6 motel rooms as late as 1980. To my astonishment, not only was he alive but working as a car salesman and residing in a nice house in a solid old neighborhood of Fresno. The front yard was a reassuring tableau of family life—balls and bats, bikes and trikes. He had turned his life around, a friend told me, put away the demons. Would he risk his new life to help me answer my past?

I approached the door at night, my heart never beating faster, and in the blue flickering light of the television I could see Rutledge reclining on the couch. He was wiry with a slight paunch, a forty-two-year-old man whose pug nose forever locked him in childhood. He saw me through the big window and opened the door before I knocked.

"Hello. My name is Mark Arax."

"Who?"

I repeated my name and he seemed genuinely bemused.

"My father was Ara."

"Oh, Ara's son. I've forgotten Ara's last name."

He admitted weeks later, after he had grown comfortable, that he feared

I was armed and might try something crazy. I reeled off the standard line, that for years I had been looking up people from my father's past to determine what kind of man he was, if he took a shortcut with drugs and if that shortcut got him killed.

I told him I knew about his phone call to Tracy Stockwell the morning of the murder, how she placed the receiver to her chest and asked Linda Lewis to work for her. I had talked to the ex-prosecutor in Phoenix who believed he had solid information tying Nunez to the murder.

Rutledge took a deep breath and asked his two small boys to join their mother in the other room. Then he explained to me the dynamics of a federal snitch, a junkie trying to finagle the best deal he could.

"The night your father was killed, we got a strange call from Frank Nunez telling us that Ara had been shot. We were doing a big dope haul at the time and Nunez was calling us three and four times a day. I didn't think anything about Ara's murder or that phone call until I returned to Fresno and read the newspapers. The timing of your father's shooting and the timing of Nunez's phone call were so damn close that I wondered if Nunez had some kind of prior knowledge."

"But there must have been something more you've forgotten," I insisted. "You must have had some solid information on top of the odd timing of the phone call."

"If I did, I just can't remember. I'm sorry but you're talking about a lot of years and a lot of drug abuse."

"That's not the way Patricia Whitehead recalls it. She said you wouldn't go to Fresno police because they were corrupt and you were scared your information would get you killed."

"During my meetings with the feds, I tried to impress them with what I knew. That's the way it works. You give them more and more and more about Nunez, so they need you more and more and more."

"But how about your phone calls to Stockwell?"

"I was frantic and needed her to greyhound me some heroin. We didn't think it was going to take more than a day or two to haul the stuff back from Mexico. But Frank had some trouble putting the deal together. I didn't have access to any stuff and I was getting desperate. So I called Tracy."

"So Nunez's role in my father's murder was basically speculation on your part?"

"The timing of that phone call from Nunez was awfully spooky," he said, shaking his head. "He knew about Ara being shot almost right as it happened."

"And that's it?"

"Unless there was something else. But if there was something else, I just don't remember."

If he was lying, I thought, he was awfully good. I caught him cold and his explanation accounted for everything—the phone calls to his girl-friend Stockwell, why prosecutor Whitehead would believe he had specific knowledge and why, in reality, he did not.

I went home disheartened and spent a month doing nothing. As tanta-lizing as my theory was, I had nothing in the way of hard evidence. Yes, my teenage hunches had been backed up by Sergeant Estilarte, the lead in-vestigator in the case. Yes, I had a money trail from Dad to Hornig to Nunez, a conforming pattern of phone calls and drug flights, and I had any number of sources recalling my father's contacts with state and local law enforcement—all pointing to the same motive. But I had no one on the inside and nothing that tied Nunez to any hitmen. By all accounts, Nunez was at the center of it all. The cops had come to the same conclu-sion twenty years earlier. And the same dead end.

○ ○ ○

Frank Hinsley Nunez was born in Arizona in 1943, the only child of Mag-daleno and Mollie Nunez, simple laborers who returned to their native Mexico to raise him. He became ill almost as soon as they crossed the bor-der and lingered near death for a year. They came north again and after a brief stay in Arizona made their way to California's farming heartland. Petrochemicals and federal farm subsidies were opening the door to a new era of plenty for the Armenian, Italian, Volga German, Japanese and Russ-ian immigrant farmer and tractor salesman and mechanic; everyone but the Mexican who actually picked the crops and carried home the poison in his pores.

The *bracero*, the stoopback in the fields, was the final indignity in a cen-tury of defeat and capitulation. It was the Latino, after all, who gave this valley its name, *San Joachin*. He was the first to farm its fecund land and the first to graze cattle, horses and sheep. It took California only two years after seizing Mexico's northern province to declare the Mexican persona non grata. In 1850, the state legislature passed the Foreign Miners License Act which required all foreigners—read Mexican—to pay a monthly $20 tax. Only after the exclusion of its cheap Chinese and Japanese labor in the early 1900s did California welcome back the Mexican, and only then to pick its crops.

They were herded into labor camps and remained there, docile, until the 1940s when gangs of zoot-suiters, sporting their baggies and duck-tails, swaggered and swelled through the streets of downtown Fresno. The *pachucos* always paid the price for their evanescent freedom, regularly being beaten by police working in concert with soldiers on weekend leave.

Here is where the Nunez family decided to plant roots, where their son grew up between generations, too late to be a zoot-suiter and too early to be a proud Chicano. He became a Mexican-American the same way my uncle became an Armenian-American, learning to internalize the hurt of exclusion, promising to get even one day by making it big.

The photo on his first driver's license shows a brown-skinned kid in black horn-rimmed glasses with no visible expression. Photos in years since show the same deadpan. My friend, a Chicano scholar and poet, knows this face well. The reticent Mexican. The mask of shame.

Classmates in high school don't recall much beyond the fine, stylish, al-most conservative way Nunez dressed. He seemed to have decided early on to reinvent himself from the outside in, and his first jobs upon graduation were in clothing shops. He bought a '64 Corvette and married an attrac-tive white girl and played golf with a group of white hustlers.

"Frank was a classy guy," said Stan Paramore, who sold clothes with him at Coffee's men's store. "He dressed sharp all the time. He could play a wonderful acoustic guitar and sing real well. And he was a great golfer."

More than anything, Nunez wanted to run his own men's apparel shop and in early 1969 he traveled south to Mexico to stake his dream. He was caught north of the border wearing his finest suit and toting seventy pounds of Mexican marijuana in the trunk of his sparkling car. He would have made it if not for the suspicious behavior of a friend, an Armenian, who was following close behind with his own stash. Nunez told U.S. authorities he had gone to Mexico to negotiate a deal to build a golf course, a story he would use again and again in later busts. He pleaded guilty, paid a small fine and spent the next two years perfecting a better method.

By early 1971, he had assembled a Mexico-to-Fresno marijuana and heroin smuggling syndicate complete with airplanes, pilots, ground crew, trucks and stash houses. When the feds brought down the Lambe–Simone organization that summer, it created a vacuum into which the twenty-nine-year-old Nunez stepped.

"Frank came to me after he had put it all together," Stan Paramore recalled. "He said, 'I've got a proposition for you. I'm going to be a millionaire and I want you along for the ride. I've got the connection down south. I've figured it all out. If you want in, you're in. If you don't, nothing more will be said.' I told him thanks but no thanks."

His supplier was Pepe Fernandez, the same Mexican who had furnished the Lambe–Simone ring. Pepe fronted Nunez a good portion of the dope, requiring payback only after Nunez had sold the load to middlemen. This allowed him to operate without financiers and maximize profits. Nunez was riding high. There was a house in Tahoe, a house in the Bay Area, a ranch in New Mexico and a clothing store in Fresno called the Fashion Revolution. He bought diamonds and indulged his newest fancy, to breed the greatest thoroughbred in the world.

Then came a series of bungled loads in the spring, summer and winter of 1971 that led to the arrest of his right-hand man, Richard Morgan. Pepe was no longer willing to front the dope. To recoup the losses and cushion against future ones, Nunez was forced to recruit a number of financiers. This is when Dan Hornig and Leonard Maselli and Herman Theroff and possibly the Simones entered the picture.

When federal agents busted the Nunez operation in the Arizona desert a week after Dad's murder, they seized 1,100 pounds of marijuana, a stash house, airplane and two pickup trucks. Three of the mules were arrested immediately but it took five months for the federal grand jury to indict Nunez. As agents put the handcuffs on him, he pleaded, "You've got the wrong guy. I'm a pro golfer. I just won a big tournament and they've invited me to play in the U.S. Open."

He hired Oscar Goodman, the Las Vegas attorney-to-mobsters later profiled on 60 Minutes, to defend him. The trial lasted seven days and the only mention of my father's murder came as Goodman cross-examined an Arizona sheriff's deputy who assisted in the bust.

"In that initial conversation with Fresno authorities, did they advise you of a homicide in Fresno?" Goodman asked.

"Yes."

"You had no knowledge of this homicide prior to placing the phone call?"

"None whatsoever."

"Do you know who was killed?"

"A man named Ara is all I know. A-r-a."

"Do you know when he was killed?"

The judge interrupted. "Is this really material to what we are here for, as to what the details of some murder charge in Fresno were?"

"No, your honor," Goodman replied.

"Let's get on with it, then."

In December 1972, one year after the murder, Nunez was found guilty of nine counts of drug smuggling and sentenced to ten years in federal prison. Thirteen months into his term, his wife, Diane, wrote a long letter to U.S. District Court Judge William Copple pleading for his early release. She talked about the burden of raising three young children without a father and the pain of not having an answer for her smallest one, Rick, who constantly asked, "When is Daddy coming home?"

"I know my husband well enough to say that if you modify his sentence he will walk a straight line forever," she wrote.

Frank Nunez served eighteen months. After his release, he would be popped three more times for cocaine smuggling and spend a total of twelve years behind bars before returning to Fresno, nine months after my own return home.

In the depths of my funk, I constructed a chain from the murder all the way back to the misfiring of the electrical system on one of Nunez's planes and the miscalculation of gas and his hiring of an inexperienced, frightened pilot. I picked out the snags, the small, remote and seemingly unrelated missteps and malfunctions that had to align for tragedy to find its spark. Each snag was a blunder and each blunder exposed Nunez to risk and each risk made murder that much more thinkable.

Nunez himself was a snag, dazed mind and fractured spirit. The mind seized on the notion that my father, a problem at a time of high risk, had to be eliminated. The spirit dangled between worlds, a set of Mexican friends and a set of Anglo ones, alienated from both. He had seen a lifetime of humiliation in the eyes of his father who busted his ass from one simple job to the next, and along comes my father, whose anger was partly fueled by Nunez calling him a "cheap Armenian." Dad knocked Nunez on his ass in front of his investors and gambling buddies, all white. Shame exploded against shame. My father's reaction was immediate, visceral and easily passed. Nunez's was darker, planned, hatched, malignant.

These were the impulses, the breakdown and disorder, my father and Nunez were powerless to change. And chaos enveloped that day—six bullets and not a killer shot among them, the gun Dad wrested only to jam in his hand, the uncommon strength in his body that led to miscalculation at St. Agnes, the surgeon who froze, the electrical system that failed to type and match his blood. Had just one thing gone the other way, it might have changed everything.

ooo

I had spent four years trying to place my father in a context of events. I did this by focusing on his known business associates rather than on unnamed hitmen, whose identities promised nothing but frustration. Still, there were a few suspected gunmen I just couldn't resist chasing, two in particular from the San Fernando Valley who had moved dope for Nunez. The homicide detectives never found out about this pair and I came across them only after pulling criminal files on every person Nunez called in the weeks before the killing. They had pleaded guilty to a marijuana sales charge and appeared before a sentencing judge on January 17, 1972, two weeks after the murder. One requested a stay of his jail term so he could be treated for injuries sustained in a recent "industrial accident."

"He suffered a broken finger and a severe back strain or even possibly a more severe injury," his attorney noted.

My father twisted the gun from the hand of one shooter, and he insisted he fired a shot and struck one in the back as they turned and ran. The two young men appearing before the San Fernando Valley judge roughly matched the description provided by Lewis. There was even an eerie bit of bad karma that made me believe I had stumbled upon the right ones.

One of them had been killed inside a bar in Sylmar in 1987. A drug deal apparently soured and a Mexican Mafia enforcer slit his throat and stabbed him twenty-eight times.

I found the older sister of this man listed in the phonebook in the canyons near Magic Mountain. "Vietnam killed my brother," she told me. "He was class president and a straight-A student at Sylmar High. Then he got drafted and came back an addict. He was moving weed for a big-time dope smuggler."

"Did he ever mention the name Nunez?"

"No. But I found that name in his notes recently. On a little pad. N-u-n-e-z."

"I know this might sound strange but did he ever tell you that he killed a man in Fresno?"

"No. But it wouldn't surprise me."

"Do you remember a leather jacket he had."

"Sure. With fringe on it?"

"Yeah. Fringe."

"Sure."

I was going to drive down to the Canyon Country and take a look at her photo album, but by the time I got around to it, her phone was disconnected and she had moved. It was no major loss, I thought. Even if her dead brother and his friend were, by some stroke of marvelous fate, the two hitmen, they were merely the how, the device, of my father's murder. And I was too busy chasing the whys.

I went back to my charts, the day-by-day and month-by-month movements of the major drug rings surrounding our two bars, trying to establish with absolute certainty that Nunez and Hornig and Maselli and the Simones were together in one grand drug conspiracy threatened by my father. But I kept running into the same problem: Fresno was a small world and its world of drug financiers, pilots and money launderers was smaller still. There was bound to be some overlap, some association, and it did not necessarily equate to murder. Still, the relationships were strong and teased me to the end.

Anthony Simone Jr.'s ties to Hornig were especially suggestive. After the murder, Hornig tried to sell The Forum to Simone's older brother, but state alcohol regulators traced the money to a safety deposit box belonging to Anthony and killed the deal.

A source told the homicide team that a state senator from the valley was involved in a big narcotics ring connected to the Arax murder. The detectives neglected to talk to the state senator or follow up this lead in any way even though he was known to associate with the Fresno mob. The senator's name had come up numerous times in the Lambe–Simone case. Federal drug agents wondered why a powerful legislator who had no expertise in criminal law was defending one of the drug pilots. I had my own question: Was the state senator the person my father was referring to when he boasted that his revelations would be felt "all the way to Sacramento," the state capital?

Vince Todisco, the criminal attorney, was another strong link between Hornig, Nunez, the Simones and the dirty cops who headed the police intelligence unit. Todisco ran the strip shows and crap tables at the Italian Dante Club. He was half a wiseguy, always talking up the cases he'd fixed and the cops and prosecutors and judges he'd bought.

Todisco was another one who died before I could talk to him. At his funeral, his half brother, Cheech, eulogized him: "Loophole Louie. Vinnie the Loop. Give him a long cigar to suck on and a silver cloud to lay on. God, you've got your district attorney now." Nunez attended. So did the Simones. I stood in the rear of St. Anthony's Church and left before "Ave Maria."

And then one fine spring day I finally came face to face with Frank Nunez. He was sitting in the lunch bar of a local health club with a group of Latino handball players, his longtime friends. His eyes were cast down, disengaged from the banter and beer drinking, and when he looked up at me in my sweats and weight belt, he registered not one thing. Remember this moment, I told myself. This man doesn't even have the decency to know who I am. Recall every detail and every feeling. Do something worthy of retelling, a gesture, a confrontation. I was no longer feeling so much as I was conscious of feeling. I thought for a few seconds and then I decided. I'll walk up to the woman at the front counter. I'll page "Ara Arax" and walk back and then watch the look that freezes on his sleepy face, my confirmation. But my feet wouldn't move. Much later I thought that maybe no look would have registered at all and I would have been left wondering more than I'm left wondering now. I circled him once, twice, less in the manner of a bull moving in for the charge than a long-laboring scientist who had come upon the flesh and blood embodiment of a whole life's work, awestruck, and then realizing at almost the same instant that his specimen—grand by so many conjurings—was faceless, without aura, without resonance. He was completely oblivious to my movements. Not once did he give me a second glance. I thought, *Mister, I know everything about you.* I know how your parents got to this country and how you nearly died your first year. I know your IQ and the size of the surgical scar on your left inside knee. I know the year you became a father and the sordid details of each of your busts. I know that you smuggled marijuana, then heroin and then cocaine and the cops believed you fenced stolen diamonds and that your wife was a full partner in your schemes, right down to the ledger she kept. I know that you talked in golf parlance whenever you dealt with someone you didn't trust. You'd ask a prospective buyer of heroin, "Do you want to see my clubs?" I know that witnesses who turned against you in two of your cases were threatened and that behind bars, on Sundays, you gave Bible readings to your fellow inmates. I know that you lapsed into a coma after a motorcycle accident in Mexico in 1980 and brain surgery saved your life. You're missing your temporal lobe. I know that you're still living off the misery of others and if I were alone in this world, I know what I would do.

c h a p t e r 38

She was standing in the front yard when I arrived, feeding vanilla ice cream topped with Pepto-Bismol to the dog.

"Daisy's got a little nervous stomach."

Her voice was flat and her body bent. In the sunlight, I could see the whiteheads that had petrified and become part of her face.

"What wrong, Grams?"

"Looks like I'm having a nervous breakdown, sort of."

"What?"

"Grandpa had a small tragedy last night. He picked up this white sprinkler pipe and was going to hit the mirror. That's what hit him in the eye. It looks pretty bad. Would you come in and see?"

The neighbors had twice reported her to the county for not supervising him. But short of a leash, there was no way to contain him. When she tried locking the front door, he kicked at the screen, kicking and kicking. The moment she gave in, he ran. My brother found him a mile from home in a frantic trot. "Mister! Mister!" he screamed. "Help me!" A police officer found him in a schoolyard in the rain. He hugged the cop and groped at his gun. "I love you," he said. "I'm glad somebody loves me," the cop said, smiling. He disappeared like that, out the front door, down the block, past the irrigation canal, into a neighbor's parked car, gone for hours, hunting down his mind. They brought him home the same way he left, all music and hum. One mad opera.

Now, Pop was asleep. I asked Grandma what happened.

"I had the worst Sunday. No one was around to help. And I'm stuck with a certain person all day. I found him on the floor naked. He had pee-peed all over himself.

"So finally I get him into bed and in a few minutes I saw a shadow going straight into the big mirror, you know that big mirror we have in my bedroom. He had that white plastic pipe. So I grabbed it from him and he got mad and tried to grab it from me and the end hit him right in the eye. So I put peroxide on it and it looks pretty bad.

"When I tried to pull the pipe, he pulled it back. . . . It looks like I did it. I mean, the way it looked like."

She had taken some time getting the story right and even managed to not completely exonerate herself. But I knew it to be a lie. I had learned far too many things about my grandmother to believe otherwise. She had hit my Great-grandmother Azniv in a dispute over a toaster the old woman gave to her daughter. She took a broomstick to the head of the big Mexican woman who provided day care during the week. My uncle explained her anger this way: "You know she was so much fun when we were little. Your Dad and I would tickle her and make her laugh until she peed in her pants. Then she had my sister and that female surgery and change of life and all of sudden she went cuckoo."

Pop came down the hall, his diaper *whisk, whisking,* a trail of urine on the wood floor. Pus sealed shut his one good eye and the other was a black and blue mess, an inch gash from the tear duct down. He was looking for his testicles.

"I want to tell you about my *go-gos.* They're missing. Some-onnnnnnnnnnnne chopped them off. Someonnnnnnnnnnnne."

I checked his bad eye and he reached to hug me. Psoriasis covered his body except for his hands, which had the tender, diaphanous look of a baby bird, rendered see-through from years of blister, scab and rebirth.

"I lovvvvvvvvvve youuuuuuu. One hundred bare-breasted coeds at the gates of Sorbonne. Aram Arax, we love you. His mind is *tres biennnnnnnnnn.*"

I kissed him on the forehead and he made the sign of the cross.

"Drop down the rope so I can climb to heaven," he said.

"So you believe in God, after all?"

My grandfather, the lifelong atheist, didn't miss a beat. "If there is a God, I believe in him."

It was inevitable, I guess. Fresno's criminal underworld, including some of the drug smugglers tied to Nunez and Hornig, found out about my book. I had gone to the apartment of a woman named Marie who in finer days had been a trophy piece for so many local gangsters. Only later did I find out she was on the periphery of a methamphetamine operation that involved the Simones, father and son.

I was passing through a highly charged Fresno, a town not unlike the one that took my father. My talks with local, state and federal cops—all in pursuit of the past—had been misread. The gangsters were whispering that I had returned not so much to find the truth about my father but to settle old scores with those I believed responsible. And since I couldn't prove them as murderers, why not the next best thing—a newspaper exposé on their present drug trade that would force the hand of law enforcement. Some even thought I was passing information to the feds.

In visits with Marie, I took pains to underscore my interest in my father's era only.

"You can't separate what happened to your father from what's happening today," she insisted. "His murder was the beginning. It's all the same players."

Her life was in danger, she said, and she had informed the "Fresno Mafia" that if anything happened to her, "Mark Arax of the *Los Angeles Times* has the complete story of the methamphetamine ring."

"That's a lie, Marie."

"Yeah, but they don't know that."

I tried to appeal to logic. "I don't want to be your bargaining chip. And if you think you've bought yourself some protection, you'd better think again."

"It was your dad's life then and it's my life now. He made a decision to go to the law and was killed. I've made a decision to go to the Fresno Mafia and tell them I've got you."

"You're holding me out as your threat and you have no fucking right," I shouted. "You don't know the position you're putting me in! Now, every question I ask about my father carries this double whammy."

"You don't know the position you put me in when you came knocking on my door. All of a sudden they had more reason to fear me. Remember, you're the one who entered *my* life. Now I have to do what I have to do."

Marie taught me a lot about power and the way it played out in the shadow world where she lived. I had trusted someone desperate enough to use me as a pawn. I knew the game. I was playing it myself, maneuvering Marie for my own lofty ends. She just happened to be doing it better.

My wife knew all about Marie and most of the others. She stayed up late into the night trying to absorb all the zigs and zags of my search. Often, my take on a key person changed a half dozen times, and I expected Coby to keep it all straight in her mind. She tried for the longest time, and then she lost patience—with me, with my investigation, with all the grotesques who invaded our bedroom hours. She had warned me about Marie, then started taking chances of her own. She confided to casual friends the real nature of my book and invited neighbors to our childrens' birthday parties—normal things, to be sure, in normal times. She was no longer willing to back up my lies to family. She poked fun at my paranoia.

"You loved this thing in the abstract," I chided. "It gave us a chance to come back home. But whenever it gets a little tough, you fold. 'I can't do it. I won't do it. I want out.' "

My wife was the one person I got to choose in my life, a selection made in part because she was so different from the Armenian girls—blonde, hazel-eyed, hesitant, the daughter of an IRS accountant and a fourth-grade teacher. We were earthy, volatile, parading in our underwear, a mad knot of feuding brothers, sisters, aunts, uncles and cousins. For better or worse, she became part of the clan. She learned to cook Armenian and she learned to disregard the stares of Armenians, their chocolate eyes saying, "Who is that blonde *o-dar* with one of our boys?" Not even my grandfather, the priest, cared to learn her name. Till the day he died, he called her Lady. My wife endured all this with a shrug. But a murder that would not go away was no longer going to be part of the bargain.

"I married you—not your murder!"

I ticked off a list of her family baggage. "You married all of me," I said snidely. "Just like I married all of you."

"Go open and close the shutters," she mocked, referring to my newest late-night habit. "The big bad man is coming."

Voices exploded. Our five-year-old daughter ran back and forth trying to negotiate peace. "Daddy, this is not fun. I'm not having any fun. Daddy-daddy. Please come into your office. Please, Daddy. Don't fight. Please, Daddy. I love you."

Then came the invitation from the other side. Anthony Simone Jr. wanted to see me. His private eye had come across my tracks at federal archives in San Francisco. It seems I had been the one person who actually checked out the old Lambe–Simone case file and left behind my name. An intermediary put us in touch. Simone wanted me to know that he knew what I was up to. He wanted me to know that he knew I suspected him and his father of a part in the murder.

"I'd be asking a lot of questions, too, if my old man was killed," he said over the phone. Then he gave me directions to the ranch house next to his father's fig packing plant west of town.

What was I to make of this man whose presence I had felt from the moment I first read the murder report five years earlier? Simone Jr., then twenty-two, was the first person at The Apartments after the two gunmen shot my father. He got there just as the ambulance was driving away. A few weeks later, Dan Hornig hired him to manage The Forum, in effect to replace my father.

At the Madera dope trial, Simone's daily attendance as a spectator seemed to go beyond his friendship with defendant Richard Lee Morgan. The court reporter later recalled Simone's outbursts during testimony and the rumors swirling about the courtroom that his father, Mr. Fig, was allied with Nunez and worried that his name would come out.

When pilot Charles Johnson decided to name Nunez, Hornig and Maselli as principals in the smuggling conspiracy, it was Simone Jr. who stalked Johnson at work and at the Madera courthouse and threatened to kill him. Later, he was the only family member to serve time in the Lambe–Simone case.

The more I delved into the murder, the more I glimpsed a connection between Nunez and the Simones. And they were the real McCoy, the big bad men Coby was referring to. That night, as I drove out to the country to meet with the son, I thought back to what an undercover operative for the feds had told me months earlier.

"If the Simones were involved with Nunez, and your father was threatening to expose that, it would be just like the movies. You don't cross people like that."

I had met the federal mole in San Francisco and after three beers and an hour of sweet talk he was still skittish. He had been sent to Fresno in 1974 to infiltrate Simone Sr.'s inner circle. Armed with a phony name, phony rap sheet and phony Mafia credentials, he was working for the federal strike force that had busted Simone Jr. and the Lambes a few months before the murder.

The Simones were back in the drug business. The same M.O.: Guns and cash to Mexico in exchange for marijuana and now cocaine. Armond Bletcher was their hired muscle. Tony Simone Sr. boasted of benefactors high up in local law enforcement. Undersheriff Harold McKinney was practically in his rear pocket, he bragged.

The feds decided to infiltrate the Simone operation through his mistress, a private eye named Sandra Bending. "Sandra Bending didn't know if I was coming to town to take over the local boys or to offer them a deal," the undercover operative told me. "She had been shown my file and long rap sheet. It was all made up. Even my name. I was Al Palmieri."

They spent a month getting to know each other. Mafia bona fides or not, Palmieri had to be checked out in every way before he could be introduced to Simone. Bending asked to feel his hands. You've never done any manual work, she said. No, he replied. And I don't intend to. Then she took a picture of his driver's license and gave it to Simone. You'd better be legit, she warned him. The old man doesn't fool around.

"Mr. Simone was a very careful man. I later found out that his friend, Undersheriff McKinney, ran a state check on me and a guy in the D.A.'s office ran a federal check. Mind you, this was just to meet the man. To say hello."

He sat behind his desk at the fig packing plant, a little man with graying hair and stubby cigar and diamond pinky ring. A wannabe Godfather. I hear good things about you, he said. Palmieri smiled. I'm glad you did.

"Sandra said the meeting went well but 'Just don't get nosey. Don't fuck around with him. He's hired people out of LA before who will kill you.' I was given the name of an Italian man in Los Angeles—Joe Sica, I believe—who was Simone's connection to the outside Mafia."

Over a period of weeks, as Simone gained confidence in Palmieri, he revealed more and more of his criminal enterprise. The fig business provided the perfect wash to launder the illicit gains.

"He let Anthony do the dirty work. This way the old man was insulated. But he complained that the kid wasn't smart enough to run the gambling business. That's why he needed me."

Simone offered Palmieri a healthy cut of the action. Palmieri told him he had to check first with his people in San Francisco.

Three generations of Simones—the bootlegger, the gun runner, the drug smuggler—had made a trifle of the law, parlaying a half century of crimes into a multimillion-dollar farming and land empire. Palmieri was about to redeem that history, to do what the local cops never saw fit to do, but first he needed a badge. He approached Tom Kotoske, head of the organized crime federal strike force in San Francisco. Their conversation went something like this:

"Tony Simone has asked me to join him. He wants me to take over his gambling operation."

"That's great," Kotoske said. "Do it."

Palmieri was working as a contract employee for the feds. He told Kotoske he wanted a real job with the agency. "I need a badge. I'm not going to infiltrate this guy's organization and testify against him without a federal badge. He's too dangerous to do otherwise."

Kotoske, who had jursidiction in eleven states, from Alaska to Guam, told Palmieri he had bigger fish to fry. "Can't do it," he said. "Sorry."

Sitting in that hotel bar, the story rushing back to him, Palmieri smiled the wry grin of someone who should have known better. "They can always do what they want in a community that doesn't care. I'd be willing to bet that within a few days of your father's visits to the police, the other side knew about it and made the decision to stop him.

"I was close," he said, shaking his head. "I would have nailed the whole stinkin' bunch of them if Kotoske had given me a lousy fucking badge. Kotoske said no, and I said good-bye."

○ ○ ○

On a summer night in 1993, the dank dust of sulfur in the farmer's air, I found myself in a vineyard with Anthony Simone Jr., so close I could almost smell his breath. He was standing in the front yard when I drove up, shirtless and shoeless in blue jeans with a big silver belt buckle. He was short and stout, a thick Zapata mustache and a long scar that ran from his shoulder to his neck, the bad boy of Fresno.

I might have expected some trepidation, but I was calm as could be as he extended his nubby hand and I shook it.

"You've got a lot of balls coming out here at night by yourself. . . . You're pretty buffed."

He was referring to my body, still clinging to its old weight lifting exploits. "Not anymore," I said.

We sat in the backyard and he told me to ask any question I wanted. But before I did, I should know for the record that he knew nothing about the murder. He couldn't even recall the rumors of the day.

"I'm sorry, 'cause I know you came here wanting to know. It's a big mystery to me. Have you checked his love life? Maybe he was messin' with some broad he shouldn't have."

"I think it had to do with drugs."

"I can tell you this—your old man wasn't involved."

He said his file at federal archives was missing and I was the last person to check it out. He knew from friends I was asking a lot of questions.

"So you think we were involved?"

"I think one of the smugglers of that era might have been. That's why I went to federal archives. I got copies of the file, if you want it."

He was playing with me now. "Well, I guess you think it was me 'cause I was the first one at the bar after the shooting. The cops saw me there. They didn't bother to tell me to leave."

"That would be pretty stupid," I said. "Showing up at the scene of your own crime?"

"Either stupid or real smart," he grinned. "It would take a lot of balls."

I asked what he recollected of that night, the details of the crime, and this was where he made his first mistake. It was around seven, foggy, he recalled. Ara was in the office. It was opened. The two gunmen were playing pool in the back room. They left and came back. Both fired shots. He died at the hospital. It was a lot of detail to summon up for someone who pleaded ignorance to the old rumors. When I bluffed about money missing from the safe and the chance that it was robbery after all, he recalled that no money had been taken.

Then he began to fish. Let me ask you some questions? What have you found out? Who have you talked to? What ever happened to Dan Hornig? Is he alive or dead? How about a guy named Frank who sold real estate and helped Hornig put together a deal to sell The Forum bar?

This last question was fascinating for the information it imparted. First, he wanted to see my reaction to the name "Frank," without giving away the last name, "Nunez." Second, he made "Frank" into a composite of Leonard Maselli, the real estate agent, and Nunez himself, who had put together a deal for Hornig to sell The Forum to Simone. This was the deal that, in the wake of Dad's murder, fell through when state regulators discovered that Simone was using his brother as a front to buy The Forum.

"Was Frank an Italian?" I asked.

Simone hesitated. "Uh, uh . . . no, he's not Italian. He recently came back to town. He meets my father for breakfast once in a while."

We talked two more hours, until midnight brought a chill to the air. He said he was steeling himself to spend four years in a federal prison camp for his role in the methamphetamine ring. His coconspirator and the man who had turned on him was none other than Richard Lee Morgan, his longtime friend and Nunez's former right-hand man. Simone's father had financed the deal and misled the grand jury. The feds agreed not to prosecute the old man in exchange for his son's guilty plea. Simone Jr. was doing time for Simone Sr. again.

"My dad told me I was stupid to plead out. But he doesn't understand. They were going to take him down. And prison ain't no place for a seventy-year-old man with one lung."

As a writer, I told him, I was drawn to the family story, how his grandfather, Mauro, parlayed bootlegging into a fortune in farmland and how he and his father were able to keep it going through hard times by smuggling drugs and running guns, the feds never really touching them.

"Maybe we should write a book," he said.

"It could be about the pioneers of drug smuggling," I said with a smile.

"We'd have to be careful, though. We'd have to make sure all the crimes had run their statute of limitations."

He was turned sideways, gawking at the moon. "That's the thing about murder," he said, shaking his head and yawning. "There's no statute of limitations."

The fog hit all of a sudden. The phone rang. It was my grandmother.

"Grandpa passed."

He began singing Turkish songs three days before and didn't stop.

"Maybe he sang too hard," Grandma mused.

He had died of pneumonia, nursing home euthanasia. I drove to her house and thought how every person I had ever loved and lost in my life left me in this month, in this fog.

Grandfather, Pop, my touchstone. I owed him an enormous debt. It was he, and Grandma, against all odds of Fresno's nouveau-riche upbringing, who shaped my view. I was more idealistic and less materialistic than my friends because of them. It was Pop, along with the cynicism imposed by the murder, who gave me an alternative perspective. It was his voice inside me that drove me to the streets to write about the black underclass and the Asian gangs.

But I had come to see through the many years of digging other truths as well. His communism seemed to me at one time to be risk taking. It defined him in my eyes as a man of guts and commitment. Now I sensed that his politics, like the rhetoric in some of his poems, reflected mainly nostalgia and longing and slogans. He picked his spots to be brazen. His diatribe against capitalism was conducted inside ethnic walls—the Armenian press and Armenian political gatherings and picnics. He engaged in none of the self-examination and asked none of the penetrating questions that wrenched so many members of the party after Stalin's crimes were revealed. In fact, he dodged the questions that consumed much of the Left during the forties, fifties and sixties. He did not see how far from Marx and Engels the Soviet Union had strayed. He didn't question the contradiction between Marx's commitment to democracy and the Soviet Union's rendering of Marxism.

Even the issues that consumed him were different. He was a nationalist. He wanted what was best for Armenia. His role as liaison between Soviet Armenia and the United States was not a completely imagined one. He was tight with a succession of the Soviet consul generals in San Francisco and got invited to all the big shindigs. American students who wanted to study in Armenia had one sure way of getting there—the signature of Aram Arax. But what happened in his adopted country was of much less interest. He invented his own world here and it had nothing to do with what was happening or who was suffering in Hollywood or New York or Washington.

When I would ask him about the brutality of Stalin, he would respond with jargon: "What do you expect, *tsahkis.* Excesses are part of the correction." He was cynical in this way, the delegate, the party minion, the small, frightened immigrant who threw in his lot with the organization and in return became part of an immediate extended family. He did not question. And his wife, my grandmother? Well, she was simply along for the ride, his parrot. "You know they have millionaires in the Soviet Union," she once told me. And of course she was right.

I will always remember my grandfather's beautiful handwriting, calligraphylike, for it came to represent for me his life of ornament, the surface art and surface utterances. He could recite old lines of Verlaine and Baudelaire but he thought of them as simple symbolists writing about the sun, the moon and the flowers. In his art, nothing got past the ornamental with Pop. It was so much idolatry.

He was consumed by politics and tormented by his silences as a writer, half here and half there, no longer certain of his voice. He was not the perfect father. But never did I doubt his love for family, his children and grandchildren and especially me. To stand in for my father, this was his deepest choice, and he was true to it always.

○ ○ ○

Driving blindly in the fog to comfort my grandmother, I broke into laughter at the irony of my grandfather, eyes sealed shut with mucus, chest rattling, singing Turkish songs until the breath had gone out of him.

We reached my uncle late that night. Josette came to the house with him. It was a measure of my grandmother's discontent that her daughter-in-law had stepped foot inside her house for the first time in three years and stayed in the other room.

Grandma was pouring a cup of hot water when Navo walked into the kitchen. "Hi, Ma. What are you doing?" He asked this with the fullness of a question that needed an answer.

"I'm drinking some hot water," she replied without irritation.

Daisy had twisted herself into a pretzel, trying to snatch a flea from her hind leg.

"Ma, Ma. What's that dog doing? That crazy dog. Look. Look."

He called Jack Sarafian at Yost and Webb. They decided on a Tuesday funeral.

I offered to write the newspaper obituary and pick the pallbearers. Uncle Navo and Brian would pick out a casket and meet Sarafian at the funeral home. My sister, Michelle, would order the flowers. We knew what had to be done. It took about twenty minutes.

His daughter, Jeanette, flew out from Cleveland the next day. We found a short bio and final thoughts he had written fifteen years earlier when he thought he might not survive surgery. We had it translated into English; at his direction, it was read midpoint in the service.

He began by thanking his uncle, Ervant, for bringing him to the San Joaquin Valley in the spring of 1920. He said he would miss Fresno, its cool summer breezes, its searing sun, its vineyards, the shade of its acacias. Most of all he would miss Alma, his "dear fawn." He recalled the village of his birth, the harvest weddings, the family members who died in the massacres. He cherished his work on behalf of socialist causes and the splendor of seeing Armenia reborn. He grieved the loss of a child, the pain that would not sleep.

"It has been a wound in my heart," he wrote. "An incurable wound.

"I have no hate in my soul, but I despise killers. My dearest grandchildren, love America and also the root of your ancestors. Fight for peace of the world. Only peace. I depart with the song of love in my soul. Good-bye all."

○ ○ ○

I waited for the forty-day mourning period to pass before I confronted my uncle, at his house, in his living room. I laid out my theory beginning to end, as if he had never heard it before.

He didn't budge. "I think what really happened was the Mexican had a bitterness in him because Ara threw him out of the bar physically. I think that was the whole thing. But I don't know that it makes a helluva lot of difference what the reason was, Mark."

"It makes all the difference in the world, don't you see? It takes it out of the realm of a cheap fight with Nunez. He died because he gave a damn and had the guts to try to better this town."

"Maybe you want to believe it was something more. But maybe it was just that. A cheap fight. If you're looking to connect all these guys to the murder, you'll never do that. Ain't no fucking way. You can connect the friendships and maybe the drugs. But that's all."

I had lost my patience with his stonewalling; I let my accusation fly.

"I can connect a lot more than that. This is what I find so curious about you: Everyone has always compared me to you. Mark and Navo. But I wear my emotions right here. You hold everything inside. The truth. This was your brother. These were your friends. And if by some chance you didn't know, why haven't you put the pieces together all these years since? Let me be candid. I think you might have been involved in their shenanigans."

"Mark, you really don't know me, do you?"

"I guess I don't."

He raised his voice at me for the first time.

"Well, I'm going to tell you something about me and then fucking put it to rest. Okay? I don't break the law. You fucking understand that?"

"I'm not saying . . ."

"Hold on. And I don't go for cockamamy scheme fucking deals like that. I don't ever have done it."

"I accept that. I accept that. But you're hiding something. Something that can't be shared."

"I'm not hiding anything! I don't know what else to tell you. I want you to understand something. If I knew, for five minutes, for sure, if I knew those guys were involved in your dad's murder, I'd . . ."

"I know. I know."

"I know you want to write about this. But maybe it's a story that should never be told. How important is that story? Is it going to bring your father back? All it's going to do is give you a little self-satisfaction. Is that worth the risk? They shot and killed your father. And if they were capable of that, what do you think you are? A big deal? Maybe you're just trying to find out who your father was. But we can all ask those questions if we want to about our fathers. I mean, I don't know if it's all that fucking important sometimes."

Brandishing my logic and circumstance, I had tried for four years to get him to confirm that his golfing and gambling buddies had betrayed his brother and this betrayal set in motion the murder. Had I really, truly imagined I could budge him, get him to admit that the outcome might have been different had he taken the time to discern what was behind his brother's fear? Was this such a consuming lust that I needed to take away his shield, force him to face the battering truth, crush him? Hadn't he told me he needed pills to find peace? *You're going to have to give me something more, Mark, before I delve that deep and reopen this wound. You're going to have to trot out the indisputable before you get me to relinquish this belief. Yes, it was Nunez but it didn't involve drugs or my friends. It was no more complicated than Ara's loss of temper and the Mexican's need for revenge.*

His concealment, I decided, had nothing to do with any involvement in the Nunez drug ring. Rather, he was trying to hide from himself the tragic consequences of his lifelong detachment. Since childhood, he had been forced to detach himself from the situations around him. His father's politics and wanderlust. His mother's craziness. His own ethnic stature. He was a little man before the age of fifteen, smoking cigarettes and playing poker and making up for Grandpa's shortcomings. Detachment was the way he protected himself from the restrictive real estate codes and blackball and "Bignoseian" jokes. The dollar became his God, the very thing his father preached against. He so detached himself from his first wife's behavior that he was blind for years to her indiscretions. Detachment was the way he dealt with us. You've got the house, he told my widowed mother, the bar, two cars, $75,000 from insurance. You're going to be just fine. And he walked out our door and married Josette and never really walked back in. Like my father, he found a way to detach himself from the dangers of the men he chose as companions. The difference was he knew when to dance in and dance out. So, yes, it was possible that the older brother keen to danger, the older brother acutely aware of the capacity for violence around him, did not know—or did not want to know—the danger my father was in.

He was clearly not well. He had paid the price for whatever he overlooked and neglected to do. For all his cunning and evasions and failure to do right by us, I loved him. I loved him, just like I loved my father now, for all his faults. He had tried hard over the past three years to bring me back into his life. I felt his love again and respect and saw the delight in his eyes the first time he held my son. And yet this patriarchal role conflicted with his better judgment. His distrust of the journalist. His need to conceal. His fear what the truth might do to his son. What it might do to me.

And there was something else he was telling me: These things do not belong to you exclusively, Mark. This is my history, too. You have failed to exercise prudence, to adequately consider family honor. You are commiting thefts from my parents' cellar and attic and dinner table to satisfy this glutton in you. Under the sway of greediness, this passion to shine with a book, you have deceived me and our family. We are not playthings for your frivolous shows. We are not smoke and wind.

oοο

"Let your grandfather's bones rest in peace at Ararat Cemetery," my grandmother wrote to me. "You are monkeying around with too many things."

The ostensible subject of Grandma's letter was my brother, Donny. She had asked him to move in with her after Pop's death and now she wanted him out. She accused him of stealing her keys, toenail clippers, purse, the left hand from two sets of evening gloves.

"Your precious Donny has locked me inside," she screeched on the phone. "He told me, 'I'm going to drive you to the insane asylum and I'm going to come and visit you and laugh.' I'm not crazy! . . . You don't believe me?"

She tried to hit him with the broomstick and he grabbed it from her hands and broke it in half, the same thing my father had done forty years earlier.

"Now I know what was going on all those months Pop was sick," Donny berated her. "You were beating him."

She ran into the kitchen and brandished a knife and began jabbing the air: "I'll kill you! I'll kill you!"

A few weeks later, on the twenty first anniversary of my father's murder, she called the cops to kick my brother out. The two young officers were leaving the house when I got there.

"What happened?" I asked the taller one.

"Something about her grandson cooking pasta with garlic past the dinner hour." He smirked and shook his head and I glanced at the name on his uniform: MARK KEENEY. He was son of Coke Keeney, one of the members of the intelligence unit with whom my father supposedly met.

I jumped all over her. "For cooking pasta at eight at night you called the police? You put so much goddamn faith in them? Did it ever occur to you that the police may have been involved in your son's murder!"

She was crouched, ready to pounce.

"He shouldn't have been snitching," she said. "He was a Simple Simon."

I was stunned into silence. Where she picked this up, I cannot say. If there was something else spoken between us as I walked out her door, I do not recall. All night and all morning the words, her indictment, rang in my head. Your father, the dreamy boy, was a snitch and a simpleton. He failed to understand Fresno. He failed to understand that the chief preoccupation of power is preserving itself. He got what was coming to him.

It wasn't like I hadn't been warned. Jeanette, her daughter, had cautioned me, "You don't know Grandma. You don't know her capacity to hurt." She was always able and willing to disguise it from me. I was her favorite, her kisses almost too wet. Now senility had snatched away her finesse. She wasn't the same player. A few weeks earlier she confided that my mother had fallen in love with Uncle Navo when they worked side-by-side at the bank in 1954. He spurned her. "If I can't have Navo," Grandma's story went, "I'll have his brother." It was one of her more savage myths. Dad reduced to stand-in, an agent of my mother's vengeance.

I could never own up to her sickness, dismissing the stories of my Aunt Jeanette and Uncle Navo who used words like "sociopath" and "diabolical" to describe her. "Calling her a liar isn't good enough," my brother insisted. "Grandma's classic" is all I could muster.

You have to understand: Holidays, especially Christmas, didn't thrill my mother. It was Grandma who made them special. She prepared a wonderful table on Christmas Eve and made a big deal out of Brian and me dressing up as Santas and handing out the presents. She knitted the best slippers and beanies. We all went to her when we got sick. Everyone but Dad. She massaged our feet and fixed us root beer floats. She rubbed a silk scarf over my sister's tummy, rock hard with Mediterranean disease.

If she wasn't stuffing food down your throat she was sticking some knickknack or toy in your pocket. You didn't leave her house empty. All Michelle had to do was admire one of Grandma's costume jewels and it was hers. This generosity extended to strangers as well. I don't recall Grandma ever turning away a Girl Scout or Little Leaguer or broom peddler for the blind. The table next to the rocking chair sprouted stacks of magazines. *The Nation, Esquire, Atlantic, Harpers, Soviet Life, Prevention.* She entered all our names in the Publisher's Clearinghouse Sweepstakes. **MARK RANDY ARAX. MILLION-DOLLAR FINALIST.** When public television finally came to Fresno she was one of the first subscribers.

My uncle and aunt and brother didn't know the things I knew, the verse and affliction and curse she revealed to me. There was a poem she had written in January, 1979, about the fog.

> In the shadow of its veil
> I hear the past
> Ringing bells
> Some with a joyous note
> Others too sad
> The day is done
> What will tomorrow bring?
> More echoes?
> Which ones?

On a drive to the country to see the farm where my father was born, she told me that her first memory of life was seeing her younger sister, Siranoush, one moment singing like a bell and the next moment toppled over into a bucket of scalding water. "She might have lived if she was naked," she said. "But the layer of clothing trapped in the water. When they took off her dress, her skin peeled right off with it." For three days, her mother pounded her thighs with the hands that filled the bucket, hands knotted like an oak burl. The day of the funeral her mother couldn't walk. She crawled for months after.

"My father was an old man, very neurotic, a nonperson," she said. "He wanted to separate from my three uncles but my mother wouldn't let him. She felt he couldn't provide for us. Those uncles all wanted her attention. They were all living together. They were living an unnatural life."

When I asked her to elaborate, she said her brother, Shant, the youngest, was actually a half brother.

"I used to see them roaming around. Waiting for turns. I was very alert. Sex looks ugly afterwards. My sister, Roxie, didn't believe me. 'You're making it up. Mama must have been raped.' Roxie could fall asleep and think the whole world was just wonderful when she awoke. She didn't see the bad things. Me, I saw and heard everything. My mother once told me, 'I have sinned. I'm not going to heaven.' I told her, 'I don't want to hear those things.' You know what I thought about years later? It was like the Mormons who had several wives. Only this was turned around."

The anguish of home life, she said, made her an easy mark for Grandpa's chicanery. She was between classes at college when Uncle Ervant drove up in his Model T with Grandpa in the rear seat flat on his back. "Aram is dying of a broken heart," Ervant motioned to the car. "You're going to go off and get married and don't say no because I've already sent your uncles a letter saying that you two are in love."

"That was dirty, Mark. There would be big bloodshed. My uncles, you don't know. Those ignorant people, what they are. It was all framed up. An ugly trap. Your grandfather stole me. I didn't get to finish school. I didn't get to pursue my art."

"Why didn't you just go home and tell your uncles the letter was bull?"

"I was so confused. I guess I became attached to him because that's all there was."

I asked if she had learned to love him. She said she learned to respect him, his mind, but it wasn't love. Then, in a box of keepsakes she had entrusted to me, I found a card she had written him on the fortieth anniversary of their wedding. The cover was three dried flowers pressed flat beneath rice paper.

"Our love persevered through all these years like the flowers on this card. We gave each other, besides ourselves, three lovely flowers. We shall cherish them with all our love. Also my love to you always. With gratitude and respect, Alma."

I felt sorry for her. She was, after all, the one who held the family together while he moved them pillar to post. My father's murder shook deeply her creed about treating bad people good and rooting always for the underdog. But instead of adopting a halfhearted approach, she redoubled her efforts and carved out a new life of volunteerism at the local juvenile hall. "Her boys," she called them, a flock of tattooed Latino thieves and killers whose art she hung in the dining room and whose sad stories of victimization we were made to listen to. She tried to set them straight with the story of her son's tragic end, which she described as a botched robbery by two thugs at his "store."

She grew more fearful and despairing, less capable of laughter and physical love. She poured herself into her cooking, into the achievements of her grandchildren, especially me, and the unrealized potential of her adopted grandchildren behind bars.

Because she felt sorry for me, I was never a target of her spite, and I failed to appreciate how much she defined us, good and bad. Not until she began to unravel and her stories lost their finesse and reflected more bitterness did I recognize the far reach of her distortion. Her fears had become our fears. Her judgments our judgments. Her lies our truth.

"Don't sit under that framed painting," she once told me, "It might fall on your head." Water triggered a panoply of fears. She repeated a hundred times the story of opening up the icebox late at night, knocking back a glass of cold water and passing out on the kitchen floor. She invented corkscrew ways around town to avoid ditch banks. This wasn't easy considering they lived three doors down from one of the biggest irrigation canals in Fresno.

Danny, her son-in-law, was a good Jew, a righteous Jew. But others were not to be trusted. When Coby and I made an offer on our first house, freshly painted with lots of shiny brass fixtures and polished hardwood floors, we took Grandma by for a look. At first blush she loved the place. Then she noticed a gold menorah on the mantel and everything changed. "Look at the dustballs. It's nice but it sure is filthy. Look at the cracks in the ceiling. What do you want an old house for?"

I caught her one day listing her daughter's good and bad points on paper—three good, seventeen bad. "I had surgical menopause at 33," she said. "It was after Jeanette's birth. They found a little tumor in there. Maybe it hit her on the head." She chuckled in a way that said, I know I just said something nasty and maybe I'd better wash it down with a laugh.

Jeanette had moved to Cleveland with Danny in 1972 and had remained there ever since. Invariably, whenever I called to talk, she was upstairs in her bedroom with a migraine headache. She had put 3,000 miles between her and Grandma. She told me she wanted to escape the family history, as Joyce wanted, she said, to escape his nightmare. She was a fine painter whose folk art preserved a kind of sweet mythology of their lives—the ranch in Manteca, her two brothers playing backgammon, the perfect sunflower that covered the huge round antique oak table, the seeds they picked and roasted. She wondered about Navo and me, about our relationships to this history, to the family honor. She had decided that we each wished to preserve it, her oldest brother with his silence, and me, her oldest nephew, with his questions.

Each trip home, clutching another book on mother-daughter hangups, Jeanette vowed to survive a period of days under the same roof with her tormentor without returning the cruelty, without seeing that part of herself she shared with her mother. Always she failed.

"Freud said it first," she told me. "The family is a tyranny ruled by the most neurotic member. Don't you see, Mark. She's one of these people that everything she gave she extracted. If your finger was cut at the knuckle, hers was cut at the wrist. She always had it worse. She's like that woman in the movie, *Woman in the Dunes*, who lived in a cave beside the water and spent her life moving sand. I always thought of my mother like that. In her kitchen."

I reminded her of our virtues. "We're not such bad people, Jeanette. And I think Grandma deserves some of the credit."

"I agree we're not bank robbers or drug dealers or alcoholics but what are we, Mark? Navo's sixty years old and he's so shut off from himself that he can't express a simple emotion. When he finally sheds a tear at his father's funeral we all find it remarkable. I'm a forty-eight-year-old woman still trying to break free of my mother and I may never succeed. Your dad would be alive today if it weren't for her. He was so far out there without any grounding. He lived in a fantasy land."

W e bought an old house in a tucked-
away neighborhood not far from where I grew up. It was a fig orchard once
and the roots of the old trees still hung on, firing up new shoots in crevices
beyond my shovel's reach. I was soon engaged in an old battle, pruning
them off at the base only to have them say hello to me again the next
spring. The lot was big and it felt like country again. I planted a vegetable
garden around the pool.

I told a few neighbors my real name and that I was a journalist with the
Los Angeles Times. I mentioned nothing about my father or the book. The
neighborhood was quiet and the streets curved in a way that discouraged
any outside traffic.

Which is why the boxy charcoal Plymouth stood out.

Coby noticed it one morning moving slowly past the house. Our new
neighbor, a wily cowboy from Oklahoma, had told his wife he spotted the
same car seven or eight times. Two white men in their mid-forties wearing
suits, he said. They drove by at different times of the day and slowed down
to rubberneck our house.

"Are you sure it's my house they're interested in?" I asked him, knowing he had his own tangled past.

"Yeah. It's like they're measuring your movements."

A few nights later, he heard a car door shut at three in the morning and grabbed a rifle. The charcoal car was parked behind bushes with a perfect view of our house. This time the two men weren't wearing suits, he said. They saw him coming and tore off.

"You got any protection?" he asked me.

"A thirty-eight."

He motioned me to the trunk of his car and reached inside. "Well, you might need this."

"I've never fired a rifle."

"It's simple," he said, demonstrating the single-bolt action.

He had access to bear traps. All I had to do was ask and he would rig the perimeter of the house. I decided to rake the flower beds to track any footprints and stand watch through the night again.

I was nodding off that first night when a light suddenly spread across the shutters. I opened the wooden slats and saw a beat-up white car lingering at our house. No one took this route by day, much less at two in the morning, with only parking lamps on.

I grabbed the rifle and waited. Sure enough, the jalopy returned, this time without lights. In the faint glow of our lamppost, it looked like a farmworker's car, windows smoked in dust. Those two guys in suits were setup men, I calculated. These guys were trouble. Or maybe it was the same pair trying to cover tracks with a different car.

It slowed to a crawl at our mailbox and I bolted out the front door to the middle of the lawn. I stood there screaming in my underwear, "Come on, motherfuckers!"

I shoved the bolt back and then forward and took aim toward the front end. I could feel my legs go numb and finger pull at the trigger. I braced myself for the kick but it never came. I had failed to lock down the bolt. The driver floored the gas and disappeared into darkness.

Coby had watched the whole thing from the office window. We tried not to awaken the children as we plucked them from their beds and carried them to the car.

"What's wrong, Daddy?" my daughter whispered.

"The air conditioning broke, Ash. We're spending the night at Gram's."

"I want my bed," my son cried. "I want the Mickey Mouse pillow."

I looked in the rearview mirror for any movements and then roared out of the garage. It had come to this, what my mother feared. We were being driven from our house. Under the cover of night, we were leaving. I damned my father and then I damned myself. What was real? What was happenstance? Was it my neighbor's past come to visit? Was it mine?

Coby tried to calm me. "It's all right, honey. You're just tired."

"I would have shot those bastards if it hadn't stuck. What if they were just farmworkers?"

○ ○ ○

I found my answer to the most important questions—Did my father die on the right side? Was he motivated by a sense of community or by greed?—all at once. It came in a series of unimaginable encounters with people who crossed paths with him in the last week of his life and had been waiting all these years for me to find them.

My mother never wanted my life to be this search, and yet she realized that the past couldn't so easily be discarded, not like the shabby house in the old neighborhood. Before she died, she opened up about my father—his indiscriminate generosity, his seat-of-the-pants business deals, his invincible optimism. She believed his murder was somehow tied to the $18,000 he invested with Hornig in The Forum, but she remained adamant that I steer clear of anyone associated with the bars. If I had to talk to someone, she said, there was only one person who might know something and could be trusted: Dad's longtime friend, Tommy Bayless.

They were an unlikely pair, my father and Tommy. Tommy was Volga German, the tribe of wheat farmers lured to Russia by Catherine the Great and forced out by the Bolsheviks. A sizeable contingent settled on the west side across the Southern Pacific tracks from the Armenians, too close for their pleasure. It was Tommy's link to the old neighborhood that intrigued me. He had grown up with a number of Volga Germans who joined the police force. Lieutenant Eddie Heizenrader used to play marbles down the street.

"I always told my wife that Markie's going to find out," he greeted me. "Someday he's going to call on us."

Arthritis laid claim to his body and he sat clumped in a recliner, puffing a pipe. He had worked as a repossessor for the bank and used his tracing skills to ask questions about the murder, a search that lasted two years. "I picked up a lot of stuff from the streets. Problem is, I can't remember who it came from."

He knew that my father had visited police headquarters days before the shooting. He knew about Hornig's role in the Nunez drug ring, about Dad striking Nunez and the ring's rumored connection to larger operations, including the Simones. He wondered about my father's involvement.

"Ara could be persuaded," Tommy said. "Ten grand will get you twenty. A one-shot deal. If he had his back against the wall."

"What doesn't make sense," I interjected, "is why would he threaten to expose a drug ring in which he was involved?"

"That's what puzzled me," Tommy said.

He paused, motioned nervously to my tape recorder on the table and asked me to shut it off. Then he leaned as far forward as his knotted body would allow. From that moment on, I didn't need any tape to remember.

"Your dad called me three days before he was killed. We hadn't talked in some time and he was in a very excited state. He said, 'Tommy, there's things going on in Fresno you won't believe. Bigger than you can imagine. I know things I shouldn't know.'

"He said he could put some important people behind bars. In fact, he said he was going to do it. He said, 'Tommy, there are names you won't believe.' He said the police were crooked. Some organized group was controlling them. 'I'm going to do something about it,' he said."

Tommy was frightened and asked Dad not to tell him anymore. Dad told him he had confronted someone at the bar and threatened him with exposure.

"I told your father, 'God, I wish you hadn't done that, Ara.' He said, 'Don't worry, Tommy. It's going to be all right.'"

My uncle, according to his first wife, had recounted very nearly the same conversation with my father. The line Dad had crossed was irredeemable, Tommy feared.

"I got off the phone and I told my wife something bad is going to happen. 'Ara's going to get killed.'"

I asked him why the murder report made no mention of this last conversation.

"I never told anyone. First of all, I didn't trust the two detectives investigating the murder. That phone conversation. . . . That was something that could have ended with me on the witness stand."

Tommy reached into a basket next to his recliner and pulled out a newspaper a few days old. He read a column noting that the former police chief, sheriff and several former officers (all known to be crooked) had met with current high-ranking officers in the back room of a Chinatown fish market. Twenty years, old age, had done little to calm his fears.

"This crap is still here," he bristled. "This town is still dirty. If the police get ahold of your tape, they're likely to wonder why I never went to them about Ara's phone call. He was mad as hell at Eddie Heizenrader."

My father and Heizenrader had grown to hate each other, and this ill will stemmed partly from a fight at the bar, which ended with Heizenrader flat on his back. "Eddie was drunk and popped off and got the crap beat out of him. Your dad wasn't even at the bar at the time, but Eddie still held it against him."

My father complained to Tommy that Heizenrader was giving him all kinds of problems about underage girls at the bar. And Heizenrader had a lot of gall because he was involved in some real dirty things.

"Your dad said, 'Tommy, I'm going to blow this town wide open.'"

It was no coincidence that my father was killed shortly after visiting the second floor of police headquarters, he said. This is where the intelligence and vice units were housed.

"I didn't tell those homicide detectives anything because I felt Heizenrader may have been the one who tipped off the bad guys. Ara wouldn't have gone to Eddie directly because he didn't trust him. But Eddie had to hear about Ara's visits to the police department. If there was a leak, it came from Eddie."

Tommy wondered if I knew that Hornig and Heizenrader were close friends.

"I know they knew each other," I said. "But I just figured it was a bar owner and drunk cop thing."

"It was a lot more than that, Markie. Don't underestimate the German connection."

It could be no more complicated than small talk over a drink at The Forum while my father was off playing golf. "Heizenrader lets it slip that

Ara is making all sorts of noise. The word gets back to Nunez. Nothing else would be needed, Markie."

That afternoon, we took a drive to the west side and Tommy pointed out the houses where he and Heizenrader, who had died a few years earlier, grew up. He looked me right in the eyes. "Don't think that meeting in Chinatown between the old guard and the new guard was just a meeting. . . . Don't believe that for one minute or you're getting too relaxed. These people aren't the kind of people who get together to chew the fat. Your father wasn't afraid enough. Call me paranoid. Anyone can. But I'm alive."

I had gone to Linda Mack to learn more about the politicians and builders who had subverted local zoning and planning laws for thirty years. She founded a good-government group in 1971 and a few years later was elected to the city council, one of the few far-seeing leaders in the town's history. We spent almost two hours talking about Fresno corruption then and now. As I got up to leave, I could feel her taking measure of me, a funny half-grin on her face.

"How old are you?"

"Thirty-six."

"Was your father Ara Arax?"

"Yes," I nodded.

"I met with him four days before he was killed."

He had called out of the blue one day, not unlike my call to her, and asked about the Committee for Responsible Government, the group she helped organize to expose a single builder who controlled the city council and board of supervisors through bribes and threats. The leaders of the group agreed to meet with him at The Apartments. It was midday, and the place was empty. My father offered them drinks and said he was encouraged by their work but that local corruption ran far deeper and involved much more than they knew.

"He was very angry and he went on and on about drugs and how devastating it was to the kids and how every morning he swept up his nightclub and found these drugs on the floor. He said there were some very influential people in town making money on narcotics. He said Fresno had become a distribution center for the state. He said the police department was corrupt and protecting the traffic. He said there were payoffs going on."

"Did he mention any names. Heizenrader? Morton?"

"I can't remember any names he mentioned. But he talked in terms of doing something. He indicated that he was going to expose something very big."

He wanted to lend his support by offering the bar for the group's next fund-raiser a few weeks away. They accepted and the day Linda Mack was to pick up the tickets at the printer, she opened the newspaper and read that he had been murdered. The group decided not tell anyone about the meeting.

"We had never heard this stuff before. We were fighting corruption in planning and your father wanted us to broaden our approach to include drugs and police corruption. We came away wondering why he was talking to us. We were just a small group, twelve to fifteen people, and we were just getting our act together."

He had nowhere to turn, I explained. The D.A. was a closet homosexual who gave Chief Morton and Lieutenant Heizenrader the means to control him. Local FBI agents hunted and fished with Morton. City hall was run by Mayor Ted Wills, Heizenrader's buddy. The newspaper, managed by a bunch of cowed hacks, was no option either. The federal drug agency didn't have an office in Fresno. Dad did manage to contact the one competent state narcotics agent in town. The agent never got back to him.

"After the murder," she said, "there was a real effort to discredit your father. But we had no reason to doubt his sincerity. The murder opened our eyes. This man wasn't just whistling Dixie. . . .

"Something else was going on with your father, if I may say. He said he had a son that age, fifteen or sixteen. He said he saw how devastating drugs were and he didn't want you to become involved."

She had no idea the piercing blow of these last words, and I didn't show it. It was only later, when my wife had asked me how the day had gone, that I felt them puncture me.

One day after his meeting with Linda Mack's group, my father was golfing at Fig Garden when he casually pulled aside his young playing partner, Bob Mackechnie, on the twelfth tee. He confided that his life was in danger.

"You know life can be fucked sometimes," Dad began.

He talked about playing ball at USC and having to come home to work the family business and losing the grocery stores and then buying the bar and seeing it destroyed by drugs. And now that his children were getting older, he could see how it could affect them, too.

"Why he chose me, I don't know," Mackechnie said. "But he was talking about you. He was watching you and he was afraid you could be swallowed up by this thing."

Bob Mackechnie was one of the names I had jotted in the little book I kept in my dresser drawer as a kid. When I finally got around to contacting him, I had no idea who had given me his name and why he was so important.

"The cops killed him," he said, shaking his head. "The cops had him killed."

"How do you know?"

"That day, he told me that he never had a problem with the police department until he tried to stop the drug traffic. He said he had gone to the police with information and that's when his troubles began. He said he couldn't trust them. They were involved."

"Did he mention the name Eddie Heizenrader?"

"Yes. He talked about Heizenrader a lot."

"Did he mention Morton?"

"H. R. Morton? The police chief who married the madam? Yes, he mentioned him. Your dad said Morton knew all about it. He said he had to go outside of town now because he couldn't trust the authorities in Fresno."

"Did he mention anyone else?"

He thought for a moment. "He said his business partner, and he didn't mention his name, had done some bad things. I remember him saying, 'I can't sit by and watch it happen. I'm going to do something.'"

"Did he ever say what?"

"No. And I didn't ask. I just stood there slackjawed. I knew Fresno was wide open. I had heard a few stories. But I thought that ended in the sixties. He said he was trying to put an end to it. Then three days later, I'm driving out to the college and I heard the news on the radio: 'Ara Arax was shot and killed.' I've never looked at Fresno the same since."

I had managed to bottle up my emotions while listening to the accounts of Bayless and Mack, transfixed by the suddenness of what they were telling me. But Bob Mackechnie was just a kid back then, only three years older than me, and the portrait he offered of my father saddened me no end. To contemplate the truth of this fetid town. To know that it offered him no other way out. To know that he was alone. My desperate father in the days before his death, calling an upstart committee he had read about in the newspaper and pouring out his anger, confiding his fear and regret to an eighteen-year-old kid at the golf course, trying to find some way out of the mess that enclosed him, and me. I felt pity (for him? for me?) and I finally broke, a stinted, stifled cry that squeezed in my throat and showed only in my eyes. Mackechnie glanced away.

To live in Fresno was to participate in a lie. It was expected, part of the compact. Only a fool did otherwise. My father was that fool, and Mackechnie felt sorry for me and my miserable situation, about which he could do nothing except remember.

"Years later, Eddie Heizenrader joined Fig Garden. He was a big tall guy with a broad smile. Always smiling and laughing and slapping backs. But I never looked at the smile. All I could see were his eyes. They weren't the eyes of a man you could cross and find yourself in a back room with. I thought, 'How can you smile, you SOB? You killed Ara Arax.'

"He didn't pull the trigger. He probably didn't even hire the guys. But that's who your dad traced his troubles to. Heizenrader and Morton. They were involved up to their eyeballs in what was troubling your father. And if Ara talked to me, he talked to others.

"I have a theory. It's nothing novel. But I have a theory that you can tell everything about a man from the way he plays golf. My friend and I did this all the time. We could call a personality after one hole. The asshole. The hustler. The cheater. The fraud. It was right there in the way they played golf. Your dad wasn't any of those things, Mark. Your dad was a good man."

Tom Bayless, Linda Mack, Bob Mackechnie. My father reaching back to me, the words they could not kill. This portrait of a desperate man, to which I now had to add misgiving. The knowledge of being stalked, of an unwise decision about to backfire, irrevocable. And to have them confirm what I had presumed from almost the day he was killed, that his final resolve was strengthened by the fear that I, his oldest child, was playing with drugs. In truth, I had barely flirted with them. But that didn't matter. He was convinced that the scourge of his bars had spilled over into his home. I remembered the last fight we had a few days before the murder when he confronted me about my odd behavior and I told him I wished I was dead and collapsed on the floor like a rag doll, and he raged. "You wish you were dead? You wish you were dead?" he screamed, pulling me up by the shirt.

It was about me after all.

Dominic Estilarte, the lead homicide investigator, knew this visit was different. There were no scrapbooks trotted out. No offers of ice tea or lemonade. He had scarcely opened the front door and invited me to sit down when I knocked him back with my accusation:

YOUR DEPARTMENT WAS INVOLVED IN MY FATHER'S MURDER.

"And I think you covered it up. Not because you were dirty. But because you were afraid. I mean, it involved Morton and Heizenrader. How could your investigation be anything but a whitewash? It was either that or risk your own life over a man who was already dead."

Perhaps if I had caught him a year or two earlier, weak from heart surgery, he might have answered me differently. But the face he shot back, open and sincere and just a slight bit befuddled, clearly had not contemplated this question, or if it had, it had been long forgotten.

"You don't have the full report," he said, as if that was enough.

"What do you mean, I don't have the full report? I've got everything that was in that box."

The box was only half of it. There were notes passed back and forth between him and another detective. For their eyes only. This was done to keep the intelligence unit in the dark. Knowing Heizenrader's close friendship to Hornig and others in the Nunez drug ring, it was the prudent thing to do.

"So you're telling me you suspected your own intelligence unit in the murder?"

He shook his head no and launched into a long-winded and fantastic explanation of how Heizenrader or Coke Keeney or Moose Nyberg or Orndoff or private eye Butch Turner could have leaked Dad's visits to Hornig and Nunez. But he suggested that this leak was inadvertent, the kind of thing friends let slip to friends over a couple drinks. How were they to know that Nunez would risk murder?

"You're dancing around it!" I snapped. "Heizenrader and Morton were protecting these guys. They were part of the drug ring. It was no inadvertent leak. Heizenrader and Morton might as well have pulled the trigger."

What seemed so obvious to me was one of the mysteries that could never be answered to Estilarte. He was like my uncle in that way, questions better left to the past with all the other what-ifs and could-bes and whodunits.

"To my knowledge, the intelligence unit never protected criminals," he insisted. "They were just a bunch of freeloaders. As long as Hornig fed them drinks and broads, they were along for the ride. Eddie probably got drunk and let loose that Ara was visiting the police department. And the boys got nervous."

I didn't bother to recite the long history of Heizenrader's dirty deeds to Estilarte. Here was a man who had survived thirty honest years in the Fresno Police Department by striking himself blind. Who was I to disabuse him?

The most compelling evidence of all came from inside the police department itself. In the summer of 1986, a former Fresno homicide detective named Leonard Wood locked himself in his bathroom and blew out his brains. His wife found this note:

Got started with the wrong police department as you know. Lots of tapes and history. Nothing to come of it. Prostitution, gam-

bling, drugs, murder. Very sad. Two police department murders
in house.

Wood had told friends that one of these "in-house" hit jobs was the Ara
Arax murder. He believed that Chief Morton and Lieutenant Heizenrader
had used Armond Bletcher, the behemoth who always dreamed of being a
cop, to set up the kill. The motive, he told friends, was to prevent my father from exposing a major narcotics ring with ties to the police department.

Jackie Gere, a friend of Wood's wife, recalled Wood's frustration: "He
told us that when he was investigating Bletcher's murder he picked up a
lot of leads on your father's murder. He said it involved narcotics and corruption. He said Ara was trying to expose it all. Every trail in your father's
murder, he said, led right back into the police department."

Wood's own trouble began in the spring of 1977 when he crossed Po-
lice Chief Hal Britton, one of Morton's jade ring boys who had taken over
the reins. Wood discovered that Chief Britton was protecting Gary
Prestidge, the pimp and bookie now smuggling cocaine. Wood told
Deputy Chief Jim Packard, one of the few honest men at the top, that
Prestidge had been paying off the department for years.

Deputy Chief Packard took the allegations to the mayor, city manager
and assistant city manager—three men who had assumed office in the
high spirit of reform.

"Your father's name surfaced in our first conversation," the assistant city
manager told me. "The allegation was that members of the police department knew something about his murder and had covered it up.

"I guess like your father we didn't know where to go with these charges.
And going to the wrong place was enough to get you killed in Fresno. We
couldn't go to the locals and we couldn't go to the state. We had letters
from the state attorney general praising the hell out of the Fresno Police
Department. We had letters from the FBI's resident agent saying he
trusted our officers completely. So we took it to Tom Kotoske of the organized crime strike force in San Francisco."

This was the same Kotoske and the same federal strike force that failed
to pursue Tony Simone Sr. and his protectors in law enforcement three
years earlier. This time, Kotoske was inclined to turn the Fresno Police

Department inside out, but he couldn't find a cop willing to wear a wire and he couldn't assuage the concerns of the city manager and mayor, who both feared what a bloodletting might do to the department's morale.

The city manager, backed by a council that now included Linda Mack, did agree to fire Chief Britton and clean up the intelligence unit. A local hearing detailed the unit's improper relationship with private eye Butch Turner and other misdeeds. Blackmail, bribery and murder involving the head of the unit, Eddie Heizenrader, never came up. Coke Keeney was demoted to patrolman and Moose Nyburg quietly retired. The Hank Morton era, thanks in part to my dead father, had finally come to an end.

The federal strike force had been summoned to Fresno three times in the years after my father's murder to ferret out ties between law enforcement and organized crime. Three times it left without indicting a single police officer. When I asked Kotoske, the former head of the strike force, why, he cited the town's indifference.

"Lots of cops in Fresno came to us. But when it came time to go into that grand jury room, when it came time to putting their hands on the book and telling us what they knew, they were a bunch of gutless jerks. I'm talking jellyfish. Some departments have guys with guts and gumption willing to open their mouths and pay the ultimate price. Not in Fresno. You need evidence. You need names, times, dates. Chitchat ain't shit. I've heard stories down there, some gut-wrenching stories. Homicide? Hell, yes. Rogue cops are absolutely unmerciful. But where does that leave you?"

It left Leonard Wood, the homicide detective whose allegations touched off Chief Britton's firing, a broken man. "Leonard was terrified. He said if he stayed in Fresno, he could be killed," recalled Gere. Wood quit the department and moved to the Bay Area and never worked in law enforcement again.

I wondered if Wood knew it was the Nunez operation my father threatened. Did he know that Dan Hornig and Leonard Maselli were drinking and gambling buddies of Morton and Heizenrader? Wood was six years dead when I got around to asking these questions and his widow and lover couldn't say.

Wood did tell friends he could never determine the purpose behind my father's visits to the police department. Was Arax there to issue a threat in person? Or was he there to cover up for his loose mouth and try to fool Morton and Heizenrader into believing he really wasn't a risk?

In my vain attempt to discover everything Wood knew, I was led to another key piece of the puzzle: the strange movements of the last person in the bar before my father and the gunmen arrived.

The bar was empty when this customer, a longtime patron who did remodeling work for my father, walked in between five and six o'clock. A plumber by trade, he made his real living peddling drugs and pimping girlfriends. He snooped around and engaged in small talk with barkeep Linda Lewis. It was his twenty-ninth birthday and Lewis offered him a drink. The plumber refused. He stayed all of three minutes, and before he left he asked Lewis for her phone number, address and the name of her roommate. She thought this odd but gave him the information just the same. Fifteen minutes later my father showed up and a short time later so did the killers.

He was the plumber who installed our joke of a sprinkler system as a way to work off his bar tab. The first time I read the murder report, I wondered if he might also be the fingerman, the accomplice who waited outside the bar and confirmed for the out-of-town shooters that the stocky, thin-haired man in the office was Ara.

I had nothing connecting the plumber to any shooters or the men suspected of hiring them. Even though homicide detectives believed the same—that the plumber helped set up the murder—they waited four months to question him, too late to determine if a huge gap in his account of that day resulted from faulty memory or deceit. He refused to take a lie detector test.

I knew from the phone records that the night before, a Saturday night, Armond Bletcher called the plumber from San Jose. Bletcher's phone records are noteworthy for the number of long-distance calls he made and the brevity of those conversations. Most were over in a minute or two. The conversation that night with the plumber lasted more than an hour.

Then I learned this from a former colleague of Detective Wood: The plumber and Frank Nunez had been friends for years. If Nunez needed a third party to help carry out the murder plot, it probably wouldn't have been Hornig or Maselli or any of the other white businessmen and golfing buddies who financed his drug venture. He would have picked the plumber, a Mexican-American from the old neighborhood, to introduce the hitmen to their target.

I called my old high-school friend at the *Los Angeles Times* and told him what I had discovered. "You're finished, buddy," Pete King said. "There's nothing more you need to know."

Could I call my search complete without trying to find and confront Dan Hornig? While I no longer believed that he had a direct role in the murder, he was the one who became entangled with Nunez and set my father's tragic course in motion. I had watched him from a distance at Maselli's funeral and tried to write him off as dead. But he had managed to leave Fresno and start a new life in the construction business without ever answering the key questions:

Why wasn't the partnership contract with my father signed? How much of the $18,000 did you turn over to Nunez? What was my father's reaction when he found out?

I tracked down Hornig through court and property records. He was sixty-seven years old and living in Discovery Bay, 170 miles north of Fresno. The country club and marina community had been built on asparagus fields where the San Joaquin and Sacramento rivers meet.

He and his second wife, who once worked for him as a cocktail waitress, lived with their schnauzer in a modest tract he helped build along the golf course. I talked my way past the guard station. A silver-blue Thunderbird with the license plate HORNIG was parked in the driveway.

He answered the door looking like he had just finished a round of 18. His legs, the only fit part of him, were tanned to the sock line. I introduced myself and he hardly missed a beat, pumping my hand and asking me inside and offering a cold drink.

I was a little nervous, filling the air with too many words. He couldn't have seemed more pleased—and poised—to see me. (I would learn later that he had been tipped off to my inquiries by a golf pro who had once been tight with Nunez.)

I told him I had questions about my father, and he suggested we take a drive to the harbor. He parked the car next to the yacht berths and shut off the engine. He made a half turn toward me but I kept staring straight ahead, my eyes fixed on a line in the parking lot.

"Your father's word was good. We never needed anything in writing. He was straightforward. The only thing was, Ara was the type of guy who thought he could reform people. He always thought he could be the good guy."

He was talking faster now and his voice had a tiny flutter.

"What about your partnership in the summer of 1971?"

"Ara gave me $7500, but I'm fuzzy on the details."

"Any theories or rumors?"

"Want me to be real honest with you? I didn't hear any rumors, Mark. Honest to God."

This was the same disclaimer my uncle once issued, and it struck me as preposterous. I told him the theories I heard as a kid—drugs, a beef with a drug smuggler, bookmaking. None of them rang a bell with Hornig. He advised me to ignore them.

"Rumors are going to happen. Everybody thought I burned my bar down for the insurance money. Everybody. And a lot of people thought I was involved with dope. I never was."

I had come armed with court documents and telephone tolls that told a far different story. I had jotted the questions he surely didn't want to hear into my notebook. But as he sat there rattling on, not once mentioning the name Nunez, chalking it up to a robbery gone bad, I couldn't even muster the energy.

I drove back home through the delta swamp. The moon was full and orange and low over the asparagus fields. A brilliant streak of light fell from the eastern sky. I walked in late and couldn't sleep. My wife and I made love, and I dreamed that Hornig and I were driving in his car around Fresno when he suddenly pulled into the old bar, exited quickly and out from the shadows came Nunez.

The next day I dialed his number.

Yes, he admitted, it was $18,000 my father gave him, not $7500.

Yes, he was involved in the Nunez drug ring but it was only one failed load.

Yes, he was struggling financially but the money he invested (five or 10 grand?) didn't come from my father. My father never knew about the drug deal until after the planeload of marijuana was discovered in Madera. When Hornig confided his involvement, my father took the news well.

"If I would have done that with your dad's money, that's traceable, Mark. And I'm smarter than that."

"So what did you do with his $18,000?"

"I don't remember. That was 25 years ago."

"You cashed his $10,000 check at the bank," I shouted. "A few weeks later you recruited Charles Johnson to fly the load. You cashed the money and gave it to Nunez."

"It didn't happen. You'll never show that. You can't prove it. If I cashed it or whatever, it didn't happen."

He was adamant that he knew nothing about the murder, before or after. And he didn't know about any fight between Dad and Nunez a few weeks before.

"You witnessed the fight, Dan," I persisted. "You described the entire incident to the homicide detectives."

"I don't remember it. How can I get that clear to you? Nunez never entered my mind until I talked to you today. That's the God's truth."

I*t's 6:10 at night. January 2, 1994. It's been dark nearly an hour. The parking lot is empty. The façade, rock and stucco, is just like you left it. So is the tall sign topped by a martini glass. Only the words, Ara's Apartments, are gone. This is a cowboy bar now, and it looks too small, too bereft, for the shadows it has cast. Alone in the car, I give myself a moment to feel something, to let whatever is going to come, come. I'm not sure what I expect. Maybe some electric, clenched-fist, manic bolt of joy. Maybe the easy tears Mom and I used to cry watching* Madame X *and* Backstreet. *I feel neither. Instead, my mind trips back to your funeral, to the old lady chanting her village curse against the gunmen, "Why weren't their fingers broken? May they wake up with their fingers broken," and then to a swim party at Dan Hornig's house in the summer of 1971 to celebrate your partnership in* The Forum.

It is one of the few moments of my childhood that comes back with absolute clarity. There is Dan Hornig and Ingrid Hornig and their two kids, Uncle Navo and Brian, the five of us and Frank Nunez and his wife and two small children. What I recall so clearly, almost perfectly preserved, is not the party itself but a snippet of conversation between you and Mom as we drove home.

"Who's Frank Nunez anyway?" Mom asked. "He's sure got the look of easy money."

"You don't want to know who Frank Nunez is," you replied. "He's bad news."

And yet after that night you became familiar with Nunez and played golf with him and kept his phone number in your notes and visited his clothing store once or twice. For a time, at least, you looked the other way and then humiliated him in one fatal burst.

At this moment, exactly twenty-two years ago, you drove the Firebird into this parking lot and opened the bar's thickly cushioned front door and stepped into darkness. Did you have an inkling what awaited you? I close my eyes and fantasize about a return back. To be the man I am and know precisely what is about to happen. You're inside. Linda Lewis is inside. And the two killers drive up. I wait, .38 revolver in hand. You're working on the books, groaning about taxes and bills. Linda is blasting Don McLean. And I make my move.

Are the killers somewhere nearby marking their own anniversary, a ritual reunion? Do they drive their friends or wives by here and point out this spot? A scraggly man in leather jacket and jeans and a big belt buckle walks toward my car. He moves closer and closer. He stops at my window and peers inside. Shoot the motherfucker! Shoot the motherfucker!

Is this where it ends, all untidy? Do I hunt down Nunez, this time just him and me? Do I play your little boy with Nunez's friend and accomplice, the plumber? Do I piss on the graves of Morton and Heizenrader? See, Dad, I am standing at the same place you stood when you raced up the stairs of the Fresno Police Department. I am facing the exact moment of judgment you faced. Do I listen to my head or to my heart? How far do I take things? Who must I make answer?

You somehow failed the process, made the wrong judgment, misread your world. You forgot that the way these people use power is fundamentally different from your way. I tell myself not to be angry. You didn't have the luxury of knowing fully the family you came from. There is a mark on our blood. Yours was one misstep on a long road of missteps back to the old land. You were born to a place that was far dirtier than you could have imagined. You got into something that was far bigger than you understood.

I know these things. I have the benefit of our history, the benefit of your mistakes. I have the luxury of someone like Uncle Danny. It is over, he tells me. There is nothing ideal or even essential in facing down and outbraving the men I believe responsible.

"The justice of facing these guys eye-to-eye is a moment," he said. "The look in your eye won't brand them. Your words will."

So why does his advice feel like the easy way out? I've spent half my life imagining what it would be like. I've worked six years positioning myself for just such a moment, plotting what to ask, how to ask it? These bastards have never had to answer a single question about you. Who, if not me?

What goes around, comes around. It was your favorite saying. But it's not like the movies, Danny says. It is my words that must create the justice, my words that must last out lifetimes. The guts are in my words. "Give him something back with your words, Mark."

My words slice two ways. My sharpest questions must be turned back onto you. Did you truly believe you could involve yourself with the corrupt and not become obligated to them? At the height of your discontent, you plopped down our life savings in a second bar. Your new partner, Dan Hornig, was suspected of burning down an earlier nightclub and staging a burglary to collect the insurance. It was all over town. Was it possible you didn't know?

To simply chalk up your blindness of people and motives as naïveté or immaturity or foolishness is to let you off easy. And no one reading this now would accept that. You betrayed us, Dad, and it wasn't the few affairs you had or the physical abuse you sometimes inflicted or even your desire to be guru of your world. No, your deepest betrayal was deceiving yourself that you could cater to scum, play the financial game with the town's crooked German connection, and still retain your innocence.

Yes, I have pressed many things too far. I have put myself and my family at risk. But I want you to know that I am savvy enough not to repeat your mistakes. This notion that I can trick them out of their secret, scare them, charm them, is the same ego that got you killed. What had my meetings with Anthony Simone and Dan Hornig proven if not the futility of such an encounter, a fool's gold. Sure, I might get a stutter or stare or a concession by default, but it is nothing to hang my hat on. What were these guys going to tell me two decades later? That they were sorry? That the triggermen were so and so? That you died a hero?

I don't need any more rumors. I don't want to hear any more explanations. I don't want to place myself in any more of harm's way. It's okay, Mark, I can hear you saying. Let it go, son. You talk to me even as I continue digging to find Mary Santana, the young woman (lover?) to whom you supposedly entrusted a "black book" on Fresno drug corruption. You tell me I have done all that is expected of me even as I drive by Frank Nunez's house contriving a chance encounter that will never come.

I want you to know that you didn't die in vain. If my playing with drugs is part of what motivated you, you must know that the experiment ended with your death. I'm a straight-arrow guy. It was my promise to you, the one promise I kept.

Sometimes I catch myself thinking: What if you had lived, what if the emergency room staff at St. Agnes had quickly typed and matched your blood and Dr. Marius, arriving ten minutes earlier, found and sewed up that hole? Or what if you had never been shot, never wreaked havoc with your noble gesture? What then would have become of me, of you and me? In a lifetime of questions, this is the one question I have never attempted to answer.

I think it is an impossible question. I was your shining hope and yet you saw something of your brother in me, and you felt threatened. I speak a language you may not have understood. We would have had some serious battles, Dad. But I am also certain that the love we had for each other would have won out in the end.

There was so much I didn't know, would never know.

I found my father to be a man who cared, a man who trusted people and tried to make a difference. He cared especially about his town and the kids who grew up there. Some people demand more of a community, of life, than the structure of life can give. So they crack open that structure with their demands. My father was that sort of person. He was a reckless spirit who didn't belong to his father's traditions and didn't belong to his brother's. He didn't quite understand that there are people out there who don't care if you're a nice guy with a big heart. They care only about their business, and their crimes are justified along those lines. He didn't know he was in over his head until it was too late.

In the end, he was stopped the only way such a man can be stopped, an early casualty in the fight against drugs. There were no certificates of appreciation or city proclamations honoring him. Rather, his reputation had been dragged through the mire. Honest cops like Dominic Estilarte kept the truth of their findings from the public to keep their own dirty bosses in the dark, bosses who played a central role in the murder. *They killed my father and then they killed his good name.*

Yet that vindication, that truth, was so complex and layered. It was enriched and distorted all at once by the lives and motives of family, friends, history, city and culture, and above all by the complexity of my father himself.

So much of who my father and his brother were came down to their differing notions of what it meant to be a citizen. For Uncle Navo, it was enough to be a good provider and make sure that no risk he took in business or his social life came back to hurt the hearth. For Dad—and this was his glory and his fatal risk—it wasn't enough to raise your family safely and securely if you closed your eyes to the surrounding community.

The bar business, spiritually and financially, was his rebirth. If his lax ways helped bankrupt the grocery stores, he saw no reason to change. To be someone for the bar people, it filled a great need in him. Everyone has hopes that they can help others, but in my father this yearning grew so great and was bound to such insecurity that his patrons became extensions of himself. He had plans for them.

Likewise, the rhetoric of Grandpa and Grandma's lives wasn't a notion he could so easily discard. From the time he fought tooth-and-nail with a friend who popped off about Grandpa's communism, Dad was proud that his parents stood for something. And he tried to fit that something into his own brand of capitalism, however perverse the accommodation. Uncle Navo, on the other hand, was able to distance himself nearly completely from Pop's rhetoric. Indeed, he laughed at it, an immigrant's naïveté.

In those old home movies, Pop is always sitting on the couch, eternal pipe, slightly removed from us, slightly mocking, dandling the youngest on a knee. About Grandma, the most he could muster was, "I have no trouble, Mark. She's a wonderful cook. She loves her grandchildren. She is loyal. But she says some things you cannot digest sometimes."

He represented a sweetness and gentleness in our lives but he refused to be a buffer between his children and wife, who had the energy and will of three women. He allowed her to weave her web of disruption in return for her wonderful meals and gracious hostessing and love for grandchildren. When Grandma's pokes at the Jews made life miserable for Danny and Jeanette one summer, Pop refused to intervene. "What can I do?" he told Danny. "You're going to have to leave. This tension is not good for any of us." He did the same when Grandma intruded on my father and uncle, never allowing a real relationship to develop between brothers.

Pop had a defense of silence, the *tsk, tsk, tsk.* He was gentle but irresolute. Grandma, by contrast, watched closely for who had power and made sure she was protected against those people by having a story or stories to assassinate their character.

I tried to imagine being brought up in such a household: Navo recruited at age six to help in the stores, cheated out of childhood. Was it any wonder he mastered the strategies of survival and cynicism? My father, the experiment, handed no responsibility and no discipline, forever the child. Was it any wonder, then, that anyone who flattered my father was a friend? Was it any wonder he tried to become his brother's equal by going into business with his brother's good friend, Dan Hornig, whose conceit and double-dealing he did not fully comprehend until it was too late?

My grandmother recognized my father's self-destructive force, a force she sought to control. On his birthday in 1966 she gave him a book, *Renew Your Life Through Yoga.* I don't think he read it or at least I can't ever recall him assuming a lotus position. The fire that made him such a force on the football field he never reined in. "When you get mad," he counseled me, "count to ten. I know it sounds simple, son, but it works." He did not heed his own advice.

I want to believe it was a truer world he lived in, a world in which instinct ruled over consciousness. But my father's failure to suppress his instinctual side, his belief in only his own power, was a serious flaw.

He came in contact every day with evil but he refused to see it for the longest time. A friend recalled the shock in his face when confronted with the indisputable evidence of a patron's drug dealing. "Not Mike," Dad insisted. Mike happened to be a true pioneer, one of the first and biggest drug smugglers in town.

My father overcame cynicism by blocking awareness, by remaining idealistic and innocent above all about himself. One day he awoke from this dream, struck himself sightful, and was suddenly angry at himself and his world for playing him the sucker. So he made one cleansing pass at redemption, only to fall on his sword. His death was of a piece with his life—the logical extension of his failure in judgment. Violence and devastation erupted from the innocence that didn't know itself.

I had to give my uncle his due. For Navo, the question wasn't a matter of a good citizen doing his duty versus a poor citizen shirking his. He believed you must never put preservation of the community over self-preservation, the first duty, the highest obligation. He knew the limits and costs of dealing with the underworld in Fresno, and he exercised a caution and restraint that my father did not comprehend. My uncle was there for his son, always. My father left me dangling between worlds, a kid and a man.

In my search for the murder itself, I had charted the most intricate of movements, developed elaborate lists linking names, dates, and addresses. I had logged thousands of miles in my car and interviewed more than three hundred people. I grew fat on the secrets of Fresno, the peccadillos and adulterations of a small circle of men. I could recite every scandal in the hundred year history of the police department and a good share of the ones in the sheriff's office as well. I grew dizzy in the minutiae, the documented stories of judges and cops and elected officials bribed with small change. I struggled to discern incompetence from corruption, inertia from complicity. I saw how years before the sergeant became a cop, years before the drug smuggler became a bandit, they grew up on one block, heard parents tell stories of the same faraway land, wore the same baseball jersey and left for war as part of the same unit. When the cop and the criminal were young and soft, these allegiances were formed and they transcended any job, any uniform, into adulthood. Over all this, I laid my father's movements and financial transactions and indiscretions.

And this is what I seemed to have found: My father bought a bar, The Apartments, in the mid-sixties and turned it into the hottest nightclub in the Central Valley. It overtook him. At some point, too late, he came to the realization that he could no longer control his patrons, their drug taking and drug dealing. He tried to remove himself by buying an interest in The Forum, a bigger nightclub in a better part of town. So what happened to the money he invested in this venture, his future? The timing indicated that Dan Hornig handed over at least a portion of it to Frank Nunez and a drug ring involving prominent citizens and the highest levels of the police department. Lieutenant Heizenrader was making life miserable by pressuring state alcohol regulators to close The Apartments as a public nuisance. My father began to realize the danger this world posed to me and the kids he coached. For all these reasons—redemption, revenge, civic re-

sponsibility, fatherly duty, ego—he decided to expose the ring and its protectors. So few choices. Where to go? He sought out state narcotics agent
Dick Walley. He called the attorney general's office. He thumped Nunez:
"I want your drug smuggling ass out of here." He telephoned Tommy
Bayless and launched into a harangue about Heizenrader and police corruption. He did the same with Linda Mack and Bob Mackechnie. He was
going to blow open the town and it would be felt "all the way up to Sacramento." Those words again. Murder seemed so remote back then. He visited the police department. Whom he was seeing—the crooked members
of the vice and intelligence units and their cohort, private investigator
Butch Turner—I know. What he was telling them, I cannot say. Maybe he
tried to negotiate a deal. *Leave my bar alone and I'll keep quiet.* Maybe he had
gone to threaten them face-to-face. I know he left one last meeting at police headquarters buoyant, or at least appeared that way to a friend standing at the foot of the stairway. The sanguine fool who thinks he pulled it
off? Or just a smile for a friend in a moment of crisis? Suffice to say, he
didn't allay any concern. The last person to arrive at the bar before the
shooters: Nunez's longtime friend, the plumber. The first person to arrive
after the shooting: Anthony Simone. The cop who secured and oversaw
the crime scene: Lieutenant Heizenrader.

Or maybe, just maybe, before my father could act and before his antag-
onists could react, two robbers came in and killed him. Can you imagine
the glee on the faces of Nunez and Morton and Heizenrader? Their problem had been removed, plucked right off, and they didn't have to so much
as raise a finger. Sure, it was far-fetched, but without the shooters, without
a smoking gun, I could never be certain it didn't happen just this way, or
some other cheap, mutant prospect yet considered. Pimp Gary Prestidge,
for one, had bragged to his wife that he bought the contract—payback for
the thumping Ara gave him. Others believed the bar manager at The
Apartments, Mike Garvey, was involved with a drug smuggler named
Buddy Barnard and it was this ring my father threatened. In other words,
I had unearthed a mass of circumstance and context but none of it was
quite enough to overcome the lapse of years. No one person I found could
replace the voices lost and addled, frightened and complicitous. I lacked
the immediacy of the crime. I lacked the tools of law enforcement to co-
erce witnesses and the tools of the courts to compel them. Murder, at least

the class performed by hitmen and conspirators, is a crime that never completely yields its secret.

When I look back on a hundred years of family history I am tempted to say that my father's quirk of grandiosity and temper was a family marking as surely as the big ears on the soft face. It reached at least back to his father's grandfather, Jonig Agha, the double-dealing taxman hacked into a hundred pieces in the village below the mountain of mist, not by Turks but by Armenians. He actually believed his killers had convened a banquet to honor his good Turkish deeds. It touched the murdered man's son, my grandfather's uncle, who killed a coworker in the Bulgarian coal mines because the man happened to slight him, and it touched Uncle Harry, the cop killer, who did not believe he deserved poverty. "Some poor people do without because they're scared," Harry told me. "I had no fear." Their reactions differed only in degrees from the way my father responded to the slights of Terry, the man who bought our old house, or of Van Keyes, the young friend who implied that Dad was a liar, or of Frank Nunez himself, who referred to Dad as a "cheap Armenian."

And what about me? I used to believe the murder changed everything about me. It explained my passions and fears, the scowl etched down my brow and the earnestness a little hard to take. It was the reason I became a journalist and the kind of journalist I became. It alone accounted for my outrage and righteousness. But am I his son for nothing? Surely their traits extended to me, my inflated view of self and what I could achieve because I was aggrieved and right. My own betrayals of family. The self-deception that allowed me to go on in the face of danger. What moves me now, isn't it what moved him then? My father, the crusader without a pen. How this town might have been different had he found a way to tell his story. So it got passed to me. Mine to tell.

I could press on and spend the rest of my life trying to unearth one person with one complete answer. How many Tommy Baylesses and Linda Macks and Bob Mackechnies are out there that serendipity has not yet taken me to? How many people who crossed paths with my father in those last elusive days? I have chosen instead to be content with a picture of my town and my family, a snapshot in time, that could never be rendered in a courtroom. It is over. Nothing like my best dreams.

A few months after I put away my notebook and tape recorder and T-shirt with the hidden pocket and all the other unseemly accoutrements and guises and put-ons of the past six years, I went to see my grandmother with nothing more in mind than a nice chat.

She greeted me at the door the same way she had greeted me for years. "I was just thinking about you. 'This is the day Mark should be coming.' Do you believe in mental telepathy?"

She had turned the house into a giant calendar, notes affixed to walls, appliances, the bed post, reminding her of pills and vitamins to take, dog to feed, lawn to water.

"Do you want to eat some strawberries, Navo?"

"No thanks, Grams."

"Look at me, I'm thinking of Navo. Mark, I've made some nice boiled chicken. Do you want some?"

"No, I'll pass."

"Then what should I do? I feel like making you something."

"I'm really not hungry, Grams. How about sitting down and talking?"

"Wait a minute, now." She opened the freezer and pulled out two TV dinners. "Or how about some braunschweiger?"

"Sit down and relax. I'm full."

"I can't. I'm having a nervous spell right now."

She held a bottle of Librium and read the label in a cracked, pitiful voice. "I was going to ask, don't laugh, I was going to ask who is Navo's mother? . . . I'm Navo's mother."

"Don't worry, Grams."

"Did I have a child who died?"

"Yes. Ara. My father."

"Oh, Ara. He loved to dance. He used to put the classical music on and he was a beautiful boy, beautiful, and he'd dip this way and that way. Then he didn't do it anymore. He said if I'm going to be a football player, I can't do that. He always got by with everything. I never used to stay mad at him because there was a spirit about him. He was a very dreamy boy.

"I never hit Ara but I hit Navo. That was another ugly thing I did. I expected Navo to be able to handle Ara. How could he handle a brother only two years difference?"

She began to recall the night my father was killed and the way Navo broke the news to her. "He came up to me right here and said in the cruelest way, 'Ara's dead.' He didn't even give me any preparation . . . Did we come to your house that night?"

"Yes."

"That's right. You were hiding behind the curtain and you asked me, 'Grandma, what am I going to do? How am I going to take care of us?' I'll never forget that."

"Don't be down. You've got us and the great-grandchildren. Just remember that."

"You know, Ara was not a bar man. He was innocent. There's a lot of monkey business going on in the bar. That awful guy. What's his name? Hornig. He was a fascist. Navo knows a few things. Maybe they scared Navo, too. Well, that's too late. We can't do anything about it now."

"Who scared Navo?"

"The men who killed your father. Maybe they scared the other one, too."

"What men?"

"Hey, I've got an idea. Why don't you get close to Navo and ask him. Tell him everything's in the past now."

"You think Navo knows?"

"Sure he knows. They were Navo's friends who did it."

"What friends?"

"Your father was very innocent. They knew he knew too much and there was a secret of some kind. Some secret. They knew all about it and Navo knew it, too. Why don't you tell Navo it's in the past and I'm not going to write about it. Because he's nervous you're going to write about it. They're all nervous.

"They thought that Ara knew too much. They were bad men. You know Ara was too innocent. Now if *you* were in there, you'd catch on real fast. He didn't catch on fast. I begged him. Please don't have a bar. I'm going to tell you something about Grandpa. He's too easygoing. He didn't teach the boys."

"So you think Navo knows."

"He probably won't tell you. His friends know. These people are still alive. Some of them.. . . How come Navo was friendly with them? They ate together. That Hornig. They went on vacations with them. Navo knows."

"Do you think he felt guilty?"

"For a long time he did. I think he felt involved in it. I think this even . . . Navo knew too much. He was scared."

My grandmother—the oldest child who knew all the family secrets, who saw and heard and what she didn't see or hear she supposed, snooping around bedroom corners—knew this secret, too. My grandfather surely knew. He knew all about Hornig and the $18,000 and Dad's threats to expose everything. He must have tried to dissuade him, either directly or through Navo. That's what he was telling me all those years ago in allegory. I remember the old guy saying:

"If Ara-boy wanted to do something, it was impossible for us to change his mind." Then he proceeded to tell me how Dad burned himself on the farm when he refused to heed Grandpa's warning and poured gasoline on green fig cuttings against a strong wind. "You see he wanted. . . . When he got it in his mind, he had to do it. He had to conquer. He had to be hero. He's like that."

Half my life a riddle, half my life a search, and the answer was no more distant than their kitchen table. A friend later wondered if I felt betrayed, not so much by my uncle's evasions because his motives could be understood but by my grandparents, who owed me something, too. No, I told him. Imagine the rock climber who scales the top of his mountain, preserving in his mind's eye the vistas but all but forgetting the scraped knees. That was me, too weary for anything but compassion.

And yet when my grandmother caught herself coming clean, caught senility talking, she tried one last frantic time to snatch it back.

"Who killed Ara? Let's see. They shot him early in the morning. He was counting the New Year's money and I guess they tried to rob him. And that girl in the front had something to do with it. Because she told them where Ara was."

Her eyes darted here and there across the cluttered room. "Robbery. I begged Ara. Please don't go into the bar business. Was he the older brother or were you the older one? *Oooff,* I have to drink a ton of something to make me forget. But I don't drink, do I? I don't know how I'm going to sleep tonight. You know Grandpa had a lot of fault. He didn't have a damn head. He should have told the boy, 'No. This is not your business.'"

"Calm down, Grams."

"Maybe they scared Navo, too. Navo was a close-mouthed person. How come he told them all that? They forced him to say something. I don't know why I'm talking like this. Let's see. . . . Ara was an honest person. There was some secret. Why don't you ask Navo? Years and years have passed. Only don't ask him too much at one time."

NAVO WAS A CLOSE-MOUTHED PERSON. HOW COME HE TOLD THEM ALL THAT? THEY FORCED HIM TO SAY SOMETHING. THERE WAS SOME SECRET. My God, I thought, there it was. The last piece. *Uncle Navo was living with Grandma and Grandpa at the time. He and Dad meet the morning before the murder. Navo is caught between brother and good friends. Tell your brother to keep his big mouth shut. Navo tries to talk some sense into Dad but he persists. He's going to blow open the town. Hornig later joins them at this meeting. My father leaves.* THEY FORCED NAVO TO SAY SOMETHING. THERE WAS SOME SECRET. Is it never going to end? I had it all figured out and now this. Let it go, Mark. Let it be. The woman's not well. The woman's senile. All her vigilance, all her energy, and she could not save her dreamy child. Her anger and guilt got heaped onto Navo, as if to say, "I was only his mother. This was a world I did not grasp. But you, his brother, you, your friends."

○ ○ ○

A little more than a year later, my uncle called to say that my grandmother had taken ill at the small nursing home she shared with five other women.

"She's incoherent. I hope I'm wrong but she looks like my grandma the night before she died. Isn't it crazy?"

He was on his way to see her, and it seemed to me he wanted company.

Danny believed I owed Uncle Navo one more chance. Did I not see the hypocrisy, the confusion in motives, in continuing to accept his dinners and holiday parties while risking his psychological destruction with my book?

I thought I had given him plenty of chances to respond over the years, but Danny believed I was just shooting questions at him. I was stonewalling him as much as he was stonewalling me.

"You owe your uncle the truth about your book and a chance for him to respond, knowing the stakes. It's amazing that you wrestled for so long with the idea of confronting the killers but you won't do the same for your uncle."

We had been driving only a minute or two when he asked how the book was going, and I told him I was having a hard time framing the questions. "I don't think you realize you are a major character. And you're not going to like it. There was a time I suspected that you and Dad were involved in this ring."

He tried to laugh but it came out tinny.

"Fine, but I contemplated the question. And it's in the book. So are the recollections of your first wife. You went to her a few days after the murder. You told her that Dad was going to expose the town. You tried to mediate but he wouldn't listen."

"That's not true."

"You were afraid. You were carrying a gun."

"That's so fucking stupid." His voice was more stubborn than angry. "Ara never told me a thing."

Then he repeated the story about the breakfast meeting the morning before the murder, Dad talking crazy about "people blowing up the house" but nothing more. Only this time my uncle pretended not to recall the third party who was there with them.

I challenged him. "You've told that story a dozen times to me. And each time you never hesitated to say it was Hornig. Why now?"

"Well, yeah, you know," he muttered.

"This is what I'm wrestling with. God knows I haven't been straight with you about this book. But I'll tell you right now. You have not been straight with me about Dad's murder."

"You're wrong, Mark. You're absolutely wrong. You want me to shit out something I don't have. Your dad. He was a funny guy. God, he was very innocent. But he never told me anything."

We had driven past the nursing home once already, and the bottle of orange juice he brought for Grandma was getting warm in his hand. I expected him to do what he always did when our conversation took an uncomfortable turn. Find cover, seize pretext, preserve his mystery. But he kept circling the block, once, twice, three times, waiting for some resolution, I believed. I thought to myself: He allowed no one, not his wife or his son or his golfing mates, to press him in the way I had pressed him these last seven years. He would shut them off like that. His son was easy on him, he once told me, by way of saying that I was hard.

Why was it necessary to turn your back on my sister, brother and me? Was it guilt? Was it because we reminded you of your pain?

"I made a mistake, Mark. But you could have called me."

"I was fifteen, Unc."

He wanted me to see that we were alike in that way. Both of us forced to grow up too soon by our father's failings, each of us reacting to the loss of childhood by detaching ourselves from feelings. He was driven further into silence, into emotionally closing down, by my father's murder, a death that resulted from associations both brothers chose to risk. And I had been driven in the opposite direction, a life of questions that could not have conflicted more with his need to be left alone, walled in by his silence.

"I want you to know this book has weighed heavily on me," I said. "I can handle the investigation. The fear. What I can't handle is the thought that this might destroy what you and I have built again."

"I can't be your conscience, Mark. I can only tell you not one time do I know something you don't know. It's just that simple. I don't have to cover anything."

"You lost something."

"I lost a part of me."

"No. Something else. You carried a little . . ."

The car was idling in the driveway of the nursing home, a late summer day he believed my grandmother was dying, when he cried to me, "You want the truth?

"I should have gone to him 'cause you know he was like a son to me. I should have said, 'Ara, what's happening here?' But I was so deep in my own shit that I didn't do that. That failure. . . . I've taken medication because of it. I almost had a nervous breakdown over it. I mean, what more can I give over it?

"I want you to know, honey, I love you like you're my own son. I want you to know that."

"I know that, Unc."

"And maybe I don't always show it. But I have never lied to you regarding your father's situation. I just don't know. I don't know."

It didn't matter anymore if I believed him on this singular point or not. He had come as far as he was going to come, and it was far enough for me.

"If I seem aloof it's because I'm basically a very closed person. I don't even know what the reason is. Even Brian says the same thing. Well, what the fuck. You know. Why do I have to run my feelings all over my goddamn ass?"

"I know."

"I wracked my brain already. I've been through all these fucking exercises. And you know what? It's not worth it. You've got a life to live, Mark. I have a life to live. And I'm going to live it. It may sound selfish, but hey, I was in my front yard and Josette had to call Brian because I was going to kill myself. Now I've been that far with this thing. Okay? I'm not going to go through it again. So you've got to take it."

He told this last story hoping to make it sound like it was something

out of the faraway past, back when the murder was fresh and he was struggling with his choices. But I knew from his son that it was me and my
questions that had driven him to the edge only a few years earlier.

"For a while after the murder, I would just get in the car and drive and
talk to him. Things I was never able to tell him. That I loved him. That I
was sorry I let him down. The one thing I learned is when someone is in
that situation and they're talking and they're in obvious fear, take the
time to see what's behind it. Take the time to see what's causing it, and I
didn't take that time and I've lived with that guilt."

My grandmother had never forgiven Navo for being the one who told
her the news that night, for being the survivor. She pounded him with her
fists, damned the ambivalence of his face. "You're lying! Ara's not dead.
You're lying!" I know, because I had never forgiven him myself.

"You couldn't have saved him, Unc," I said, my voice breaking. "Not
unless you were willing to take the bullet yourself."

This was the only thing I ever gave my uncle that he, as patriarch, did
not protest taking.

"I just want to apologize for the lies I've told."

"Bullshit! There's no need to apologize, Mark. I'm all right with the
book. The family will be all right. Come on, let's go inside and see
Grandma."

He grabbed my head and buried it in his midsection. I could feel him
tremble, or maybe it was me trembling off him. "He was a tornado going
through the world." he said. "You're a lot like him sometimes, you know.
Except you're smarter than he was."

"He betrayed me," I wept. "The fucker betrayed me."

"No, he didn't betray you, son. How did he betray you? He died."

"He died because he was stupid. He died for nothing. This community
wasn't worth it."

"Mark, every community is worth it. Every community needs someone
to stand up. . . . It was an act of decency."

ooo

Back home, my son greeted me at the front door. "Daddy, Daddy. Upee.
Upee."

I swept him into my arms and squeezed him tight and thought about all the life I had missed ransacking lives that had come before, lives that were not my own. I thought about my father and what he tried to give me and what I tried to take, and what got passed on without either of us trying.

"Oh, Dad," I muttered. "I miss you."

"Daddy," Joseph mimicked.

"Yes, son. My daddy . . . so much."

"So much."

"Yes, Joseph."

"I want to read, Daddy. Read book. Read book."

He pointed to the bookcase and began to cry.

"Read book, Daddy! Read book! Upee."

I lifted him onto the ledge and he grabbed his favorite story, about a farmer and spring. I sat him back down on my lap.

"When the bees sing in the flowers . . ."

My father's eyes, eyelashes, looked up at me, smiling. My father's hands turned the page.

Reckoning the town's history was like holding a ball of kite string, webbed and layered, and watching as it played out straight and taut. It leaped from one era to the next, scarcely a century in time, the same crimes, the same sorry responses, all the way up to my father.

I cannot help believing, after excavating its past, that Fresno, the town, its citizenry, its institutions, its cops and district attorneys and judges and elected officials and the whole accumulation of its history played a part in the murder.

I cannot help thinking that it might have been different if the community's newspaper, the Bee, hadn't been so feckless. It took Drew Pearson, a columnist from Washington, to look up county property records and discover that Police Chief Wallace held a fortune in land. The Bee editorial staff was made up of Fresnans who went to school, played ball and spent off-hours drinking at the Hi Life with Chief Morton and Lieutenant Heizenrader. Familiarity bred indolence. When City Manager Hunter approached the Bee in the mid-sixties with evidence of Morton's wrongdoing, the city editor listened politely but never assigned a reporter to investigate. Hunter later learned that the editor had been arrested numerous times for drunk driving, his record wiped clean thanks to Morton.

Then there was Edmund G. "Pat" Brown who did nothing to pursue the widespread vice and corruption in Fresno while serving as attorney general and then governor. Brown and Hank Morton were buddies. The squat and genial Irish politician counted on Morton and his police relief association to raise funds and help deliver the vote in Fresno County. "Hank Morton is one of the best chiefs in the state," Brown declared during a campaign stop in Fresno in the late 1950s. "You should have seen this town years ago."

And what about the federal government? J. Edgar Hoover's boys were still tethered to the old bugaboos, too busy chasing dissidents and "Comminists" to worry about local corruption and depraved cops. The FBI amassed more than 1,000 pages of reports on my grandfather, Aram Arax, the fanciful Bolshevik, during a forty-two-year investigation that ended when he was eighty-three years old and blind. The FBI file on Eddie Heizenrader, one of the biggest crooks to ever hide behind a badge, ran thirty-three pages. And most of those pages pertained to Heizenrader's official dealings with the bureau.

Coming home to write about my father's murder, about Fresno then and now, I told myself it was all right to feel things deeply about the town. But even before I finished my quest, I had rejoined the *Los Angeles Times* as a state correspondent based in the San Joaquin Valley. It now fell to me to report and write dispassionately on Fresno. I knew from the years of book work that the town still suffered because of its geography. The outlaw white boys still controlled the flow of drugs, and the public—its cravings fed a steady diet of two-bit Latino and black peddlers brought to justice—never complained.

The local offices of the FBI, Customs and DEA, and to some extent that of the U.S. Attorney, were like baseball farm clubs stocked with rookies eyeing the bigger city and tired veterans eyeing pensions—breeding ground for complacency. The Fresno cop was better educated, better trained, than his brethren in the sixties and seventies, and there were no Mortons or Heizenraders enshrined at the top. Still, a rot lingered.

I knew that state agents trying to bust a large steroid and cocaine ring ran across Fresno police officers as customers. One high-ranking narcotics cop, a steroid user himself, kept tipping off the ring to the movements of investigators. The D.A.'s office and the department's internal affairs conducted sloppy probes that ended without charges or disciplinary action.

Knowing how much heat I brought to the subject of Fresno, my editors at the *Times* naturally wondered if I could exercise the proper distance. I wasn't sure myself. My solution those first months back at the paper was to write about everything else—about Hmong refugees and the funky new architecture of city hall and the water wars that continued to define this region.

As it turned out, there was nothing to worry about. As soon as I put on my *Times* cap, a familiar set of journalistic imperatives took over. Of course, I could still smell a good story, and some of the stories I set about unearthing did little to ingratiate me with the men who wielded the power and pocketed the riches in Fresno. They weren't strangers to me. Some I had known all my life, and they began to talk about Ara's son—the one with the chip on his shoulder—who had returned to Fresno to dump on the home team.

I discovered that politicians had parceled out huge subsidies to the construction industry, which, in turn, subsidized their election campaigns. I wrote that a decade of gung-ho growth had nearly bankrupted the town. For every dollar that development brought in, two dollars went out the window to service the growth. It was a $67-million-a-year losing proposition, not counting the environmental degradation.

The *Fresno Bee's* neglect to cover this and other stories in any meaningful way bred in the whole town—its businessmen, politicians, bureaucrats, prosecutors, judges, grand jury—an arrogance and insolence. It was so rare for the powerful to be roughed up, asked the tough questions, made to account for their decisions that they reacted to the slightest oversight and criticism like incredulous children. I wasn't the journalist asking the tough questions journalists asked, but the aggrieved son of a murdered man looking to get even. Builders took out an advertisement in the *Bee* accusing me of cooking figures and making up quotes. When I later caught a city councilman selling his vote for a $500 campaign contribution, he ranted to the *Bee* reporter. "His father was a goddamn drug dealer who got killed and he's been trying to save the world ever since."

My friends ask where I will go once this book is published: Surely you cannot stay in Fresno. Surely you cannot indict a town, hold it up for ridicule and stick its face in its own mess, and expect to live there in peace. My young cousin in Cleveland asked his father, "How can Mark think he can take on that world of idiots, appoint himself watchdog? He is a fool like his father if he thinks he can do better." I have no death wish, I assured them. There was a good chance we would sell the house once the book was done and I would ask the *Times* for another assignment in a different part of the state. But there was also an equal chance that I would find a way to stay on, stop running, replant roots, send up shoots like those diehard figs.

My ambivalence, my stubbornness and obligations, remind me of a time back in college when I went to see Charles Garry speak at an Armenian political club downtown. The radical lawyer who had defended Huey Newton and Eldridge Cleaver and the Reverend Jim Jones grew up in nearby Selma, the son of an Armenian peasant farmer named Garabedian. Garry hadn't been home in fifty years.

He stood stupefied over the podium. For a full minute, it seemed, he did not utter a sound. His eyes welled tears. His whole body shook. Finally, he shrieked: "I hate this place. I hate Fresno County. I hate every part of it right down to my guts. I have sensed and felt racism to its highest intent here. I learned what it is to be a member of a minority. I learned what it is to be scorned upon, despised and hated."

Every day one of his schoolmates disparaged his Armenian heritage and every day Garry answered with his fists. Sometimes the older boys would knock him down but never did he accept defeat. If he couldn't beat them with his hands, he went after them with a stick.

"Yes, I have hate in my heart and I don't intend to give it up. . . . You never overcome things you yourself lived through."

I wonder about that seventy-year-old man who died a few years ago still clenching his hate, as I wonder about my own relationship to Fresno. This place that took my father and took my youth and who knows what else it will take before it has finished with me. I try to feel hate but all my history—the ballroom where my parents met and where twenty-five years later I met my wife, the church where Hyreek dispensed his burning sermons and where each of us married, the bars, the hospital, the cemetery—is here. So are my sister and brother and aunts and uncles and the men who killed my father. I want to say I hate it, right down to my guts, but hating Fresno means that I live only in its past and relinquish any voice in its future. Maybe I am my father's fool, but in moments of anger I think, let Fresno wonder about *me.* Let it wonder where I lurk, and where I might strike next, Ara Arax's boy.

ACKNOWLEDGMENTS

Many of the relatives, friends, mentors, and colleagues who shaped my life or assisted in my search appear in these pages. I can only hope that I have portrayed them in a way that makes clear my gratitude and love. This small nod at the end is for some of the others—my teachers, coaches, fellow members of the Red Top Gang, and the friends I shared newsrooms with in Baltimore and Los Angeles.

In particular, I want to thank Uncle Arsan, Aunt Roxie Iskendarian, and my wife's grandmother, Agnes Hoogveld, for their generous financial support along the way. I am grateful to Mike Mosettig, one of my journalism professors at Columbia, who persuaded me that the last thing the world needed was another lawyer. I owe much to *Sacramento Bee* reporter Denny Walsh and former *Modesto Bee* reporter Jim McClung for their exhaustive files and stories on the "Fresno Mob," stories that appeared in the late 1970s and tried to redeem the years of *Bee* neglect.

As for my own newspaper, the *Los Angeles Times,* it has bent over backward to help me meet my obligations to family and book. For this, I want to thank Shelby Coffey, Carol Stogsdill, and Noel Greenwood. It was Noel whose eagle eye ("Mark, now I'm just a dumb reader but . . .") helped me tame the beast of what was surely a 600-page book. When that trickster inside me kept insisting I was finished, my uncle, Danny Melnick, and friends and colleagues Peter King, Rick Wartzman, Steve Braun, Judy Pasternak, Jesse Katz, Sheryl Stolberg, Gary Taubes, and H. Roger Tatarian kept showing me a better way.

My agent, Kris Dahl, never lost her enthusiasm for this book, not when the two-year project became four years and the four years became eight. I am indebted also to my cousin, Brian Arax, and best friend, Warren Paboojian, for reminding me that there was a world out there beyond 1972. Above all, I want to thank my wife, Jacoby, whose love and support got me through the darkest hours.

—M. A.